Time Well Spent

Time Well Spent

Subjective Well-Being and the Organization of Time

Daniel Wheatley

ROWMAN &
LITTLEFIELD
INTERNATIONAL
London • New York

Published by Rowman & Littlefield International Ltd
Unit A, Whitacre Mews, 26-34 Stannary Street, London SE11 4AB
www.rowmaninternational.com

Rowman & Littlefield International Ltd.is an affiliate of Rowman & Littlefield
4501 Forbes Boulevard, Suite 200, Lanham, Maryland 20706, USA
With additional offices in Boulder, New York, Toronto (Canada), and Plymouth (UK)
www.rowman.com

British Library Cataloguing in Publication Data

A catalogue record for this book is available from the British Library

ISBN: HB 978-1-7834-8425-6

Library of Congress Cataloging-in-Publication Data Available

ISBN: 978-1-78348-425-6 (cloth : alk. paper)
ISBN: 978-1-78348-427-0 (electronic)

™ The paper used in this publication meets the minimum requirements of American National Standard for Information Sciences—Permanence of Paper for Printed Library Materials, ANSI/NISO Z39.48-1992.

Printed in the United States of America

For Taid, 1923–2016, and Indy, 2008–2016

Contents

Acknowledgements ix

1 Subjective Well-Being and Time-Use: An Introduction 1

2 A Pluralist Perspective on Time-Use 29

3 Time-Use: The Historical and Policy Context 53

4 Work-Time, the Quality of Work, and Well-Being 73

5 The Household Division of Labour and Flexibility in Paid Work 101

6 Care and Volunteering: The (Feel) Good Samaritan? (Irene Hardill and Daniel Wheatley) 125

7 Where to Next? Travel-to-Work and Travel-for-Work 151

8 Leisure Time: The Pursuit of Happiness? (Craig Bickerton and Daniel Wheatley) 173

9 The Organization of Time and Subjective Well-Being: Key Findings and Implications for Public and Organizational Policy 199

Bibliography 221

Index 255

Acknowledgements

I wish to thank all of my collaborators past and present, and colleagues at both the University of Birmingham and Nottingham Trent University. Particular thanks go to Craig Bickerton for his contributions to the book, and to Professor Irene Hardill and Dr Bruce Philp, who are both long standing collaborators and mentors. I also wish to thank my family for their support. Thanks also go to the team at Rowman & Littlefield International for their support in the development and production of this book.

Chapter One

Subjective Well-Being and Time-Use

An Introduction

1.1 SUBJECTIVE WELL-BEING AND TIME-USE IN CONTEXT

This book explores the relationship between how we use our time and well-being, with reference to empirical measures of self-assessed well-being usually referred to as 'subjective well-being' (Pavot and Diener, 2013, 134; Diener et al., 1999). Time-use has become increasingly complex in recent decades, as changes in technology and the progressively flexible nature of paid work have blurred the boundaries between work, leisure, and other uses of time (Bulger et al., 2007; Pyöriä, 2003, 166; Wheatley, 2012b). Technology has led to an increase in opportunities to work from home or on the move, engage with colleagues or clients in different locations/countries, socialize in new ways both face-to-face and virtually, and travel internationally for both business and leisure purposes (Felstead et al., 2005). The impacts of these changes are well documented in academic literature and the media, but often accounts fail to consider the broader picture of how we use our time and the relationship this has with well-being. This book offers a theoretically nuanced approach to the investigation of well-being. It aims to enhance our understanding of subjective well-being by exploring the impact of the organization of time. Using contemporary empirical evidence drawn from the United Kingdom as an example of a post-industrial society, this book offers important insight, extending our understanding of how we use our time and how we feel about it. Important to note at the outset is that this book is not focused on providing a detailed account of subjective well-being as an approach to understanding well-being, although it does reflect on definitions, measures, and key contributions to the literature. It does not centrally focus on debates over the measurement of subjective well-being, or indeed, on comparing subjective well-being with other measures of well-being. A number of contributions have already provided important insight into these issues, including, for example, works by David et al. (2013), Diener (2009a, b, c, 2013), and Frey and Stutzer (2002b). This book, instead, focuses on exploring how we use our time and the relationship this has with self-assessed well-being.

An expanding and interdisciplinary range of research in psychology, economics, and the broader social sciences has centred on generating a greater understanding of what individuals value and the factors affecting their well-being (see Comim, 2005, 162), exploring links with life satisfaction and happiness (see Clark et al., 2008; Dolan et al., 2008; MacKerron, 2012). Self-assessment of an individual's overall well-being has become increasingly topical given the growing awareness of the limitations of existing measures of well-being. This body of literature is based on the work of Kahneman (e.g., Kahneman et al., 2004; Kahneman and Krueger, 2006), Diener (e.g., Diener et al., 1999; Diener, 2009a, b, c, 2013; Pavot and Diener, 2013), Dolan (e.g., Dolan et al., 2008), Frey and Stutzer (2002a, b), Easterlin (1974, 2001), and others. It has been partly driven by acknowledgement of the limitations of relying on economic data, including gross domestic product (GDP), which is arguably the single most important economic statistic in public discourse, as a measure of welfare (Hicks et al., 2013, 74). These measures, never intended as complete measures of progress, have been criticized for not accounting for all relevant production, income, and wealth, and for failing to capture the value of relationships, health, and happiness (Weijers and Jarden, 2013, 1–2; Stiglitz et al., 2009). Despite high profile acknowledgement of these flaws, including a speech famously delivered almost five decades ago by Robert F. Kennedy at the University of Kansas in March 1968, GDP has remained the principal measure of economic progress. Recent public debates regarding the role of GDP and its profile in policy-making though, have prompted movements by governments and international organizations (e.g., EU, OECD) to explore alternative/complementary measures of well-being (see Stiglitz et al., 2009). Measuring quality of life has been identified as fundamental in assessing the relative progress of societies and as having relevance for both monitoring and policy-making purposes (OECD, 2013). In the United Kingdom, under the coalition government, the Office for National Statistics (ONS, 2014c) developed a 'Happiness Index' to complement GDP, as a traditional economic indicator of societal improvement. The ONS has collected data on happiness since 2011 to measure well-being through consideration of 'GDP and beyond' (ONS, 2014c). Surveys such as the Integrated Household Survey and Understanding Society have since this time asked respondents to answer a range of questions focused on self-assessment of well-being, including: how satisfied are you with your life nowadays? How happy did you feel yesterday? How anxious did you feel yesterday? To what extent do you feel the things you do in your life are worthwhile?

Time-use represents both an innovative and an appropriate lens through which to approach the investigation of well-being. The organization of time involves both choice and constraint. Time comprises a range of different uses, each one distinct but at the same time closely tied to the others, creating blurred boundaries and complex routines. Time-use changes throughout the lifecourse of an individual, influenced by changes in societal norms, policy intervention, and technological development. Post-industrial economies have witnessed a polarization into work-rich-time-poor and work-poor-time-rich households (McDowell et al., 2005), while technological developments including Wi-Fi and mobile devices have created a blurring of the household-workplace interface (Bulger et al., 2007; Felstead et al., 2005), and spillover between different time-uses and leisure. Time-use is explored in this book with reference to: (1) work, (2) household, (3) care, (4) travel, and (5) leisure as summarized in figure 1.1. Important in the consideration of time-use applied in this book are the blurred boundaries present, for example, between forms of unpaid work which may take place within the workplace, that is, unpaid overtime, within the household as acts of care, or through a voluntary organization. Meanwhile, time spent in the household can be used to perform housework, childcare, or as family time which itself reflects a blurring of leisure and care. Notably, the book is not exhaustive in its consideration of all uses of time. Detailed reflection is not, for example, given to the impact of time spent sleeping. This time varies between individuals, although on average individuals often report between six and eight hours of sleep per day. Evidence is largely consistent in showing that the quality of sleep has a positive relationship with reported subjective well-being (Kahneman and Krueger, 2006), although the causality of this relationship is less clear, that is, does good sleep quality increase well-being, or is it the case that happier individuals enjoy better sleep?

Approaches to understanding time-use in mainstream economics, typified by the work of Gary Becker (1976, 1985), simplify their analysis of how we use our time to a rational choice between work (a bad which is consumed to generate income) and leisure (a good), subject to a budget constraint. However, alternative perspectives are critical of mainstream approaches. Radical and Marxian approaches, for example, identify the presence of conflict over the length of the working day, with structural and social forces playing a major role in determining work-time patterns (Laibman, 1992). Moreover, it has been asserted that work-time can be a source of fulfilment (Spencer, 2009, 105), and that any resistance or aversion to work may be culturally determined (99). Feminist perspectives, further, highlight the role of gendered norms in the household division of labour, and subsequently labour

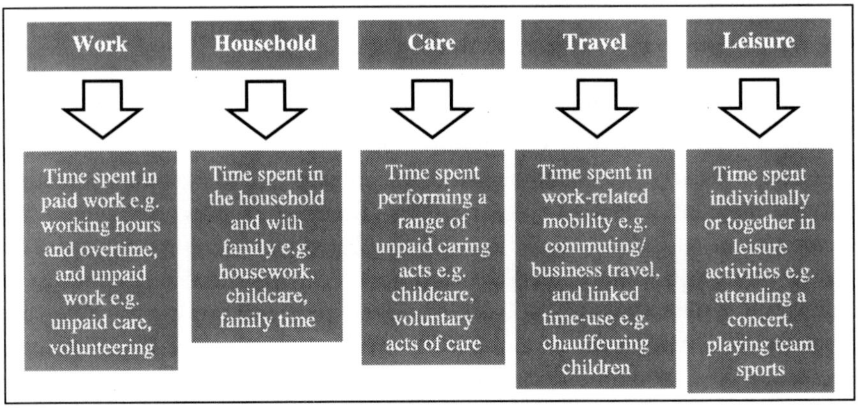

Figure 1.1. Aspects of Time-Use Investigated in this Book.

supplied to the capitalist sphere, which may reflect inequality and gender oppression (Folbre, 1994; Sirianni and Negrey, 2000). The debate present in the extant literature, which is reflected upon in more detail in chapter 2, is evident of the fact that time-use is itself complex and subject to spillover between activities, referring to work or non-work influencing/impacting the other in either a positive or negative way (Guest, 2002, 258–59). Moreover, time spent in a range of activities can equally act as a source of satisfaction *or* dissatisfaction depending on the constraints faced and the preferences of the individual. Achieving a desired balance in the use of time should, in principle, increase happiness. How we use our time is thus highly relevant when exploring happiness and well-being and requires thorough investigation.

1.2 DEFINITIONS OF SUBJECTIVE WELL-BEING

Subjective well-being is a self-reported, or self-assessed, measure of well-being, consisting of emotional responses, satisfaction with specific domains of life, and satisfaction with life overall (Diener et al., 1999). It is a 'stated preference' measure of well-being, in contrast to more traditional 'revealed preference' measures often favoured within the economics discipline.[1] It reflects experienced feelings, which can be both positive and negative. Embedded within these feelings are both 'cognition' (an evaluative/judgemental component) and 'affect' (a pleasure-pain component of well-being) (Stutzer and Frey, 2010, 683). Within the subjective well-being literature 'affects' are often separated into negative influences, referred to as 'negative affects' (NA), and positive experiences, referred to as 'positive affects' (PA). A number of scholars have thus identified subjective well-being as having three separate but linked components: NA (affect), PA (affect), and the overall judgement of life (cognition), usually termed 'life satisfaction' (Diener, 2013, 663; Pavot and Diener, 2013, 135). It should be noted that by its very nature measuring well-being in this empirical manner is subjective, that is, it is an expression of the experience of an individual. Experiences are thus likely to have different impacts on the feelings of different people.

There remains some debate in the extant literature regarding whether subjective well-being is an internally determined stable state of personality, often referred to in reference to 'top-down' theories of subjective well-being, such that there is some underlying process which renders certain individuals more or less happy throughout their lives (Diener, 2013, 663; Pavot and Diener, 2013, 136). Alternatively, subjective well-being has been argued as a variable state determined by a range of external events and activities undertaken throughout the lifecourse, reflected in 'bottom-up' theories. Within the 'bottom-up' approach it is, nevertheless, usually accepted that, while variable, individuals' subjective well-being returns to particular 'set-points' (Headey, 2008).[2] Important, therefore, to 'bottom-up' theories is the presence of causality between self-assessment of well-being and life events and activities. Individuals may, at different times, exhibit different happiness set-points, that is, those with a happier disposition may be more likely to participate in, or derive more or less pleasure from, particular events or activities. Present evidence, however, suggests that subjective well-being is the product of both personal traits (top-down factors) and life experiences (bottom-up factors) (Pavot and Diener, 2013, 137).

Also important to acknowledge is that reporting higher levels of subjective well-being reflects both an absence of negative influences and the presence of positive ones. Moreover, it is argued that subjective well-being represents a global assessment of well-being, not just assessment of a single domain (Pavot and Diener, 2013, 135). This does not, however, render assessment of different life domains irrelevant. Assessing specific domains of life, referred to in the literature as 'domain satisfaction' (van Praag et al., 2003, 30), offers the opportunity to generate a more nuanced perspective on the experience of subjective well-being for individuals and/or groups, and may be particularly important when investigating certain aspects of life or the arrangement of time, for example, work or health (Pavot and Diener, 2013, 135). Schimmack (2008), for example, has reported that changes in domain satisfaction may influence overall life satisfaction. This book considers both measures of 'aggregate' or 'overall' life satisfaction and general happiness, and satisfaction with individual domains of life in the context of the use of time, for example, job and leisure satisfaction.

Box 1.1 Measuring Subjective Well-Being

From a measurement perspective there is an important distinction between objective and subjective measures of well-being (see Galloway et al., 2006, 19–22). Objective measures of well-being typically take the form of a basket of indicators or a composite index such as the *Measure of Domestic Progress* (Cobb and Daly, 1989) and its successors. They capture material conditions that influence well-being. These measures adjust GDP in a number of ways that attempt to capture non-market activities (e.g., adding the value of domestic labour or subtracting the costs associated with crime). Measures of subjective well-being, in contrast, capture how people experience the quality of their lives, and incorporate emotional responses and cognitive judgements. Subjective well-being, though, has itself been the subject of significant debate, not least in regard to its use as a substitute, or complement, to long-standing revealed preference and income-based welfare measures within economics (Kesebir and Diener, 2008).

Subjective well-being measures provide a proxy for 'utility' and there is a large body of literature exploring potential arguments for this proxy utility function (see Frey and Stutzer, 2002, 405). This 'experienced' utility is empirically measured using either a 'single-item scale' or 'multi-item measures' (MacKerron, 2012, 709; Downward and Rasciute, 2011, 333). The two most common single-item scales are 'happiness with life' and 'satisfaction with life' (Dolan et al., 2008), measures which have been shown empirically to generate largely consistent responses (Smith and Exton, 2013). Some surveys and studies of well-being consider multi-item scales. These have included, for example, the Positive and Negative Affective Scale (PANAS), the Satisfaction with Life Scale (SWLS), and the General Health Questionnaire (GHQ), the latter often included in a shortened form (e.g., GHQ12) containing a number of satisfaction questions focused on the measurement of subjective well-being (Dolan et al., 2008, 95). Studies exploring the determinants of well-being usually adopt the following approach to the measurement of subjective well-being (see 95):

$$\text{SWB}_{\text{report}} = \text{r(h)},$$

where self-assessed well-being, often a response to a single-item scale, for example, life satisfaction, is a reporting function (r) of 'true' subjective well-being (h). 'True' subjective well-being is itself determined by social, economic, and environmental factors (X's). The relationship is usually expressed as an additive function in the following form:

$$\text{SWB}_{it} = \alpha + \beta_1 X_{1it} + \beta_2 X_{2it} + \beta_3 X_{3it} + \cdots + \varepsilon_{it}.$$

Various methods of modelling responses to subjective well-being questions have been applied in existing studies. The key differential in approaches to modelling rests in whether responses are treated as cardinal or ordinal. Cardinal variables are those where responses are provided on a numerical scale, for example, number of hours worked per week. Ordinal variables differ in that the possible responses represent discrete ranked, or ordered choice, categories, for example, dissatisfied, neither satisfied or dissatisfied, satisfied. There are well-documented limitations to the use of linear models, treating subjective well-being measures as cardinal, in analyses of subjective well-being. The ordinality of the data, measured on a ranking scale, renders assumptions of cardinality difficult to accept in most cases (see Fielding (1999) for an extended discussion). Increasingly, the ordinal nature of the dependent variables is observed, and ordered logit or probit techniques are applied to the analysis of subjective well-being measures (Stutzer and Frey, 2010, 688). These models provide an appropriate method of analysis as there is an inherent ordering to the dependent variables, and an assumption that the same response by different individuals represents a similar level of satisfaction (van Praag et al., 2003, 34).

As stated preference measures, subjective well-being measures capture how individuals feel about their life on 'aggregate' or 'overall' (life satisfaction or happiness), and in individual domains, for example, job and leisure satisfaction (van Praag et al., 2003, 30). Measures of subjective well-being tend to be derived from survey questions, of the form 'All things considered, how satisfied are you with your life as a whole these days?', where responses are provided on a Likert scale usually comprising either five, seven, or eleven categories ranging from 'not at all' or 'completely unsatisfied' to 'completely satisfied' (Hicks et al., 2013, 78; Helliwell et al., 2015). An example question on job satisfaction from the UK Understanding Society survey is as follows:

Q. On a scale of 1–7 where 1 means 'completely dissatisfied' and 7 means 'completely satisfied', how dissatisfied or satisfied are you with your present job overall?

7	6	5	4	3	2	1
Completely satisfied	Mostly satisfied	Somewhat satisfied	Neither satisfied or dissatisfied	Somewhat dissatisfied	Mostly dissatisfied	Completely dissatisfied

This book considers both 'overall' (life satisfaction and measures of general happiness) and domain satisfaction (e.g., job and leisure satisfaction). In this regard these measures allow individuals to express their relative satisfaction and/or happiness, offering a key indicator of quality of life and well-being. Also important to note is the distinction between 'momentary' and 'reflexive' well-being measures. Momentary measures are conducted while the respondent is participating in an activity, capturing feelings experienced while engaged in the activity. These contrast 'reflexive' measures which consider experiences in the present/recent past, usually presented in social survey questions in terms of 'these days' or 'nowadays' (see Bryson and MacKerron, 2013). The latter, reflexive measures, are used in the majority of research and in the empirical analysis reported in this book.

Some scholars maintain that revealed preference measures (i.e., reporting on the actual choices of individuals) offer a more suitable approach to measurement of well-being, however these measures themselves are problematic due to the presence of, for example, bounded rationality (i.e., decision making based on limited information/understanding) which may result in individuals making choices which do not reflect their 'true' preferences (Kahneman and Krueger, 2006, 3). Measurement validity is a concern with the use of ordered response Likert scale questions regarding well-being. There is also debate regarding the validity of studies which use small-scale primary data collection, often present in the psychology literature, against large-scale datasets preferred by economists, which allow for the inclusion of a range of control factors in the analysis (Dolan et al., 2008, 96; Brown et al., 2012, 1009). Meanwhile, within the economics discipline radical perspectives are critical of the mainstream acceptance, at face value, of measures of happiness and satisfaction. Caution is necessary in the interpretation of self-reported well-being. It has been argued, for example, that measures of subjective well-being fail to account for the structural reasons for dissatisfaction with work, and that norms and expectations may influence relative satisfaction levels (Spencer, 2009, 130). Nevertheless, a substantial and growing body of evidence supports the validity and comparability of subjective well-being measures as measures of well-being (see Stutzer and Frey, 2010, 684–87).

1.3 SUBJECTIVE WELL-BEING: KEY CONTRIBUTIONS

In recent years a substantial body of literature on subjective well-being has developed. A number of authors have provided substantive reviews of this work, for example, Frey and Stutzer (2002a), Di Tella and MacCulloch (2006), and more recently Dolan et al. (2008) and Frey (2008), from which this section draws a number of references to key contributions. Within the extant literature a broad range of potential factors have been considered in respect of their effects on subjective well-being, including: (1) personal characteristics such as gender (Hodson, 2005; Garcia et al., 2007; Philp and Wheatley, 2011); age (Blanchflower and Oswald, 2004, 2008); health and disability (Lucas, 2007) and ethnicity (Luttmer, 2005); (2) relationships, for example, the presence of dependent children (Garcia et al., 2007); (3) socially developed characteristics including education (Blanchflower and Oswald, 2004, 2008; Khattab and Fenton, 2009) and economic activity (Frey and Stutzer, 2002b; Stutzer, 2004); (4) income, which has been the focus of a significant portion of the research within economics linked to welfare (see, e.g., Easterlin, 1974, 2001; Clark et al., 2008; Jorgensen et al., 2010; Kahneman et al., 2006); (5) wider macroeconomic factors including climate change and the environment (Ferreira and Moro, 2010; Welsch, 2006) and the social and political environment (Jorgensen et al., 2010); (6) technology and use of information and communication technologies (ICTs) (Amichai-Hamburge and Hayat, 2011; Buglass et al., 2015; Contarello and Sarrica, 2007; Putnam, 2000); and (7) elements of time-use including working hours (Blanchflower and Oswald, 2004; Wheatley, 2012b) and the commute (Kahneman et al., 2004; Ettema et al., 2010, 2012; Wheatley, 2013). The following discussion outlines key contributions in a number of these areas. It is not exhaustive, but provides a summary of research, including a number of key contributions, exploring a wide range of factors affecting well-being. This discussion also provides an explanation for the inclusion of a number of these factors as controls in the empirical analysis that follows in subsequent chapters of the book. Factors associated with how we use our time are only briefly considered here, as specific details are provided in each of the remaining chapters of the book.

1.3.1 Gender

Research focusing on gender differences in subjective well-being generally suggests that women report greater levels of satisfaction and/or happiness (Alesina et al., 2004), although certain groups of women including mothers may report lower well-being. Women have also been found to often report lower scores when asked multi-item well-being questions, including those from the General Health Questionnaire (GHQ) (see Clark and Oswald, 1994). Women's satisfaction levels may be lowered as a result of household responsibilities including care (Garcia et al., 2007; Philp and Wheatley, 2011). Research considering satisfaction with domains of life in reference to home-based teleworking, further, identified gender differences in satisfaction with job, working hours, and especially leisure. Women in all cases reported lower levels of satisfaction (Wheatley, 2012a). Where women report greater satisfaction it has been suggested this could simply reflect that they compare their relative satisfaction on a lesser scale, and/or are less willing to communicate their dissatisfaction (Hodson, 2005), further evidencing the potential relevance of both happiness set-points and expectations to subjective well-being.

1.3.2 Age

Age provides interesting, and relatively consistent, results across existing studies. Most research finds a negative relationship between measures of subjective well-being and age, but a positive relationship between subjective well-being and age-squared (or age^2/100 which is used in some studies). The findings suggest a non-linear, u-shaped relationship is present between satisfaction and age. Satisfaction increases with age, but importantly diminishes in the middle part of the lifecourse (Blanchflower and Oswald, 2004, 2008). This has also been evidenced in regard to specific domains of life, including work and leisure (see, e.g., Wheatley and Wu, 2014). Explanations of this non-linear relationship are often linked to other factors relevant at this part of the lifecourse, including the impacts of paid work and the presence of dependent children. It should also be noted that evidence has suggested that well-being diminishes among the elderly, but that this is often associated with ill health or ill health among family (Plagnol, 2010).

1.3.3 Health

Health has been shown to have a strong relationship with reported well-being (Michalos and Kahlke, 2010, 2008; Plagnol, 2010). Both physical and psychological health have been shown to have significance, with psychological health notably appearing more highly correlated with subjective well-being

(Dolan et al., 2008, 100). Health has also been found to become more relevant to well-being throughout the lifecourse (Plagnol, 2010, 754). The presence of a long-term illness or disability has a strong association with lower satisfaction levels (Lucas, 2007). However, some studies have reported differing results. For example, Khattab and Fenton (2009, 20–21) found no significant relationship present. Adaptation may also be relevant to reported well-being. Oswald and Powdthavee (2008), for example, offered evidence that in some cases individuals adapted to their disability status. The negative impact of disability on subjective well-being may therefore diminish with the length of time a disability is experienced.

1.3.4 Ethnicity

Research has indicated some distinction in subjective well-being by ethnicity, although results are subject to particular limitations as a consequence of data limitations pertaining to categorization of ethnicity in much existing research. Differences have been reported between white and non-white categories, with the latter reporting lower levels of well-being (Luttmer, 2005; Thoits and Hewitt, 2001). In addition, some research has indicated an interaction with age: there tends to be less difference in the reported well-being of older people as a function of ethnicity (Baker et al., 2005; Greenfield and Marks, 2004). However, problems exist in assessment of the relevance of ethnicity to well-being, due to data limitations which often result in ethnicity being considered in terms of white and 'other' categories. This often results in statistically insignificant empirical results, while the 'other' category is difficult to interpret due to its inherent diversity.

1.3.5 Family, Relationships, and Marital Status

Married people usually report higher levels of subjective well-being (Qari, 2014, 37), while those who are separated often are associated with the lowest levels of subjective well-being, even in comparison to those who are divorced or widowed (Helliwell, 2003). Some arguments suggest the positive association between marriage and well-being may be a result of happier individuals being more likely to get married, happiness acting in this case as a cause rather than effect of marital status (Pavot and Diener, 2013, 140; Diener, 2013, 664). In addition, others suggest that the positive impact on well-being of getting married reduces as time passes – individuals adapt to their marital status – although research on this is conflicting (Qari, 2014, 29). Spousal and wider social relationships are also relevant in terms of the broader benefits associated with feelings of closeness, intimacy, and community. For example, Bryson and MacKerron (2013, 9) found that among thirty-nine types of activity intimacy and lovemaking rank first and second as activities which increase happiness (relative to not doing these activities). These findings are indicative of the benefits of regular human interaction, corresponding with Headey (2008), who identified family, friends, and community as being associated with higher levels of satisfaction. Visiting friends and relatives has been found to significantly and positively contribute to subjective well-being (Brajša-Žganec et al., 2011, 88). There may be certain exceptions to this general pattern, however, as Martin and Westerhof (2003) report lower satisfaction levels where contact with friends/family involves caregiving or receiving, while potential problems may also exist in managing relationships when adults continue to live with their parents (Pichler, 2006).

1.3.6 Children

Children are associated with more negative than positive effects on subjective well-being, reflecting the presence of additional pressures (financial, time). The presence of children also has related impacts on time-use as it increases working hours among men (Knoester and Eggebeen, 2006, 1554) as they often take on the role of primary earner within the household, but reduces time spent in paid work among women. This often results in lower life satisfaction overall among women, due to challenges associated with the provision of care (Della Giusta et al., 2011, 17–18). Parents of dependent children, especially mothers, face additional time constraints which may have particularly negative impacts on satisfaction with leisure (Garcia et al., 2007). However, beneath this broad trend important nuances are found. Negative impacts may be most evident among those with school-age dependent children, often associated with difficulties in combining work and childcare (Wheatley, 2012b). In addition, stronger negative effects are reported by single parents, divorced mothers, following changes in residence, in lower-income households, and where children are ill or require additional care (see Dolan et al., 2008, 107; Alesina et al., 2004).

1.3.7 Education

Education generally provides less clear results in existing research. A positive relationship has been reported in some studies between subjective well-being and education, such that each additional broad level of education, for example, in the case of the United Kingdom a move from GCSE/A level (high school/further education) to degree (higher education) is associated with higher levels of reported well-being (Blanchflower and Oswald, 2004, 2008). Other research, though, has suggested that mid-level education is associated with the highest levels of life satisfaction (Stutzer, 2004). Extending these findings, it has been argued that those with degree level education may report lower satisfaction (in particular with job/work). This is argued as being a result of their expectations, which may not be met at least early in the career (Khattab and Fenton, 2009, 18). Also relevant to education is that obtaining educational qualifications is likely to be related to a range of unobservable personality traits, including intelligence, motivation, and family background (Dolan et al., 2008). Education is, further, likely to exhibit a positive relationship with both income and health, and thus needs to be carefully treated in analyses with respect to controls.

1.3.8 Economic Activity

In regard to economic activity, evidence generally shows that those in work, education, or retirement are more satisfied than those unemployed or economically inactive (Frey and Stutzer, 2002; Knabe et al., 2010; Krueger and Mueller, 2012). This is not to suggest work is an entirely positive activity, but rather that the negative effects of unemployment have a considerable impact on well-being. Meier and Stutzer (2006) suggest that the relationship between hours of work and life satisfaction has an inverse u-shape where greater engagement in work increases satisfaction levels up to a point beyond which further increases in working hours result in reductions in well-being. Empirical research considering life satisfaction as a continuous, rather than a discrete ordered choice, variable (a discussion of this distinction is provided in section 1.2) found between 5 percent and 15 percent lower satisfaction scores among the unemployed compared with the employed (Frey and Stutzer, 2002). Moreover, the unemployed additionally report lower positive impacts than the employed from engagement in comparable activities including leisure (Knabe et al., 2010, 875; Krueger and Mueller, 2012, 598–99). It has been suggested, though, that the unemployed may be able to compensate some of the negative impacts of being out of work, through using their time enjoyably while the employed are at work (Knabe et al., 2010, 879). Men's well-being appears to be more strongly negatively impacted as a result of unemployment (Lucas et al., 2004), especially among the middle-aged (Pichler, 2006). Some studies have suggested that the negative effects of unemployment are significantly reduced when financial status is controlled, suggesting that income and concerns surrounding future income is a key driver of the negative impact of unemployment (Haller and Hadler, 2006). However, the majority of research evidences a significantly lower level of happiness among the unemployed even after controlling for a range of factors (Blanchflower and Oswald, 2004; Deaton, 2008). Consistent with these findings, empirical analysis of the full panel of the British Household Panel Survey found that preferences for reduced working hours decreased as unemployment rates increased (see Philp et al., 2015). Employees are more likely to accept lengthier hours of work, at a given wage rate or salary, in order to retain their employment, as unemployment is perceived as having a number of significant negative impacts, especially where unemployment rates are high.

Research exploring the relationship between retirement and well-being is somewhat inconsistent with evidence finding both potential negative and positive effects (Kim and Moen, 2001). The transition into retirement is central to understanding the relative impacts. For example, involuntary retirement, associated with redundancy or ill health, is likely to have an overall negative effect. In addition, the effects of retirement often differ between domains of subjective well-being, as satisfaction with leisure time has been found to increase, while negligible effects may be found on overall life satisfaction (Bonsang and Klein, 2012). Retirement can also act as a trigger for engagement in certain uses of time, for example, volunteering (Van Willigen, 2000; Grimm et al., 2007). It has been argued that a number of factors are key in driving the specific impacts of retirement on well-being, such as financial security, family and social relationships, and individual characteristics including health and certain personality attributes (Kim and Moen, 2001).

1.3.9 Income

Income has been the focus of a significant amount of research into subjective well-being within the economics discipline, often linked to debates surrounding welfare. Clark et al. (2008) provide an overview of literature on the relationship between income and well-being. Most studies tend to report a u-shaped relationship, with positive but diminishing returns from increases in income (Mentzakis and Moro, 2009), but findings are not without some conflict and contradiction. Easterlin's (1974) seminal work reported a surprising finding, termed the 'Easterlin paradox'. He found that while income differences between individuals are reflected in differences in subjective well-being, evidencing a positive correlation, national income increases do not generate an identifiable increase in subjective well-being. Similar findings have also been reported in more recent work (e.g., Blanchflower and Oswald, 2004). In explanation of this finding, relative income is argued as, perhaps, being more relevant. Easterlin (1995), for example, found in later research that cross-sectional data analysis usually reveals a positive relationship between wealth and happiness, but that subjective well-being does not continue to increase as general levels of wealth rise. He suggested this finding is a result of relative income having a greater influence than absolute income. Further work has strengthened the focus on relative income to include perceptions of wealth and financial status, highlighting its relevance (Mentzakis and Moro, 2009).

Other contributions have suggested that increases in income among wealthier individuals may not be met with long-run increases in subjective well-being, as additional income increases expectations of 'necessary' income (Stutzer and Frey, 2010, 691). Kahneman et al. (2006) offer an alternative explanation of the relationship which they link to time-use. They posit that the reason wealthier individuals do not continue to report increases in satisfaction levels is that they spend more and more of their time in activities, linked to work, which are associated with lower subjective well-being, including activities which cause stress and tension. Consistent with the findings of Knabe et al. (2010) with respect to differences between the employed and unemployed as discussed in the previous section, this suggests that other causal factors may be responsible for some of the differences observed in relation to income. Jorgensen et al. (2010, 621) report on the relevance of household income. They found higher levels of life satisfaction reported among individuals from higher income households compared with lower income households. Research also suggests some gender distinction in the relationship between income and subjective well-being. Income has been identified as a central driver of the satisfaction levels of men, but this may not be as prevalent among women (Della Giusta et al., 2011, 22; Wheatley and Wu, 2014, 455).

1.3.10 Wider Macroeconomic Factors

As well as personal and other demographic factors, and those related to economic activity, the existing literature also identifies a range of wider macroeconomic influences on subjective well-being. Economic crisis has been shown to have a u-shaped impact on well-being, with initial high magnitude negative impacts, which diminish and are eventually followed by increases in the level of well-being to previous and even above pre-crisis levels (Graham et al., 2010, 742). Meanwhile, unemployment rates within an economy may reduce subjective well-being, while a higher rate of unemployment welfare (benefits replacement rate) relative to expected wage rates increases life satisfaction for both the unemployed and the employed (Di Tella et al., 2003). Higher levels of democracy are also associated with greater satisfaction (Dorn et al., 2007), although income may have a mediating effect.

Evidence pertaining to the effects of the environment we live in, and pollution, on self-assessed well-being is limited (Dolan et al., 2008, 110). However, some contributions have found statistically significant relationships between pollution and subjective well-being. For example, Welsch (2006, 811), using a panel of ten European countries, found evidence in support of air pollution having a negative effect on subjective well-being, evident in willingness to pay for improved air quality. Other research has found consistent evidence showing negative impacts on well-being of reduced air quality, and positive impacts derived from living in a warmer climate (Ferreira and Moro, 2010, 264). Living in large urban areas, especially in a deprived area, has also been shown to have potentially negative effects on life satisfaction, while rural residential location may be beneficial (Shields and Wheatley Price, 2005, 533).

1.3.11 Technology and the Use of ICTs

ICTs are used for a range of purposes including work, study, research, engaging with friends and family, gaming, and meeting new people (Contarello and Sarrica, 2007, 1022). Indeed, many individuals are spending more and more time engaged in social media and using wireless technologies (Buglass et al., 2015). Use of technology can create a range of opportunities (e.g., for working on the move using Wi-Fi), but also blurring of boundaries between work and home/family (Bulger et al., 2007; Hislop and Axtell, 2009; Lowry and Moskos, 2008). The relationship between Internet use and subjective well-being has generated a number of conflicting results. Some studies suggest negative impacts, including loneliness and social isolation, resulting from increased Internet use reducing physical interaction with family and friends (Putnam, 2000). Meanwhile, other research suggests Internet use is associated with a number of social benefits, including interacting with friends and colleagues, which are likely to increase well-being (Amichai-Hamburge and Hayat, 2011, 587–88; Contarello and Sarrica, 2007, 1029). Watching television is often reported as one of the most frequently engaged in activities during leisure time (Brajša-Žganec et al., 2011, 88). However, studies have suggested it has little positive impact on subjective well being relative to other leisure activities (Knabe et al., 2010, 875) while some studies have actually shown a negative impact, specifically among those reporting heavy consumption of television (Frey and Benesch, 2008).

1.3.12 Time-Use

The relationship between time-use and subjective well-being is of specific interest in this book. Past research is indicative of work-time being associated with a number of negative influences on subjective well-being including stress and tension (Kahneman et al., 2006), while long working hours have also been found to generate dissatisfaction (Philp and Wheatley, 2011). Household activities including housework, and the provision of care, have generated some conflicting results in the literature, but often are associated with negative impacts on subjective well-being especially for women (Della Guista et al., 2011). Meanwhile, volunteering is generally argued as having positive impacts (Morrow-Howell et al., 2003, S143), although Haller and

Hadler (2006) found no significant relationship between volunteering and life satisfaction or happiness. Lengthier commutes are generally regarded as generating dissatisfaction (Stutzer and Frey, 2008), although among women shorter commutes may be associated with lower levels of subjective well-being due to difficulties in combining the commute with household responsibilities (Wheatley, 2014, 193). Evidence on travel-for-work, including business travel, suggests a range of potential benefits, for example, career development, getting to see the world, but also a number of potential negative well-being effects (Gustafson, 2006, 2014). Studies have also suggested a range of leisure activities may have positive effects on subjective well-being. For example, Brajša-Žganec et al. (2011) consider engagement in a range of different leisure activities, and find that engagement in cultural events helps to explain reported well-being: visiting exhibitions, the theatre, reading books, and attending concerts are all associated with higher levels of subjective well-being. More detailed discussion of the impacts of these different elements of time-use is offered in each of the subsequent chapters of the book.

1.4 OUTLINE OF THE BOOK'S AIMS AND APPROACH

1.4.1 Aims of the Book

This book aims to explore subjective well-being through the lens of time-use, specifically focusing on the nature of different forms of time-use present among individuals in a post-industrial society. This approach is focused on enhancing understanding of the complex interaction between different uses of time, including the opportunities and challenges presented by modern technologies. The book comprises discussion of existing research in this area, and draws on published empirical research including Philp and Wheatley (2011, 2013), Wheatley (2012a, b, 2013, 2014, 2016, 2017), Wheatley and Bickerton (2016a, b), and Wheatley and Wu (2014).

1.4.2 A Mixed Method Approach

The empirical work presented within the book is both quantitative and qualitative in nature, reflecting a mixed method approach to the analysis of subjective well-being and the organization of time. This approach acknowledges the role of the lifecourse in how we use our time. While the book does not apply a lifecourse approach throughout, reflections are given to the role of chronological age and key transitions in the lifecourse. A lifecourse approach is applied in chapter 6 and further details of this approach can be found in this chapter. Mixed methods are applied in the book comprising use of large-scale secondary data extracted from a range of relevant surveys, complemented by quantitative-qualitative data from a number of smaller-scale primary research projects. The qualitative data is used to support standard measures of subjective well-being extracted from large-scale surveys, and collected in primary surveys, offering more detailed insight into the responses provided by individuals pertaining to their well-being.

As all methods have limitations, researchers have increasingly recognized that a mixed method – or multi-strategy – approach may help to avoid the biasing effects of any single approach, which could otherwise have significant impacts on the reliability and validity of research (Cresswell, 2013, 203). Mixed methods differ from multi-methods in that multi-method approaches comprise a range of methods of data collection and/or analysis which are located within a single research paradigm, that is, either quantitative or qualitative. In contrast a mixed method approach, such as that applied in this book, uses a complementary mix of both quantitative and qualitative research techniques. While the use of mixed methods is in no way unique in research within the social sciences, it does differ from the majority of research within economics pertaining to time-use and subjective well-being. Mainstream methods in economics tend to rely exclusively on mathematical and statistical modelling (Spencer, 2009, 129). These specific methods of analysis are founded on a number of methodological assumptions, which have been criticized for lacking relevance in an open social system (Lawson, 2003). It is therefore beneficial to approach research with methodological pluralism, combining a range of methodologies and techniques, contra much research within mainstream economics. This book combines quantitative data with qualitative aspects, integrated within a case study approach, allowing a more comprehensive analysis of the organization of time.

A mixed method approach allows both quantitative and qualitative research practices to be employed, and integrates the data at different stages of enquiry (Cresswell, 2013, 204). This method allows the research to 'generalize the findings to a population as well as develop a detailed view of the meaning of a phenomenon or concept for individuals' (16). A multi-strategy approach of this nature is able to reveal much more than would have been found through a single approach (Bryman, 2012, 631). A mixed method approach can suffer from too much diversity, resulting in both quantitative and qualitative elements being compromised in order to undertake both (Pawson and Tilley, 2006). However, mixed methods, utilized appropriately, combine the best of the statistical robustness of mathematical quantitative techniques with the detail and nuances of qualitative research (Bryman, 2012, 631). Combining methods offers the researcher the opportunity to neutralize any biasing effects that may result from employing only quantitative or qualitative techniques. The classification of mixed method or multi-strategy approaches has been attempted in a number of ways (see Cresswell

Table 1.1 Mixed Method Research Designs (see Cresswell and Plano Clark (2011, 70–72)

Convergent	Comprises data collected and analysed separately using quantitative and qualitative methods which is combined during overall interpretation
Explanatory	Quantitative data collection is followed up using qualitative data collection to explain the findings
Exploratory	Initial exploratory qualitative data collection is followed by quantitative data collection
Embedded	Both quantitative and qualitative data are collected within a single research design
Transformative	An approach in which the researcher interacts with participants during the data collection process, with a focus on employing a range of methods which may provide benefits to participants of the study
Multi-phase	Comprises multiple phases or connected studies which employ quantitative and qualitative methods

and Plano Clark (2011) and Bryman (2012) for fuller discussions). Cresswell and Plano Clark (2011) outline six major mixed method research designs, summarized in table 1.1.

Important to mixed methods is the ability to triangulate findings (see Hammersley, 2008). Triangulation can be used to cross-check and give wider context to the findings of one research strategy through use of a method associated with an alternative research strategy (Bryman, 2012, 633–34). It is thus often associated with convergent mixed method research design (Cresswell and Plano Clark, 2011, 77). However, triangulation can also be used to provide complementary data that explains different aspects of the phenomena being researched (Hammerlsey, 2008, 33). In economics the use of triangulation is often limited, 'beyond the weakest form of the interaction of modeller and model' (Downward and Mearman, 2007, 80). This book, in contrast, applies 'between method' methodological triangulation, effectively combining quantitative and qualitative methods to the analysis of how we use our time (81).[3] A mixed method approach is applied in this book in order to not only triangulate, but also explain and enhance the research findings. Enhancement, which refers to the use of mixed methods to extend the findings made using one strategy with additional evidence drawn from a separate approach (Bryman, 2012, 633–34), is applied to enrich and add robustness to the empirical work conducted. The approach applied in this book also responds to Brown et al.'s (2012, 1016) calls for an interdisciplinary, mixed methods approach to the assessment of satisfaction levels, including those associated with work. It applies this approach, combining quantitative analysis of survey data from both secondary and primary sources with qualitative evidence extracted, for example, from semi-structured interviews, allowing analysis of individual attitudes and behaviour which is sympathetic to the social context that shapes the attitudes and behaviours observed.

The mixed method approach employed in this book is subject to certain limitations. Combining methods and data-sets, while providing the analysis with a range of useful data, is challenging not least as in the latter case data sources contain inconsistencies in their approach to capturing certain relevant data as a result of the distinct scope and aims of different surveys, as well as the differing points in time in which the data is captured. In addition, it should be acknowledged that use of a specific panel of individuals contained in certain data sources, for example, Understanding Society, and certain aspects of the qualitative data including life history reflections in the care and volunteering case study outlined in the next section, may render some findings representative of a cohort effect, influenced by a particular economic, political, or social policy environment (see Lindsey et al., 2015, 53). However, together the quantitative and qualitative data sources used, and the data collection and analysis methods employed, provide both complementarity and comparison, ensuring a robust approach in the research presented in the book.

1.4.3 Data Sources Used throughout the Book

As well as drawing on the results of published work by other scholars, this book presents results from the analysis of a range of UK empirical data from both secondary data sources and primary research projects. Data sources are as follows:

Secondary Data Sources

- *Annual Survey of Hours and Earnings (ASHE)*: ASHE is one of the largest surveys of earnings in the United Kingdom. Although it collects fewer demographic characteristics than the Labour Force Survey or Understanding Society, it collects data on wages, paid working hours, and pension arrangements for an approximately 1 percent sample of the UK working population. ASHE was created as a replacement for the New Earnings Survey (NES) in 2004, although the ASHE methodology was applied to earlier data from the NES to provide ASHE datasets from 1997 onwards (ONS, 2016e). ASHE is used in this book to provide contextual data on, for example, the gender pay gap in the United Kingdom.
- *British Household Panel Survey (BHPS)*: The BHPS provides data collected from households on a year-on-year basis reflecting on various aspects of time-use and satisfaction. The main objective of the BHPS was to further understanding of social and economic change at the individual and household level in Britain, and to identify, model, and forecast such

changes and their causes and consequences in relation to a range of socio-economic variables. It was designed, using a stratified random sampling method,[4] as an annual survey of each adult member (aged sixteen and over) of a nationally representative sample of over five thousand households (ten thousand individuals). Between 1992 and 2009 individuals were successively re-interviewed and, if they left their original households, all adult members of their new household were interviewed. Children were interviewed once they reached sixteen years of age. From Wave 9, two additional samples were added to the BHPS from Scotland and Wales, and at Wave 11 an additional sample from Northern Ireland (Northern Ireland Household Panel Study or NIHPS) was added to increase the sample to cover the entire United Kingdom (BHPS, 2010). The book uses data from the combined panel of the BHPS and Understanding Society, as the latter subsumed the BHPS in 2009.

- *British Social Attitudes Survey (BSA)*: BSA is an annual survey of three thousand individuals conducted by the National Centre for Social Research. Conducted since 1983, it considers attitudinal movements reflecting on life in Britain and the political environment. A set of core questions are asked, but the survey includes new questions each year reflecting current issues (National Centre for Social Research, 2009). The 2009 BSA is used in this book as certain questions, for example, regarding time spent grandparenting which is used in chapter 6, have not been included in subsequent surveys.
- *Community Life Survey (CLS)*: The CLS was commissioned by the UK Cabinet Office in 2012–2013. It captures data on patterns in a range of areas, including volunteering, charitable giving, community cohesion and participation, and subjective well-being. It is an annual household survey with a sample of 5,000–6,000 adults (aged sixteen years and over) resident in England. It was initially conducted through face-to-face interviews, but moved to online data collection in 2014. The CLS is used in this book, in chapter 6, to consider patterns in both formal and informal volunteering.
- *Labour Force Survey (LFS)*: The LFS is a survey of the employment circumstances of the UK population. It is the largest household survey in the United Kingdom and provides the official measures of employment and unemployment (ONS, 2016a). It uses international definitions of employment and unemployment and economic inactivity, together with a wide range of related topics such as occupation, training, hours of work, and personal characteristics of household members aged sixteen years and over. Collected since 1973 (initially biennially), it moved to become quarterly in 1992, with a quarterly sample size approximately equivalent to that of previous annual data. The survey since became known as the Quarterly Labour Force Survey (QLFS). Comprising a sample of approximately

130,000 individuals, the QLFS questionnaire comprises a 'core' of questions which are included in every survey, together with some 'non-core' questions which vary from quarter to quarter. The questionnaire is divided into two main parts. The first part contains questions on the respondent's household, family structure, basic housing information, and demographic details of household members. The second part contains questions covering economic activity, education and health, and also may include questions asked on behalf of other government departments, for example, Department for Work and Pensions. The survey is used to provide a range of contextual and descriptive data throughout the book, including in particular in chapter 4 and 5.

- *Understanding Society*: Alternatively titled the United Kingdom Household Longitudinal Study (UKHLS), Understanding Society is a multi-topic longitudinal survey of a nationally representative sample of forty thousand households, conducted annually, which were selected for inclusion in the survey in 2008. Face-to-face and telephone interviews are used to capture data from each adult member of these households each year. The survey aims to improve understanding of social and economic change in Britain at the household and individual levels (Understanding Society, 2015). It is anticipated that over time the study will permit examination of short- and long-term effects of social and economic change, including policy interventions, on the general well-being of the UK population with a strong emphasis on domains of family and social ties, work, financial resources, and health. This data source is used throughout the book.
- *Workplace Employment Relations Study* (WERS): WERS (2013) is a series of national surveys of employment relations at the workplace level. Six surveys have been conducted, in 1980, 1984, 1990, 1998, 2004, and 2011. The aim of the WERS series is to provide an evidence-base about a broad range of employment relations and practices which is large-scale and statistically robust. WERS2011, used in this book, collected data from a representative sample of 2,680 British workplaces. Within each of these workplaces data was collected from a workplace manager responsible for employment relations and personnel. In addition, data was collected from 1,002 worker representatives and 21,981 employees (WERS, 2013).

Primary Data

The book draws on three separate case studies which involved primary data collection conducted within the United Kingdom. Two of the case studies were conducted in the East Midlands, while the third (and most recent) was conducted using a sample drawn from the wider Midlands regions (East Midlands and West Midlands).[5] A case study can, dependent on research questions, design, and purpose, be quantitative, qualitative, or mixed methods in its approach (Cresswell and Plano Clark, 2011, 193–94). Two of the case studies detailed here are mixed methods, while the other used a qualitative research strategy. In each instance, a case study approach was adopted to enhance understanding of the causal processes underlying the relationships observed (Yin, 2008). While specific findings may relate only to the location studied, the representativeness of the case studies enables some generalizability of findings to a broader context, justifying the use of single cases in the analysis presented (41; Rueschemeyer, 2003, 309). Two of the studies reported were funded by the UK Economic and Social Research Council (ESRC). Details of the studies are as follows.

Complex patterns of time allocation among dual career households

This research project was an ESRC-funded PhD Studentship (award no. PTA-030-2005-00807). It comprised an in-depth mixed method case study of dual career households[6] with data collected through organizations and employees in Greater Nottingham,[7] a regional employment centre in the East Midlands region of the United Kingdom, conducted in 2006 (see Wheatley, 2012b). The case study adopted a convergent mixed methods design, collecting data in separate, but linked, strands using different methods (Cresswell and Plano Clark, 2011, 181). It developed the themes of an earlier study, the 'Location and Mobility Decisions of Dual Career Households' project funded by the Leverhulme Trust (grant F/740), reported in Hardill and Watson (2004). The findings of this study are reported in particular in chapter 5. The study comprised semi-structured interviews with human resource managers (HRMs, as representatives of organizations) and a survey of highly skilled employees (and their partners):

- *Interviews with human resource managers*: Evidence was gathered from ten semi-structured interviews with HRMs. Large employers were chosen, employing a total of fifty-seven thousand individuals in 2006. The selection included four organizations ranked in the largest fifteen employers in Greater Nottingham in 2006 (Nottingham City Council, 2006). They included both public and private sector organizations, and a voluntary sector organization, in various industries. Prior to the interview the HRMs were provided with an interview schedule which was divided into relevant themes including organization policy on working hours, flexible working arrangements, and travel-to-work. The semi-structured approach also permitted some time to digress. The interview transcripts were analysed using a simplified version of the cross-sectional thematic coding method (Ritchie and Spencer, 2003).[8] The HRMs were also used as gatekeepers to access employees at each organization to conduct a survey.

- *Employee survey*: Data was collected from eighty-one dual career households, where at least one partner was employed at one of the organizations studied. The other partner could have worked for any employer in any location. The questionnaire, which was predominantly quantitative in nature, drew on that used in the previous Nottingham case study (Hardill and Watson, 2004), and comprised mostly closed questions. The questionnaire was divided into sections exploring household characteristics, working patterns, and commuting patterns of both the respondent and their partner. In total responses from 142 individuals were included in the analysis (after the removal of invalid/incomplete responses), approximately 52 percent of which were women. Almost 32 percent of respondents reported the presence of dependent children, and the average age of the men and women sampled was 44.2 and 41.8 respectively. The sample comprised 64 managers and senior officials, 50 professionals, with the remainder in associate professional and technical occupations. Approximately 87 percent of the sample was full-time, and 66 percent employed in the public sector.

Doing one's duty: a case study of volunteering in a deprived community

This ESRC-funded (award no. R000-22-0592) micro-sociological case study was conducted in a small former-industrial town in the East Midlands region of the United Kingdom in 2004. The study adopted a qualitative approach focusing on care and volunteering among older adults (see Hardill and Baines, 2011). Four case studies of volunteer organizations were conducted, where each organization was responsible for provision of social welfare services, employed paid workers, and used volunteers (197 volunteers reported in total).

A combination of techniques were employed to gather data: repeated, systematic observation; collection of documentary evidence; interviews with key informants (officers in local economic development and social inclusion, managers and workers in organizations using volunteers); focus groups; and 'life history' interviews with a selection of volunteers. This combination of data gathering was intended to provide a careful and authentic description of ordinary conscious experience and explore the meanings and explanations that individuals attribute to their experiences. In total twenty-seven interviews were conducted with volunteers and with paid workers. Life history interviews were structured around the 'volunteering journey', with reference to paid work and family commitments. Additional documentary evidence was collected and focus groups also conducted. In the book, evidence is drawn from individuals at a range of stages in the lifecourse (see chapter 6 for a more detailed discussion of the data collected in the case study). They reported diverse household structures, some living alone, while others lived with their partners, children, and grandchildren. Some of those interviewed reported paid work, others had already retired, but all were active in the community helping and caring for neighbours and family/friends informally, as well as giving time formally via volunteering through an organization. Findings from this study are reported in chapter 6.

Travel-to-work and travel-for-work: blurred boundaries and complex patterns of time-use

Referred to as the Travel-for-Work Research Project, this mixed method case study of organizations and employees focused primarily on patterns of travel-to-work (i.e. commuting) and travel-for-work, conducted within the Midlands (East Midlands and West Midlands) of the United Kingdom in 2015. This project is reported, in particular, in chapter 7. The case study adopted an explanatory mixed method design, with a smaller qualitative follow-up phase, comprising semi-structured interviews, being used in part to explain and enhance understanding of the responses given in an online survey (Cresswell and Plano Clark, 2011, 181):

- *Online survey of employees*: Primary data was collected from a sample of highly skilled workers using an online questionnaire, publicized using a large database of contacts in senior roles within Midlands-based organizations. The survey comprised open and closed questions, focusing on travel behaviours, subjective well-being, and individual and household demographic characteristics. Particular focus was given to incidence of travel-for-work and its impacts including capturing employee's opinions on this activity through responses to open questions. The survey received a total response of 141 individuals (after the removal of invalid/incomplete responses), approximately 61.4 percent of which were men. The average age of the men and women sampled was 46.3 and 40.4 respectively, and approximately 48 percent of respondents reported the presence of dependent children. Around 90 percent of the sample reported working full-time, and 72.3 percent were working in the private sector. All were employed in highly skilled occupations, including senior managerial and professional occupations.
- *Semi-structured follow-up interviews*: The survey data is complemented by data captured through follow-up semi-structured interviews with a stratified 10 percent subsample comprising fourteen highly skilled workers, providing a cross-section of employees by gender, age, and other characteristics, offering insight into travel-for-work among those with family responsibilities, in different occupations and career stages. The interviews captured employee perspectives pertaining to their preferences and

experiences of travel-for-work including frequency of travel, ownership of travel time, work-family conflict, and well-being. The interview data was analysed, consistent with the dual career case study, using a thematic coding method (Ritchie and Spencer, 2003), alongside the survey to triangulate research findings.

1.5 CONTRIBUTION OF THE BOOK

Through the lens of time-use this book offers a broad exploration of factors influencing subjective well-being, incorporating standard measures of life satisfaction, as well as satisfaction with specific domains of life, including job and leisure time. This book approaches this increasingly relevant topic from a pluralist, that is, non-mainstream, economics perspective, including drawing on the work of radical and feminist economists. The book offers a critical exploration of the effects of the organization of time. The blurred and complex nature of how we use our time is considered, while the book also offers deeper investigation, taken one-by-one, of the different ways in which time is used, and of the preferences and constraints determining time-use, from work-time to leisure and other uses of time. The book includes contributions drawing on the extant literature, while a number of chapters draw directly on empirical evidence from a variety of UK contexts, extracted from both large-scale secondary data sources (e.g., British Household Panel Survey, Labour Force Survey, Understanding Society) and smaller-scale primary research. This book's specific contribution is in exploring, in detail, the impact of differences in the organization of time, the preferences and constraints determining time-use, and the reported well being of individuals, considering the policy implications in the context of contemporary post-industrial societies.

Are employees happy with their job? Does flexibility in work increase happiness? Why do individuals choose to volunteer? Do workers enjoy their commutes and/or travel-for-work? How do we spend our leisure time, and do we enjoy it? These are just some of the questions to which this book provides important insight. Following this introduction the remainder of the book is structured into eight further chapters. Initially the focus falls on the relationship between paid work and other uses of time. Chapter 2 outlines key conceptual approaches to time-use, including the development of norms, as well as the preferences and constraints present in the determination of work-time. One of the main contributions of this chapter is to consider the complex, and often blurred, relationship between various uses of time. Chapter 3 considers the historical context for the current organization of time and also reflects on the UK policy context, setting the scene for the subsequent chapters which consider specific elements of time-use separately. Chapter 4 offers a critical perspective on mainstream economics approaches to work-time to consider the length of the working day, the quality of work, and relative satisfaction with work-time. The chapter builds on published empirical work reported in peer-reviewed journals including Philp et al. (2015), Philp and Wheatley (2011, 2013), Wheatley et al. (2011), and Wheatley (2017), using the UK Labour Force Survey and the combined panel of the BHPS and Understanding Society. Chapter 5 moves the context to the household to consider the household division of labour and its impact on time-use including housework and paid work, for example, through use of flexible working arrangements. The chapter builds on further published work including Philp and Wheatley (2011), Wheatley and Wu (2014), and Wheatley (2016). Gender is a key theme throughout this chapter, centring on the debates regarding relative equality within the household and its impacts on time-use, and in turn subjective well-being. Chapter 6 moves the focus to forms of care (childcare, ill/elderly care) and the impacts of volunteering on the subjective well-being of individuals throughout the life-course. The chapter draws on feminist economics and social policy literature, and empirical analysis of a number of data sources including Understanding Society, the Community Life Survey, British Social Attitudes Survey, and the Doing One's Duty case study. The chapter, further, builds on published work including Baines and Hardill (2008), Hardill and Baines (2007), and Philp and Wheatley (2011). Chapter 7 reflects on time used for work-related activity, specifically travel-to-work and travel-for-work. The chapter builds on the empirical work published in Wheatley (2013, 2014), and draws on the Travel-for-Work Research Project reported in Wheatley and Bickerton (2016b). Chapter 8 focuses on the impact of engagement in different forms of leisure activity, drawing on work published in Wheatley and Bickerton (2016a). The relative impact on well-being is explored with reference to existing literature and UK empirical data from Understanding Society. This chapter contributes to our understanding of the the relationship between how we use our leisure time and subjective well-being. Chapter 9 then draws together the different aspects of time-use to consider holistically the organization of time and its impact on subjective well-being. It offers a summary of key findings from the book, and a more holistic discussion of how time is organized in contemporary post-industrial societies. In the discussion of these themes, this chapter draws on work from economics, economic geography, HRM, psychology, and the broader social sciences. This final chapter reflects on the impact, and effectiveness, of the range of policy which influences how we spend our time. The chapter further considers the validity of subjective well-being as a measure of economic well-being, the role of technology in both aiding and creating challenges in how we use our time, and potential future policy development and avenues for research into the complex relationship between how time is spent and subjective well-being.

NOTES

1. 'Stated preferences' refers to the preferences of individuals considered in reference to the responses they give to questions, for example, the responses given to a question regarding well-being with domains of life, or life overall. 'Revealed preferences', an approach that is often favoured by mainstream economists, is in contrast founded on the assumption that by examining different combinations of goods preferred outcomes can be inferred, thus revealing the preferences of the individual.
2. 'Set-point' refers to an individual's stable, chronic level of subjective well-being, which is linked to the personality traits of the individual (Pavot and Diener, 2013, 137).
3. 'Between method' triangulation contrasts 'within method' triangulation, the latter referring to combining different varieties of the same method, for example, applying different econometric techniques (Downward and Mearman, 2007, 81).
4. Stratified random sampling refers to a random sampling method where the wider population is divided into subgroups by the researcher determined by some particular criteria. For example, researchers collecting survey data may structure the data collection so that they generate a sample which is representative of a broader population by gender, or from each department within a firm (Bryman, 2012).
5. The Midlands regions of the United Kingdom provide an instructive case, and are representative to some degree of other regions both in the United Kingdom and Europe with regard to industrial and occupational breakdown, hours worked, and travel-to-work patterns (Green and Berkeley, 2006; Hardill et al., 2006).
6. Dual career households are households in which both partners are employed in managerial, professional, or associate professional occupations.
7. Greater Nottingham is comprised of Nottingham City, the Boroughs of Broxtowe, Gedling and Rushcliffe, and the Hucknall part of the district of Ashfield (Nottingham City Council, 2010).
8. The themative coding conducted involved initially identifying themes from the research aims. The interview data was then extracted using a coding table to identify further common themes and sub-themes, for example, flexible working policy for which flexi-time was a sub-theme. Using the themes identified from the coding, quotations were then extracted from the interview transcripts.

Chapter Two

A Pluralist Perspective on Time-Use

2.1 INTRODUCTION

This chapter outlines key conceptual approaches to time-use. Relevant to this discussion is the concept of rational choice, as well as norms, preferences, and constraints present in the determination of how we use our time. One of the main purposes of this chapter is to outline the complex, and often blurred, relationship between various uses of time which is not well explained by mainstream economic theory. Drawing on published work including Philp and Wheatley (2011, 2013), this chapter provides theoretical context for the subsequent chapters which consider specific elements of time-use separately. It explores a range of theoretical approaches to the allocation of time. Particularly important to this book are concepts of time allocation which recognize not only the individual, but also the household. Theory must also acknowledge the different choices and constraints faced by men and women in the use of time, including the impact of such activities as work-related travel and care, which form the focal points of the discussion in chapters 6 and 7.

Key to the debate in this chapter is the concept of constraint. It is essential, therefore, to define this term in reference to its use in this book. When used in mainstream utility theory, as described in the next section, 'constraint' refers primarily to the idea of the 'budget constraint', that is, the set of combinations of goods (including leisure) just obtainable given a level of income. Extensions of mainstream theory, such as Becker (1976), consider a range of constraints faced by economic agents, including time and goods constraints, as well as production relations. Becker suggests these can be grouped into a single 'total resource constraint'. In general, mainstream approaches view constraints as fixed or exogenous. Institutional economists, in contrast, see constraints as more fluid, influencing and forming social norms and behaviours, while radical and Marxian approaches emphasize the role of power and conflict in the determination of patterns of time-use, including working hours. Feminist economists, such as Folbre (1994), have also recognized the influence of external factors. Collective bargaining, for example, results in the development of social norms. This leads to the creation of 'structures of constraint', which limit individual decision-making (6–7). Also of key concern to feminist theorists is the concept of the household and how the household influences individual decision-making and can act as a constraint. This broader notion of constraint is applied in this book, with the exception of the discussion of mainstream theory in the next section.

This chapter begins with an exploration of the mainstream economic approach to labour supply, as well as Becker's (1976) extension of this theory incorporated in his theory of the allocation of time. It then continues with a discussion of Hakim's (2000) gendered extension of mainstream theory, which offers specific insight in considering the heterogeneity of women's preferences. These approaches are critically reviewed with reference to heterodox perspectives, including institutional, radical and Marxian, and feminist economic theory. Institutional theory is discussed through the work of such theorists as Ayres (1951), Commons (1931), Veblen (1909), and Hodgson (1988). Institutional perspectives highlight the importance of habits and norms and the effect of institutions in determining patterns of time allocation. The discussion of radical and Marxian approaches draws on the work of Laibman (1992), Philp (2001), and Spencer (2009). Finally, the discussion of feminist theory offers further explanation of how we use our time, drawing on the work of Folbre (1991, 1994) and Nelson (1995, 2004), among others.

2.2 MAINSTREAM APPROACHES TO THE ALLOCATION OF TIME

When conceptualizing the use of time, a critical discussion of mainstream economic theory (i.e., mainstream labour supply theory) provides a suitable foundation. This section explores mainstream approaches to how we use our time, which centre on the trade-off between 'work' and 'leisure', where initial focus is given to decisions over time spent in paid work in particular. The discussion draws on the seminal contributions of Becker (1976, 1985), and more recent contributions including that of Hakim (2000, 2004).

2.2.1 Mainstream Labour Supply Theory

The foundations of mainstream economics can be traced back to the 1870s. At this time there was growing focus on the concepts of marginalism and utilitarianism. The term that developed to describe this change in the nature of economic theory was 'neoclassical' (Colander, 2000, 131). This description was initially coined by Veblen (1899a), in describing the work of Marshall. At this time neoclassical theory was not 'mainstream'. However, by the late 1930s the term 'neoclassical' had extended to encompass all marginalist theory including that of Jevons and Menger. Subsequently, it has been used in a much broader context to refer to the use of calculus, marginal productivity theory (Colander, 2000, 131), and a focus on simultaneous relative price determination through the interaction of supply and demand. Neoclassical, or mainstream, labour supply theory is founded on the model of rational choice. The concept of rational choice is itself based on a series of axioms. These characterize the 'rational' behaviour of an individual and begin with the concept of 'preference'. Preference denotes, for example, that if situation A is preferable to situation B, then the individual will be better off under situation A. This relationship assumes three basic properties. The first is that an individual can, without indecision, rank their preference for two or more alternatives, referred to as completeness. The second property, referred to as transitivity, is that an individual will be consistent in their decision-making, so that if they prefer situation A over B, and B over C, then they will also prefer A over C. Finally, the concept of preference also assumes continuity, that is, if A is preferable to C, then situations close to A will be preferred over situations close to C.

The mainstream approach to an individual's choice concerning their time spent in paid work, in its simplest form, involves a choice between 'work' and 'leisure', subject to an income or budget constraint. The model begins with the premise that an individual will obtain a level of utility contingent upon income derived from work and leisure time. It assumes the only utility generated from work is the income received. Leisure also acts as a source of utility. Marginal utility of leisure is assumed to always be positive, so that greater hours of leisure are always preferable; this has been critically referred to as an assumption of 'leisure-as-bliss' (Spencer, 2006), and is discussed later in this section. Implicit here is the non-satiation axiom. The 'rational' individual wishes to maximize their utility, and is assumed to be 'free' to determine the hours they wish to work. The relationship is shown diagrammatically in figure 2.1.

The choice of how much labour to supply (hours worked), and how much leisure time to take, is made simultaneously. The model assumes the two are mutually exclusive.[1] For an individual the maximum length of the working day is represented by H_m. This may reflect physical, mental, or legal limits. It is important, too, to consider the existence of non-linear income (i.e., the presence of welfare benefits for the unemployed) which may impose a floor, represented by 0b in figure 2.1. There are different wage rates in the example

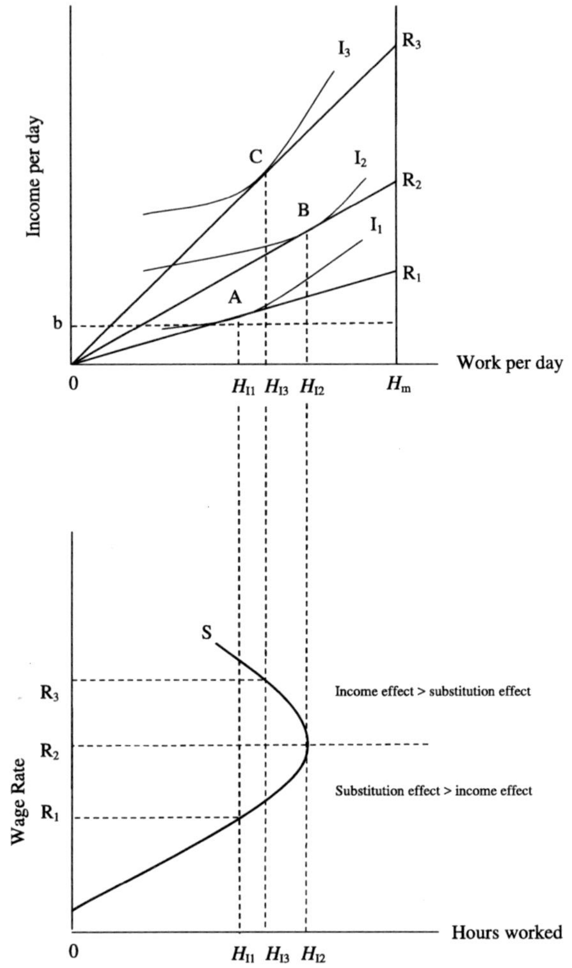

Figure 2.1. Neoclassical Income-Work Trade-Off Determining Individual Labour Supply.

depicted in figure 2.1, given by R_1, R_2, and R_3. Preferences are reflected in the indifference curves I_1, I_2, and I_3. Given the particular preferences of the individual a backward bending labour supply curve can be observed, as depicted in the lower set of axes in figure 2.1.

Concentrating on the labour supply curve, as the wage rate increases from R_1 to R_2, the individual offers to work longer hours, at the cost of leisure time. The individual experiences both a 'substitution effect' and an 'income effect' concurrently. The substitution effect is greater below wage rate R_2. The increase in the wage from R_1 to R_2 will result in the individual tending toward work as the relative cost of leisure increases. The income effect, however, is greater beyond wage rate R_2. The individual will tend toward leisure and offer fewer hours of labour beyond R_2 as they are able to have more income and leisure by working fewer hours at the higher wage rate. The individual's labour supply curve is therefore backward bending. Hours worked can be represented by the function,

$$H = f(w,b)$$

where, for a given individual's set of preferences, working hours (*H*) are a function of, and therefore determined by, the real wage (*w*), and real non-labour income (*b*).

A number of objections have been made to the assumptions made in this model of labour supply. For example, Spencer (2006, 461–62) highlights two issues with the assumptions of the mainstream model, specifically in relation to leisure time. The idea of 'leisure-as-bliss' is criticized, as it is suggested that the marginal utility gained from leisure is heavily dependent on the nature of leisure time. For example, spare time for those on welfare payments is unlikely to be used in the same way as it will be by wealthier individuals. Second, it is important to acknowledge that unemployment is not the same as leisure time. As such unemployment cannot be classified as leisure. In addition, the residual time not considered in this model, that is, time not spent in paid work or leisure, which includes sleep and other necessary activities including eating (which sit outside of the physical limit of time which could be spent in paid work H_m), undoubtedly has influence over any such trade-off present. Issues relating to the classification of leisure time are returned to throughout this chapter, and in more detail in chapter 8. What this discussion highlights, though, is that it is inappropriate to treat a number of work-related and household activities, including, for example, the commute and caring, as forms of 'leisure' in analyses of how we use our time. However, simply excluding them from the analysis by incorporating them into the residual time ignores the influencing and constraining effect these uses of time will have on time spent in paid work and leisure.

Revealed Preferences for Work

A simplified version of mainstream preference theory, which does not rely on a complete preference map, has been offered by Samuelson (1948), who considered an individual's choice between two goods. It is suggested that by examining different combinations of goods, in this case income and work, preferred outcomes can be inferred, thus revealing the preferences of the individual. For a given budget constraint the individual will choose their preferred combination of goods in each situation. The combinations of goods which lie on the same indifference curve as the preferred outcome are neither better nor worse solutions for the individual, that is, the individual is indifferent towards them. The budget constraints, R_1, R_2, and R_3, from figure 2.1 can, therefore, be used to observe an individual's 'revealed preferences' at points A, B, and C.

Neither indifference curve analysis nor the revealed preferences approach, though, recognize the constraining role of institutions, as argued by institutional economists, in moulding preferences through customs, norms, and habits. Nor does it acknowledge the role of gendered and household norms influencing individual behaviour which conflict with assumptions of self-interest, as does feminist economics. These perspectives are discussed further in this chapter. The representation of the derivation of working hours presented by mainstream theory, and in Samuelson's (1948) preference determination, is limited in its uses due to oversimplification. The simple work-leisure trade-off model of an individual's labour supply neglects a number of important factors including evolving constraint, which will be explored in the next section. However, this model is important as it provides a foundation for our understanding of how we use our time, and indeed offers important insight into the distinction between 'revealed' and 'stated' preferences. This provides a basis from which to further explore conceptual explanations for decisions over how we use our time, including extensions and alternatives to mainstream theory.

Working Hours under Constraint

A number of alternative arguments have been presented which build on the mainstream rational choice model, but place greater emphasis on the effect of a time-constraint. Past research by Tummers and Woittiez (1991, 409–10), for example, argued that the mainstream approach to working hours is deficient. Exploring the effect of restricted hours caused by job availability, they found that where restricted hours were present, this creates a non-linear budget constraint as wages decrease with hours worked. It is suggested that this non-linear budget constraint provides a better estimation of the distribution of working hours. For example, women work fewer hours per week than men as their hours are under greater constraint as a result of their greater household contribution (Fagan et al., 2012; Garcia et al., 2007, 2011). In other research Böheim and Taylor (2003, 113–14) reject mainstream labour supply theory. Using empirical evidence from the British Household Panel Survey (BHPS) they argued that working hours cannot be varied continuously at the discretion of the individual. Instead they are a product of employer preference, the level of local labour demand, individual demographics, and unobserved effects specific to the individual,

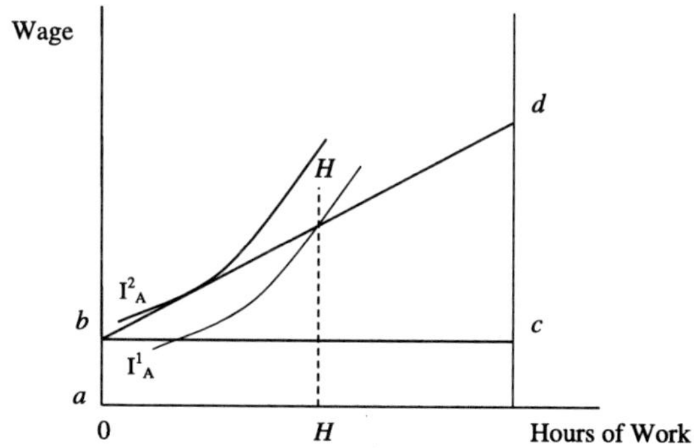

Figure 2.2. Constrained Working Hours. *Source*: Bosworth et al. (1996, 24).

which vary with time. These factors are likely to obstruct the individual in attaining their preferred equilibrium between hours worked and leisure resulting in constrained hours.

Constrained hours of work are represented in figure 2.2 (taken from Bosworth et al., 1996, 24). The budget constraint for the individual is represented by abd. Given this budget constraint the individual's preference may lie on indifference curve I_2. However, HH is the hours the individual is constrained to work, for example, eight hours per day. The individual must therefore choose to either work the constrained hours (at point f on indifference curve I_1) or not work at all. The individual will participate in the labour market if they can achieve a higher level of utility at the wage rate by working these constrained hours, than not working at all. Some employees will therefore work fewer or more hours than would be preferable with a conventionally drawn constraint. However, there may be a number of solutions available which allow individuals to work their optimal, and/or financially constrained, number of hours. These include, for example, holding more than one job, working overtime, or undertaking reduced hours or part-time flexible employment, although evidence is indicative of many of these 'options' themselves reflecting constraint (Atherton et al., 2016; ONS, 2015d; Wheatley, 2016).

Time-Use as a Trade-Off

The mainstream income-work trade-off model can be criticized as it does not consider time spent on work-related activity. Instead it simplifies the individual's choice of how much labour to supply into a trade-off between leisure and income. There is reason to contest this simplified representation of an individual's allocation of time. The labour-leisure dichotomy employed in the standard account of labour supply neglects time spent in work-related activity, and that spent commuting.[2] An alternative measure of productivity offered by Harvie et al. (2009), which is a more appropriate indicator of well-being, is *social productivity*. This measure considers productivity, but unlike traditional measures, takes account of the 'toil and trouble' of producing goods and services. Importantly, measures of productivity should include time forgone. However, social productivity is excluded from government measures of productivity, as it could be argued as irrelevant from the market perspective. Other past research, for example, McQuaid et al. (2001), has suggested the mainstream work-leisure trade-off should include time lost to work-related activity, including time spent commuting. A more appropriate representation of an individual's time would, therefore, account for unpaid work-related activity (including the commute) and the tasks of social reproduction. These additional uses of time have clear constraining effects, limiting or influencing individuals' preferences for hours of work. Time allocation theories founded solely on choice are therefore unsatisfactory. The analysis of alternative patterns of time-use, and constraints, presented in this section underlines the adaptability of mainstream labour supply theory. Nevertheless, the concentration of the neoclassical analysis on the choices of self-interested rational individuals, the gender blind nature of its analysis, and the questionable assumptions upon which it is founded leave it open to criticism from a number of other theoretical standpoints.

2.2.2 Becker's Theory of the Allocation of Time

An extension to mainstream theory, in the context of time-use, is offered by Gary Becker (1976). He argues that for individuals who work it is improper to focus on work-time in isolation from non-work-time. If there is a period of time when one is not engaged in work there are foregone earnings associated with this decision. Hence work-time can be expressed in terms of wages, and non-work-time can, in principle, be expressed in terms of wages foregone. Becker (1976, 91–98) therefore proposes a 'full income' approach to an individual's time-use, using an equilibrium solution concept. If full income is denoted by S, and total earnings forgone by the interest in utility, L, then (93):

$$\sum p_i b_i Z_i + L\left(Z_1, \ldots, Z_m\right) = S$$

L is a function of the commodities (Z_i) as how much is earned or forgone is dependent on the consumption set (e.g., Z_1) chosen. If average earnings, represented by $\hat{w}$, are interpreted as being constant and independent of Z_1, the equation can be can be written as (93):

$$\sum\left(p_i b_i + t_i \hat{w}\right) Z_i = V + T\hat{w}$$

with,

$$\pi_i = p_i b_i + t_i \hat{w}$$

$$S' = V + T\hat{w}$$

The full price of a unit of Z_i (π_i) is the sum of the prices of the goods and of the time used per unit of Z_i. $\acute{S}$ is a resource constraint which gives the money income achieved if all time is devoted to work, if $\hat{w}$ is interpreted as being constant and independent of Z_i. V represents other income, $T\hat{w}$ is time at work, and $t_i\hat{w}$ is time at consumption. Achievable income is spent directly on goods, $\sum p_i b_i Z_i$, and indirectly through the income forgone, $\sum t_i \hat{w} Z_i$, by using time at consumption rather than at work.

This provides the equilibrium, utility maximizing, condition:

$$U_i = T\left(p_i b_i + L_i\right) i = l, \ldots, m$$

where $p_i b_i$ is the direct, and L_i the indirect component of the total marginal price, $p_i b_i + L_i$.

In Becker's analysis the level of income earned is dependent on the consumption set chosen. Achievable income is spent on goods or, if foregone, on non-work activities such as consumption time (with the latter being viewed as a commodity). The results of Becker's analysis, when applied to the determination of working hours, indicate that a 'pure rise' in income will result in a reduction in working hours. According to Becker some activities, such as childcare, do have relatively large forgone earnings associated with them. However, childcare is not considered leisure as such in his analysis. Thus he maintains that the concept of forgone earnings is of greater importance than any concept of leisure, rendering the investigation of leisure unnecessary. Indeed Becker (1976, 100) argued that the 'economist can reach all his traditional results as well as many more without introducing it [leisure] at all'. While this may be formally correct, it is not clear why monetary equivalents should conceptually take logical precedence over expressing commodities and incomes in terms of the time required to produce them.

Mackie et al. (2001, 92–93) criticized Becker for not acknowledging that activities such as work can generate positive as well as negative utility. In addition, they argued that one of the key limitations of Becker's approach is that constraints result in some activities taking more time than would be preferable, while some activities come with a minimum time constraint, for example, working hours for salaried employees. The arguments conflict with the concept of indifference between activities, and highlight the importance of time as a unit of analysis. Given these limitations the currently accepted micro-founded mainstream position is that individuals derive utility from consumption of goods and the time spent in different activities (Hess et al., 2005, 228). Under this framework individuals are assumed to allocate their time and consumption of goods between activities, including work, leisure, and travel, in order to maximize utility. Their utility is, however, subject to certain constraints, notably the total amount of time available, wealth, and the minimum amount of time required for activities to take place. There are a number of further objections which may be made to Becker's analysis, for example, at a behavioural level. Human beings may wake up in the morning and consider what they might earn, or what they can buy. Alternatively, they may consider how they are going to pass their time, and economic concerns might be secondary to other motivations which are social, relational, or altruistic, which may, for example, drive individuals to participate in voluntary acts. This is not acknowledged by Becker (1976). For example, Becker consistently reduces one form of relationship – marriage – to a contract-based institution broadly similar to a capitalist firm. Time and relationships are thus simply extensions of market processes. As Hodgson (1999, 112) observes:

> Although modern neoclassical economists widely recognise the need to analyse the household in terms of the individuals composing it, the result is to treat all the relations between the individuals along purely contractarian lines. Symptomatically, in this approach there is no conceptual dividing line between the family and the marketplace. ... Accordingly, neoclassical economics is unable to conceptualise the specific institutional features of the household and the special human relations within that sphere.

Further criticism of Becker has been offered from a range of perspectives. For example, Spencer (2004b) argues that although Becker's analysis incorporates some of the earlier understanding of the disutility of labour into the analysis of labour supply, its focus remains too narrow. Becker suggests that work-time contributes to the creation of non-market 'goods' and 'bads', and that these commodities affect decisions regarding how we spend our time. However, the focus remains between wages and working hours, solely from the perspective of the opportunity cost of work-time. The 'disutility of labour' in Becker's analysis only alters the willingness of workers to accept the wages offered in a particular role. It has no causal effect on worker effort or motivation. Becker does not consider the possibility of workers resisting work, and of managers extracting effort from employees (Spencer, 2003; 2004a).

Meanwhile, institutional economists, including Hodgson (1988, 14), have argued that Becker's theory is limited by the assumption that preferences do not change through time. For Becker there is no social formation of preferences. This assumption not only leaves preferences outside the economic system, but incorrectly results in them being considered as constant or fixed. It is conceded, however, that Becker does acknowledge that preferences do 'change' through time, and that these changing preferences are included in the stable or fixed preferences assumed in his system (Hodgson, 1988, 111). Becker (1976, 13) argues that notions of irrational behaviour and ignorance, explained by social scientists through customs and traditions, are 'ad hoc and useless explanations of behaviour'. Hodgson (1988) labels Becker's assumptions of permanent preferences to be similarly ad hoc. Utility analysis is therefore of questionable worth and operational value in this context (117). Feminists criticize Becker for disregarding the role of care and the household (Nelson, 1995, 142). He did address a key critique from feminist economists. In a later work Becker (1985) included caring and housework in definitions of work. However, one of the key limitations of Becker's approach is that it remains grounded in rational choice theory which centres on assumptions of self-interest. It does not adequately account for the complex relationships which affect decision-making within the household (Cha, 2010; Lundberg and Pollak, 2007). Nor does it acknowledge the heterogeneity of individuals. In this sense it is limited and remains somewhat 'gender blind'. Given this limitation the next section extends the discussion of mainstream theory, considering Hakim's gender sensitive approach.

2.2.3 Hakim's Preference Theory

Catherine Hakim's (2000) approach provides a gender sensitive analysis, focusing on the employment preferences of women, and how they differ from their male counterparts. However, this approach has been subject to criticism, especially from feminist theorists, who consider it limited by its mainstream basis in self-interested rational individuals.

Female Employment Preferences

Hakim (2000) argues that the employment preferences of women represent a distinct case to that of men. In her model, men are treated as a homogenous group with strong preferences for full-time paid work (158). This assumption can itself can be criticized: men may simply be constrained to work full-time, just as women are constrained to work fewer hours, or provide care. In contrast to her treatment of men, Hakim models women as heterogeneous, displaying a range of preferences for work and family life. Hakim splits

Table 2.1 Categorization of Women's Preferences

Home centred	Home centred preferences are mainly found among those women who prefer not to undertake paid work, and for whom children and family are central priorities throughout the lifecourse.
Work centred	Work centred preferences are present among mainly childless women who are committed to work and equivalent activities, and for whom qualifications represent an investment in human capital.
Adaptive	Adaptive women have a combination of work and home preferences. This diverse category represents those who want to work, but are not committed to it. As such they are argued as being most responsive to social and employment policy.

Source: Hakim (2000, 158).

women into three broad groups in relation to their preferences as summarized in table 2.1.

Mainstream theory is criticized for assuming that all individuals are homogenous, and for being grounded solely on male behaviour (Hakim, 2000, 30–31). Hakim argues that women should be included explicitly in labour market analyses as they undertake the majority of part-time and non-standard forms of employment. They require acknowledgement in theoretical and policy analyses. In common with Becker, and somewhat controversially, Hakim maintains that most women in wealthy countries have relatively unconstrained choices. Hakim suggests that the diverse preferences of women result in a conflict between the aforementioned groups. The conflicts present in the preferences of women leaves them disadvantaged in the labour market in comparison to the more homogenous case of men (Hakim, 2000, 5).

A key critique of Hakim is that her analysis begins with clearly defined preferences. As with the criticisms levelled at Becker, institutional and radical perspectives argue that preferences are shaped in the process of social interaction. Hakim has been challenged for her lack of acknowledgement of constraint, and the gendered constraints resulting from the household dynamic. These are prevalent in feminist economic theory (see Folbre, 1994; Nelson, 1995; Bell, 1974). Women may not simply have preferences for or against paid work, but may be coerced into undertaking paid labour, or into providing full-time care for children or elderly relatives. Even where paid work is undertaken, the uneven division of labour within the household is likely to leave women under greater constraint than their male counterparts (Garcia et al., 2007; 2011). Research which has explored patterns of part-time and reduced hours work, further, highlights that women's patterns of work are dominated, not by personal preference, but instead by family and household responsibilities, creating specific challenges which may not be present among many men (Fagan et al., 2012, 23; Fagan and Walthery, 2011, 273–75; Harris, 2007, 501). These women are more appropriately described as 'aspirational but constrained' in comparison to Hakim's categories of adaptive preferences. Women may be constrained into adapting their preferences as a response to the continuing gender inequity they face at work and in the home (Leahy and Doughey, 2006). They may not pursue certain careers as they may consider them out of reach. In some cases, their preferences may therefore adapt so that they feel they do not want to work towards a career.

Hakim's approach is controversial and has been subject to criticism. Her extension of mainstream theory provides a gender sensitive approach, categorizing women by their preferences. This, as with other mainstream approaches, is founded on the assumption of choice. Hakim's approach ignores the compromises and constraints faced by many women as they combine paid employment with household obligations. In contrast, this is a key component of feminist theory explored later in this chapter. Mainstream approaches are also limited as they do not recognize that preferences are influenced and formed. This is a principal focus of alternative approaches, for example, institutional economic theory.

2.3 ALTERNATIVE PERSPECTIVES ON TIME-USE

A number of alternative perspectives on time-use offer, perhaps, a more comprehensive explanation of the processes involved in determining how we use our time, including those of radical and Marxian, institutional and feminist economists.

2.3.1 Institutional Economic Theory

Institutional economics offers an alternative perspective to mainstream economic theory. Historically there have been three meanings to institutionalism (Samuels, 1948, 1–2). First, the term has been used to refer to a movement against the dominant mainstream approach to economics. Second, it has been used to refer to problem-solving: seeking to work out solutions to the problems of advanced industrial economies, largely in areas relating to welfare and labour. Third, institutional economics has attempted to create a body of knowledge which differs from mainstream economics, as it seeks to explore the organization and control of the economic system, especially in terms of power relations. Institutional theory is widely regarded to be an American phenomenon. Leading early institutional theorists included Veblen, Commons, Mitchell, and Ayres (Rutherford, 2001, 173). A strong European branch developed in the latter half of the twentieth century, particularly through the work of Hodgson (1988), which forms a significant element of the discussion in this section. The key argument of institutional theory is that social institutions form a central and essential role in moulding the preferences and guiding actions of individuals and firms (Hodgson, 1988). The term 'institution' covers a variety of notions and concepts. An institution as defined by Commons (1931, 648) is

> collective action in control, liberation and expansion of individual action. Its forms are unorganized custom and organized going concerns. The individual action is participation in bargaining, managing and rationing transactions, which are the ultimate units of economic activity. The control by customs or concerns consists in working rules which govern more or less what the individual can, must, or may or may not do. These are choices resolved into performance, forbearance or avoidance while participating in transactions.

Institutional theory follows the perspectives of behaviourism. This approach locates human action within institutional structures – norms, customs, habits – as an alternative to the mainstream approach which is focused on individual preferences (Dugger, 1979, 903). Veblen (1909, 239), another of the founders of institutional economics, defines institutions as, 'settled on the habits of thought common to the generality of men'. Institutions are described by Veblen as the primary form of social structure – a set of norms and customs which are imperfectly reproduced through habituation – and thus habits are the primary form of human practice (Lawson, 2003, 213). Customs form a primary focus as it is argued that collective action is more universal in the unorganized form of custom than it is in the organized form of concerns (Commons, 1931, 651). For example, in addition to the employment contract, customs and norms at work may determine acceptable dress, workplace etiquette, and indeed working hours, including widely acknowledged 'normalized' patterns of work such as working Monday to Friday from 9 a.m. to 5 p.m. The preferences of an individual develop out of these norms, customs, and habits. Norms are reproduced through the development of habits in each generation of individuals (Dugger, 1979, 902). Customs and habits may change with shifts in economic conditions. Present institutions consist of the 'residue' of ancient institutions, and are also influenced by changes in technology. Technology has a key role in shaping society, increasing the significance of mobility and the fluidity of modern institutions (Ayres, 1951, 51).

Institutions mould the preferences of individuals (Veblen, 1899a). This is a departure from mainstream theory which regards institutions simply as tacit or given constraints, which restrict otherwise free behaviour. For institutionalists the individual is 'free' to make choices within the constraints they face in the present. These choices, although 'free', are a product of routine and habit, and are influenced by the structure and culture of the system. Mainstream theory, in contrast, does not view 'free' behaviour in the present as a 'reproducer of routine', which may develop into constraint in the future (Hodgson, 1988, 134). Institutional economics rejects mainstream economic theory.[3] It argues the economy is inseparable from a host of social and political institutions. In contrast mainstream theory, such as labour supply, offers detached understanding and is founded on a number of assumptions, including the questionable axioms of rational choice (Ayres, 1951, 49). Becker's and Hakim's extensions to mainstream theory similarly suffer on the basis of these assumptions. Institutionalists maintain that social and economic change cannot be explained by human wants or scarcity – both of which are determined by institutions and technology – but can only be explained in reference to social forces (50). Institutional theory replaces homo economicus – 'economic man' – with what is termed 'institutional man'. The former offers a methodologically individualistic account of human behaviour. Institutional theory instead derives institutional man from observed behaviours, taking into account different forms of behaviours and norms in different societies (Kapp, 1968, 2). The importance of institutions is that they create the consistencies found in the mass behaviours of individuals which empirical quantitative studies analyze (Mitchell, 1925). Institutions influence behaviours and create societal norms.

Mainstream theory supposes a closed system, where a variable environment denotes equilibrium which may or may not be reached. The environment is assumed to consist of fixed functions which govern the preferences of individuals, and productive techniques (Hodgson, 1988, 19). Economists regularly use the term 'ceteris paribus', and it is the factors held constant which institutionalists suggest limits the arguments of mainstream economists (53–71). Institutionalists argue that the socio-economic system evolves. As Veblen (1899b, 190) states, 'by one method or another, institutions change and develop … the development of these institutions is the development of society.' Social patterns are not the outcome of individual acts, but instead individuals and their actions are the outcomes of social patterns. In contrast, the mainstream approach results in social phenomenon being explained through the summation of individual parts to social wholes, ignoring the importance of social processes in shaping individual preferences and habits. The continuing influences of social institutions – the household, the employer, social culture or roles – are not recognized by mainstream theory (Hodgson, 1988, 68). Moreover, Hodgson (1999, 101–16) contends that empirical evidence casts doubt over the non-satiation axiom, and that the accumulation of skills and habits, rather than rational deliberation, causes social change. The indifference curves which form the foundations of mainstream approaches to labour supply are problematic. As Dugger (1979, 902) argues, institutional structure determines the range of alternatives available to the individual. The preferences of a household are thus not simply decided by the individuals within it, but are continuously influenced by social institutions and culture (Hodgson, 1988, 68–69).

2.3.2 Radical and Marxian Perspectives

Mainstream theory considers the number of hours worked by an individual, and therefore time spent in leisure, to be determined by their exogenously given preferences for income and leisure, subject to a budget constraint. This relationship is also reliant on the axioms of rational choice theory detailed in section 2.2. Marxian political economy has traditionally viewed labour-time as an essential element in analyzing distribution in capitalist economies. As such the focus on work-time is clear in such an approach. However, though Marxian political economy can be used to analyze contemporary patterns of work-time, it has had less to say about time-use in general. Laibman (1992) has, though, sought to address this conceptual weakness and to unify Marxian exploitation theory with the analysis of time-use and inequality within the household. In the Marxian theory of capitalist exploitation the length of the working day is divided between the time required to produce profit, interest, and rent, and the time during which workers produce the equivalent of what they consume. The ratio of the former (surplus labour time) to the latter (necessary labour time) is the rate of capitalist exploitation. This is a measure indicating distribution by class – defined by income source – in work-time terms. Marxian political economists, following Marx, decompose the exploitation rate to show how it is directly affected by various forces, specifically: (1) the real wage; (2) the productivity of labour; and (3) the length of the working day. The third element provides an analysis of extensive labour extraction that can be used to explain work-time patterns in different periods of capitalist development. In this approach conflict arises over the length of the working day, with structural and social forces playing a major role in determining work-time patterns. Laibman (1992) connects the theory of conflict over work-time to intra-household conflict. Production in the economy as a whole (including household production) involves two subprocesses (59–61): (1) in the household sector the time taken to produce wage goods is added to household labour to produce total social labour, and (2) in the capitalist sector 'current' labour, that is, labour employed by capitalists, is combined with raw materials to produce the capitalist sector output. Capitalist production, therefore, involves transforming labour employed in the capitalist sector and the commodities used in the production of goods to produce the output of the capitalist sector. Likewise, for the household sector, production combines household labour and market goods to produce social labour.

In order to integrate the analysis of intra-household conflict with the theory of absolute surplus-value it is important to recognize that the household and capitalist sectors are interconnected and that there are flows between them. The outcome of conflict over work-time (positive or negative absolute surplus-value) is manifest in the amount of current labour supplied to the capitalist sector. The flow of goods to the household sector is a further point of conflict, as employees bargain over real wages. Thus, the distributive conflict between the household and capitalist sectors is reflected in the flows of current labour and wages (Laibman 1992, 61). There emerge, in Laibman's reformulation of the Marxian theory of exploitation, two aspects that are especially relevant. First, in contrast to mainstream approaches, hours worked are argued as being an outcome of conflict and structure rather than individual preference. The flows of current labour and wages are also elements in this conflict-process and the structural forces only reflect the desires of employees with respect to the relative balance of work and leisure by chance. Second, the flows of household labour and labour supplied to the capitalist sphere may not be equal for men and women, generating inequality and reflecting gender oppression.

Radical theorists further criticize mainstream approaches, such as Becker's, for ignoring capitalist exploitation, and importantly, power (Spencer, 2000, 547). For example, work by Philp (2001) and Philp et al. (2005) has argued that the power of respective classes is important in generating outcomes in contemporary conflict over the length of the working day. In this sense management and hierarchies may have an important role in imposing work on employees, and thus in determining working hours at the organization level. This will be returned to in chapter 4. The axioms of mainstream theory have also come under significant criticism. For example, labour should not be considered homogenous. Among other things, this neglects the impact of work on human welfare (Spencer, 2009, 95). Schor (1993) also reported that individuals tend to 'adapt' to their environments. Their preferences, as such, adjust over time (129). Contrasting the mainstream view that work is associated with disutility, it has been argued that any resistance or aversion to work may be culturally determined (Spencer, 2009, 99). It is further argued that an individual may actually gain utility from work up to a point. In some cases they may work over the hours required to complete their tasks, that is, they may want to do a 'good' job (Spencer, 2009). These approaches have also offered reflection on institutional perspectives. For example, if forty hours per week is the work-time norm for a particular historical period, why have the accepted hours become forty hours? Institutional theorists including Commons (1931), and Marx (1976), both recognize the importance of the legal framework, social norms, and struggle between capital and labour. Conflict over working hours may well involve individual decision-making, but irreducible social forces have a considerable part to play as well (Philp et al., 2005). Mainstream theory can therefore be criticized for reducing the hour-determination process to simple individual optimization. Philp et al. argue that even if individuals have some control over their working hours, it is likely that this 'choice' is less significant than the institutional and evolutionary forces which determine the constraints they face (81). Mainstream models, and their extensions, which are based on choice can therefore be considered severely limited (80).

2.3.3 Feminist Economic Theory

Feminist economic theory is critical of mainstream theory for its focus on a self-interested rational individual. Institutional perspectives deliver a more appropriate view of decisions over work-time and Hodgson's work, for example, includes some discussion of the household. Feminist theory considers the centrality of the household. This section outlines feminist economic theory. It explores women's roles in paid and unpaid work, and how they differ from their male counterparts. Feminist critiques of mainstream approaches to labour supply are discussed. Applications of feminism to some of the key themes of this book are also explored, including notions of the division of labour within the household, gendered decision-making, constraints regarding paid and unpaid work, and time-constraints.

Feminism, in the economics discipline, developed in three key stages or waves. First wave feminism occurred between the mid-nineteenth and early twentieth centuries and focused on gaining equal rights of contract and property, and opposing the ownership of married women (and their children) by their husbands (Folbre, 1994, 147). Second wave feminism developed in the period from the 1960s to 1990. The focus of second wave feminism was highlighting gendered economic differences and the role of women in economics. During the 1970s and 1980s a number of mainstream economic theories were criticized by feminists, including the microeconomics of the household and labour markets, macroeconomics, and international trade (Peterson and Lewis, 1999). However, some have argued that it was during the third wave of feminism, in the 1990s, that feminist economic theory found its voice. It should be noted this was later than in other social science disciplines (Ferber and Nelson, 2003). Meagher and Nelson (2004, 102–3) suggest that the slow adoption of feminist thought in economics was led by two factors. First, economics, unlike many other disciplines, is dominated by a single paradigm – neoclassical theory – and a single methodology that puts a heavy emphasis on quantitative mathematical and statistical analysis (Spencer, 2009, 129). Second, the assumptions found in the models, methodology, findings, and policy prescriptions of economics are male-centred. Economics consistently reflects only the 'masculine' argument.

Feminist analysis of the mainstream approach to labour supply reflects on its disregard for social and emotional dimensions of human behaviour. Feminists, including Nelson (1995, 137), argue this should be considered a serious limitation, rather than a sign of rigour as it is often perceived by mainstream economists. The model of individual choice in markets is considered the distinguishing characteristic of economics by Becker (1976, 5). Similarly, Lucas (1987, 108) stated that the assumptions of the mainstream model provide 'the only "engine of truth"' in economics. In contrast, feminists contend that both of these approaches do not reflect robustness, but instead promote the continuation of gendered bias in economic modelling and analysis (Nelson, 1995, 137). Although families are considered by many mainstream economists, including Becker, they are only 'economic' if they can be modelled in terms of choices and markets. Feminist theorists contend that for women the family has, historically, been more directly 'economic'. The family, in this context, provides economic security for women. This remains the case for some as their fortunes are tightly associated with the economic and social status of their partner. Importantly, given the focus on this book, it is worth noting that a number of past debates between economists, and indeed census takers, have centred on whether to classify time spent performing unpaid household tasks in the home as work or as leisure (Folbre, 1991).

Feminists argue that individuals are embedded in a household context and that individual choice is constrained by others. A person's ability to participate in the labour market, undertaking paid work, is dependent upon the amount of unpaid work they undertake, and their responsibilities within the household. The labour market participation of men and women is therefore distinct. The economic lives of men and women have converged in the past fifty years, however important divisions persist within the household (Lundberg and Pollak, 2007, 6–7). Women still undertake the bulk of unpaid work in most households, including the majority of housework, as well as acting as primary caregivers (Garcia et al., 2007, 2011). Unpaid housework has been recognized by some economists, including Becker, as an important variable in rational choice models of labour supply. There is also an admission that housework is not a subcategory of leisure, which had previously been the assertion of mainstream theory (Faulkner, 1986, 56). Definitions of unpaid work have been broadened by feminist theory to include housework and, importantly, caring (Himmelweit, 1995). However, the idea of ubiquitous 'choice' for many is still questioned. Women, particularly those that are married/cohabiting and/or have dependent children, can only 'choose' between paid work outside the home and unpaid work inside the home (Bell, 1974, 621). Increasing pressure is felt by households for both partners to remain in some form of paid employment as a result of political, social, and financial drivers (Lewis and Campbell, 2008). Many women's choice may thus be limited to unpaid work in the home plus either full-time or part-time paid work outside the home.

Many economists do not consider humans to be 'homo economicus'. However, human behaviour is modelled in this way, as it appears the most useful and rigorous starting point for objective economic analysis. But, this results in significant gendered bias (Nelson, 1995, 136). The 'economic man' of mainstream economic theory is rational, independent, property owning, and self-interested with no regard for others. Faulkner (1986, 60) argues that this describes white male opportunity only, and has little relation to the experiences of women. The dominance of mainstream theory limits the exploration of any behaviour other than that of the self-interested individual. Analysis should acknowledge that we are born, and require a significant input from our parents (or others) in terms of care, not to mention the role they play in moulding preferences. Family provides social contact early in life, before colleagues and friends. The home also provides sustenance. These facts are frequently disregarded by mainstream economic analysis. They are considered unimportant, intellectually uninteresting, or natural. These areas of life are those thought of as 'women's work'. Feminist theorists have argued that modelling human behaviour requires greater acknowledgement of all the above factors (Nelson, 1995, 136). They are characteristics of all economic agents, whether they be men or women.

Feminist theorists further contend that the mainstream approach is inadequate for exploring women's decisions to work or care, for example, for women when they become mothers (Himmelweit and Sigala, 2002). It assumes individuals will choose the option which gives them the greatest utility, based on certain assumptions. However, mothers may not simply make their choice whether to continue in paid work in this manner. Any decision could be inputted into the rational choice model. However, it ignores the real processes involved in decision-making (Himmelweit and Sagala, 2002). In particular, the decision over whether to offer care to another (whether a child or relative) will not simply reflect self-interest and be made solely taking account of the individual's own preferences (van Staveren, 2010, 1129). Mainstream economic theory does provide conditions under which a non-self-centred approach to decision-making can be modelled using the concept of the family or household. Mainstream approaches in economics, though, are founded on a unitary model of the household in which the household is considered a single decision-making entity, led by a male 'dictator'. While this allows analysis into decision-making, it only fits the model of the male-breadwinner, female-homemaker, severely limiting its application to contemporary analysis. Regarding their labour market participation and work-time, women should be considered as decision-makers (Himmelweit and Sigala, 2002, 3). Indeed, with the increasing fluidity of work and rising household working hours the male-breadwinner, female-carer model, no longer offers an appropriate reflection of social reality (Crompton et al., 2007).

A major constraint faced by women is whether it is financially worthwhile for them to remain in the labour market. This choice must be given significant consideration with a number of factors affecting the decision, including costs of caring, cost and time associated with travelling to work, loss of time with their child, and loss of time to perform household tasks (Himmelweit and Sigala, 2002, 12; Wheatley, 2013; Wheatley and Wu, 2014). Where women are in dual earning households only those in paid employment with high earnings (including managerial and professional occupations) are likely to remain in full-time employment. Even then, women often compromise their careers as the household and personal relationships are central influences on their preferences and decisions (Harris et al., 2007). Women, as a result, may reduce their working hours, while some leave the labour market entirely to care for their children (Sirianni and Negrey, 2000, 62; Drinkwater, 2015). However, increasingly women display a greater commitment to the labour market, remaining in full-time employment for a significant proportion of their careers.

Commitment to the labour market does not, though, substantially alter the number of household tasks women perform. Nor does it result in a significant redistribution of household labour between men and women commensurate with their paid labour (Garcia et al., 2007, 2011). The availability of new household technology has also failed to create a substantial shift in household labour. As Schor (1993, 86–88) argued, this is because technology creates new tasks (while reducing the burden of others), and may create higher standards within the household environment. In this sense the household can be considered a site of conflict and inequality, as gendered norms influence the allocation of household tasks. Many women who undertake paid work perform a 'second shift' of unpaid work within their home. Women's time-use is, therefore, often particularly complex and demanding. For women who are employed outside the home, this results in a 'double shift' becoming the norm (Jones, 2003, 7). Women are subject to paid work *and* unpaid work within the home creating significant time inequalities between men and women. Married/cohabiting women employed outside the home in highly skilled occupations have the longest working weeks of all (Wheatley and Wu, 2014). MacDonald et al. (2005) use Canadian data to show that this results in greater levels of stress among women as they combine paid work with lengthy hours of unpaid work. Time spent on household responsibilities, and caring for elderly relatives, may also be more stressful for women than paid work. Indeed, lengthy hours of care (adult and child) have been shown empirically, using panel data from the BHPS, to have negative impacts on satisfaction with life overall among women (Della Giusta et al., 2011, 17–18). Paid work and household work combine to create a significant 'time squeeze' (Sirianni and Negrey, 2000, 62). Women's time is thus subject to much greater constraint.

The analysis of feminist theory presented in this section has highlighted a number of weaknesses and concerns regarding the use of mainstream economic theory in modelling how we use our time. The lack of consideration for the differences in the habits, behaviours, and constraints of men and women renders mainstream models inappropriate. This is particularly notable for the analysis of mothers. Feminist theory extends the perspectives on work and the household, introducing the broader notion of constraint defined at the beginning of the chapter. This section has highlighted how gendered norms within the household can result in women feeling a greater 'time-squeeze' (Schor, 1993; Southerton, 2003) and in high levels of stress for women (MacDonald et al., 2005), particularly among those with greater responsibilities in the labour market. The uneven division of household time may also have significant impacts on their careers should they, for example, attempt to utilize flexible working arrangements in order to balance paid work with the household (Lewis and Humbert, 2010).

2.4 CHAPTER SUMMARY: PLURALISM AS AN APPROACH TO UNDERSTANDING TIME-USE

This chapter has provided a conceptual discussion of the nature of time-use. In summary, this chapter has argued that mainstream economists' approach to time allocation, typified by Becker, is unsatisfactory with regards to examining household and workplace activities. The mainstream approach to labour supply simplifies individual decisions over work-time, a core use of time, to a trade-off between work (income) and leisure. Becker's (1976) rational choice approach, which extends mainstream labour supply theory, suffers from oversimplification and overuse of assumptions. Becker's analysis does not adequately acknowledge that preferences change through time, and are influenced by a range of factors. Employers, for example, may have a significant influencing effect on the preferences of employees. Moreover, Becker's analysis is largely 'gender blind'. Hakim offers a further extension of mainstream theory, which provides a gender sensitive analysis. She criticizes mainstream theory for assuming all individuals are homogenous, and for being grounded solely on male behaviour (Hakim, 2000). Hakim suggests women are heterogeneous, displaying a range of preferences for work and family life (158). However, her approach is limited as it assumes women make free choices which reflect their preferences. This ignores key issues of constraint and inequality. Mainstream approaches can also be criticized from a radical perspective for ignoring key issues of power in determining behaviours and constraining choice (Philp, 2001; Philp et al., 2005). Laibman (1992), for example, identified class and gender power relationships, and the structure of capitalist society, as being integral in explaining patterns of work-time and household activity.

Institutional theory critiques mainstream approaches, and Becker in particular, for ignoring the continuing influences of social institutions. These mould the preferences of the individual, whether originating from the household or the firm, or as a result of social culture or roles. Mainstream theory is inadequate because it is based on a number of problematic assumptions. Thus, it does not view 'free' behaviour in the present as a 'reproducer of routine', which can reflect constraint (Hodgson, 1988, 134). Institutional approaches suggest that the preferences of a household are not simply decided by the individuals within it, but are continuously influenced by social institutions and social culture. Institutional approaches take account of the constraints faced by households, and additionally connect different elements of time-use including consumption time and household labour time. However, little explanation is given to the complexities of the household, including the household division of labour and caring responsibilities.

The household is in contrast a primary focus of feminist theory (Folbre, 1994; Nelson, 1995; Bell, 1974). Feminist theory critiques rational choice approaches for their persistent focus on 'homo-economicus'. Mainstream economic theory has traditionally ignored the household, and unpaid household labour, termed 'women's work'. Feminists also consider the home to be a site of conflict and inequality. Women, more so than men, make decisions in the context of the household, with consideration for managing paid work alongside domestic responsibilities and care. This may result in reductions in working hours or even exit from the labour market at certain points in the lifecourse. Acknowledging the limits of mainstream theory, the contributions from alternative heterodox traditions have been explored in this chapter. These provide appropriate theoretical foundations for the empirical exploration of how we use our time, and the impacts the organization of time has on our well-being which forms the remainder of this book.

NOTES

1. It has been argued that the time taken for individuals to consume goods should be included in the analysis of time-use, but that this may generate contradictory results (Steedman, 2001, 17–19).

2. Note that although the commute is considered as a form of unpaid work-related activity in this book, it is separated from other work-related activity as there is greater choice over the (length of the) commute. However, the extent to which the commute may represent a compromise or constraint is considered in detail in chapter 7.

3. Institutional economics has itself faced a number of criticisms, not least from mainstream economists. For example, Mirowski (1981, 593) reports that institutionalism has been labelled as empiricist and lacks any coherent theory. Relatedly,

institutional economics has been labelled descriptive rather than analytical (Witte, 1954, 135). However, as Ayres (1951, 55), among others, argued, this view is mistaken. While empirical work comprises a significant portion of institutionalist studies, empiricism does not produce the body of theory found in institutional economics. In addition, many of the major advances made in economic theory are the by-product of empirical study (Witte, 1954, 135). This highlights its importance in the generation and evaluation of theory.

Chapter Three

Time-Use

The Historical and Policy Context

3.1 INTRODUCTION

This chapter considers the historical and policy context for the current patterns of time-use we observe. The way we use our time has altered significantly throughout history, driven by societal and technological change. Time spent in paid work has diminished historically since the Industrial Revolution (Bienefeld, 1972). As a result of government intervention and changing norms in work-time, opportunities to engage in paid work have increased, and continue to do so, for women (Lewis and Campbell, 2008). The structure of the economy and the types and ways in which we work, and engage in work-related and non-work activities, have also changed dramatically. Paid work remains central in the time-use of many individuals, and in turn households, influencing and constraining other uses of time (McDowell et al., 2005; Philp and Wheatley, 2011; Wheatley and Wu, 2014). Developments in technology, including information and communication technologies (ICTs), have created opportunities to reduce the burden of paid work, but have also created challenges associated with the blurring of activities (Felstead et al., 2005; Wheatley et al., 2008). This chapter explores the drivers of change in how we use our time, including past and recent policy interventions. The focus here is on the United Kingdom, but broader context and examples are provided where relevant. Specific attention is given to the developments of norms in work-time and the differing constraints faced by men and women. In providing an overview of historical developments and the current policy environment in the United Kingdom, this chapter sets the scene for the empirical investigations presented in subsequent chapters.

3.2 A BRIEF HISTORY OF TIME-USE

In the United Kingdom, the development and standardization of how we use our time can be traced as far back as the sixteenth century. During this period, there was large-scale scarcity of labour. This period witnessed an increase in real wages at the same time as there was unmistakable evidence of reductions in the hours spent at work (Bienefeld, 1972). As the century proceeded, trends of reductions in working hours began to be reversed. In the seventeenth century this continued with the abolition of holidays by the Puritans. Increased annual working hours were associated with the emergence of the Protestant work ethic, a term used to describe Protestant values which emphasized hard work and the accumulation of wealth, first coined by Weber in his work *The Protestant Ethic and the Spirit of Capitalism* (1976). By the eighteenth century real wages recommenced their upward trend and hours once more declined, such that a working day of ten hours, from 6.00 a.m. to 6.00 p.m. (with two hours of breaks) came to be the accepted norm. In other words there developed 'usual and acknowledged hours of daily labour' (Bienefeld, 1972, 40).

With the advent of the Industrial Revolution came an important change in the structure of paid work, which has significant relevance to how we use our time. Specifically, a spatial separation of home and work occurred as factories developed to house large machinery, concentrating economic activity into particular geographical locations. The technological advancements witnessed during this period, particularly the growth of the rail transport network, allowed increased mobility among the labour force. The movement of labour on a frequent, including daily, basis to these centres of economic activity resulted initially in large-scale rural to urban migration, but also in the widespread emergence of the commute. Locating workers within fixed environments has historically been advantageous to employers as it facilitates monitoring and enforcement of 'normal' working practices, not least in relation to the length and timing of the working day (Marglin, 1974).

One problem encountered early in the Industrial Revolution was enforcing work discipline. The practice of Saint Monday – workers taking time off work to engage in leisure activities – persisted from the seventeenth to the twentieth century (Reid, 1996). Capitalists, and managers and supervisors, were drawn into conflict with workers, who exhibited strong preferences for leisure. The 'leading-sector' in the Industrial Revolution in the United Kingdom was the cotton textile industry. By the end of the eighteenth century some cotton mills operated for thirteen hours or more per day, driving conflicts over working hours and practices (Bienefeld, 1972). It should be noted, however, that a number of firms and industries did not experience conflict of this nature, as they opted for reductions in hours, seeing the potential gains in terms of increased productivity. Reductions in hours were realized through the introduction of shifts, and were administered in a number of industries, including the machine lace workers of Nottingham (210). Initial legislation targeting reductions in working hours, enacted in 1802 and 1819, was ineffective, largely as a result of employer interests controlling the 'legislative and repressive apparatus of the state' (34). The Factory Acts, beginning in 1802, summarized in table 3.1, were a series of acts which aimed to improve factory working conditions during the Industrial Revolution. Further legislation restricting hours was passed in the period 1820–50 and as a result, from the middle of the nineteenth century, employers began to focus on productivity increase, that is, intensive labour extraction (Hobsbawm, 1968). In 1872–1874 there was a comprehensive reduction of normal working hours driven, in part, by the strength of organized trades and craft unions.[1] Further reductions in hours came with the development of new unionism in the 1880s; this largely affected unskilled and low-skilled workers.

The growth of large firms, seeking to maintain their position in industry, resulted in further standardization of hours. This reflected the realization that long hours were not of great benefit to the employer, and as such a restriction on hours was deemed an adequate barrier against entry into the industry (Bienefeld, 1972, 210–11). Reductions in hours through gender neutral legislation, and from collective bargaining (162–78), became standard practice by the middle of the twentieth century (Figart and Golden, 1998, 412).

3.2.1 Production and Working Practices in the Twentieth Century

The new production and working methods which emerged in the twentieth century were theorized, initially in 1911, by Frederick Taylor (1967). Taylor

Table 3.1 The Factory Acts

1802	The first Factory Act was 'an act for the Preservation of the Health and Morals of Apprentices and others employed in Cotton and other Mills, and Cotton and other factories'. It prohibited the employment of apprentices at night or for longer than twelve hour days. However, this act was never enforced.
1819	Robert Owen, an influential figure during the Industrial Revolution who was a successful and philanthropic factory owner, a pioneer of cooperation, and a thinker who inspired socialist movements in many countries, had successfully campaigned for an Act of Parliament to be passed restricting the hours of all children to twelve hours per day, excluding meal times.
1825	Legislation was passed limiting the working week to sixty-nine hours. But problems were again present with respect to enforcement.
1833	The Factory Act of 1833 was limited as it restricted hours for women and children only, although this may have had a side effect of reducing hours for men.

Source: Figart and Golden (1998, 412).

adopted a scientific approach to management, termed 'Taylorism'. His approach extended Adam Smith's (1981 [1776]) division of labour concept, first published in his book *An Inquiry into the Nature and Causes of the Wealth of Nations*, but focused on changing working conditions as scientific management aimed to increase productivity through reductions in inefficiency caused, for example, by malfeasance. Taylor (1967, 15) believed that by eliminating malfeasance, higher wages, shorter working hours, and better working conditions would be possible. Scientific management made use of a number of innovations including time and motion studies, plus the adoption of standardized tools and time saving devices. Task allocation was fundamental to scientific management, and the subdivision of carefully specified tasks was thorough. Under Taylorism there was a movement of responsibility from the individual worker to the manager. This increased the control available to the manager, but resulted in significant reductions in levels of autonomy for the worker. The essence of Taylorism is that there should be little, if any, initiative on the part of the worker or producer, an aspect of Taylorist work organization which has since been heavily criticized (Kelly, 2000). Indeed, it has been argued that any discretion on the part of the worker would be considered as a potential threat to productivity under Taylorist work organization (Choi et al., 2008, 423). Taylorist (1967, 33–34) methods, nevertheless, were important in the development of modern managerial practice, where knowledge is used to generate rules, laws, and formulae for workers to adhere to, with each manager having 'initiative' over their workers. This process of mechanization and extensive industrialization also influenced the precise measurement of time in the work context. As Thompson (1967, 61) stated, 'Time is now currency; it is not passed but spent.'

Production and working practices in the twentieth century were revolutionized with the advent of Fordism. It has been argued that 'Fordism was Taylorism plus mechanization' (Lipietz, 1997, 2). This analytical concept, based in both name and content on the production techniques of Henry Ford's Ford motor company, between 1913 and 1914, was characterized by the notion of the 'five-dollar day'. High-wage workers were seen as beneficial as they sustained high levels of consumption and aggregate demand. As productivity increased, wages charted a parallel growth in order to maintain consistent consumption levels. This consequently maintained profitability (see Figart, 2001, 406–8). It extended the division of labour and displaced skilled craft-based workers for low-skilled employees working on an assembly line. Automation through mass production was the most important technical feature of Fordism, however equally important was control of labour (408). The subdivided tasks of Fordism were specified in detail by management and significant mechanization was adopted, thereby allowing greater control by management and supervisors over the pace and regularity of production.

The power of managers to control and regulate the conditions of work was heightened. By the 1970s there was, however, a significant shift in paradigm towards *flexible specialization*, as mass production of highly standardized goods was no longer competitive in many industrialized countries.

3.2.2 Deindustrialization in the United Kingdom

One of the key changes which occurred in the United Kingdom, and in many other industrialized economies, during the latter part of the twentieth century was the decline of industrial activity, termed deindustrialization (Martin and Rowthorn, 1986). Explanations of deindustrialization vary as the reasons behind this phenomenon are complex. Singh (1977, 134) argued that exports failed in the manufacturing sector due to a loss of competitiveness, and this was responsible. Other factors highlighted by Townsend (1997, 80–81) include the recessions of the 1970s and early 1980s, which resulted in the loss of manufacturing jobs, devastating many industrial towns. Further explanations have been offered which implicate loss of competitiveness, poor management, and poor labour relations (Hardill et al., 2001).

During the 1970s a range of factors acted as drivers for poor economic performance in the United Kingdom. High marginal tax rates made the UK economy less conducive to investment and growth (Kilpatrick and Lawson, 1980). Kilpatrick and Lawson also argue that lack of efficiency was a major source of problems in the United Kingdom, and that poor industrial relations and the strength of unions may have exacerbated these issues. An alternative explanation is that of the UK economy reaching 'maturity'. A high income elasticity of demand for services, coupled with increased low-cost competition from abroad, reduced demand for indigenous industrial output (Kitson and Wilkinson, 2007, 812). The Conservative governments of the 1980s viewed deregulation, privatization, and reductions in direct taxation and union power as highly desirable (Crafts, 1996, 176). However, by the 1980s UK industry was in widespread decline. Whatever the cause, the decline of manufacturing industry led to the loss of millions of jobs in 'blue-collar' occupations. Nearly 1.9 million manufacturing jobs were lost between 1966 and 1977 (Bazen and Thirlwall, 1989, 11). Jobs in manufacturing declined a further 9.24 percent between 1981 and 1991 (Hardill et al., 2001, 20). The share of the world's manufacturing trade generated by the United Kingdom fell from 20.9 percent in 1973, to just 9.1 percent by 1979 (Crafts, 1993, 20). The impact of these changes on the economy is illustrated by the reduction in relative per capita incomes. The United Kingdom, ranked ninth in the world during the first half of the 1960s, dropped to fifteen by the beginning of the 1990s (Quah, 2000). Some jobs were lost abroad where lower labour costs were attractive to organizations. However many were lost due to improvements in technologies, and the drive to decrease costs to improve profits. The restructuring of the UK economy also resulted in an increase in the North-South divide, broadening inequalities between regions (Hardill et al., 2006). The decline of industries such as ship building impacted greatly on the North East and Scotland, and the decline of coal mining during the 1980s had devastating effects on large areas of the United Kingdom, including the Midlands (174). This loss of industry resulted in a significant shift in the structure of the UK economy.

3.2.3 The Emergence of a Post-Industrial Economy

The contemporary economy of the United Kingdom is, perhaps, most appropriately defined as a post-industrial economy. It is characterized by the growth of the service sector, sometimes referred to as tertiarization. A 'post-industrial economy' is defined as one where the majority of the labour force is no longer employed in agriculture, mining, manufacturing, construction (and associated storage and transportation), but is instead dominated by the service sector comprising employment in retailing, teaching, office work, transport, administration, entertainment, personal care, and the finance, real estate, and insurance industries (La Jeunesse, 2009, 95). The service sector is responsible for the majority of employment within the United Kingdom. Estimates from the UK Census of Population, summarized in figure 3.1, show the changes that have occurred in the industrial structure, with the service sector increasing slowly from 33 percent in 1841 to 34 percent of all workers in 1901, and 46 percent by 1951. However, stark increases have since been

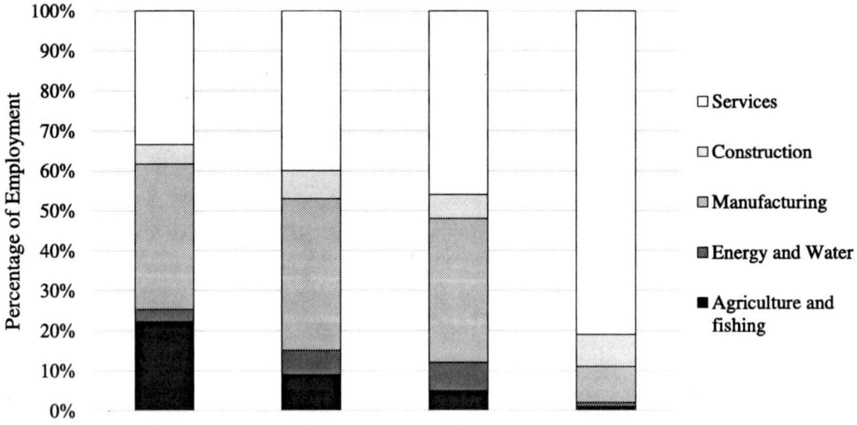

Figure 3.1. Industrial Structure in Great Britain/England and Wales (UK Census of Population).

recorded with services accounting for 70 percent of employment in 1991 (Lindsay, 2003, 137), and 81 percent in 2011 (ONS, 2013a).[2] Expansion has also occurred in flexible and part-time working, led not only by the growth in participation among women for whom reduced hours employment remains more common, but by a bigger movement from standard (full-time) to non-standard (part-time, self-employed, temporary) employment. These changes have increased insecurity among many occupations resulting in the loss of a 'job for life' or 'stable career'. The growth of insecurity in the labour market has affected many groups of workers from the lower skilled to the professions and even management (Rifkin, 1995, 101). Sennett (1998, 120) suggested these changes mean a career can no longer be regarded as a 'well made road'. However, tertiarization and the flexibilization of employment are only part of a more complex set of changes which characterize post-industrial economies. Technological change has aided globalization, through enabling instant communication, reduced transport costs, and by facilitating international flows of labour and capital. Meanwhile growth in services, alongside changes to social and employment policy, has increased female labour market participation rates, and the retention of older workers within the labour market (La Jeunesse, 2009, 97).

A number of scholars have attempted to encapsulate the changes to the economy and labour market which began, arguably, in the case of the United Kingdom in the 1980s, and continued into the 1990s and 2000s. As well as the moniker 'post-industrial economy' used in this book, these changes have been conceptualized in a range of alternative ways, including the 'new' economy, the 'knowledge-based' economy, and the 'service' economy. There exists no formal definition for a 'new' economy. Quah (2001, 16) defines the 'new' economy as being composed of: (1) ICT, including the Internet, (2) intellectual assets, (3) electronic libraries and databases, and (4) biotechnology, that is, carbon-based libraries and databases. For Quah, the distinguishing characteristic of these categories is that they represent goods and services which hold the same properties as knowledge, which is itself a key characteristic of the changing nature of the economy. Other broad definitions of the 'new' economy describe it as comprising or containing elements of: (1) the emergence of ICT, (2) the growth of the service sector, and (3) the effect of globalization and deindustrialization on the economy (Nolan and Slater, 2003, 58–60). Two distinct perspectives exist in relation to defining the 'new' economy. First, there are those that see the changes to the economy as being driven by ICT and the sectoral consequences of its advances. Alternatively, the new economy has been argued as representing the post-industrial form taken on by the entire economy (Coyle and Quah, 2002, 6). Quah (2001) suggests two distinctive features of the 'new' economy. First, the productivity improvements associated with ICT have rippled strongly throughout the entire economy, 'affecting everything from mergers and acquisitions in corporate finance, to factory-floor rewiring of inventory management mechanisms' (10). Second, ICT products behave like knowledge. They hold all the relevant economic properties of knowledge, characterized by near-infinite expansibility and a disrespect of geography. Goods and services that behave like knowledge are becoming more important in two respects: as a fraction of total consumption, and in their increasingly direct contact with a growing number of consumers.

Beyers (2002, 28), in contrast, argued that the changes in the structure of the economy should be considered to be characteristic of the emergence of 'a service economy supported by goods and service producing sectors' rather than as a 'new' economy. Indeed, it has been suggested that the changes in the structure of employment in the United Kingdom are better encapsulated in the term 'service economy', given the large proportion of workers now employed in the service sector (Nolan and Slater, 2003, 77). The post-industrial economy of the United Kingdom, as it is referred to in this book, has also been termed the 'knowledge driven' economy and the 'new knowledge based' economy (Nolan and Slater, 2003). The application of 'smart' technologies, and globalization have triggered the emergence of a knowledge economy which is centred on the exploitation of intangible assets, including knowledge, ideas, and information, which are used to generate intangible outputs in the form of knowledge and services.

Consistent in these various definitions and explanations of the changes in the economic structures of many societies is the central role given to developments in ICTs. Through facilitating changes in the nature of paid work, including globalization, advances in technology and ICT have, at the level of the individual worker, been argued as playing a central role in the increased intensity, duration, and participation of paid work (Perrons et al., 2005). ICT is credited with adding to work-related stress, not reducing it. Doyle and Reeves (2001, 30) contend that ICT should be used to replace the standard working day, rather than simply extending it. The boundaries around work have dissolved as individuals are never off-line (Perrons et al., 2006, 3), and work can be conducted on the move, during travel, and from home (Hislop and Axtell, 2009; Bergman and Gustafson, 2008). There has, however, long been an appreciation for the revolutionary nature of ICT, as it links jobs and enables virtual contact (Castells and Aoyama, 1994, 26). The impact of ICTs also extend well beyond paid work influencing, for example, the way we travel and spend our leisure time.

Beck (2000) raised concerns regarding the impact of the emergence of the post-industrial economy in changing the nature of work. In particular, recent decades have witnessed a reduction in job security and increases in inequality (e.g., in pay). Changes in patterns of paid work are apparent resulting from sectoral change in the composition of the United Kingdom, including longer hours for highly skilled workers, increases in flexible and part-time work, and increases in mobile working (Hislop and Axtell, 2009; Wheatley, 2012b). The labour market increasingly favours polarized skill levels. Those with advanced cognitive skills, such as programmers and management consultants, are located at one end, and those who are 'unskilled', such as carers and cleaners, are at the other (Coyle and Quah, 2002, 8). The modern workplace requires individuals and their households to be well informed, highly organized, and stable, allowing support for both working individuals and their children. The new work environment requires increased flexibility, and is characterized by instability (Wheatley et al., 2008). The post-industrial economy is argued as being characterized by a 'digital duality or divide' (Perrons, 2003, 68), between what can be referred to as the 'information-rich' and the 'information-poor' (La Jeunesse, 2009, 97). This divide is generated by low level jobs created by high level managers and professionals. It may result in increased divisions and inequalities in social class, ethnicity, and between regions. Regional variations associated with the manufacturing economy have dissolved, but have been replaced with growing regional disparities in incomes generated by the growth of high status professional occupations in finance in the London and South East regions of the United Kingdom (McDowell, 2004, 149). The working environments present in the post-industrial economy may also exacerbate divisions between genders (Perrons, 2003, 68), in part owing to the differing constraints present in employment among men and women resulting from the household division of labour and caring responsibilities (Garcia et al., 2007, 2011).

3.2.4 Feminization of the Labour Market

The feminization of the labour market represents a key change in the structure of employment, and importantly has a range of effects in regards to how we use our time. The share of paid employment in the United Kingdom undertaken by women has increased in almost all industries and occupations. This is most notable in certain professions, clerical and service occupations (McDowell et al., 2006). Whereas the UK Labour Force Survey reported 53 percent of women were engaged in waged employment in 1971, this figure had risen to 67 percent by 2013 (ONS, 2013c, 3). During this same period rates of employment among men decreased from 92 percent to 76 percent. The service sector, as already discussed, has increased in size substantially since the latter part of the twentieth century, and has been a particular growth area for women's employment. It employed 60 percent of men and 82 percent of women in 2004, and by 2011 the UK Census of Population showed that 71 percent of men and 92 percent of women in work reported employment in the service sector (ONS, 2013a). Women have since the early 1990s accounted for approximately half of the labour force in the United Kingdom (Nolan and Slater, 2003, 60), and command an 'increased political voice' (Walby, 2002, 25). They are demanding, and winning, greater equity, enabling access to paid work, although this does not always result in equal wages (Carnoy, 2000, 108). Indeed, recent UK evidence from the Annual Survey of Hours and Earnings (ASHE) suggests that the gender pay gap still stands at around 10 percent among full-time workers, although in 2015 the gap was recorded as 9.4 percent which was the lowest recorded since the ASHE survey began in 1997 (ONS, 2013b, 2014a, 2015a). When factoring in the greater propensity of women to work part-time the pay gap remains closer to 20 percent.

The growth in women's labour market participation is attributed to changes in women's expectations and aspirations, and key legislative changes which have increased opportunities within the labour market. In particular, legislation was enacted in the 1970s, beginning with the Equal Pay Act of 1970, which prohibited unequal treatment of men and women with respect to pay. Other policy included the Sex Discrimination Act of 1975 which focused on the promotion of equality of opportunity between genders, and the Employment Protection Act of 1975 which made it illegal to terminate women's employment due to pregnancy and introduced statutory maternity provision (ONS, 2013c, 3). Women have been able to take advantage of greater educational opportunities, while the rising cost of living also renders many households dependent on two incomes. There has also been a shift in employment and welfare policies, in particular, during the period of the New Labour government in the United Kingdom from 1997 to 2010 (McDowell et al., 2006, 144). Mothers – including single parents – are now expected to either be in employment or looking for work, rather than relying on welfare (Lewis and Campbell, 2008, 535–36). New measures have also been put in place to improve 'work-family' policies. These have been made to ensure women are able to manage work alongside the home and especially childcare (McDowell et al., 2006).

The increase in the size of the service sector, which as was noted earlier is a sector in which women are significantly represented, has occurred during the same period as traditionally male dominated sectors, such as manufacturing, have declined. The long-term decline in blue-collar work and the increase in white-collar occupations has reduced the need for a workforce consisting of physically strong workers, who tend to be male. Historically male manual workers could expect up to double the pay of women. This resulted from differentials in strength, and the principle of a 'family wage' being paid to men, but not women (Hakim, 2000, 63). In contrast white-collar occupations do not require physical strength, and as such allow women the same opportunities as men. A new division of labour has arisen between 'masculinized' labour in possession of high skill levels and career positions offering prosperity. This contrasts with 'feminized' labour of both sexes which is low-skilled with minimal levels of job security and low incomes (Castells, 2000, 11–12).

Gendered divisions, though, remain apparent in the labour market in both vertical and horizontal forms, resulting in segregation between industries and occupations (Teasdale, 2013, 400; Hakim, 2000, 65). Horizontal segregation – in which certain industries experience dominance by a single gender – remains evident as women are employed mainly in service activities, while men undertake managerial, manual, and technical jobs (Fagan and Burchell, 2002, 17). For example, around 70 percent of those employed in the public administration, education, and health sector are women (ONS, 2013a), while certain industries such as retailing employ large proportions of women (Broadbridge, 2008; Foster et al., 2007). Among the professions large numbers of women are found in education. Meanwhile, others areas of employment remain dominated by men, for example, construction and engineering (Kusku et al., 2007) where only around 12 percent of workers are women in the United Kingdom (ONS, 2013a). Men continue to dominate at the highest levels of many industries, particularly in government, management, and professional occupations. Data from the 2014 UK Annual Population Survey shows that 12.7 percent of men report employment as managers, directors, or senior officials, whereas only around 7.3 percent of women report employment in these occupations (NOMIS, 2015). Moreover, recent data from the UK ASHE reveals that men continue to occupy the majority of the highest earning jobs. Within the top 10 percent of earners, 69 percent are men (ONS, 2013c, 18). There remains a 'glass ceiling' within workplaces, sustained by workplace cultures and informal procedures that render women at a disadvantage when attempting to reach higher levels of management (Fagan and Burchell, 2002, 20). Where women do reach higher levels of management the horizontal segregation present in many occupations and industries often means they are likely to manage other women.

Developments in ICTs and wireless technologies have been argued as extending the opportunities for those with caring responsibilities, guiding a reduction in gender inequality (Perrons, 2003). This is driving increases in the numbers of dual earning and dual career households (see Wheatley and Wu, 2014). In addition, a number of employers now offer a range of 'concierge services' to their employees, including catering, shopping services, and the provision of care through crèche services (Perrons, 2004, 103–4). Much of the flexibility on the part of the employer is put in place to ensure retention of highly skilled women, employed in senior positions. These workers are 'time-starved', creating a demand for low-paid, low-skilled, services. However, many managers remain averse to supporting greater levels of flexibility among employees. This limits the ability of those under significant constraint, including those with caring responsibilities, to engage in paid work (Sullivan and Smithson, 2007; Lewis and Humbert, 2010).

Gender divisions within the household continue to constrain women with housework and caring (including both child and elder care) responsibilities (Garcia et al., 2007, 2011; Lundberg and Pollak, 2007; Perrons, 2004). This is not least evident in the proportions of women employed part-time. Part-time work accounts for approximately 40 percent of employment among women (Connolly and Gregory, 2008, F52). The household division of labour and caring responsibilities have resulted in an increase in low-skilled, low-paid female workers undertaking caring and domestic work for highly skilled, well-paid female workers. There exists a divide between 'career' women who are highly educated, and command well paid employment, and those who are in less secure, lower paid work, some of whom exit the labour market at certain points during the lifecourse as they cannot afford care (Drinkwater, 2015, 284). 'Career' women although income rich, it can be argued, are time poor (McDowell et al., 2005). Schor (1993) suggests there may have been a reduction in female household labour, due to increases in female employment rates. Men now perform a larger proportion of household tasks than they did previously (Sullivan, 2010; Schwanen, 2007). However, employed women's lives remain dominated by the household. Women still perform the majority of household tasks (Harris et al., 2007). Those women who perform two tasks, paid employment and household work, endure a 'double-shift' (Jones, 2003, 7). The success of flexible working is currently limited by enduring links between full-time work and perceived professional and labour market commitment. The issue remains that the productivity levels of workers are often deemed less significant than the concept of commitment linked directly to hours of work (Harris et al., 2007, 501). This requires not only full-time hours, but long hours associated with 'time-devouring male employment' cultures (Sirianni and Negrey, 2000, 72). Career progression suffers for those who do not, or are unable to, adhere to this culture. Opportunities for promotion are only offered to individuals who consistently work full-time throughout their careers, contrasting starkly with the lived reality of many women's careers (Lewis and Humbert, 2010).

3.3 THE UK POLICY ENVIRONMENT

The UK economy continues to be characterized by a liberal stance on employment, welfare, and wider social policy (Lewis and Campbell, 2008, 535–36). Following the neoliberal approaches of the Conservative governments of the

1980s and 1990s, associated with, among other things, privatization and a reduced role for the state, the New Labour governments from 1997 employed a hybrid 'liberal collectivist' model (Clarke, 2004) which acknowledged the need to address widening inequality and the decline of public infrastructure (Grimshaw and Rubery, 2012, 106). Key developments in the period of the New Labour government included the National Minimum Wage (1998), the Working Time Regulations (1998), family leave policies, part-time and fixed-term worker regulations, and a right to union recognition (Smith and Morton, 2006). However, in recent years there has been a return to the neo-liberal approach since the Coalition government was voted into power in 2010. Reductions, and in some areas withdrawal, of state provision have changed the economic and social environment. These changes are of concern as the United Kingdom, common with many other post-industrial economies, faces a number of challenges associated with changing social structures and attitudes, including: (1) the reduction of support for training and/or pensions by employers in the labour market, while increased pressure is placed on individuals and the government to invest in an educated workforce; (2) an ageing population associated with rising costs in elderly care; (3) changes in the structures of families and support networks including through geographical dispersion; and (4) changes in individual and societal norms and attitudes, including towards gender roles, which increase the demand for policy to support parents (Grimshaw and Rubery, 2012, 108).

3.3.1 Working Time Regulation

Since 1973 the United Kingdom has been subject to European Union (EU) policy.[3] One such EU policy, the European Working Time Directive (EWTD), was adopted in the EU (except the United Kingdom) in 1993. It imposes a maximum forty-eight-hour working week for employees. It protects against the possible negative effects which long working hours may have on the health of individuals (European Commission, 2005). The Directive (Council Directive 94/103/EC) does provide the option for member states to impose an opt-out, but this is only permitted under certain conditions, specifically where no signature is requested from the worker during the first month of employment, there is no victimization for not signing or withdrawing from an opt-out, and employers keep records on the working hours of opted-out workers. The United Kingdom adopted the Directive in the form of the Working Time Regulations (WTR), implemented on 1 October 1998, and amended in 2002 and 2007. In contrast to a number of other member states including France, the UK WTR did include an opt-out from inception. Many employers, both in the public and private sector, have promoted this to employees, through waivers. The main characteristics of the WTR are (Department for Business, Innovation and Skills, 2011b):

- a limit of forty-eight hours per week which the worker can be required to work, averaged over a period of seventeen weeks (although workers can choose to work more using the 'opt out' agreements);
- a maximum average of eight hours of work in twenty-four for night workers;
- free health assessments for night workers;
- an entitlement to eleven hours of rest each day;
- an entitlement to a day off each week;
- an entitlement to an in-work rest break if the working day is longer than six hours;
- an entitlement to four weeks of paid leave per year (pro rata for part-time employees); and
- entitlements for adolescent workers.

Continued evidence of long hours in the United Kingdom, and a number of judgements at the European Employment Council on 9 June 2008 regarding the working conditions of doctors, oil rig workers, and those whose job involves being 'on call', led to a series of revisions seeking stronger application of the EWTD in the United Kingdom. However, in recent years the UK government has sought to further relax the application of the work-time legislation (see, e.g., Guardian, 2011). This recent policy agenda contrasts starkly with the potential benefits derived from reductions in work-time, which have been argued to include the redistribution of hours of work across the labour market, reductions in levels of capitalist exploitation, and a more equitable society (La Jeunesse, 2009). Reductions in hours could also offer greater opportunities for engagement in the 'third' or voluntary sector, something which some scholars argue is likely to become an increasingly important extension/alternative to paid work in the economy as the effects of technological progress create a decline in service sector employment through automation of routine and repetitive tasks (101) – a change already evident, for example, in the growth of self-service check-outs – and as a result of reductions in public funding of services since the 2007–2009 economic crisis.

3.3.2 Equality and Work-Life Balance Policy

Legislation targeting greater equality in paid work began with the abolition of the 'marriage bar' from 1945 in the United Kingdom.[4] This was replaced by equal opportunities and sex discrimination legislation in the 1970s, including those described in section 3.2.4. By the 1990s equal pay and comparable worth policies had made notable inroads into eliminating sex discrimination

Box 3.1 Work-Time Regulation in France: an Alternative Approach

In contrast to more liberal approach adopted in the United Kingdom, France opted for a stronger application of work-time regulation. Initial policy was enacted in 1996 through the Robien Law which offered financial incentives to firms creating jobs and job shares. This was accompanied by the reduction in the legal working week from thirty-nine hours to thirty-five hours through the Aubry Laws (law No. 2000-37), effective from February 2000, which were named after the Employment and Solidarity Minister at that time, Martime Aubry. The Aubry Laws legislated for a statutory maximum work week of thirty-five hours for companies employing more than twenty people in exchange for social security rebates paid to firms for each employee. These laws focused particularly on employment generation and productivity benefits. Work-time reductions were to be achieved with no loss of pay, in exchange for work-time reorganization and labour flexibility (Fagnani and Letablier, 2007). Evidence suggested that the French economy experienced an initial positive economic response to reductions in working hours, including reductions in unemployment rates (from 12.2 percent in 1997 to 8.6 percent by 2001) and the curtailing of up to seventeen thousand redundancies/lay-offs (LaJeunesse, 2009, 213; Hayden, 2006; Durand et al., 2004). The majority of employees reported improved work-life balance and positive reactions to their increased leisure time (Fagnani and Letablier, 2007). However, it has since been argued that these positive outcomes were a coincidence of economic recovery in France at this time, and that initial implementation may have actually retarded the French economy (Philpott, 2005), and increased work intensity and stress for a significant minority of workers (Fagnani and Letablier, 2007). Moreover, the policy created short-run freezes in income, while lower and middle income workers experienced reduced income, as they became unable to work additional hours of overtime (effectively creating underemployment among these workers). Additional leisure time was therefore offset by reductions in real wages. A number of amendments, including the addition of an opt-out in the private sector, have since relaxed work-time regulation in France. Although these changes have been met with demonstrations by unions, further relaxation of the legislation continues to be sought by the French government (Chazan, 2016).

in pay (Hakim, 2000, 60–61). From the late 1990s the New Labour government promoted greater movement of women into paid employment. This was done through linking welfare payments and tax credits to labour market participation, and by providing better education opportunities (McDowell et al., 2005, 446). Until recently coping with the interface between work and home, and equality within the home, have largely been considered private matters. During the past two decades, however, work-life balance and equality between genders have been pushed to the forefront of public policy. A series of measures have been promoted, many under the banner of 'work-life balance', to ease the conflicts for individuals who find their work demands encroaching into other areas of family life. Work-life balance or 'integration' aims to improve conditions for all workers by altering work practices (Atkinson and Hall, 2009, 652; Fagan et al., 2012). It is defined as the ability of individuals, regardless of age or gender, to combine work and household responsibilities successfully, or with minimum conflict (Clark, 2000, 751). The household-workplace interface has become increasingly blurred (Bulger et al., 2007), creating a range of challenges for workers and their households. The Work-Life Balance Campaign (WLBC), which was launched in spring 2000, aimed to raise employers' awareness of the benefits to business of introducing policies and practices which help employees obtain a better balance between work and home (Department for Business, Innovation and Skills, 2011a). For Clutterbuck (2003) central to the notion of work-life balance is 'choice' since work-life balance involves: being aware of different demands on time and energy; having the ability to choose how to allocate time and energy; knowing what values to apply to choices; and making choices. Through a range of mechanisms, including provision of advice, case study research, partnerships with twenty-two leading employers, and modest financial support to help employers access consultancy services to develop new policies and practices, the campaign encouraged employers to provide flexible working options for their employees (Arrowsmith, 2001).

Since inception, the WLBC has driven a rise in non-standard employment contracts, and increased emphasis on flexible working (Lewis and Plomien, 2009). The UK government has developed and implemented a number of legislative acts to aid this process. The Flexible Working Regulations (FWR), outlined in box 3.2, offer workers a range of leave options and the legal right to request a flexible working arrangement (see Deakin and Morris, 2012, 750–52). In the United Kingdom working women are able to take up to twenty-six weeks of ordinary (paid) maternity leave, and a further twenty-six weeks of additional leave (one year total). Fathers are entitled to two weeks of paid paternity leave, and until recently have been able to take up to twenty-six weeks of paternity leave (when meeting certain criteria). In December 2014 new rules for Shared

Box 3.2 The UK Flexible Working Regulations

The Flexible Working (Procedural Requirements) Regulations, SI 2002/3207, and the Flexible Working (Eligibility, Complaints and Remedies), SI 2002/3236, are amendments to the Employment Act 2002, s47, consolidated in the Employment Rights Act 1996, ss80F–80I. Initial policy applied to parents of young and disabled children. It was extended to include carers of certain adults and parents of older children in 2007. Employees with parental responsibility for children under sixteen were included from 2009. From June 2014, the 'right to request' a flexible working arrangement became available to every employee after twenty-six weeks of employment service. New laws on leave options included extensions and changes to eligibility for parental, paternity, and adoption leave, while maternity leave rights were also extended under the regulations.

Parental Leave and Shared Parental Pay were introduced through *The Share Parental Leave Regulations 2014* presenting greater options for parents of babies born after 5 April 2015 to determine how to structure work and caring responsibilities, offering the ability for parents to share up to 50 weeks of leave (37 weeks of which is paid) subject to certain eligibility criteria (Gov.uk, 2016b). Some employers, though, focused on 'employer-friendly' flexibility – for example, zero-hour contracts, on-call systems, and shift-work – may be unwilling to offer the same flexibility they expect from their employees, creating difficulties for workers in achieving desired work-life balance (Gregory and Milner, 2009, 123). In particular, employers make 'allowance decisions' (Poelmans and Beham, 2008) and can reject requests for flexible working citing 'business need' (Department for Business, Innovation and Skills, 2011a), where decisions are based on justifications set-out in the Flexible Working Regulations: (1) cost of accommodating the request; (2) difficulty finding replacement cover; and (3) impacts on the quality/delivery of service, all of which are difficult to objectively evaluate. This raises questions regarding the relative success and impacts of flexible working, something that will be considered in chapter 5. It should also be noted that while these policies focus on increasing opportunities for continued labour market participation, this is against the backdrop of an ageing population and reductions in public sector services in the aftermath of the 2007–2009 global economic crisis. This has increased the demand for voluntary provision, a particular focus of chapter 6, while creating specific challenges for those attempting to combine paid work with caring responsibilities.

Box 3.3 Examples of Flexible and Family-Friendly Working Policies in Europe

Finland

Finland, and other Scandinavian countries including Norway and Sweden are known for progressive flexible working and family-friendly policies providing legislative support for women throughout their careers. These countries have open labour markets, high levels of educational attainment among women, and a liberal legal and social environment. In Finland there is an equal gender split in participation in the labour market, although common with the United Kingdom and many other post-industrial economies, there remains 'a great deal of both horizontal and vertical occupational segregation' (Kyro, 2009, 394). Parents have, since 1990, had legal rights to day care in Finland. 'In some Nordic countries as in Finland, the day care is a so-called subjective right of a Finnish child: she is entitled to day care by birth' (Arenius and Kovalainen, 2006, 37).

Germany

Germany has introduced a number of family and employment policies aimed at improving labour market participation, opportunities, and conditions, with a focus on 'free-choice'. Since 2002 policies have been introduced aiming to promote part-time work, commitment to re-employment after maternity leave, training support during maternity leave, and leaves of absence for ill/elderly care. Social security thresholds, and social attitudes, promote women exiting the labour market for extended periods when dependents are present (O'Reilly and Bothfeld, 2002). In 2007 the Elterngeld (parent's money) was introduced allowing parents to take paid leave of up to fourteen months following childbirth (providing a variable-rate benefit equal to two-thirds of previous earnings), in an attempt to make a faster return to work more acceptable for parents. A lack of childcare availability acts as a significant constraint. Meanwhile, slow changing social attitudes form a further barrier (Pfau-Effinger, 1998, 184). Women returning to work, in some cases, may be labelled 'Rabenmutter' or raven mother as they are considered 'bad mothers' for returning to work and abandoning domestic responsibilities (Evans, 2011).

Norway

Norway offers significant paid parental leave entitlements. In Norway leave entitlement is either fifty-four weeks at 80 percent of previous wage, or forty-four weeks at 100 percent of previous wage, but with a maximum monetary limit (Brandth and Kvande, 2009, 192–5). Norway has developed some of the strongest parental leave entitlements for fathers, although evidence suggests that long hours norms limit take-up of these leave entitlements (Pascall, 2008). Consistent with the United Kingdom, significant gender variations remain in Norway in respect to long-term use of part-time work, which is more common among women. This is driven by their need for flexibility to ease work-family conflict (Kjeldstad and Nymoen, 2012, 103–4).

Sweden

Sweden has been identified as offering arguably the most egalitarian economic and social environment. For example, it was ranked first in the Economic Intelligence Unit's Women's Economic Opportunity Index (EIU, 2012)*. Sweden has some of the highest female labour market participation rates in the world. It was the first country to introduce paid leave for fathers, and has one of the highest proportions of female representation in parliament (over 40 percent). Sweden offers significant paid parental leave entitlements to both mothers and fathers. Consistent with policy in Finland parents have, since 1990, had legal rights to day care in Sweden. Arenius and Kovalainen (2006, 36) argue that 'universal day care, irrespective of family form, family income or women's employment relationship is a prerequisite for women's high labour force participation'.

* The Women's Economic Opportunity Index is calculated using twenty-six indicators in five key categories: (1) labour policy and practice; (2) access to finance; (3) education and training; (4) women's legal and social status; and (5) the general business environment (EIU, 2012).

3.4 CHAPTER SUMMARY: A CHANGING ECONOMIC AND POLICY ENVIRONMENT

This chapter has outlined the way in which historical developments have influenced and led to a relative standardization of the way we use our time. Changes during the Industrial Revolution, the impacts of deindustrialization, and the emergence of a post-industrial economy in the United Kingdom have all greatly affected the way time is spent. The UK policy context has also been considered, providing a platform for the exploration of how we use our time presented in subsequent chapters of the book.

The historical evidence presented highlights how the way we use our time has become normalized since as early as the sixteenth century. Developments during the Industrial Revolution placed further emphasis on the standardization of routines of work and non-work time (Bienefeld, 1972). Technological developments, including the rail network, in turn led to the development of the commute as we understand it today. A key feature of the normalization of work-time has been the focus of employers on the extraction of labour. Initially efforts focused on extensive labour extraction, that is, long hours, but the advent of Taylorist and Fordist methods of work organization by the early twentieth century shifted the focus to intensive labour extraction (Figart, 2001; Choi et al., 2008). As many advanced economies deindustrialized during the latter part of the twentieth century, resulting from a range of political and competitive drivers (Crafts, 1996; Hardill et al., 2001, 2006), this led to the emergence of the post-industrial economy. Characterized by the growth in services and ICTs (Quah, 2000, 2001; Nolan and Slater, 2003; Perrons, 2003), a post-industrial economy brings both opportunities and challenges, for example, through increases in female labour market participation, but also a blurring between work and non-work time.

Throughout history, the role of intervention has been significant. The Factory Acts, enacted in the nineteenth century, through to recent amendments to Flexible Working Regulations in 2014, are examples of intervention by government to address concerns regarding the impact of paid work on the well-being of workers. Policy has also sought to enable and promote greater labour market opportunities among women (Lewis and Campbell, 2008). As women's labour market participation has increased since the middle of the twentieth century, many women (and some men) are ever more constrained into performing two jobs – paid employment and household work – leaving them under significant time constraints (Jones, 2003). This is particularly acute among 'career' women, who while working full-time often continue to undertake significant household and caring responsibilities (Garcia et al., 2007, 2011; Lundberg and Pollak, 2007). Policy has attempted to facilitate a better balance between these activities, providing greater flexibility in paid work (and recently parental leave), but employers retain significant control over the implementation and use of flexible working arrangements (Gregory and Milner, 2009; Poelmans and Beham, 2008). The impact of the changes in paid work on the household, and also time available to devote to other activities, including volunteering and leisure, is of considerable importance and is explored in this book. A number of the specific issues identified in this chapter will be considered in detail in the subsequent chapters, including the impact of intensive and extensive labour extraction in chapter 4; the blurring of work and non-work time, and the use of flexible working arrangements, in chapter 5; the relationship between paid work, volunteering, and care in chapter 6; and the role of travel between home and work and travel undertaken to conduct work in chapter 7.

NOTES

1. Unions desired reductions in hours in order to reduce unemployment, based on the assumption that if each employee works fewer hours, there will be employment for more individuals (Bienefeld, 1972, 194–95).

2. Data for 1841 and 1901 covers Great Britain. Data for 1961 and 2011 is for England and Wales. This follows changes in the structure of the sample collected for the UK Census of Population which moved from covering Great Britain to England and Wales in 1921.

3. The future of the UK policy environment, and specifically the role of the EU in UK policy, has become uncertain since the UK voted to leave the EU in July 2016.

4. The marriage bar was a prohibition on married women's employment put in place to ensure jobs, especially 'white-collar' jobs, were the exclusive domain of men (Hakim, 2000, 59).

Chapter Four

Work-Time, the Quality of Work, and Well-Being

4.1 INTRODUCTION

Work, in the broadest sense, includes both paid and unpaid work (Hardill et al., 2001, 74–75). Paid work can be paid work for an employer or paid work as a self-employed worker. Unpaid work can take the form of unpaid work for an employer, formal and informal voluntary work, or unpaid activity undertaken within the home, encompassed in the term 'tasks of social reproduction' (Glucksmann, 1995). Time spent in paid work accounts for a substantial portion of time-use among a significant share of the population. Around 73 percent of the UK population reported being economically active in 2015, while similarly around 73 percent (22.8 million) of those in work reported full-time employment, that is, report working thirty or more hours per week (ONS, 2015e). However, paid work has historically been the site of considerable conflict over both the length of the working day and working conditions, and also represents a source of great inequity. The propensity of individuals to engage in paid work is affected significantly by a range of factors, including the ability to access labour markets, physical and mental well-being, and the distribution of household labour including care. Given the historic conflict surrounding work-time, as outlined in the previous chapter, it is not surprising that mainstream labour supply theory in economics begins with the assumption of paid work as an economic bad. Indeed, paid work has often been defined in regard to performing an arduous task (Weiss and Kahn, 1960). However, the relationship between work and our well-being is more nuanced. While work can be a source of significant dissatisfaction, it equally represents a potential source of achievement and fulfilment (Spencer, 2009, 105), and provides both social networks and personal identity (Sparrowe et al., 2001).

This chapter explores historical and contemporary work-time, while also reflecting on broader patterns of time-use. A critical perspective is provided on mainstream economics approaches to work-time using radical economic perspectives, drawing on concepts of exploitation of labour to consider the length of the working day and relative satisfaction with work-time. Consideration is given not only to the extent of work-time, but also to the quality of work reflecting on the relative levels of autonomy present in paid work, and the relationship between control over various aspects of paid work and subjective well-being. The chapter uses data from the UK Labour Force Survey and the combined panel of the BHPS and Understanding Society, and refers to work published in peer-reviewed journals including Philp et al. (2015), Philp and Wheatley (2011, 2013), and Wheatley et al. (2011). It is also further developed in Wheatley (2017).

4.2 EXTENSIVE AND INTENSIVE WORKING ROUTINES

Despite the presence of work-time regulation for almost two decades, lengthy hours of work remain evident in the United Kingdom, and in many other post-industrial economies (Messenger, 2011). In part, this is a product of long hours remaining equated with commitment in the eyes of many senior managers (White et al., 2003). Long working hours can be defined as working over forty-eight hours per week, following the maximum EWTD/WTR forty-eight-hour working week, while 'very long hours' are defined as working over sixty hours per week (Hogarth et al., 2001, 20). Data for the period 1995–2006 found 'excessive hours', that is, hours over forty-eight hours per week, among 17.7 percent of employees (Messenger, 2011, 302). According to the 2015 Labour Force Survey (April–June) around 15 percent of UK workers report working over forty-eight hours per week inclusive of overtime. Long hours are more common among men: 21 percent of men report long hours, compared with 7.8 percent of women, driven in part by the greater propensity of women to work reduced and part-time hours. With respect to the lifecourse, working long hours is also most prominent during middle age (between forty and fifty-nine), and least common among those aged under twenty-one and over seventy. Long hours continue to be a feature of full-time work in the United Kingdom, both in aggregate when compared to other EU nations (Philp and Wheatley, 2013) and among specific groups, for example, managers and professionals (Ford and Collinson, 2011; Philp and Wheatley, 2011). The sources of longer working hours can be summarized as follows: work pressure including increased workloads, greater competition, fewer staff, smaller budgets, and increasingly demanding customers; individuals feeling a genuine strong commitment towards their work, colleagues, customers, and clients (Kodz et al., 1998); managements' demand for commitment to the firm (White et al., 2003); and the pressure to complete tasks, equal the long hours worked by management, and improve take-home pay through overtime payments, commission, and performance-related pay (Kodz et al., 1998). It has been argued from a radical perspective that workers are coerced into working lengthier hours for the benefit of the capitalist employer. For example, Philp (2001) and Philp et al. (2005) argue that power of respective classes is important in generating outcomes in conflict over working hours. Indeed, as Marx (1976) suggested, in this sense, employees may be considered to be exploited under capitalism through unpaid work, as unpaid labour time benefits the employer (Spencer, 2009, 54). It should be noted that in some cases workers may feel the desire to work extensively, termed 'workaholism' (Schor, 1993, 70), although it may more often be the case that individuals simply feel they must spend extra time working in order to get the job done (Bergman and Gustafsen, 2008; Kodz et al., 1998, 21–23).

Salaried workers, especially in managerial and professional occupations, are likely to work longer hours (Ford and Collinson, 2011; Messenger, 2011, 302). These longer hours are, in many cases, not rewarded with additional pay. The emphasis is instead on the completion of tasks with less regard for the time this may take (Kodz et al., 1998, 32; Wheatley et al., 2011). Past research in the United Kingdom suggests that senior managers are the least likely to feel they have time to complete their tasks within normal working hours. While management may be a necessary function in organizations, evidence suggests that many managers work long hours and expect the same from their employees (Kodz et al., 1998, 32). This may, though, perpetuate a culture of long hours. A range of research has shown that there exists a greater resistance to work-time reduction among those in managerial employment (e.g., Bielenski et al., 2002, 13; Wheatley et al., 2011). But it is managers that enforce (supervisory function) and monitor the work-time of others. The primary responsibility of managers is in assigning tasks and extracting effort from workers (Wheatley et al., 2011). Moreover, managers are often rewarded for the performance of their workers (den Dulk and de Ruijte, 2008). The role of managers in endorsing long hours cultures and presenteeism among workers is, therefore, a key concern. Because of the requirement for managers to supervise, their role requires presenteeism to ensure the company or organization interests are in safe hands. Those undertaking management roles may well be self-selecting, because they are attracted by the governing nature of these occupations. Cultures of long hours, monitoring through frequent meetings, and the presence of meetings cultures extends the working day and also limits the ability of employees to benefit from flexible working arrangements and discretion over the timing and location of work.

Working long and inflexible hours may have significant implications for individuals and their households, causing dissatisfaction, reducing productivity, limiting career progression, and resulting in health problems. Where long hours cultures are not embraced workers may face significant career implications, as managements equate long hours with commitment (White et al., 2003). This, however, perpetuates gendered social constructs and inequity at work and home (Lewis and Humbert, 2010, 242). Extensive hours of labour, moreover, may generate particularly negative outcomes for employees. Excessive working may result in increased levels of stress (Green, 2001; Burchell and Fagan, 2004, 634), while Meier and Stutzer (2006) suggest that the relationship between hours of work and life satisfaction has an inverse U-shape (see chapter 1). Consistent with this assertion, it has also been argued long hours have a negative social impact and adversely affect the health and well-being of working individuals (Philp et al., 2005; Kahneman et al., 2006). Employees in some occupations, however, may trade-off lengthy hours of work in return for the greater job satisfaction available in these roles (Taylor, 2002). In addition, for these individuals work is likely to have an important social impact as it forms an integral part of their life and identity (Sparrowe et al., 2001). Those who don't enjoy work, in contrast, are likely to simply work to earn and leave all thoughts of work at the workplace when they go home (Doyle, 2000, 9–13). Working hours also have an important relationship with leisure. Lengthier working hours reduce time available for leisure, and evidence has shown a strong negative effect on leisure satisfaction (Ateca-Amestoy et al., 2008; Van Praag and Ferrer-i-Carbonell, 2004).

Changes in the structure of work, including Taylorist work organization, and advances in technology and ICT, have had a central role in the increased intensity of paid work (Figart, 2001; Perrons et al., 2005). However, the

Box 4.1 Work-Time Reductions and Equity

Some scholars have argued that reductions in hours of paid work could increase equity in society. For example, LaJeunesse (2009) argued that governments could use work-time regulation as a tool for increasing equity through redistributing hours of work across the labour market. This would result in reductions in work-time for some, in principle those currently subject to the greatest degree of exploitation by capitalists, while others would benefit from gaining employment (or increasing their hours of work). Reductions in work-time would mediate the negative impacts of capitalist activity which damages the environment, and has negative physical and social impacts through extensive labour extraction. In this model, individuals no longer see themselves only as paid employees, but more holistically in reference to their work, family, and social relationships, shifting society towards a model of greater freedom.

intensification of work, and associated reductions in task autonomy, increase work strain (Green, 2004, 622) and may reduce job satisfaction among workers. High-performance and high-commitment managerial practices, put in place to increase employee work effort, place additional pressure on workers and can form barriers to work-life balance (White et al., 2003). Meanwhile, managers exhibit considerable influence over the use and success of work-life balance practices within organizations (McCarthy et al., 2010). Unsupportive managers may create work-stressors – that is, work experiences that generate stress – due to the presence of task ambiguity and work overload (Greenhaus et al., 2012). Reductions in autonomy, limited flexibility, and the presence of extensive and intensive labour extraction are evident in many occupations, including the professions. For example, Ogbonna and Harris (2004, 1198) explore levels of work intensification within UK higher education, a sector historically associated with greater autonomy. They found increased levels of stress and reduced interaction between colleagues as a result of the intensification of work. These negative impacts are driven by time constraints and increased competition between workers, and performance-related remuneration systems, which do not reward team work. While the intensity of paid work has clearly increased, control over the timing and nature of the tasks completed during paid work may have actually declined (Green, 2006).

Long hours, and variable and unsocial hours including complex travel routines in particular, may make it difficult for individuals to perform activities together. Friendships, even marriages, may be constrained into operating without the frequency and regularity possible for those who work shorter and more regular hours. Married/cohabiting couples may only spend two or three hours together per day in shared activities. These activities tend to be eating, housework, and watching television (Gatenby, 2004). Meanwhile, impacts are likely to differ by gender as inequalities between men and women remain in the home and at work, despite increasing numbers of women participating in the labour market, and the changes in the nature and occupational structures of work (Perrons et al., 2005). These inequalities at work and within the home are explored in chapter 5, while the impact of intensive travel routines is reflected upon in chapter 7.

Box 4.2 A Note on Self-Employment

Approximately 15 percent (around 4.6 million) of those engaged in the labour market in the United Kingdom in 2015 reported being in self-employment, equivalent to the highest rate in the past forty years. Much of the growth in total employment since the global economic crisis (see section 4.5), has been driven by more flexibilized employment including part-time (and other reduced hours), temporary, and self-employment.

It is also important to note that at the same time as there has been a growth in self-employment, the financial returns from this form of work are reported as having declined significantly, by around 22 percent since 2008–9 (ONS, 2014b). Movements between employment and self-employment may be motivated by 'entrepreneurial pull' or 'unemployment push', with the latter estimated as accounting for up to 48 percent of movements into self-employment (Dawson and Henley, 2012). In the prior case, high-pressure, high income careers may be traded for a more desirable 'lifestyle' offering improved balance between work and home, and a less frantic and more creative life, through self-employment (Morrison, 2006; Drew, 1998). Self-employment may, further, represent a way of avoiding career stagnation when flexibility becomes a necessity as a result of increased household responsibilities. However, in recent years casualization of the workforce, and the replacement of secure paid employment with short-term contract work (Raess and Burgoon, 2015, 95–6), encapsulated in the term 'gig economy' or 'gig work' (Friedman, 2014), has resulted in self-employment offering the only viable option to work for some individuals.

Self-employment has the potential to provide significant flexibility, autonomy, and liberation (Fraser and Gold, 2001), however this is often combined with uncertainty, stress, and anxiety (Fenwick, 2006, 76). Evidence does suggest that drivers of movements into self-employment differ between genders. In particular, it has been argued that women's careers are characterized by transition periods where their career decisions are influenced by their stage in the lifecourse. For those with caring responsibilities this may result in family-related career breaks, interruptions to their working lives, or movements into self-employment (Cabrera, 2007; Hytti, 2010). Self-employment in these cases may represent a career stage, rather than a permanent movement. Schmid (2010) suggests that dependent children are likely to act as a key driver for non-standard employment among women. Home-based self-employment is also more prevalent among women, and is a product of both the greater household constraints faced by working women (Garcia et al., 2011; Wheatley and Wu, 2014), and the lower capitalization associated with women-owned businesses (Hundley, 2001, 827). However, the burden of household responsibilities and childcare can limit the scope of entrepreneurial activity, reducing income and the intensity of work effort (Hundley, 2001). Meanwhile, the home-based self-employed are more likely to have secondary sources of income, often from other employment (Mason et al., 2011). This may be driven, for example, by limited client bases, resulting in difficulties in securing comparable rates of pay to those employed in the same sector (Stanworth and Stanworth, 1995, 227). Moreover, exogenous factors including economic crises can put particular short-term pressure on the financial viability of many entrepreneurs businesses.

Longer working hours are often a feature of self-employment, in part driven the lifestyle benefits derived from this form of employment, although hours differ by gender as a result of the varying drivers of self-employment (Lee et al., 2007, 112–13; Hundley, 2001). Evidence suggests hours are somewhat polarized between those working long hours, that is, over forty-five hours per week, and those working short hours of less than eight hours per week. Patterns in hours in recent years are also highly gendered as around one-third of men report working over forty-five hours per week, whereas only around 15 percent of women report long hours. A greater proportion of women, accounting for just under a quarter, report up to fifteen hours per week (ONS, 2016b). In some cases the self-employed may take on a second job which may also result in lengthy overall hours of work. Second job holding may be driven by a range of factors, including: (1) retention of links with previous employers or clients, especially when self-employment is viewed as a career 'stage' rather than a permanent commitment (Hytti, 2010); and (2) wider macro-economic conditions which place pressures on smaller enterprises requiring a second job to supplement the income from the owner-managed business (Flandez, 2009). In the latter case self-employment associated with amenity value is likely to require second job holding, even in the medium to long term, as individuals are less concerned with the financial returns from running their business than with the amenity value they derive from self-employment. Motivations to stay self-employed thus extend beyond financial returns to qualitative benefits, and effects, including perceived greater autonomy and satisfaction obtained from the business venture (Blanchflower, 2000; Eckersley, 2007) and/or work-life balance benefits. Indeed, recent research reported in Atherton et al. (2016) has shown that some self-employed individuals take on second jobs in order to maintain businesses which are otherwise not economically viable, as a result of the amenity value (including flexibility) offered by self-employment.

4.3 THE QUALITY OF WORK

The quality of work, including the level of autonomy and control present in paid work, has been shown to have some mitigating effects on the impact of lengthy working hours and employer-driven flexible work schedules, which have particularly negative impacts on the well-being and work-life balance of employees (Fagan et al., 2012, 40). Work intensity may have increased within many occupations, and while changes in the occupational structure of the labour market has increased opportunities for flexibility and autonomy, this varies considerably between occupations and sectors. There has been a degree of polarization of 'good' and 'bad' jobs, although even 'good' jobs, that is, those which are highly paid and exhibit high levels of autonomy, do exhibit a number of 'bad' characteristics including intense work routines and work-family conflict (Kalleberg, 2012, 433). Evidence focusing on the period prior to the global economic crisis (1998–2004) identified some improvement in job quality attributed particularly to a strong macroeconomic environment and rising employment rates, rather than through specific attempts by government and/or employers to improve the quality of jobs (Brown et al., 2007). As supervisors, managers have a key role in determining hours of work and 'job quality' at the organization level. This is not to suggest that employees do not make 'choices'. Individuals make decisions about careers, promotion, and so on, but these decisions are often constrained by personal and household circumstances, especially among women (Hardill, 2002), and as a result of the presence of institutional rigidity which maintains norms in paid work routines. While it has already been acknowledged that paid work can be a source of achievement and fulfilment (Spencer, 2009, 105; Gallie, 2007), it is important to highlight that it has also been argued that autonomy and control are central to employees 'enjoying' work (Spencer, 2009, 66).

4.3.1 Job Quality and Autonomy

Job quality refers to the degree to which a job exhibits characteristics that generate benefits for the employee, including to physical and mental well-being (Green, 2006). A number of different categorizations have been offered for the relative quality of jobs, as summarized in table 4.1. Broadly, jobs can be categorized into the following categories (see Holman, 2013, 477–78): (1) low-quality 'low-commitment' and (2) high-quality 'high-commitment' where jobs fitting the prior category are likely to exhibit characteristics of Taylorist work organization including low autonomy, skill, pay, training, security, and employer-driven flexibility. Meanwhile, jobs fitting the latter category exhibit autonomy, variety, skill, opportunities for training/development, better pay and security, and opportunities for flexible working. Bartling et al. (2012), identify 'good jobs' as those that exhibit high levels of discretion, pay, and rent-sharing. They argue that offering discretion to employees can produce optimal outcomes for employers as long as this discretion increases productivity, employers pay high wages which are reciprocated through higher levels of work effort among employees, and employees are screened on the basis of past performance. Karasek and Theorell (1990) categorize four types of job quality by relative task discretion and demand. Active jobs generate positive outcomes for employees with respect to well-being, due to the increased control even given demanding work routines. Meanwhile, low autonomy in demanding jobs (high-strain jobs) generates incidence of work-stress. Employees in job types 3 and 4 (see table 4.1) are likely to exhibit low to moderate levels of well-being derived from paid work. More recent research by Holman (2013), using cluster analysis, extended this taxonomy to identifying six types of job also summarized in table 4.1.

Table 4.1 Taxonomy of Job Quality

	Job Quality Categories	*Key Features*
Karasek and Theorell (1990)	(1) Active jobs	High autonomy, high demand
	(2) High-strain jobs	Low autonomy, high demand
	(3) Passive jobs	Low autonomy, low demand
	(4) Low-strain jobs	High autonomy, low demand
Holman (2013, 477–8)	(1) Active	High autonomy, social support, complexity, security, and moderate pay and workloads
	(2) Saturated	High demands, long hours, high pay
	(3) Team-based	High autonomy, high demand, frequent team-working, high security
	(4) Passive-independent	Low demand, low autonomy, infrequent team-working
	(5) Insecure	Temporary employment, low demand, low pay
	(6) High-strain	Low autonomy, high demand

Within each of the categorizations autonomy has a fundamental role in the relative 'quality' of jobs. The efforts of management to reduce employee autonomy has resulted in low discretion work becoming the norm (Houlihan, 2002, 69; Choi et al., 2008, 423), and is a characteristic of many low quality jobs. Even with the decline of the industrial sector and growth in the service sector, evidence highlights the continued presence of Taylorist work organization in many post-industrial economies. Past studies have identified a Taylorization of employment in the service sector through standardization, prescription, and routinization, and limited autonomy as a result of strict managerial controls (Bain and Taylor, 2000). These methods of work organization have been widely criticized as they remove the factor of aspiration from work and have potentially negative consequences for employee morale (Kelly, 2000, 8). Among other things, the assumption of homogenous labour extracted through hierarchical relationships with management neglects the impact of work on human welfare (Spencer, 2009, 95). Research has shown that even in service employment such as call centres, often associated with more standardized labour processes, the uncertain nature of customer interactions and requirement for workers to undertake not just physical tasks but 'emotional' or 'interactive' labour, limits managerialism and affords a level of autonomy (Jenkins et al., 2010, 561; Sallaz, 2002, 396). Centrally, it is also asserted that this comes at a low cost to the employer, but is often embedded within an intense and highly routinized working environment (Sallaz, 2002, 399). Where specific efforts are made by employers to reduce levels of discretion among groups of employees this can have negative impacts. For example, Eustace (2012) considered the impact of attempts to appropriate the speech of call centre employees in Scotland. Findings indicated that 'low-discretion' measures had little positive effect on customer service, and further resulted in indirect discrimination against some employees who were left with feelings of insecurity and subordination due to their accent and dialect.

Control and autonomy in work, usually correlated with higher quality jobs, has been identified as aiding reductions in work-life conflicts for both men and women. Greater control, through autonomy over decision-making and use of flexible technologies, has been shown to have positive relationships with management of work and family (Batt and Valcour, 2003, 215). Autonomy may also generate specific benefits for women, offering the ability to better manage their dual responsibilities of work and home (Hochschild, 2003). Gender divisions in autonomy may reflect the impact of horizontal and vertical segregation which remains present between industries and occupations (Teasdale, 2013, 400). Men continue to dominate at the highest levels of many industries, particularly in government, management, and professional occupations. This, however, limits women's access to autonomy which could facilitate work-family integration (Padavic and Reskin, 2002). Greater proportions of women (31.9 percent) than men (14.6 percent) do, however, work in the public sector (NOMIS, 2015), which has been shown in the past to offer greater access to flexibility (Wheatley, 2012b). The segregation present in the labour market may have implications with regard to relative control and flexibility available to working men and women. Research has argued that even after controlling for occupational variations a gender gap is present in relative job quality (Stier and Yaish, 2014, 16–18). It has been argued that these patterns may represent women being offered lower quality and less rewarding labour market positions by employers due to their inferior power position in society (Findlay et al., 2009). Evidence is conflicting, though, as Galinsky et al. (2011, 145), reporting on US data, found that similar proportions of men and women, and parents and non-parents, reported having 'complete' or 'a lot' of control over the time and location of their work. As a result of their greater household contribution, women (especially mothers) more often require flexibility, reflected in their use of flexible working arrangements. However, these arrangements may disadvantage them in their careers (Fagan et al., 2012, 23–24), limiting opportunities and impairing wage growth, especially among working mothers (Glass, 2004, 387). For a more detailed discussion, see chapter 5.

4.3.2 Autonomy and Subjective Well-Being

Control over work is important in determining the quality of working life (Eckersley, 2007, 148), enabling employees to use their creativity and develop their skills (Gallie, 2007, 212). Control over the timing and location of work has been shown to offer specific benefits through reducing work-life conflict and enhancing job satisfaction (Costa et al., 2006). Past research conducted in the United Kingdom, using the 2000 Working in Britain survey, suggested control over working hours to be strongly correlated with greater job satisfaction (Doyle and Reeves, 2001, 22–23). Meanwhile, Humphrey et al. (2007) reported greater levels of perceived job autonomy may have positive impacts for employees on job performance, job satisfaction, organizational commitment, and intrinsic motivation. Autonomy in paid work has also been found to reduce levels of work-related stress and 'work-family conflict' (Grönlund, 2007; Kalleberg et al., 2009). Flexible schedules, control over work tasks, and social support are all identified as reducing the level of stress generated by paid work. Meanwhile, more recent research by Boxall and Macky (2014, 9) and Galletta et al. (2011, 13) found that higher levels of control over work generates positive feelings and attitudes among employees, while reducing work-related stress, fatigue, negative work-non-work spill-over, and turnover intention with potentially significant benefits for employers in employee retention. Greater control and autonomy could, though, have some negative consequences for the employee. For example, it may be awarded to the employee alongside more intense routines of paid work, potentially offsetting some of the benefits to well-being (Boxall and Macky, 2014, 4). Meanwhile research reporting on a sample of Internet-based workers, considering the self-employed, suggested that even where autonomy and control is high workers may still report low job satisfaction as a result of work routines conflicting with social norms, reflecting the influence of social expectations regarding patterns of work and non-work (Lee and Lin, 2011, 464).

4.4 CHANGING PATTERNS OF WORK-TIME

While conflict remains over the extent of time spent in paid work, historical changes in work-time evidence long-term reductions in hours of work, in part driven by government intervention beginning with the Factory Acts outlined in chapter 3. Figart and Golden (1998, 412) suggest that the institutional arrangements of the twentieth century aided a division of labour between home and work, and between genders. This extended the separation of home and work which began in the Industrial Revolution. It facilitated men working full-time to support women homemakers. Average weekly hours remained fairly constant throughout this period, particularly for white men in their prime earning years. Average annual hours decreased as a result of the growth of paid holidays and time off work. Average annual hours experienced reductions from 2,984 hours in 1870, to 1,489 hours by 1998. These decreases in working hours are shown in figure 4.1, which summarizes normal full-time hours since 1860 and average weekly hours since 1856 (Bank of England, 2015; Weale, 2016). Hours of manual workers, for example, fell from 53 hours in 1943, to 43.5 hours by 1987 (Lindsay, 2003, 140). Hewitt (1993) highlights the decline in basic working hours during the twentieth century, but suggests that while basic hours have declined, hours inclusive of overtime may have increased, at least in some occupations and/or industries, for example, highly skilled occupations (Ford and Collinson, 2011; Philp and Wheatley, 2011).

While the post-war era in the United Kingdom has been characterized by further reductions, followed by relative stability in hours of work (Boulin, 1993), the synchronization of work and leisure which existed during the twentieth century has diminished due to the emergence of a more globalized 24/7 working environment, characterized by intense working routines and a flexibilization of the labour market (Wheatley et al., 2008). Indeed, since the global economic crisis in 2007–2009 some increase in hours has actually been recorded, while there has been a growth in non-standard working routines including part-time and other forms of reduced hours. It should also

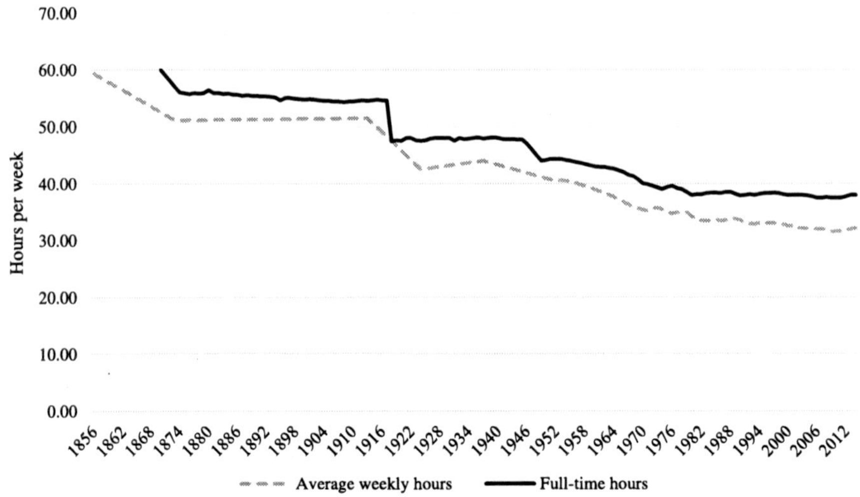

Figure 4.1. Historical Hours of Work in the United Kingdom.

be noted that while figure 4.1 offers useful insight into hours of paid work, it provides only a partial perspective with respect to all forms of work undertaken, as it excludes certain forms of unpaid work, including housework, childcare, and voluntary activity which account for substantial amounts of work in a broader sense, and all of which can be marketized.

4.5 RECENT DEVELOPMENTS IN THE LABOUR MARKET

While patterns of full-time and average weekly hours offer important insight into the changing patterns of time spent in paid work, it is also important to recognize the increasing diversity that exists in labour market participation, including between genders and across the lifecourse. In recent years there has been a growing emphasis on flexibility, adaptability, team-working, and individual responsibility, in both the private and public sectors (Wheatley et al., 2008). However, in particular since the 2007–2009 global economic crisis, the flexibility present in employment has shifted to more often reflect 'employee flexibility for the employer' (as recognized by Costa et al., 2003), characterized by less secure, reduced hours, and 'temporary' employment focused on providing employers with a flexible workforce, as well as a growth in self-employment including employment in gig work where workers are categorized as self-employed 'independent contractors'. It has been argued that this is a result of the fragile state of many economies following the crisis, as Gerwyn Davies of the Chartered Institute of Personnel and Development (CIPD, 2012) stated in the post-crisis period in 2012, 'Many employers remain cautious about adding to their long-term cost base. Business confidence has improved … but is still fragile.'

While growth has been recorded in part-time and other more flexible forms of work, it has been shown that full-time jobs only account for around one in forty of the net jobs added to the UK economy between 2008 and 2014 (Trade Union Congress, 2014). Part-time employment stood at 8.31 million, accounting for 26.8 percent of the workforce in April–June 2015, an increase from 7.5 million (25.3 percent) seven years earlier in 2008 (ONS, 2015e). Part-time work remains especially prominent among women, driven by their greater household contribution (Connolly and Gregory, 2008, F52; Garcia et al., 2007, 2011; Lundberg and Pollak, 2007). Data from the 2015 UK Labour Force Survey (April–June 2015) confirms the continued gendered patterns present in part-time work, which accounted for approximately 41 percent of employment among women but just 11 percent among men (ONS, 2015e). Perhaps of greater concern have been movements toward more 'flexibilized' employment (Raess and Burgoon, 2015). Employers have sought to increase the flexibility of their workforce, including through the use of zero-hour and temporary contracts. Zero-hour contracts are a non-guaranteed hours form of paid employment. Employees on these contracts do not receive the same rights as full-time employees, including holiday and sick pay, and these employees have no guarantee of work or pay from week to week. While controversial, in the United Kingdom these contracts have become more common, although legislation has been enacted since 2014 banning exclusivity clauses in zero-hours contracts (Department for Business, Innovation and Skills, 2014). This ensures those workers subject to these contracts can seek secondary employment. Around 744,000 UK workers reported being on a zero-hours contract in April–June 2015 representing around 2.4 percent of all in employment, an increase from 622,000 in April–June 2014. As well as zero-hours contracts other temporary forms of work, including agency work account for a notable portion of the labour market. A further 307,000 UK workers reported agency 'temporary' jobs in April–June 2015. It is also important to note that many of those on zero-hour contracts, and engaged in temporary work, are young workers: in 2015 around 34 percent of those on zero-hours contracts were aged sixteen to twenty-four (ONS, 2015c).

These trends are particularly problematic as evidence suggests that the flexibility present among workers is not being returned by employers, for example, in the form of greater flexibility over the arrangement of work-time, and that a notable proportion of those working flexible and/or reduced hours show preferences for full-time work. Indeed, the UK Labour Force Survey captures data on reasons for engagement in part-time work. In 2015 over 15 percent of those working part-time reported that they do so due to lack of full-time opportunities, an increase from around 10 percent in 2008 (ONS, 2015d). Evidence is indicative of Taylorist work organization, and the prevalence of employer-driven flexibility in the UK labour market as employers apply both numerical (fixed-term, agency, mandated part-time work) and functional (shift-work, overtime, varying work weeks using balancing-time accounts) flexibility to their workforce (Raess and Burgoon, 2015, 95–96).

4.6 WORK-TIME, THE QUALITY OF WORK, AND WELL-BEING: EVIDENCE FROM THE BHPS AND UNDERSTANDING SOCIETY

Patterns of weekly time-use among full-time and part-time workers are summarized in figure 4.2 using data drawn from the BHPS and Understanding Society covering twenty-two years from 1992 to 2013/14. This includes: (1) hours spent in paid work; (2) overtime (which may be paid or unpaid); (3) time spent travelling to work, that is, commuting; (4) the amount of time devoted to housework; and (5) time spent caring for ill/elderly relatives and friends. Importantly, these estimates do not include time spent caring for dependent children, which is likely to form a key element of time-use among parents and many part-time workers, especially working mothers. Moreover, these surveys do not consistently capture data on time devoted to volunteering (this has been included every other year since 1996), or time spent in leisure activities. These are not, therefore, included in the analysis presented, but this time use is given specific consideration in chapters 5, 6, and 8 respectively.

Examining the patterns of time-use over the past two decades a number of key trends emerge. Time-use among full-time men has remained relatively static over the period, with a substantial amount of time devoted to paid work each week averaging 45.1 hours inclusive of overtime over the sample period. These patterns are consistent with the presence of long hours already noted from the UK Labour Force Survey. Meanwhile, women reporting full-time employment report working just under 40 hours per week inclusive of overtime. Full-time women have reported some reduction in hours devoted to housework, although their overall time-use recorded in figure 4.2 continues to be lengthier than full-time men as a result of their greater household contribution (also including ill/elderly care). Given the continued evidence of women remaining the primary caregivers for dependent children in most households (Garcia et al., 2007, 2011; Lundberg and Pollak, 2007; Perrons, 2004), this additional burden, which is not included in the patterns observed in figure 4.2, is likely to leave many women with quite intense schedules where they continue to work full-time. The noted reductions in time spent performing housework may, in part, reflect the

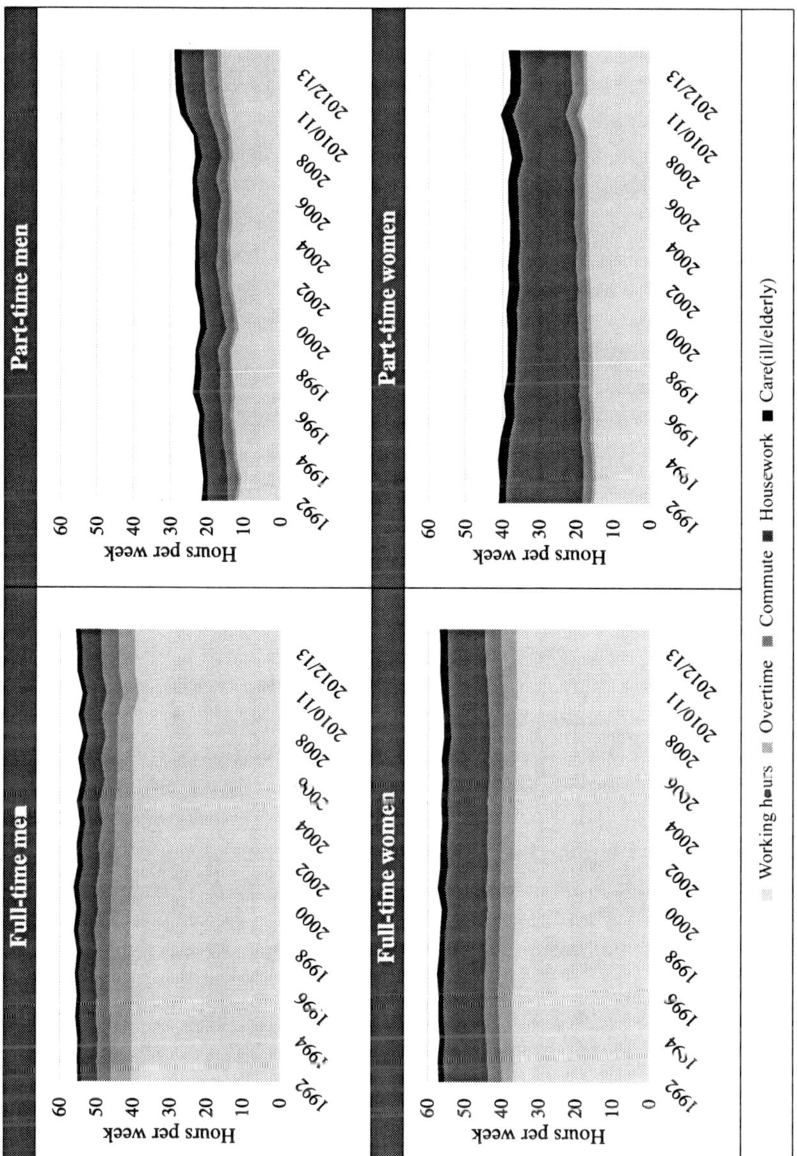

Figure 4.2. Weekly Patterns of Time-Use, 1992–2013/14 (BHPS/Understanding Society).

impact of technological change in aiding the completion of a number of household tasks, although as Schor (1993, 86–88) argued technology creates new tasks (while reducing the burden of others) and may create higher standards within the household environment. The observed change is also likely to reflect the marketization of certain household tasks, for example, cleaning, household maintenance and gardening (a further discussion is offered on this in chapter 5), and the reduction in household labour felt by women as a result of the marginal increase in housework reported among men (Sullivan, 2010; Schwanen, 2007). Commutes act as an important additional time constraint. Commutes are longer among men in all occupation groups, averaging approximately 4.9 hours per week, which is equivalent to a 30-minute home to work travel time (assuming a five day per week working pattern). In contrast, women commute, on average, 4.3 hours per week. Further discussion is offered on patterns of travel, including gendered distinctions, in chapter 7.

Gendered patterns of time-use are starker among part-timers. Women working part-time report substantial time spent on housework (averaging 16.5 hours per week between 1992 and 2013/2014). Although time spent on housework has reduced during the sample period, the time part-time women spend on housework is relatively consistent with hours spent in paid work, although subject to some year-on-year volatility. In contrast part-time men report lower overall time-use led by substantially lesser household input, but also marginally shorter working hours. Part-time work continues to be less common among men, as discussed earlier in the chapter. Men working part-time are predominantly at either end of their careers, often combining part-time paid work with education or with part-retirement (Delsen, 1998, 64; Gregory and Connolly, 2008, F4). The residual time-use not observed in figure 4.2, which includes activities such as childcare and volunteering, is likely to be lengthier among part-time workers. Volunteering and care including grandparenting is a particular feature, for example, among many retired men (see chapter 6 for a full discussion).

As the existing literature suggests, hours differ considerably between occupations with some of the lengthiest hours found among managerial and professional workers (Ford and Collinson, 2011; Messenger, 2011; Philp and Wheatley, 2011). Indeed, as table 4.2 shows full-time working hours, and hours of overtime, are particular lengthy among men in managerial occupations, totalling around forty-eight hours per week on average. Women in professional occupations also report lengthy hours, especially with regard to overtime. Overtime hours are the longest of any occupation group, varying between seven and nine hours per week between 1992 and 2013/2014. It should be noted, though, that consistent with overall patterns observed

Table 4.2 Weekly Time-Use Among Full-Time Men and Women in Highly Skilled Occupations

Occupation	*Work Hours*	*Overtime*	*Commute*	*Housework*	*Care (Ill or Elderly)*	*n*
Men						
Managers and senior officials	41.5	6.5	4.9	4.6	1.0	689
Professionals	38.8	5.7	4.8	5.1	0.9	475
Associate professional and technical	39.0	3.9	4.9	5.4	1.0	507
Women						
Managers and senior officials	38.2	4.8	4.4	10.6	1.5	409
Professionals	37.0	7.6	4.2	9.8	1.4	423
Associate professional and technical	36.6	3.3	4.3	10.6	1.5	517

Notes: Data is for full-time employees aged sixteen to sixty-five. Figures (including n values) are averages taken over sample period (twenty-two observations). Housework hours were not collected in three years (1992, 2011/12, 2013/14).

Source: British Household Panel Survey, wave 1–18 (1992–2009); Understanding Society, wave 2–5 (2010/11–13/14).

in figure 4.2 some decline is recorded in work-time among those in highly skilled occupations during the sample period. For example, men in full-time managerial roles reported a decline from around forty-three hours per week to forty-one hours per week. However, although showing some decline, hours do remain long and close to the WTR maximum when inclusive of overtime, consistent with the findings of previous research (Philp and Wheatley, 2011; Ford and Collinson, 2011).

As well as the amount of time spent in paid work and other activities, the quality of this time is undoubtedly central to the relationships we observe with well-being. As routines become more complex, driven by developments in technology and requirements from employers for increasing levels of flexibility among workers, blurring and spillover between forms of time-use increasingly characterize how time is spent and present a number of challenges for individuals and their households (Wheatley et al., 2008). The '9 to 5' although still representing the time spent in the workplace for many workers, does not accurately account for the time actually spent in work and work-related activities. Achieving balance between activities, which may vary considerably between individuals depending on the preferences and constraints faced, is likely to have significant implications for reported levels of well-being.

4.6.1 Levels of Autonomy in Paid Work

The extant literature is indicative of autonomy generating positive effects for employees (Eckersley, 2007, 148; Batt and Valcour, 2003, 212; Kalleberg et al., 2009). One question this raises is in regard to which employees enjoy the highest levels of autonomy in paid work. Table 4.3 summarizes the responses to questions regarding levels of autonomy in various aspects of paid work by occupation group, using the UK Standard Occupational Classification (SOC) Major Groups.[1] Reported autonomy is greatest among managers. This is especially the case in regards to the manner of work (78.8 percent report 'a lot' of autonomy) and the order of tasks (80.1 percent report 'a lot'). In fact, around 90 percent of managers report having 'some' or 'a lot' of autonomy in all aspects of paid work with the exception of working hours. Professionals report relatively high levels of autonomy over various aspects of paid work, but notably less so than managers in regard to the nature of job tasks (only 44.6 percent report 'a lot' of autonomy), manner of work (44.8 percent report 'a lot'), and hours of work (30.8 percent report 'a lot'). This is an interesting finding as many professions are traditionally associated with high levels of autonomy. Evidence is indicative, though, of high intensity, low discretion work organization becoming more prominent in these occupations (Wheatley et al., 2011, 412). Those in skilled trade occupations are split between those reporting high levels of autonomy and those reporting relatively little. This is likely to reflect variations within this broad occupation group, for example, those who are contractors who will have relatively more autonomy and those working for large construction firms where less discretion is likely to be found. Lower skilled occupations, including sales and customer service, process, plant and machine operatives, and those in elementary occupations, report the lowest levels of autonomy in their roles, especially with respect to job tasks and working hours, evidencing the Taylorist work organization associated with many of these occupations.

4.6.2 Panel Probit Analysis

Reflecting on the relationship between work-time, autonomy, and subjective well-being, table 4.4 summarizes panel probit regression analysis exploring the relationship between a number of measures of subjective well-being and variables offering insight into time-use and autonomy in work, as well as occupation and demographics. The effects of autonomy in paid work are considered through inclusion of responses to a number of questions pertaining to autonomy, which all follow the form, 'In your current job how much influence do you have over …', with responses in each case comprising 'none', 'a little', 'some', and 'a lot'. Five different aspects of autonomy are considered, specifically autonomy over: (1) job tasks; (2) the pace of work;

Table 4.3 Level of Autonomy in Work (%) by Occupation Group

Autonomy over …	*Managers and Senior Officials*	*Professionals*	*Associate Professional and Technical*	*Administrative and Secretarial*	*Skilled Trades*	*Personal Service Occupations*	*Sales and Customer Service Occupations*	*Process, Plant and Machine Operatives*	*Elementary Occupations*	χ^2
Job tasks										
A lot	69.8	44.6	44.9	32.4	54.2	37.3	25.3	32.6	27.0	***
Some	22.3	36.1	31.4	32.4	24.5	30.7	32.6	25.0	28.5	
A little	5.4	12.2	13.5	18.2	10.9	15.4	17.9	14.1	16.8	
None	2.6	7.1	10.2	17.2	10.4	16.6	24.3	28.4	27.8	
Work pace										
A lot	67.4	44.8	49.1	47.0	59.9	38.3	35.0	41.4	34.3	***
Some	21.5	32.6	28.8	27.5	23.5	29.2	28.6	26.0	27.6	
A little	7.0	13.9	12.2	13.6	9.7	16.4	17.8	13.3	17.7	
None	4.0	8.7	10.0	11.9	7.0	16.2	18.7	19.3	20.5	
Work manner										
A lot	78.3	62.0	60.5	52.1	68.4	48.2	40.0	47.4	39.7	***
Some	16.6	28.8	26.0	28.6	20.4	29.9	29.3	23.4	28.0	
A little	3.5	7.1	8.6	12.1	6.7	13.3	15.8	12.9	15.7	
None	1.1	2.2	4.9	7.3	4.6	8.7	15.0	16.3	16.7	
Task order										
A lot	80.[illegible]	60.2	60.2	56.1	62.4	43.5	39.0	42.4	38.7	***
Some	16.1	28.9	26.2	27.2	22.8	29.6	28.5	23.8	28.2	
A little	3.0	7.8	8.1	9.1	8.1	15.1	13.4	12.6	14.5	
None	0.9	3.1	5.6	7.7	6.7	11.9	19.2	21.3	18.7	
Work hours										
A lot	48.5	30.8	29.3	28.0	38.2	15.8	12.9	22.8	14.3	***
Some	26.4	25.2	24.4	23.9	17.8	14.0	15.0	13.5	15.0	
A little	13.0	16.9	16.7	17.8	13.9	16.2	20.0	14.7	17.6	

(3) manner of (or way of completing) work; (4) task order; and (5) working hours. The presence of informal flexibility is considered to offer additional insight into control over the arrangement of work-time. Informal flexibility is reported in Understanding Society (2015) in reference to responses to the question, 'Aside from any formal arrangements for flexible working you have, are you able to vary your working hours on an informal basis, for example by re-arranging your start or finish times if you need to?' with responses comprising 'no', 'sometimes', and 'yes'. Note that commuting time is not included in the regression analysis due to the alternative inclusion of 'work location', which is included to offer further insight into flexibility in the location of work. Data from wave 4 (2012–2013) of Understanding Society is used. This wave is chosen as relevant modules on autonomy in work are only included biannually in the survey. Models consider satisfaction with job, amount of leisure time, and life overall. Separate models are performed for men and women given the distinct nature of their patterns of time-use evident in figure 4.2.

Work-Time and Other Time Uses

Consistent with existing literature (Ateca-Amestoy et al., 2008; Kahneman et al., 2006; Meier and Stutzer, 2006), the panel probit models identify that lengthier hours of work are associated with lower satisfaction across all of the measures considered. Additional time spent in paid work performing overtime similarly has a negative relationship with well-being, although this is only evident in satisfaction with leisure and life overall. Combined these findings suggest that incidence of extensive labour extraction, including that which may be unpaid (overtime), has negative effects on the well-being of workers. Time spent in other activities offers further insight. Hours of care (ill/elderly) are associated with lower leisure and life satisfaction, evidencing the impact of extensive hours of unpaid work on work-life balance. Housework also has negative effects on leisure and life satisfaction among women, but this is not evident among men. These findings are likely to reflect the relatively smaller impact housework has on men's time (Wheatley and Wu, 2014), and in contrast the significant impact of the greater household contribution made by many women which limits their available leisure time (Garcia et al., 2007).

Occupations

Men in managerial occupations are likely to be less satisfied with the amount of leisure time they experience. This is likely to reflect the impact of lengthy working hours in these occupations which limit time for other activities. Employment in professional occupations is associated with greater satisfaction with job and leisure (among men only) and life overall (among women

Table 4.4 Panel Probit Models: Work-Time, Autonomy, and Subjective Well-Being

	Ordered Choice Panel Probit Models					
	Men			*Women*		
Parameter Estimates	*Satisfaction with Job*	*Satisfaction with Amount of Leisure*	*Satisfaction with Life*	*Satisfaction with Job*	*Satisfaction with Amount of Leisure*	*Satisfaction with Life*
Time-use variables						
Working hours	–0.003**	–0.013***	–0.003**	–0.005***	–0.013***	–0.004***
Overtime hours	0.001	–0.016***	–0.002	–0.023	–0.022***	–0.007***
Housework hours	0.001	0.001	0.000	0.001	–0.006***	–0.002*
Caring hours	0.000	–0.020**	–0.024**	0.000	–0.028***	–0.024***
Demographic variables						
Age	–0.068***	–0.028***	–0.064***	–0.034***	–0.021***	–0.054***
$Age^2/100$	0.081***	0.037***	0.069***	0.043***	0.026***	0.058***
Marital status: reference is 'single/never married or in civil partnership'						
Married	0.048*	–0.001	0.004	0.098***	0.062***	0.254***
Separated/divorced	0.020	–0.070	–0.333**	0.044	–0.009	0.045
Widowed	0.444***	0.360***	0.010	0.218***	0.188**	0.176**
No. of children	0.010	–0.086***	–0.010	0.020	–0.118***	–0.013
Long-term illness/ disability	–0.108***	–0.115***	–0.174***	–0.112***	–0.187***	–0.263***
Highest educational qualifications: reference is 'no qualifications'						
Degree or equivalent	–0.017	–0.024	–0.021	–0.032*	–0.027	0.010
A level	0.021	0.030*	–0.006	0.024	0.018	–0.003
GCSE	0.046**	0.006	0.020	0.062***	–0.009	0.005
Occupation variables						
Major occupation group (SOC2000): reference is 'elementary occupations'						
Managers and senior officials	–0.045	–0.034*	–0.010	–0.171***	0.054	0.047
Professionals	0.088*	0.099**	0.077	–0.075	0.070	0.116**

(continued)

Table 4.4 (continued)

	Ordered Choice Panel Probit Models					
	Men			*Women*		
Parameter Estimates	*Satisfaction with Job*	*Satisfaction with Amount of Leisure*	*Satisfaction with Life*	*Satisfaction with Job*	*Satisfaction with Amount of Leisure*	*Satisfaction with Life*
Associate professional and technical	0.027	0.057	0.036	–0.130***	0.083*	0.074
Administrative and secretarial	–0.076	0.040	–0.033	–0.099*	–0.016	0.009
Skilled trades	0.103**	0.028	0.009	0.070	0.119	0.074
Personal service occupations	0.141**	0.032	–0.043	0.071**	0.021	–0.009
Sales and customer service occupations	–0.118**	0.001	–0.087	–0.102**	0.061	0.028
Process, plant, and machine operatives	0.133***	0.033	–0.044	–0.085	0.065	–0.044
Private sector	–0.053**	–0.088	–0.020	–0.047**	–0.085***	–0.062***
Monthly income (£,000s)	0.004***	0.001**	0.004***	0.002**	0.000	0.004***
Job autonomy and control variables						
Work location: reference is 'employer premises'						
Home	0.009	0.057	0.072	0.228***	0.112*	0.100
Driving/travelling	0.009*	–0.055	0.046	–0.083*	–0.097**	–0.059
Multiple locations	0.079**	0.012	0.038	–0.013	0.127***	0.068
Informal flexibility present in job: reference is 'no'						
Yes	0.146***	0.019	0.062**	0.065**	0.018	0.010
Sometimes	0.078	0.020	0.063	0.088**	0.032	0.042

Autonomy over job tasks: reference is 'none'						
A lot	0.412***	0.081*	0.072	0.341***	0.039	0.061
Some	0.218***	0.036	0.046	0.244***	0.071*	0.083**
A little	0.117*	0.024	0.028	0.064	0.020	0.007
Autonomy over work pace: reference is 'none'						
A lot	0.231***	0.256***	0.147***	0.180***	0.049*	0.041
Some	0.158***	0.179***	0.129**	0.087**	0.007	0.010
A little	0.158***	0.161***	0.062	0.082**	−0.042	−0.051
Autonomy over work manner: reference is 'none'						
A lot	0.067	−0.107	−0.016	0.075**	0.093*	0.064
Some	0.005	−0.098	−0.089	−0.005	0.010	0.005
A little	−0.048	−0.132	−0.132*	−0.016	0.066	−0.063
Autonomy over task order: reference is 'none'						
A lot	−0.181***	−0.056	−0.024	0.004	−0.035	−0.058
Some	−0.201***	−0.073	−0.076	0.027	−0.028	−0.061
A little	−0.139**	−0.084	−0.075	0.063	−0.013	−0.021
Autonomy over work hours: reference is 'none'						
A lot	0.049	0.052***	−0.030	0.131***	0.061*	0.078**
Some	0.004	−0.000	−0.016	−0.004	−0.014	0.006
A little	−0.006	−0.011	−0.046	0.036	−0.013	0.008
Model diagnostics						
Pseudo R-Squared	0.024	0.017	0.014	0.019	0.016	0.014
LR Statistic	707.615	520.302	356.744	694.697	601.482	467.532
Prob (LR Statistic)	0.000	0.000	0.000	0.000	0.000	0.000
Log likelihood	−14211.95	−14613.11	−12683.40	−17583.43	−18441.93	−16034.93
Restr. log likelihood	−14565.76	−14873.26	−12861.77	−17930.78	−18742.67	−16268.69
Avg. log likelihood	−1.582	−1.751	−1.520	−1.583	−1.766	−1.535
No. observations	8,985	8,345	8,343	11,108	10,444	10,444

Note: Significance levels of 1%, 5%, and 10% are denoted by ***, **, and * respectively.
Source: Understanding Society, wave 4 (2012–13).

only). Job satisfaction appears low in sales and customer service and elementary occupations compared to most other occupations, consistent with the low quality – including low pay, low autonomy, and low security – of many jobs in this category. Interestingly, private sector workers report lower satisfaction. This could reflect the positive effects of the greater flexibility present within many public sector occupations, as formal flexibility has been shown to have a positive relationship with subjective well-being (see chapter 5 for a fuller discussion). Income is positively associated with all measures of satisfaction considered (Jorgensen et al., 2010), with the exception of leisure among women.

Demographic Characteristics

With regard to demographics, age is found to have a non-linear relationship consistent with existing findings (see chapter 1): satisfaction diminishes with age but this effect is reversed as individuals become older (see Blanchflower and Oswald, 2008). Married individuals are, on average, likely to report higher levels of satisfaction, while those with dependent children are less likely to be satisfied with their leisure time reflecting the constraining effects of children. Also consistent with the extant literature, the presence of a long-term illness or disability is negatively associated with satisfaction (Lucas, 2007).

Autonomy and Control in Paid Work

The panel probit models identify autonomy in a number of aspects of work as having positive association with job, leisure, and life satisfaction, but with some important gender distinctions present in the results. Autonomy over the nature of job tasks is particularly relevant to job satisfaction among both men and women, as even 'a little' or 'some' autonomy in this aspect of work is associated with higher levels of satisfaction. The pace of work, reflecting control over the intensity of paid work, is highly relevant to men: it is associated with greater satisfaction with job, leisure, and life. However, among women work pace appears to have less relevance to life satisfaction, and is only relevant to leisure when 'a lot' of autonomy over work pace is reported. In contrast, autonomy over the manner of work appears more relevant to women, although the effects are only present where 'a lot' of autonomy is reported. Autonomy over the timing of work is also positively associated with all measures of satisfaction among women – although only where 'a lot' of autonomy is reported – while it is only relevant to job satisfaction for men. This is likely to reflect the particular benefits for women of being able to mould their work-time to fit their household responsibilities. It should be noted, though, that greater autonomy over task order is, interestingly, found to be negatively associated with job satisfaction among men. Task order has no statistically significant association for women. This result could be driven by the greater presence of this form of autonomy in certain sectors of the labour market, or among managers (see table 3.2) and/or the highly skilled (those reporting degree level education), who report lower satisfaction with certain aspects of life in the probit models.

Other variables offering further insight into the effects of flexibility in paid work, and associated time-use, suggest some relationship between flexibility and satisfaction, as well as highlighting gender divisions present driven by the household division of labour. The presence of informal flexibility is associated with greater satisfaction with job and life overall (men only). Meanwhile, working at home is associated with higher levels of both satisfaction with job and leisure time among women. These results are consistent with the benefits for women of flexibility in both the timing and location of paid work (Wheatley, 2012b). A further gender division is present among those driving/travelling in their job. Among women they report lower job and life satisfaction, while men in these occupations (and those working at multiple sites) report greater job satisfaction. It is likely that these types of employment would create particular challenges for women, in managing dual responsibilities of work and home, and potentially reduce levels of control over the timing and location of paid work.[2]

4.7 CHAPTER SUMMARY: HOW DO WORK-TIME AND THE QUALITY OF WORK AFFECT SUBJECTIVE WELL-BEING?

This chapter has considered the relationship between time spent in paid work and subjective well-being. Existing literature and the empirical analysis conducted in the chapter evidence a number of important relationships between paid work, broader patterns of time-use, and well-being. Historical patterns of time-use, summarized in figure 4.1, evidence a general decline in the time spent in paid work since the mid-nineteenth century. In more recent years, however, time devoted to paid work has remained relatively stable, while evidence is indicative of a growing intensification and flexibilization of employment. As figure 4.2 revealed, a trade-off is present to some extent between hours spent in paid work and other forms of time-use, especially housework. This is most apparent among part-time women who report extensive hours given to housework. Lengthy time-use is reported among full-time men and women, especially when considering work-time inclusive of overtime. The evidence presented in table 4.2, consistent with existing literature, has also shown that hours are particularly long within certain occupations, especially for managers and professionals. This is important as extensive labour extraction has a considerable negative effect on satisfaction, especially with leisure time, and is evident in both reported dissatisfaction with hours (see Wheatley et al., 2011; Philp and Wheatley, 2011), and in the negative relationships observed between lengthier hours of work and measures of subjective well-being.

Findings are also indicative of the quality of work, explored with regard to autonomy and flexibility, varying considerably between occupations. Managers report the greatest levels of autonomy. The empirical analysis finds autonomy is associated with positive outcomes reflected in greater employee-reported satisfaction. However, autonomy over different aspects of paid work has differing relevance to men and women workers' satisfaction with job, leisure, and life overall. The nature of job tasks and pace of work, the latter reflecting control over the intensity of work, have particular relevance to job satisfaction. The findings pertaining to the nature of job tasks, which is also seen to have positive impacts on leisure satisfaction, are indicative of the benefits for employees from having a greater level of discretion over the tasks they complete. Autonomy over work manner and working hours is also associated with greater job satisfaction among women, although the effects are only present where 'a lot' of autonomy in these aspects of work is found. Autonomy in these areas of paid work also has positive effects for women in respect of leisure satisfaction. These findings reflect the benefits for women, who may be able to better manage the combined challenges of paid work alongside household responsibilities through moulding how they use their work-time. This assertion is further supported by the findings pertaining to informal flexibility and flexibility over work location which both suggest particular benefits for women from increased control over both the timing and location of paid work.

While lengthier hours spent in paid work have a generally negative relationship with well-being, both the quantity and quality of paid work vary considerably across forms of work, between individuals, and during the lifecourse. Self-employment, further, creates a separate set of challenges, and potential benefits, with respect to patterns of work and impacts on well-being (Fraser and Gold, 2001; Fenwick, 2006, 76). As outlined in chapter 1, a nuanced relationship is present between paid work and relative levels of reported well-being. For example, unemployment is associated with a number of negative impacts on well-being (Frey and Stutzer, 2002b; Knabe et al., 2010; Krueger and Mueller, 2012). Loss of income creates challenges for individuals (and their households), and limits their ability to access employment opportunities (when considering transport), and engage in certain leisure activities which require expenditure or transport access (see chapter 8 for a further discussion). However, the unemployed may gain some satisfaction from using their time enjoyably while the employed are at work (Knabe et al., 2010, 879). The intensity of paid work is a concern, especially among the highly skilled. Meanwhile, underemployment also represents a growing concern, as evident in the proportions reporting part-time employment due to a lack of full-time opportunities. Growth in employer-driven flexible employment, including zero-hours and temporary agency work, in particular, are creating challenges for many workers, especially younger workers who are over-represented in these occupations. Meanwhile, challenges exist for those with caring responsibilities in participating in paid work. As caring more often is undertaken by women they remain more constrained in their ability to engage, and remain, in paid work (Drinkwater, 2015), often limiting them to part-time work or resulting in non-participation in the labour market. Those classed as economically inactive – including those in full-time education which accounted for around two million individuals in the United Kingdom in April–June 2015 (ONS, 2015e) – may, though, be more likely to engage in voluntary work. While not considered in this chapter, which focuses on paid work, these uses of time and their relationship with well-being are considered in detail in chapter 6. Overall, the findings in this chapter highlight the complex relationship present between paid work and well-being, and emphasize the importance of choice in influencing relative outcomes. While paid work is not an activity in which most would actively choose to spend more time, limited or constrained access to work remains similarly undesirable, both as a result of the loss of income generated from work but also because of the wider benefits paid work can bring to well-being.

NOTE

1. This analysis only includes data from Understanding Society as questions relating to autonomy were not included in the BHPS.
2. For a more detailed analysis and discussion of the impacts of autonomy on subjective well-being, including further depth on the differentiated effects of different types of autonomy to men and women, see Wheatley (2017).

Chapter Five

The Household Division of Labour and Flexibility in Paid Work

5.1 INTRODUCTION

Since the latter part of the twentieth century policy interventions and changing social attitudes have motivated a convergence in the economic lives of men and women (Lundberg and Pollak, 2007, 6–7). However, inequalities remain present in the lived experiences of work and home for men and women throughout the lifecourse. This chapter moves the context to the household to consider the household division of labour and its impact on time-use, including time spent in paid work. Specific consideration is given to the ways in which household responsibilities impact on the propensity of men and women to engage in paid work. Even in post-industrial economies praised for family-friendly working policies, including Sweden and other Scandinavian countries, gender pay gaps and the continued presence of the glass ceiling reflect a less than ideal outcome for many women (Hakim, 2004; Mandel and Semyonov, 2005). The United Kingdom remains characterized by a liberal stance on employment and welfare policy (Lewis and Campbell, 2008, 535–36), which may present an even more challenging environment for some working women. Recent decades have seen a feminization of the labour market, as outlined in chapter 3, with increasing numbers of women participating and remaining in the labour force for the majority of their adult lives, in part as a result of changes in the nature and occupational structures of work (Perrons et al., 2005). However, while increasing financial, social, and political pressure is felt by households for both partners to remain in some form of paid employment, women still undertake the bulk of unpaid work in most households (Garcia et al., 2007, 2011; McDowell et al., 2005).

Evidence has shown some improvement in the gendered distribution of household labour (see Sullivan, 2010), for example, men chauffeuring their children (Schwanen, 2007). However, women continue to undertake the majority of housework, as well as acting as primary caregivers to both dependent children and other kin and non-kin present in the household and in the wider community (Garcia et al., 2011; Woolvin and Hardill, 2013). This unpaid work, though, functions as a social constraint to many women's labour force participation (van Staveren, 2010, 1130). Women that are married/cohabiting and have dependent children are often faced with the practical 'choice' of undertaking paid work outside the home and unpaid work inside the home. Giving time to paid work and the home, can therefore involve a level of trade-off. This chapter builds on work published in peer-reviewed journals, including Philp and Wheatley (2011), Wheatley (2012b, 2016), and Wheatley and Wu (2014). Evidence is drawn from existing research, and from analysis of the BHPS and Understanding Society as well as case study evidence from the 2006 study of Greater Nottingham in the United Kingdom, to explore the impacts of household structure on decision-making by household members, gendered patterns in the household distribution of labour and their relationship with paid work, and whether flexible working arrangements offer an effective method of managing the combined demands of home and paid work.

5.2 HOUSEHOLD STRUCTURES AND DECISION-MAKING

Households can be broadly categorized as (1) traditional, (2) transitional, and (3) egalitarian. Traditional households are illustrated by the male breadwinner, female homemaker model. Consistent with mainstream approaches in economics, typified by Becker (1976), these households are founded on a unitary model of the household in which the household is considered a single decision-making entity, led by a male 'dictator'. Under Becker's model men's and women's time-inputs to the household are considered perfect substitutes (Lundberg and Pollak, 2007, 12). Households maximize utility, subject to time and budget constraints. Becker assumes that intra-household dynamics are harmonious, suggesting a 'fair' distribution of activity resulting in similar average amounts of residual time, for activities including pure consumption and sleep, by gender. But this mainstream model ignores the potential for exploitation and prioritization, for example, the male career taking precedence and the prioritization of 'his' career significantly influencing household decision-making (Cha, 2010). Meanwhile, women's role as primary care providers means that their behaviour does not perfectly reflect assumptions of self-interest (van Staveren, 2010, 1129). The traditional model of the household is no longer representative of social reality (Crompton et al., 2007;

Hochschild and Machung, 1990; McDowell, 2004), although it has been acknowledged that a pure male breadwinner model never existed as women have always engaged in the labour market (Lewis, 2001, 153). Nevertheless, the limitations of the traditional model have led to reinterpretation.

Transitional models of the household, include the collective model/adult-worker model family. In the collective model households are treated as consisting of several individuals with their own rational preferences (Browning and Chiappori, 1998). Household decisions under this model result in Pareto efficient outcomes (Vermeulen, 2002; Garcia et al., 2011). Game theoretic models have also attempted to explain decision-making within households (van Staveren, 2010, 1129). These include both bargaining models and consensual models (see Seiz, 1995, 610), which acknowledge that households are multi-person and that decisions are made by individuals with their own preferences and constraints (Grossbard, 2010). A commonality among these models is that they extend mainstream approaches by supposing a degree of 'jointness' in decision-making. These approaches, however, cannot easily explain the wide variety of contradicting gender norms that influence households. For example, in many households men control the income and wealth of both partners. Decisions are not made unilaterally, but instead reflect consideration for other household members. Recent empirical research by Livingston (2014 21) is indicative of men and women experiencing the household decision-making process differently. It is posited that a bargaining process occurs, including negotiation regarding the household division of labour (Bowles and McGinn, 2008) and the prioritization of careers (Livingston, 2011, 2).

The 'adult-worker model family', as defined by Lewis (2001, 154), is characterized by all adults within a household engaging in the labour market. Much of the discussion in Lewis is concerned with 'one and a half worker' (or dual earner) households where one partner is engaged in full-time paid employment while the other, often the female, is engaged in part-time work for at least part of their career (155), effectively leaving many women with the role of the secondary career within their household. In the past, women often took career breaks to have children. However, this trend has decreased in recent years as more women remain in some form of employment (Lewis and Campbell, 2008, 535–36). Women remain in employment by making use of both market and non-market, family-based care (Harris et al., 2007), including grandparenting which is considered in the next chapter. It should be noted, though, that while some wealthier dual earner couples exchange household labour for marketized labour as they can afford to make such substitutions, it is this exchange that has in the past been shown as being largely responsible for reductions in women's burden of unpaid housework, rather than men increasing their contribution to unpaid work (Gregson and Lowe, 1994).

The final household model, egalitarian, is characterized by, among other things, partners sharing housework equally (Hochschild and Machung, 1990). Within a growing proportion of households both partners more often remain engaged in full-time employment. Moreover, women in the United Kingdom have in recent years become increasingly likely to be the household's primary earner (Soobedar, 2011), hence there should be no lead career within a growing number of households. These households are often referred to as dual earner households, but the number of households where both partners engage in careers is also on the rise. These dual career households differ from dual earner households – those where both partners are in paid work – in that both partners are employed in highly skilled managerial, professional, or associate professional occupations (Hakim, 2002; Hardill and Wheatley, 2009). Partners in these households both pursue careers and engage in full-time paid work for the majority of their adult lives. The distribution of elements of time-use in these households is therefore especially interesting as there is, in principle, no obvious lead and secondary career present. In dual career households combining work (career) and home is likely to be particularly complex. Gendered expectations, though, impact outcomes for women who are perceived negatively if they 'competitively' pursue a career. Women may, therefore, more often 'accept' the role of secondary career within the household. For example, combining dual careers with the home may require the (short-term) prioritization of one partner's career at the expense of the others (Hardill, 2002).

Women in dual career households who are mothers have a stronger attachment to the labour market after childbirth than other groups of women (Hardill and Wheatley, 2009). But, greater labour market equality may not equate to an egalitarian distribution of tasks within the home (Garcia et al., 2007). Dual career households have a growing significance as a category of household in post-industrial economies, in part reflecting the general growth in employment in managerial and professional occupations relative to other occupation groups (Goos and Manning, 2007). In the United Kingdom dual career households numbered over 1.2 million in 1991. This had increased to 2.23 million (10 percent of all households) by 2001 (Hardill and Wheatley, 2009, 240), and approximately 12 percent (3.19 million) of households by 2011 (estimate from Understanding Society, 2012). Increases have been driven by female labour market participation, and polarization into work-rich-time-poor and work-poor-time-rich households (McDowell et al., 2005). Women in dual career households most closely represent 'work-centred' women, as defined in Hakim's (2000, 2002) preference theory. Even within this group of women, though, there are nuanced variations and contradictions, which render Hakim's categorization unsuitable (Lewis and Campbell, 2008).

Dual career households have the potential to be egalitarian as both partners invest in cultural and symbolic capital (of which education is a significant component), and have a deep commitment to the labour market (Hardill and Wheatley, 2009, 239). However, while decisions over paid work follow a more egalitarian model, the tasks of social reproduction remain a largely female preserve (Hardill, 2002). Commitment to the labour market does not substantially alter the number of household tasks women perform. Nor does it result in a significant redistribution of household labour between men and women commensurate with their paid labour (Garcia et al., 2007, 2011). Recent UK-based qualitative research is consistent with this assertion: younger couples, while in principle supporting equality, often do not evidence an egalitarian distribution of household labour. Meanwhile, older couples continue to report housework as a predominantly female activity (van Hooff, 2011, 26–27). The uneven allocation of household tasks reinforces fundamental inequalities in economic power between male and female partners (Hardill and Watson, 2004, 21). The benefits of flexible working may thus be especially important to working mothers (Dikkers et al., 2010, 576), although difficulties are faced in achieving balance between work and life if women are to avoid negative career implications often associated with use of flexible working arrangements (Atkinson and Hall, 2009, 663). While the economic lives of men and women may have converged to some extent (Lundberg and Pollak, 2007, 6–7), empirical evidence suggests that, even within dual career households, gender inequality in decision-making and time-use remain present (Wheatley, 2013). Some degree of both conflict and compromise persist.

5.3 GENDERED CAREERS AND THE HOUSEHOLD DIVISION OF LABOUR

The careers of men and women are distinct. Traditional conceptualizations of career centre on hierarchical models of career development, which assume upward progression through a series of related jobs throughout the lifecourse, associated with age and experience, which are ordered in a hierarchy of prestige (Greenhaus et al., 2000; Schein, 1978; Wilensky, 1960). However, while the term 'career' has traditionally been used to describe long-term progression, a ladder, or linear promotion, within an occupation or series of occupations involving increasing responsibility (Evetts, 2000), contemporary careers are progressively multi-directional, flexible, and flat in form, with acknowledgement given to both the needs of the individual and organization (Baruch, 2004, 68–70).

Entirely new career strategies have emerged as a result of both labour market and household change. For example, the concept of the protean career emphasizes the role of the individual, acknowledging that careers are driven internally reflecting the pursuit of individual values, rather than being organization-led (Briscoe et al., 2006). The protean careerist is defined as an individual that views paid work as a 'calling'. The core values of a protean career are: (1) psychological success rather than salary or position, and (2) commitment to the profession and actual work rather than organization or employer (Hall, 2004). The occupation or industry of employment can act as a career anchor or compass, which influences the identity of the individual, but at the same time remains relatively stable throughout their working life (Schein, 1978, 1996; Peel and Inkson, 2004).[1] Meanwhile, a portfolio career (Fenwick, 2006) is one characterized by the movement of workers between strategies, organizations, and even employment sectors, at different times in their careers. An alternative model, the kaleidoscope career, involves evaluating career decisions as if through a kaleidoscope lens to determine the best combination of work at any career stage while acknowledging the demands, constraints, and opportunities present and giving due consideration to life, family, and relationships (Sullivan et al., 2009).

For women in particular, traditional male-centred career models fail to acknowledge the complexity of their careers and the challenges faced in managing work and family (White, 1995). Women's labour market participation does not simply reflect labour supply preferences, but instead their culturally assigned role of unpaid worker in the household. It is women, more often than not, who compromise their career by fitting paid work around household responsibilities (Lundberg and Pollak, 2007). This is evident, for example, in that women also remain more likely than their male counterparts to quit their job where their partner is overworked (works long hours). Gendered expectations result in women's careers taking on a secondary role, especially where dependent children are present (Cha, 2010, 319–20). While no single theory has effectively explained the differences present in the careers of men and women, both demand and supply side factors are important including having children, marital status, education level, and job availability (Yerkes, 2010, 700).

Women have complex careers, which are captured by the concepts of multidirectional (Baruch, 2004), or patchwork, boundaryless, or frayed (Peel and Inkson, 2004, 544) careers. The 'typical' female career trajectory is non-linear, complex, and dynamic (Peel and Inkson, 2004; Arthur, 2008). The emergence of 'patchwork' and 'kaleidoscope' career models have attempted to capture the complexity of female experiences of work, including the career transitions women experience (Bateson, 1990). These contemporary career models (Arthur, 2008, 168) move away from the notion of a hierarchical career trajectory by highlighting how, for example, 'women shift the pattern of their careers by rotating different aspects of their lives to arrange their roles and relationships in new ways' (Mainiero and Sullivan, 2005, 111). Women's careers are characterized by transition periods where their career decisions are influenced by their stage in the lifecourse. Attitudes to work and career aspirations are subject to both change and conflict. For those with caring responsibilities this may result in family-related career breaks, interruptions or reductions in time spent in paid work, or even a move into self-employment (Cabrera, 2007; Hytti, 2010). It should also be acknowledged that these complex career paths, characterized by transitions, also often fit the notion of a protean career.

Women's career choices and success are influenced by their occupation (Crompton and Lyonette, 2011) and the gender segregation present in the industry of employment. Gendered divisions, as discussed in chapter 3, remain present in both vertical and horizontal forms, resulting in segregation between industries and occupations (Teasdale, 2013, 400; Hakim, 2000, 65). Moreover, the impact of the household division of labour, among other factors, results in the presence of an important divide among women between 'career' women who are highly educated, and command well paid employment, and those who are in less secure, lower paid work, some of whom exit the labour market as they cannot afford marketized care (Drinkwater, 2015, 284). Career women, while income rich, are time poor (McDowell et al., 2005; Jones, 2003, 7) reflecting alternative constraint.

In restricting labour market participation and/or commitment to a career (in the eyes of the employer), at least during certain stages of the lifecourse, the household division of labour results in career progression suffering for those who do not, or are unable to, adhere to cultures of full-time employment. In many cases, the productivity levels of workers may be considered less significant than the perceptions of commitment linked directly to hours of work (Harris et al., 2007, 501). The presence of dependent children, in particular, reduces work-time among women, but increases it among men, with potentially important career implications for working mothers (Jacobs and Gerson, 2001, 57). Career development and associated benefits including income growth are in some cases only offered to individuals who are able to consistently work full-time throughout their careers, contrasting starkly with the lived reality of many women's careers (Lewis and Humbert, 2010). This is reflected in the continued presence of the gender pay gap (ONS, 2013b, 2014a, 2015d). As Liff and Ward (2001, 27) suggested, 'Women who leave work at 5pm are seen as scoring own goals.' Some women thus postpone or forego a family, in order to conform to the male norm of long full-time hours, and effectively have to sacrifice their desired work-life balance, at least in the short term, in the pursuit of a career (Sturges and Guest, 2004, 17). At later stages in their careers women in some cases actively leave senior roles, in order to obtain greater flexibility, and through the desire to avoid high pressure long hours cultures (Anderson et al., 2010). To some extent the differences in the careers of men and women may also reflect differences in how commitment is perceived by the men and women workers themselves. Singh and Vinnicombe (2000), for example, have suggested that women view commitment as involvement, availability, and being concerned for others, while men view commitment as being innovative, adding value, and taking on challenges. Perception differences aside, though, the working lives of men and women clearly remain distinct and the household division of labour appears to have a central role in maintaining inequalities in experiences of paid work and a career.

5.4 THE HOUSEHOLD DIVISION OF LABOUR AND WELL-BEING

Broad evidence reflecting on the determinants of satisfaction levels suggests that individuals whose focus is on family, friends, and community generally report higher levels of satisfaction than those whose focus is on materialism and career (Headey, 2008). This raises important concerns regarding the impact of paid work and careers on the well-being of the individual and other household members. Although research has shown that women may actually report higher levels of job satisfaction than men, it has been suggested that this does not reflect better outcomes for women, but that they compare their relative satisfaction on a lesser scale, and/or that women are less willing to communicate their dissatisfaction regarding work (Hodson, 2005). The latter explanation corresponds more closely with MacDonald et al.'s (2005) findings which identified that the household division of labour results in greater levels of stress among women, as they combine paid work with lengthy hours of unpaid work. Moreover, lengthy hours of care (adult and child) have been shown empirically, using panel data from the BHPS, to have negative impacts on satisfaction with life among women (Della Giusta et al., 2011, 17–18). Indeed, the presence of dependent children creates added complexity for women as they attempt to combine work and life reducing levels of satisfaction, including satisfaction with leisure (Garcia et al., 2007). Job and income are more central drivers of the satisfaction levels of men (Della Giusta et al., 2011, 22). Women report dissatisfaction with the hours of paid work, as they are constrained by household and caring responsibilities (Philp and Wheatley, 2011). Flexibility is, therefore, essential for many working women. Some evidence suggests women working part-time, for example, report higher levels of satisfaction (Gregory and Connolly, 2008), but a trade-off is evident as they also report performing more housework than other women (Wight and Raley, 2009). Women's job satisfaction remains more likely to be negatively influenced (than their male counterparts) by conflicts between work and life, as a result of the greater propensity for them to become 'overloaded' by their household contribution (Ergeneli et al., 2010, 692).

5.5 PATTERNS OF HOUSEHOLD LABOUR: EVIDENCE FROM THE BHPS AND UNDERSTANDING SOCIETY

Patterns of housework remain starkly gendered despite increases in women participating in paid work, and working full-time for lengthier periods of their careers. Figure 5.1 summarizes patterns of time spent on housework per week among men and women, providing an average for the period 1992–2013/2014. Overall, women report approximately double the amount of time spent on tasks within the home each week. The trend is present even among those working full-time, and indeed even among dual career households (see chapter 4; Wheatley and Wu, 2014). As already noted in chapter 4, women working part-time report substantial time spent on housework, averaging 16.5 hours per week between 1992 and 2013/2014. Interestingly, self-employed women also report lengthy hours of housework, on average, consistent with the assertion of many women using self-employment as a method of obtaining greater flexibility at certain stages of the lifecourse (Cabrera, 2007; Hytti, 2010). Those inactive or retired follow the same pattern, but with lengthier time spent on housework in both cases among both men and women. Finally, those reporting education/training report notably lesser hours spent on housework, reflecting in many cases that these individuals are, on average, younger and living with kin or in short-term rental accommodation. The amount of time spent on housework by women has seen some reduction during the period observed, equivalent to around one hour per week among women in full-time employment (approximately an 8 percent reduction), and around five hours per week among part-timers (a reduction of 24 percent). Concurrently, men have reported increases in hours spent on housework although these have only been marginal (see figure 4.2 in chapter 4).

With respect to the nature of the tasks being completed by men and women within the home, clear gender divisions are also present. Table 5.1 summarizes responses to the question, 'I am going to read out some household jobs. Could you please say who mostly does this work here? Is it mostly yourself, or mostly your spouse/partner, or is the work shared equally?' The data highlights the continuing gendered nature of household tasks. Significant proportions of women report undertaking the majority of the washing/ironing (73.7 percent), cooking (63.4 percent), cleaning (61.4 percent), and shopping (51.0 percent). Men do, though, report greater contribution in regard to DIY (76.1 percent) and gardening (47.4 percent). Remaining couples (over a quarter in total) report these household tasks as being shared equally with the most commonly shared task being grocery shopping. It should also be noted that some households utilize marketized provision of some services, in particular DIY, as well as cleaning and gardening to a lesser extent. Even among those in dual career households, these patterns remain present although notably less stark and with

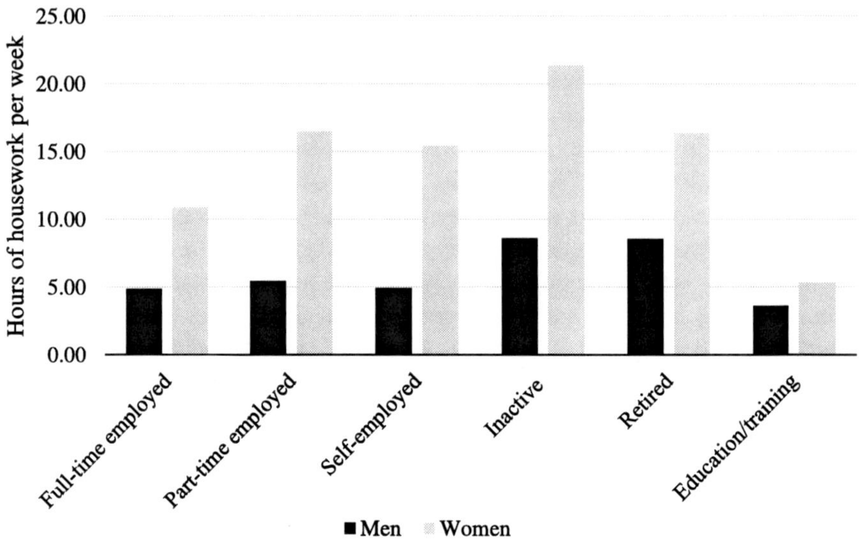

Figure 5.1. Average Housework Hours Among Men and Women.
***Source*: British Household Panel Survey Wave 1–18, 1992–2009; Understanding Society Wave 2–5 (2010/2011–2013/2014).**
***Note*: Inactive Comprises Unemployed, Long Term Sick/Disabled, Family Carers.**

some variations (see Wheatley and Wu, 2014). Further insight into household dynamics is also offered by responses to the question, 'In your household, who has the final say in big financial decisions?' Notably, in this regard men and women report similar patterns of decision-making, with just over two-thirds of households sharing decisions equally and the remainder split with marginally more men (17.7 percent of men compared to 13.8 percent of women) reporting acting as the main decision-maker regarding finances.

The number of hours spent caring for dependent children is not collected in Understanding Society (nor was it collected in the BHPS). This time-use is difficult to quantify for many individuals as to some extent it can be considered as the majority of the residual time, with the exception of sleep, for parents of dependent children. The only exceptions being time when either a child is being cared for by others, at nursery or school, or with grandparents or other relatives/friends (see chapter 6 for a fuller discussion of grandparenting). Understanding Society does, though, provide some insight into gendered patterns of childcare, as it includes the question, 'Who is mainly responsible for looking after the child(ren)?' Overall, some 59.0 percent of women report themselves as the main care provider for their dependent children. In contrast, just 3.8 percent of men report being the main care provider. Within the remaining households, around 43 percent, childcare is shared relatively evenly. Even among those in dual career households this

Table 5.1 Distribution of Household Tasks

	Men (n = 12,487)				Women (n = 14,137)			
Who Does the …	Mostly Self (%)	Mostly Spouse/ Partner (%)	Shared (%)	Paid Help Only (%)	Mostly Self (%)	Mostly Spouse/ Partner (%)	Shared (%)	Paid Help Only (%)
Grocery shopping?	14.4	42.6	42.9	0.1	51.0	11.2	37.8	0.1
Cooking?	15.9	56.9	27.1	0.1	63.4	12.9	23.6	0.1
Washing/ ironing?	7.5	67.0	24.7	0.7	73.7	5.0	20.7	0.6
Gardening?	47.4	18.6	30.9	3.1	23.9	43.2	29.7	3.3
DIY?	76.1	6.3	11.7	5.9	10.1	67.6	15.1	7.2
Cleaning?	11.0	51.9	34.0	3.1	61.4	7.5	27.7	3.4

Source: Understanding Society, wave 4 (2012–13).

pattern is evident: 48.0 percent of women careerists report acting as the main childcarer, compared to 2.8 percent of men. Clear from the patterns observed is that distinct gendered patterns remain within the household, and that the household contribution of women is significantly greater regardless of labour market status. This is likely to have a significant constraining effect, impacting the working lives of many women and generating work-family conflict.

5.6 WORK-FAMILY CONFLICT AND FLEXIBILITY IN PAID WORK

Flexible working arrangements or work-family policies, including part-time and homeworking, can be used to successfully manage home and work. In the UK context, the Flexible Working Regulations outlined in chapter 3 offer workers a range of leave options and the legal right to request a flexible working arrangement (see Deakin and Morris, 2012, 750–52). Table 5.2 provides a summary of different forms of flexible working arrangement by broad type. This includes those which focus on the arrangement rather than reduction of work-time including flexi-time, compressed hours, and annualized hours (Atkinson and Hall, 2009, 651). Reduced hours options include part-time, term-time, and job share. Finally, there are arrangements which are focused on providing flexibility in the location of work, specifically homeworking and teleworking. In addition to the formal arrangements outlined in table 5.2, it is also important to note that organizations may offer employees informal flexibility, including working at home occasionally or varying the length of the working day, as an alternative. This is often highly valued by

Table 5.2 Forms of Flexible Working

Arrangement of Work-Time	
Flexi-time	Flexible starting and finishing hours of work, often around a set of core hours e.g., 10 a.m. to 3 p.m.
Compressed hours	Work fewer but lengthier working days e.g., 4 nine-hour days per week
Annualized hours	Employees undertake contracted number of hours per year, with allocation of hours determined either through agreement between employee and employer, or by the employer in response to 'business need'
Reduced Hours Arrangements	
Part-time	Reduced hours, often defined as working under thirty hours per week
Term-time	Working only during term-times and taking extended breaks, usually in line with school holidays
Job share	One full-time position is shared between two employees. The job is divided, equally or otherwise between sharers. Salary, leave, and other benefits are divided between each worker on a pro-rata basis
Work Location	
Homeworking (including home-based teleworking)	Working at or from home. This increasingly involves use of mobile technologies, reflected in the term 'home-based teleworking'
Teleworking	Distributed work: paid work outside of the normal place of work including at home, client sites, on the move, and communicating using ICT

employees as it increases control over paid work (Hall and Atkinson, 2006, 383). However, research indicates that informal flexibility is only common among managerial and professional workers (Golden, 2009, 46–47).

Providing employees with greater control over the timing and location of paid work is sometimes referred to as 'schedule flexibility' or 'schedule control' (Glavin and Schieman, 2012, 75; Jang et al., 2011, 136). Evidence is indicative of the potential 'win-win' for both employer and employee from the use of flexible working arrangements. Employers benefit from improved customer services, employee motivation and productivity, lower absenteeism, improved recruitment and retention, and reduced accommodation costs, for example, hot-desking (Woodland et al. 2003; Department for Business, Innovation and Skills, 2010). Meanwhile, employee benefits include work-time flexibility (Tietze and Musson, 2005), reductions in work-family conflict, and alleviation of the pressures of the 'school run' by avoiding peak journey times (Wheatley, 2012b).

Women more often tend to use schedule flexibility, although access to it may be more common among men (Lyness et al., 2012). Glavin and Schieman (2012, 86), using the US Work, Stress and Health Survey, find that the presence of schedule flexibility is associated with lesser incidence of work-family conflict. However, the relationship is more nuanced in that the greater flexibility offered by schedule control is often associated with occupations which themselves are subject to higher levels of role blurring, for example, professions. Kelly et al. (2011, 267), using longitudinal data from a US organization captured prior to and after the introduction of schedule flexibility initiatives, also find that these workplace policies reduced work-family conflict. They suggest that it is particularly important as a mechanism for delivering employee benefits through flexibility, and that it has the potential to positively impact both work and family spheres. Using the 1997 Work Orientations II Survey, Lyness et al. (2012, 19–20) find schedule flexibility is positively related to both job satisfaction and organizational commitment. Moreover, the mediating effect of schedule control over work-family conflict is found to be statistically significant for women, but not men, suggesting specific benefits of greater flexibility for women.

In regard to employee well-being, greater job satisfaction has been reported among those using various flexible working arrangements (Gregory and Connolly, 2008; Hyman and Summers, 2004; Kelliher and Anderson, 2008; Wheatley, 2012a). Women, in particular may benefit from greater control over both the timing and location of work (Dikkers et al., 2010). Use of schedule flexibility may mediate the negative effects women encounter on their subjective well-being, resulting from time constraints caused by managing work and home (Nomaguchi et al., 2005). Galinsky et al. (2011, 151) find a positive relationship between flexibility and employee engagement, job satisfaction, and retention. Flexibility of this nature has been found to have a stronger effect on job satisfaction where it is combined with formal flexible working arrangements (Jang et al., 2011, 140). Home-based teleworkers, for example, can benefit from greater control over the timing and location of paid work, moulding work-time to their own preferences.

There remain concerns, however, over the extent of formalization of work-life balance policies and limited use of some flexible working arrangements (Gambles, 2006; McNamara et al., 2012). The Work-Life Balance Campaign was criticized for its 'inherent and limiting managerialism' (Shorthose, 2004, 2), and focus on preserving existing constructs of work (Fleetwood, 2007). In the private sector, it could be argued that this may reflect the nature of some businesses, including customer-facing environments which require employees to be present at certain times. Meanwhile, small to medium size organizations (SMEs) may find it particularly challenging to implement effective flexible working policies due to: (1) informal management systems; (2) the limited number of job positions; and (3) inadequate resources. These issues limit the ability of SMEs to provide flexible working arrangements at the same level as large firms (Dex and Scheibl, 2002; Maxwell et al., 2007). In some cases,

SME managers may also lack the knowledge capital required to implement appropriate systems to handle flexible working requests (Maxwell et al., 2007). Nevertheless, SME employers can, and do, accommodate requests where it can enhance their competitive position, for example, SMEs in the professional services sector allow skilled employees the flexibility to tailor work, in order to increase job satisfaction and performance (Zeytinoglu et al., 2009).

Even when flexible working arrangements are available, implementation can result in less than ideal outcomes, including the marginalization of flexible workers (Hoque and Kirkpatrick, 2003; Wheatley, 2012b). As already noted, evidence has, for example, suggested that use of flexible working arrangements can limit career opportunities and impair wage growth among mothers, especially in managerial and professional occupations (Glass, 2004, 387). Used for extended periods, it has also been suggested that certain arrangements may have negative impacts on well-being, reflecting both the challenges associated with combining work and home, and the lower job quality often associated with reduced hours flexible options including part-time work (Wheatley, 2016). Incidence of employer-friendly flexibility, driven by 'business need' (e.g., zero-hour contracts), creates difficulties for workers in achieving desired work-life balance (Gregory and Milner, 2009, 123; Poelmans and Beham, 2008; Raess and Burgoon, 2015, 95–96). Employees, further, report lesser access to arrangements where supervisors remain unsupportive of flexible working (McNamara et al., 2012, 957).

5.6.1 Flexible Working and Well-Being: Evidence from Understanding Society

Understanding Society provides useful data on patterns of flexible working in the United Kingdom. This data-set includes responses to separate questions regarding availability and use of flexible work options thus removing some of the conceptual concerns identified in existing literature regarding conflation of availability and use in many empirical studies (see McNamara et al., 2012). This chapter uses data from wave 4 (2012–2013) of Understanding Society to explore patterns of availability and use of flexible working arrangements, and the relationship between the use of arrangements and subjective well-being.

The data from Understanding Society is indicative of widespread availability of flexible working arrangements in UK organizations, as 76.2 percent of employees reported availability of at least one arrangement. This is consistent with evidence from the UK 2011 WERS. There continues to be sectoral divisions, though, as 86.6 percent of employees working in the public sector reported availability of at least one arrangement, compared with only 70.4 percent in the private sector. Variations in use are not as stark. Of those reporting at least one arrangement available at their organization,

60.7 percent reported using one of these options (58.3 percent in the private and 64.2 percent in the public sector). Meanwhile, incidence of informal flexibility is reported among similar proportions of men and women in both private and public sectors. The use of informal flexibility may provide employees with greater autonomy in the timing and location of paid work. The presence of informal flexibility is reported among just over half of all workers. The majority of managers (73.9 percent), associate professionals (58.0 percent), and administrative (62.2 percent) workers report the ability to work flexibly on an informal basis. Interestingly, fewer professionals report informal flexibility (50.4 percent), perhaps evident of the demands of certain professions, for example, those working in medicine or law. However, the aggregated data does hide variations in availability and use of different flexible working arrangements.

Table 5.3 presents data on the availability and use of flexible working arrangements by type of arrangement. Initially clear from the data are the substantial gaps between availability and use of a number of flexible working arrangements. All of the arrangements considered are more widely available in the public sector. However interestingly with regard to use, both part-time and homeworking are more common among private sector workers. In both cases this may be indicative of the potential cost reductions available to employers from the application of these options. Part-time work is the most common flexible working arrangement used by women (46.0 percent), consistent with previous evidence (Connolly and Gregory, 2008, F52). In contrast men report greater use of flexi-time (16.6 percent), especially in the public sector (25.3 percent). This is indicative of the differing constraints experienced by men and women. Men may be able to use flexi-time to manage their household responsibilities, for example, performing the 'school-run' (Schwanen, 2007), while retaining full-time employment (and pay). Meanwhile, women's greater household contribution renders it necessary in some cases to reduce working hours, involving movements to part-time. Flexi-time is often more desirable from the employers' perspective as they perceive employees using this arrangement as continuing to contribute the same work effort to their organization. Flexi-time is likely to be more popular among employers than compressed hours, for example, which results in employees not being present in the workplace for one or more days per week. Compressed hours, while available at approximately 10 percent of private sector and 22 percent of public sector workplaces, is only used by around 2 percent of employees. It creates challenges for employers, in scheduling meetings, for example. It may also be less popular among employees as they are guarded against the possibility of work leaking into their non-work day. Term-time working is found mainly in the public sector, as expected given the application of this flexible working arrangement in educational institutions. It

Table 5.3 Availability and use of Flexible Working Arrangements, *Understanding Society*

Flexible Working Arrangement	*Sector*	*Available (%)*			*Use Arrangement (%)*		
		Men	*Women*	χ^2	*Men*	*Women*	χ^2
Part-time	Private	38.1	70.5	***	18.3	51.6	***
	Public	62.2	76.2	***	13.7	39.6	***
	Total	44.2	73.1	***	16.9	46.0	***
Term-time	Private	7.1	13.0	***	1.1	3.4	***
	Public	26.7	38.3	***	6.6	17.8	***
	Total	12.1	24.3	***	2.8	10.1	***
Job share	Private	9.0	14.2	***	0.7	2.0	***
	Public	34.5	39.8	***	0.7	3.1	***
	Total	15.5	25.6	***	0.7	2.6	***
Flexi-time	Private	24.8	26.5	**	12.6	10.2	***
	Public	45.5	37.9	**	25.3	17.9	***
	Total	30.1	31.5	**	16.6	13.8	***
Compressed hours	Private	10.1	9.7		2.5	1.6	
	Public	24.4	20.2		2.1	2.5	
	Total	13.7	14.4		2.3	2.0	
Annualized hours	Private	4.9	4.2		2.1	0.6	***
	Public	12.0	10.8		2.4	1.5	***
	Total	6.7	7.1		2.2	1.0	***
Homeworking	Private	14.2	11.2	***	10.8	6.1	***
	Public	21.3	14.7	***	8.2	5.4	***
	Total	16.0	12.8	***	10.0	5.7	***
Other option	Private	19.5	17.8	***	9.2	5.8	***
	Public	25.8	19.9	***	4.9	4.1	***
	Total	21.1	18.7	***	7.9	5.0	***
Informal flexibility	Private				53.6	53.4	***
	Public				55.1	46.8	***
	Total				54.0	50.5	***
n		9,321	11,560		6,120	9,810	

Notes: Figures show percentages of employees reporting availability and use of flexible working arrangements. χ^2 significance of 1%, 5%, and 10% are denoted by ***, **, and * respectively. Data on informal flexibility pertains to use only.
Source: Understanding Society, wave 4 (2012–13).

is also used predominantly by public sector women (16.6 percent), reflecting the continuing gender norms in place regarding provision of care for school-aged dependent children (Garcia et al., 2007).

Gaps between availability and use are particularly pronounced in the use of job share. Availability of job share is reported by 15.5 percent of men and 25.6 percent of women employees (with rates over 30 percent in the public sector). However, less than 2 percent of workers in the Understanding

Society sample report using job share, and the majority of these are women. A portion of those working part-time (Durbin and Tomlinson, 2010, 633) and homeworking (Poelmans and Beham, 2008, 401) may be cases where employers consider the impact of a temporary reduction in hours can be redistributed within their organization, thus avoiding use of this less common flexible working arrangement. Homeworking is not as commonly available to employees, but is relatively common in use among both men (10.0 percent) and women (5.7 percent), especially in the private sector perhaps driven by the cost savings offered by this arrangement including reduction in the need for office space.

Reflecting on the outcomes associated with the use of flexible working arrangements, Understanding Society enables analysis of employee-reported subjective well-being among those using flexible working arrangements, summarized in table 5.4. The data from Understanding Society is indicative of important distinctions in the satisfaction levels of those using flexible working arrangements (when compared with those who do not). Overall, the benefits of the use of flexible working arrangements appear particularly evident with respect to satisfaction with leisure, although the relative association between satisfaction levels does vary by flexible working arrangement and gender. Further disaggregation of the data is consistent with that reported in the extant literature, but is evident of job satisfaction benefits among those using term-time working, annualized hours, and homeworking. Women job sharers report greater satisfaction levels, although differences in job satisfaction are only marginal. However men who job share, although a very small group, report lesser satisfaction with both leisure time and life overall. This is consistent with some of the negative impacts of this arrangement reported by Durbin and Tomlinson (2010) and could reflect the influence of other determinants (which also drive the move to job share), for example, the presence of dependent children (Wheatley, 2012a).

Perhaps most striking is that those working part-time appear less satisfied with both their job and life overall. This result is contra that reported by Gregory and Connolly (2008). It may be evidence of the, at least perceived, poor quality of part-time jobs (Fagan et al., 2012; Jacobs and Gerson, 2001), the lack of 'choice' in using these arrangements (ONS, 2015d), and low earnings and reduced opportunities for career progression (McDonald et al., 2009, 153–54). Interestingly, those working part-time are more satisfied with the amount of leisure time, a finding which is not evident among those using most other flexible working arrangements. Part-time work, it would appear, provides some benefits to experiences of leisure time, but this is traded-off against the negative aspects including receiving less pay. As already noted men using job share, but also women working compressed hours, and both men and women working from home report lower satisfaction with amount

Table 5.4 Mean Satisfaction Levels and Use of Flexible Working Arrangements, Understanding Society

	Satisfaction with Job		*Satisfaction with Leisure Amount*		*Satisfaction with Life*	
Use Arrangement	*Men*	*Women*	*Men*	*Women*	*Men*	*Women*
Part-time						
Yes	5.21	5.32	4.80	4.45	5.11	5.10
No	5.26	5.32	4.39	4.23	5.17	5.12
ANOVA	***		*		**	
Term-time						
Yes	5.40	5.49	4.75	4.39	5.16	5.09
No	5.25	5.30	4.45	4.33	5.16	5.11
ANOVA	**		**		***	
Job share						
Yes	5.42	5.34	4.31	4.43	4.74	5.17
No	5.25	5.32	4.46	4.33	5.17	5.11
ANOVA	***		***		***	
Flexi-time						
Yes	5.25	5.34	4.48	4.33	5.20	5.14
No	5.25	5.32	4.45	4.33	5.16	5.10
ANOVA	***		***		**	
Compressed hours						
Yes	5.25	5.20	4.45	4.11	5.12	5.32
No	5.25	5.32	4.46	4.34	5.16	5.10
ANOVA	***		**		**	
Annualized hours						
Yes	5.23	5.51	4.63	4.56	5.17	5.36
No	5.25	5.32	4.45	4.33	5.16	5.11
ANOVA	***		**		**	
Homeworking						
Yes	5.36	5.43	4.39	4.22	5.27	5.28
No	5.24	5.32	4.46	4.34	5.15	5.10
ANOVA	**		**		**	
Other option						
Yes	5.37	5.49	4.32	4.38	5.23	5.22
No	5.24	5.31	4.47	4.33	5.16	5.10
ANOVA	**		***		**	
Informal flexibility						

	Satisfaction with Job		Satisfaction with Leisure Amount		Satisfaction with Life	
Use Arrangement	Men	Women	Men	Women	Men	Women
Yes	5.34	5.39	4.43	4.34	5.21	5.14
No	4.99	5.18	4.34	4.29	5.01	5.04
ANOVA	*		**		**	
n	6,119	9,806	5,667	9,162	5,666	9,161

Notes: Figures are mean reported satisfaction levels where satisfaction with life, amount of leisure time, and job are asked on a 1–7 Likert scale. Between groups ANOVA significance levels of 1 percent, 5 percent, and 10 percent are denoted by ***, **, and * respectively.
Source: Understanding Society, wave 4 (2012–2013).

of leisure time than those not using these flexible working arrangements, the latter consistent with other research, for example, Wheatley (2012a). In the case of homeworking this is likely to be a direct reflection of the invasion of work into the home, resulting in blurred temporal and spatial boundaries between work and life (Felstead et al., 2005). With the exception of leisure time, though, homeworking is associated with widely positive effects among both men and women. Working compressed hours may place particular challenges on women attempting to manage work and home, as it results in heavy workloads, and those using this arrangement face difficulties in avoiding the work leaking into the non-work day. Use of flexi-time is associated with marginally greater leisure and life satisfaction among men, perhaps indicative of the benefits of retaining full-time equivalent employment. Meanwhile, informal flexibility is associated with greater satisfaction among both men and women, consistent with the assertion that it is highly valued by employees (Hall and Atkinson, 2006, 383). Overall the analysis identifies a number of gaps between current availability and use of flexible working arrangements in the United Kingdom. Use is distinct by gender, and the effects of the use of flexible working arrangements appears to vary considerably. Broad impacts are more positive from use of arrangements which focus on the arrangement of work-time and the location of paid work, while reduced hours options appear to have less positive effects.[2]

5.6.2 Case Study Evidence from Greater Nottingham

Extending the analysis of data from Understanding Society, further evidence on the use, and impacts, of flexible working arrangements in UK organizations is presented from the case study of Greater Nottingham in box 5.1.

Box 5.1 Case Study: Flexible Working in Greater Nottingham

The case study of Greater Nottingham conducted in 2006 involved interviews with HRMs at ten organizations within Greater Nottingham, and a subsequent survey of men and women in dual career households first reported in Wheatley (2012b). The organizations included in the study were drawn from the public, private, and voluntary and community sectors as follows:

Public Sector	*Private and VCS*
City Government	Optical Retailer
Government Department	Manufacturer
Higher Education Institution	Solicitors
County Authority	Telecoms
Central Government	Voluntary and Community Sector

A key feature of the case study was in exploring patterns of work among the highly skilled, including use of flexible working arrangements, and the blurring of work and non-work time. The data collected revealed the presence of spillover between a range of uses of time, including paid work, work-related activity including the commute, and household time including that spent performing household tasks and caring for dependent children.

The findings highlighted the potential benefits of flexible working, but identified that flexible working is too often employer, not employee, driven. Evidence from Nottingham, consistent with existing literature (Gregory and Milner, 2009, 123; Poelmans and Beham, 2008), highlighted the dual meaning of flexibility. While employers provide flexibility, often this will be driven by 'business need' resulting in many workers not truly being flexible as per their preferences. Being flexible entails flexibility both for the employee and their employer:

> If I decide I'm leaving early on Friday afternoon, I'll leave early. But, the double edge of that is that [my manager] will expect to be able to ring me on a Sunday. (HRM, female, aged forty-six, higher education)

It is possible to realize mutually beneficial gains from flexible working practices such as those outlined above. Employers can reduce overheads through reducing office space. Meanwhile, as some employees will arrive earlier at work, and others leave later, office hours can be extended. For example, one organization studied in Nottingham had extended opening hours, from 7 a.m. until 7 p.m. This measure increases contact time with customers, while also allowing employees greater flexibility. The dual nature of flexibility was referred to by HRMs:

> [Flexible working is] based on agreement, yes, as well as business need ... [an employee may] like to come in at 11, but actually most of our business takes place between 9 and 10:30, there might be occasions where you do need people to come in at different times, as long as your members of staff are prepared to be flexible. (HRM, female, aged twenty-eight, solicitors)

However, in some cases increased flexibility was reported as being ineffective due to heavy workloads, as workforce rationalization and increasing demands from employers result in both extensive and intensive work routines. Indeed reported hours of work were long among the highly skilled workers in the case study. Hours inclusive of overtime were 40.5 and 46.5 hours for male managers and professionals respectively, and 41.1 and 45.1 hours for women managers and professionals. Lengthy working hours such as those reported create significant difficulties, especially for partners with considerable household responsibilities. As one survey respondent described:

> Currently the hours are too long because I am undertaking almost two roles. This makes the job difficult. (Survey respondent, female, aged forty-nine, professional, higher education)

Employees may experience long hours as a result of the presence of long hours cultures. Senior managers equate commitment with presenteeism (White et al., 2003). For those with substantial household responsibilities, often women, this will be particularly problematic and can result in work-life conflict (Lewis and Humbert, 2010; MacDonald et al., 2005). As one HRM suggested:

> If it's the office culture of long hours ... it makes it very difficult for people with young children to keep up with everybody else, and that's not fair. (HRM, female, aged forty-three, government department)

In addition, the role of technology is important. It not only facilitates work, but can further burden workers with extra hours of labour, as they work on the move or at home, making use of ICTs (José de Freitas Armstrong, 1999; Wheatley et al., 2008). As one HRM noted:

> Obviously with the portability of work ... you will take things home, you will develop them at home ... you'll be delivering, you will be travelling, you will quite regularly do over your normal working hours. (HRM, female, aged 31, city government)

Considerable evidence, though, was found of some of the benefits to both workers and the organization of the use of flexible working arrangements. For example, flexitime was reported to have had significant positive effects in terms of both recruitment and retention of workers.

> I think the major reason that people [choose to work here], if you ask staff especially, what's the one thing flexi-time. It's actually a huge thing. The majority of us do work flexi-time. (HRM, female, aged thirty-one, city government)

Evidence further signalled that flexible working arrangements do have the potential to provide successful outcomes for both employees and employers, in some cases producing 'win-win' outcomes:

> Flexi-time helps work-life balance, I'm sure it does, and also it helps managers because they can manage peaks and troughs of work as well. Just having people

in 9 'til 5 doesn't always mean that we're meeting business need. (HRM, female, aged forty, central government)

[Home-based teleworking] is something that within my personal service area, simply because we do not have office space for my team, we're having to look at ... more remote working, hot-desking and teleworking. The projects, where they've been run in certain service areas, I know, have been largely successful, once the infrastructure is in place. (HRM, female, aged forty-seven, county authority)

The evidence from the case study conducted in Greater Nottingham highlights a number of the continued concerns associated with the design and implementation of flexible working arrangements in UK organizations. These arrangements offer a range of potential benefits to both employee and employer, however, a focus on 'business need' and flexibility for the employer renders these arrangements less effective in combating long hours cultures, work-life conflict, and increasing expectations for employees to be flexible for their employer.

5.7 CHAPTER SUMMARY: HOUSEHOLD TIME, CONFLICTS, AND SUBJECTIVE WELL-BEING

The household distribution of labour continues to render the lives of men and women distinct with respect to their time-use and ability to engage in paid work, at least throughout certain stages of the lifecourse. Despite changing social attitudes, reflected in changing household structures and gendered patterns of employment, many households remain less than egalitarian in their division of labour even where both partners actively pursue careers (Philp and Wheatley, 2011; Wheatley and Wu, 2014). Women continue to report performing approximately double the amount of housework of their male counterparts, as evident in the data from Understanding Society. The types of tasks men and women complete within the household also remain highly gendered. Women also remain the primary care provider within many households, with childcare representing a particular challenge which may require reductions or interruptions to participation in paid work (Drinkwater, 2015, 284; McDonald et al., 2009, 153–54). Career models have attempted to capture the complex relationship between women and paid work, reflected in multidirectional (Baruch, 2004), patchwork, boundaryless, frayed (Peel and Inkson, 2004, 544), and kaleidoscopic (Sullivan et al., 2009) careers. The uneven household division of labour, moreover, has negative impacts on well-being, including increasing levels of stress among women (MacDonald et al., 2005) and reducing life satisfaction (Della Giusta et al., 2011, 17–18).

In response to the challenges present between paid work and the household division of labour, governments, including in the United Kingdom, have intervened by enacting a range of family-friendly policy with a focus on providing a more egalitarian environment in which both men and women can engage in paid work and careers. In more recent years in the United Kingdom, this has been driven by the Work-Life Balance Campaign and the Flexible Working Regulations, which have promoted the benefits to both employee and employer of providing greater flexibility and provided a legal framework governing the provision of flexibility in paid work. Flexible working arrangements offer a potential route to effectively managing work and home. There is acknowledgement of the need for balance between creating flexibility for employees, while also ensuring businesses can continue to operate. The costs of granting arrangements present a particular concern, for example, among SMEs (Dex and Scheibl, 2001, 422). However, gaps present between availability and use of flexible working arrangements may represent 'symbolic' policy implementation among employers (McNamara et al., 2012, 938) in order to be seen as engaging in good 'HR' practice, but a lack of commitment to actively improving the welfare of their workers. In addition, flexible working policies have been criticized for their perpetuation of current models of full-time work (Hall and Atkinson, 2006), and rigid conformity to '9 to 5' norms in work-time (Wight and Raley, 2009). The evidence presented from Understanding Society and the case study of Greater Nottingham highlights both the positive and negative impacts of current constructs of flexible working in the United Kingdom on the well-being of workers, and their work-life balance. It suggests that employers need to focus on the benefits to their organization and employees of the presence of both formal and informal flexibility in work, and reconsider their approach to flexible working to broaden availability and dissolve negative career repercussions associated with flexible working (Wheatley, 2012b; Atkinson and Hall, 2009, 663). The greater likelihood of using flexible working arrangements exacerbates these concerns among women (Hoque and Kirkpatrick, 2003, 674). However, women require additional flexibility to facilitate the management of their dual role as domestic worker and mother (Sullivan and Smithson, 2007, 458). A more egalitarian environment requires changes in norms within the labour market and in the household division of labour. While improvements have been observed, enacting change is a slow process. Without change the differences observed in time spent in paid and unpaid work will continue to reflect inequality, and less than ideal outcomes for many working women.

NOTES

1. Schein's (1978, 1996) 'career anchor' concept identified eight anchors which drive a career: (1) autonomy and independence; (2) security and stability; (3) technical-functional competence; (4) general managerial competence; (5) entrepreneurial

creativity; (6) service or dedication to a cause; (7) pure challenge; and (8) lifestyle. It has, additionally, been argued that travel, which forms the focus of chapter 7, may represent its own career anchor among highly mobile workers (Suutari and Taka, 2004).

2. For a more detailed analysis and discussion of the impacts of the use of flexible working arrangements, see Wheatley (2016).

Chapter Six

Care and Volunteering

The (Feel) Good Samaritan?

Irene Hardill and Daniel Wheatley

6.1 INTRODUCTION

Volunteering is far from new, but over the past couple of decades, it has moved from the 'shadows into the policy spotlight' (Kendall, 2010, 1). Volunteering is multifaceted and by no means is all volunteering concerned with caring for others (Hardill and Baines, 2011; Rochester et al., 2010). Nonetheless, more formalized care is increasingly performed through voluntary and community sector organizations (VCSOs), where it may be paid, unpaid, or a hybrid of both (Daly, 2002). Most care, though, is unpaid and usually performed in domestic settings informally involving other household members, kin, or neighbours. The value of this unpaid care is considerable. For example, grandparenting in 2011 was estimated as having a value to the UK economy of around £119 billion (Carers UK, 2011). Care has become fragmented between different institutional settings (public, private, voluntary, and household) since Sassoon (1996, 185) described a 'patched together needs, resources and institutions' that enabled the economy to function. The decline of the state as a direct provider of welfare services is associated with the push for the voluntary and community sector (VCS) and private sector providers to deliver care under contract (Hardill and Baines, 2011). It was estimated in 2012 that the value of volunteering in the United Kingdom equated to £23.9 billion (Foster, 2013). This chapter uses the conceptual lens of care to increase our understanding of why individuals at different points in the lifecourse volunteer to help others, giving their time for no monetary reward to provide care in the home, and in the community; and at certain points in their lifecourse receive care from others. The chapter draws on work published in Hardill and Baines (2011), Woolvin and Hardill (2013), and Worth and Hardill (2015), and employs a mixed method approach combining UK empirical evidence from quantitative data sources (British Social Attitudes,

Community Life Survey, Understanding Society) and ESRC-funded (award no. R000-22-0592) qualitative research from 'Doing one's duty: a case study of volunteering in a deprived community' (see chapter 1).

6.2 VOLUNTEERING, TIME-USE, AND THE LIFECOURSE

Volunteering can be described as an activity that is freely chosen, does not involve remuneration, and helps or benefits strangers (Zappala, 2000, 1).[1] It is a form of unpaid work which can be undertaken formally through an organization or more informally as good neighbouring and time giving on a one-to-one basis, which is sometimes referred to as the 'fourth sector' (Williams, 2003, 2011). Figure 6.1, developed by Woolvin (2011; Woolvin and Hardill, 2013), provides a framework for understanding the various forms of activity which comprise informal and formal voluntary acts. Informal acts include spending time helping a friend or neighbour, participation in community action, and/or social participation which is composed of both formal and informal activity. Meanwhile, formal volunteering takes the form of committing to regular work for an organization (see also Woolvin and Hardill, 2013). Some of these unpaid formal and informal acts are concerned with caring for others to improve their well-being.

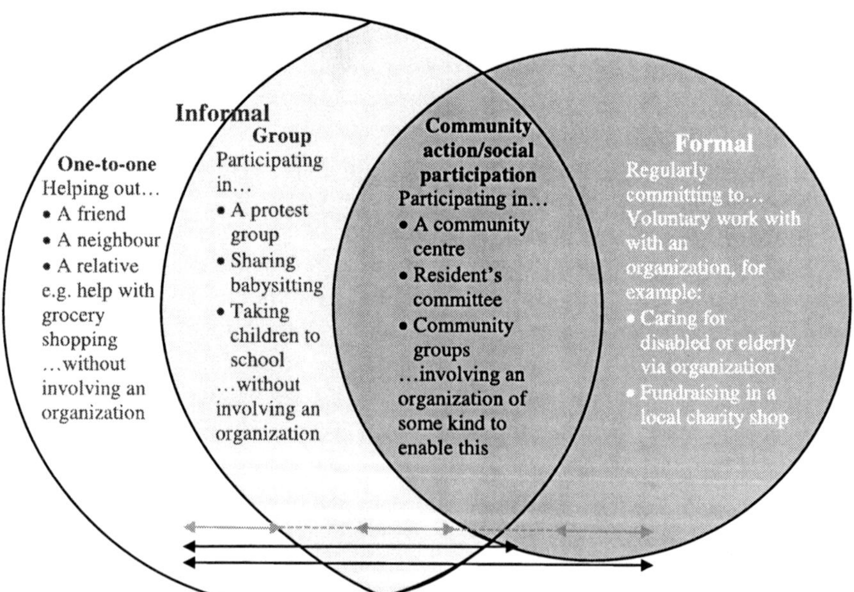

Figure 6.1. Informal and Formal Voluntary Acts (Adapted from Woolvin, 2011; Woolvin and Hardill, 2013).

With regard to the concept of care it is situated firmly within strands of feminist thought. This is novel because, in contrast to their extensive pioneering insights into paid employment and unpaid care, feminist theorists and activists have had relatively little to say about volunteering. When second wave feminism did touch upon the topic of volunteering, it was treated with suspicion as likely to keep wages low and to divert women's energies away from the struggle for change in the paid work sphere (Onyx and Leonard, 2000). We invoke the ethic of care as a conceptual lens to understand why some people give their time for no monetary reward in the home, and in the community caring for others. In this chapter a temporal dimension is added to the analysis, by examining the daily patterns of caregiving and receiving, and by applying a lifecourse perspective to consider the role of chronological age and transitions to engagement in care and volunteering throughout the lifecourse.

6.2.1 Creating Space for Volunteering: A Lifecourse Perspective

Unpaid voluntary acts can be undertaken formally through an organization, and more informally within the home or in the community (see figure 6.1). While volunteering opportunities are found in all sectors of the economy – the public, private, and the VCS – most occur in the VCS. The VCS includes a host of organizations (VCSOs) that deliver social and environmental benefits, and are neither profit making nor statutory-value driven; it is composed of charities, community groups, social enterprises, and 'umbrella' organizations that represent and support parts of the wider VCS; so not all VCSOs are concerned with the welfare of others by delivering care.[2] In liberal democracies men and women of all ages give their time to help others through unpaid voluntary work. There are different propensities to volunteer according to age, social class, ethnicity, and place of residence (Rochester et al., 2010). Motivations are complex, and the concept of the lifecourse provides a useful heuristic for understanding the changing capacities of individuals to volunteer (Hardill and Baines, 2011).

Time given to volunteering and other caring acts varies considerably between individuals and throughout the lifecourse. The lifecourse, in this context, implies not simply chronological age, but addresses individual and collective trajectories of experience – in this case giving or receiving care – in space, place, and through time as these are shaped by events, roles, memory, and retrospection (Worth and Hardill, 2015). As defined by Glen Elder (sociologist and pioneer in the field), the 'lifecourse' is 'a sequence of socially defined events and roles that the individual enacts over time' (Giele and Elder, 1998, 22). A lifecourse approach affords researchers the possibility to examine an individual's life-history to understand how events influence decisions relating to the giving or receiving of care. A 'transitions' approach to lifecourse research considers movements during the lifecourse, often contextualized with regard to specific milestones, for example, the transition from education to employment or from employment to retirement, which can impact positively or negatively on a person's ability to give time to volunteering. Work in this area has sought to explore the 'destandardization' of the lifecourse including, for example, deferred retirement (Kim and Moen, 2002).

Age is often conceptualized in lifecourse research as a social construction, which applies social understanding and significance to chronological age, for example, the age at which an individual finishes school or enters retirement. Age boundaries are thus central to how we understand the lifecourse. Within the extant literature intergenerationality has largely been explored in the context of the family, including intra-family geographies of parenting, parent-child relations, grandparent-grandchild relations, and extra-familial relations (Hardill and Monk, 2016, 5). Davis-Smith and Gay (2005) developed a typology for understanding the voluntary work undertaken from a lifecourse perspective; they identified: (1) constant volunteers, (2) serial volunteers, and (3) trigger volunteers. Constant volunteers are individuals that volunteer for the same organization throughout their adult life; serial volunteers volunteer during certain periods of their adult life and for various organizations, and; trigger volunteers only volunteer in older age. This categorization, though, focuses only on formal volunteering (Hogg, 2016). Individuals within a household continually (re)negotiate work and other commitments, including time for voluntary work (Neuberger, 2008, 16). Over a lifecourse individuals give time to others and volunteer as formal or informal carers, for example, as parents and grandparents, and are recipients of care (as children, young adults, and older adults); and this may be influenced in particular by transitions. For example, while in education volunteering may be undertaken to gain skills or qualifications, and with the support and encouragement of family. In adulthood volunteering may be squeezed by the demands of paid work, and retirement may act as a trigger to volunteer among many older adults. In addition, volunteers, volunteer efforts, and many voluntary organizations are embedded in a community context. Neighbourhood and community have different meanings to different people at different times. Each individual's activities, networks, and travel patterns shape their concept of neighbourhood and community (Massey, 1994). The community context both influences the causal processes shaping volunteering and can be the target of volunteer efforts (Williams, 2003).

6.2.2 Volunteering as an Expression of Care

Care has become a widely used concept in the social sciences; it is firmly established in feminist social science research as an activity and set of relations lying at the intersection of the state, market, and family (and voluntary sector) (Folbre, 2012). It extends into society itself, involving the networks and sets of relations of care in which people are embedded (Lawson, 2007). It is a controversial concept, viewed as an activity which generates social benefits and as a site of inequity and constraint especially for women (McLaughlin, 2006; Hughes et al., 2005). Care incorporates a range of activities, both paid and unpaid; but most care is unpaid and unrecognized as it is provided by family, kin, and friends, especially to the young, the vulnerable, the frail, and the elderly. At different points in a person's life care may be needed, and at other times care may be given to others. The ethic of care, which situates care and other household labour as forms of work, was developed by second wave feminists including Oakley (1974) and Waring (1988) as a response to notions of an ethic of work focused on self-interest, emphasizing instead care for others as meaningful and fulfilling.

A feminist ethic of care begins with a social ontology of connection: foregrounding social relationships of mutuality and trust (rather than dependence). Care is a construction, process, and achievement, reflected in both a physical activity and emotional work (Dyck, 2005), involving the provision of practical and emotional support for others (Schwanen et al., 2012, 55). Care ethics understands all social relations as contextual, partial, attentive, responsive, and responsible involving values of empathy, responsiveness, attentiveness, and responsibility – values most readily mobilized in our homes and communities (Lawson, 2007). Care, as an ethic or moral orientation, places emphasis on the welfare of the collectivity as much as that of individuals (Sampson et al., 2005). It is an embodied practice which involves giving part of one to others, impacting powerfully on identity formation, especially for women. But providing care can marginalize women as subjects in caring relationships which are considered 'other' to masculine ideologies of paid work *and* the home (Hughes et al., 2005, 265). It has long been argued that family-based care creates and reinforces inequalities within the household (Carmichael et al., 2008; Folbre, 2012; Lewis, 2002).

Although individual's care and are cared for, care is a relational concept; it can be performed as an individual act, in pairs, and in networks or groups, organized, for example, through voluntary organizations or community groups (Schwanen et al., 2012, 56), which makes it challenging to research. Caregiving operates at three spatial scales: (1) within the household, (2) to kin resident in other households, and (3) to non-kin informally as an expression of neighbourliness or organized through community groups or more formal voluntary organizations (Woolvin and Hardill, 2013; Hardill and Baines, 2011).[3] Lawson (2007) has argued that we need to think through the spatial extensiveness of care ethics, although she does not explicitly make the link to caring for others through voluntary organizations or community groups. However, care as expressed as neighbourliness, or more formally by volunteering through an organization, has long been recognized as underpinning communities of place and identity in the United Kingdom (Young and Wilmott, 1957; Hardill and Baines, 2011) and was identified by Prime Minister David Cameron (2010) as underpinning communities in the 'Big Society'. If caring – doing things/looking out for others beyond the family – is part of citizenship, some unpaid voluntary acts by individuals within communities can be readily linked to the feminist ethic of care (Williams, 2005).

The need to care for others impacts on the daily lives of individuals and their households. Paid and unpaid care remains deeply gendered; women undertake most household labour, including acting as primary caregivers (Folbre, 2012; Garcia et al., 2011), and remain in paid employment by utilizing market and non-market, family-based care (Harris et al., 2007). Providing unpaid care to others whether family members or kin can constrain women's labour market participation and the ability to volunteer in the community (Crosier and Warburton, 2001; Drinkwater, 2015, 281–4; Garcia et al., 2011; Hardill and Baines, 2011). Those providing lengthier hours of care, and for longer durations, are more likely to reduce work-time, alter the arrangement of work-time using flexible working arrangements, or leave paid employment entirely (Carmichael et al., 2008, 25). Working age women's lives have been described as 'time poor' as they juggle the competing demands of paid and unpaid work (McDowell et al., 2005), leaving little leisure time and increasing stress levels (MacDonald et al., 2005). Interestingly, women (46 percent) are nevertheless marginally more likely than men (42 percent) to volunteer (Cabinet Office, 2013). Meanwhile, evidence suggests that care, often, is undertaken unpaid within networks of kin. For example, UK data from British Social Attitudes is indicative of lengthy hours of care being provided by grandmothers, and greater incidence of care among those retired or not in paid employment (Wellard, 2011, 16). The 2011 Census of Population (England and Wales) reported that 14 percent of older adults provide unpaid care (for ill/elderly/disabled kin or non-kin), an increase from 11 percent in 2001 (NOMIS, 2013b).

6.2.3 Motivations for Volunteering and Intrinsic and Extrinsic Rewards

Providing care is accompanied by a mix of emotions, such as an increase in stress; or positive feelings of improved health and well-being (Folbre, 2012; Grimm et al., 2007; Meier and Stutzer, 2008). What moves people to care for others in the home, and community through volunteering, can be explained by reference to associated intrinsic and extrinsic rewards (Folbre, 2012; Meier and Stutzer, 2008). Intrinsic motivations centre on the notion that helping others generates increases in well-being, either as individuals: (1) care about the recipients' utility, (2) gain enjoyment from providing care in the home and community, or (3) gain utility from seeing the well-being of others increase. Alternatively, care in the home and community may be engaged in, not because these activities generate utility, but in order to generate an extrinsic reward, either as: (1) an investment in human capital, (2) an investment in a social network, or (3) to gain social approval. Models that emphasize the latter self-interested behaviour identify caregiving for family members as often being motivated by expectations of future reciprocation (Bianchi et al., 2008). However, women's behaviour, as caregivers, does not reflect self-interest (van Staveren, 2010, 1129). Care has traditionally been dependent on the labour and commitment of women (Schwanen et al., 2012). Values and norms in behaviours influence preferences, and result in the presence of constraint which may create and perpetuate inequality between genders in the provision of care (Folbre, 2012). In some circumstances care involves a trade-off as individuals forgo leisure or 'me' time. It, further, may involve negotiation with other household members, often requiring compromise, while time may be devoted to care out of necessity and prioritized before other tasks: care may be constrained.

Individuals engage in volunteering for a range of reasons, and those engaging in the same activity may indeed do so to fulfil differing needs. Six functional motivations to volunteer have been identified by Clary and Snyder (1999, 156) as summarized in table 6.1. Existing research suggests that compared to non-volunteers, volunteers may receive a number of benefits from engaging in these activities, including to both physical health and life satisfaction (Van Willigen, 2000). Meier and Stutzer (2008) found volunteering positively affected well-being as the result of rewards derived

Table 6.1 Motivations to Volunteer

Function	*Definition*
Values	The individual volunteers in order to express or act on important values like humanitarianism.
Understanding	Volunteering is used to increase knowledge of the world or exercise skills that are often unused.
Enhancement	Volunteering is used to facilitate psychological development.
Career	The individual volunteers in order to gain career-related experience through volunteering.
Social	Volunteering allows an individual to strengthen their social relationships.
Protective	Volunteering is used to reduce negative feelings, such as guilt, or to address personal problems.

Source: Clary and Snyder (1999).

from both intrinsic and extrinsic motivations. It is argued that in the majority of cases, the benefits from volunteering are a combination of these rewards. Volunteers, though, may more often be motivated by intrinsic benefits; extrinsic motivation delivers fewer benefits with regard to satisfaction with life (Meier and Stutzer, 2008). However, some conflicting evidence is found; for example, using data from twenty-four countries, Haller and Hadler (2006) found no significant relationship between volunteering and life satisfaction or happiness. With reference to the lifecourse, existing research has found divergent experiences among younger and older volunteers. Perceived benefits to health and reported life satisfaction are greater among older volunteers compared to younger individuals (Van Willigen, 2000). It has been suggested that this may be the result of younger volunteers not experiencing as significant benefits due to their engagement in volunteering more often representing an 'obligation', for example, related to parenting or training. In contrast, volunteering among older adults may be more often characterized by 'choice', and may provide them with additional benefits through granting a purposeful role in the community (Grimm et al., 2007, 4). Volunteering among older adults (age sixty and over) provides both physical and mental health benefits (Li and Ferraro, 2006). Indeed, Morrow-Howell et al. (2003, S143) reported in their study of older adults, using US data from the Changing Lives Study, that volunteering among older adults increases well-being. They also found that the number of hours spent volunteering is positively associated with well-being, suggesting that greater commitment to volunteering may deliver the greatest benefits to well-being.

6.3 CARE, VOLUNTARY WORK, AND SUBJECTIVE WELL-BEING: AN EMPIRICAL EXPLORATION

Important to our understanding of patterns of care and volunteering is not only the patterns of time-use associated with these activities on a regular, for example, weekly, basis but also how individuals engage with these activities during the lifecourse. This has become particularly relevant as a result of changes in the demographics of post-industrial societies including ageing populations and declining fertility rates, rendering investigation of patterns of care and volunteering throughout the lifecourse essential to our understanding of how we use our time.

The chapter applies a mixed method lifecourse approach, initially focusing on patterns of care and volunteering in the context of chronological age using cross-sectional data from three separate data sources: (1) the 2009 British Social Attitudes (BSA) Survey, (2) the 2012–2013 Community Life Survey (CLS),[4] and (3) the combined panel of the BHPS and Understanding Society for the period 1996–2010/2011. These data provide a snapshot of care in the United Kingdom at a time of significant labour market and welfare reform. Each of these data sources has particular strengths in the data it provides: the BSA provides useful insight into patterns of grandparenting, while the CLS provides data on patterns of both formal and informal volunteering including reasons for, and barriers to, engagement. Finally the BHPS/US provide a rich source of data which offers insight into patterns of time-use including work-time, housework, care, and volunteering over a sixteen-year period from 1996 to 2010–2011. Questions on volunteering have been included biannually in the BHPS/US since 1996. Descriptive analysis of these data sources is extended through ordered panel probit regression of the BHPS/US which considers frequency of volunteering against a range of relevant economic, time-use, and demographic variables. Through combining and comparing multiple secondary data sources the analysis provides a richer understanding of caring and volunteering behaviours and allows us to avoid some of the limitations of the individual data sources (Lindsey et al., 2015, 50). The panel data specifically offers insight into transitions and change with respondents reporting year-on-year, providing a data-set which incorporates responses that reflect the individuals 'now' (Lindsey et al., 2015, 51). The quantitative analysis is complemented by qualitative data drawn from an ESRC-funded case study conducted in a small former-industrial town in the East Midlands region of the United Kingdom (R000-22-0592, Hardill and Baines, 2011). The qualitative data focuses on those most engaged in care and volunteering throughout the lifecourse, in particular providing insight into transitions which may act as triggers. This combination of large-scale nationally representative data and case study data provides a robust evidence base with which to consider care and volunteering throughout the lifecourse with reference to the lived experiences of volunteers, reflecting on triggers and impacts on well-being.

6.3.1 The UK Policy Context

In recent decades a range of public policy has been enacted in the United Kingdom with relevance to patterns of care and volunteering, including policy focused on increasing labour market participation and social engagement throughout the lifecourse. This policy has been driven by a range of factors, including more recently austerity measures which have reduced funding in a number of areas of care provision. With respect to younger individuals, youth unemployment has remained a specific concern in recent years in the United Kingdom and beyond. Rates of unemployment in recent history among 16- to 24-year-olds peaked in the United Kingdom in 2011 at around 22 percent, while rates elsewhere have reached near 50 percent, for example, Greece and Spain. The European Commission's European Pact for Youth highlights the growing importance of labour market opportunities for young people from a policy perspective as it is 'essential for ensuring a return to sustained and sustainable growth in Europe' (Commission of the European Communities, 2005). Social engagement offers a route to such labour market opportunities, acknowledged in the United Kingdom in the National Citizen Service scheme. The scheme began in 2011 through initial pilot programmes, with the aim to provide a number of both intrinsic and extrinsic rewards, including skill development and work experience, among sixteen- and seventeen-year-olds (Gov.uk, 2016a).

For carers, the Carers (Equal Opportunities) Act 2004 (CEOPA) places a duty on local authorities to provide them with details of their rights and opportunities to access education/training, employment, and leisure (Carmichael et al., 2008, 7). Meanwhile, the Flexible Working Regulations, since inception, have offered workers with certain caring responsibilities leave options and the legal right to request flexible working (see Deakin and Morris, 2012, 750–52). However, while these policies focus on increasing opportunities for continued labour market participation, recent reductions in public sector care services are creating specific challenges for those with caring responsibilities.

Some of those exhibiting the greatest caring responsibilities are older adults. Approximately 22.6 million individuals are aged fifty or over in the United Kingdom, representing 35 percent of the population (NOMIS, 2014). Older adults face increasing uncertainty in their economic and social lives following the abolition of statutory retirement age, rising economic activity rates driven by economic necessity, and emerging changes to state pensions and the welfare state, which may impact on care networks as the over fifties undertake substantial amounts of unpaid care as parents, grandparents, and for ill/elderly kin and non-kin (Understanding Society, 2014; Wellard, 2011). For over a decade, EU policy-makers have promoted the concept of an 'active old age', in which older individuals remain in paid or voluntary work (European Commission, 2003). The UK government has adopted strategies including Opportunity Age, launched in 2005 (DWP, 2005), which aimed to, among other objectives, increase employment rates and provide greater flexibility for the over fifties in continuing careers, managing health conditions, and combining work with family/other commitments (DWP, 2005). The state pension age has been raised in recent years to sixty-five for both men and women, with further increases outlined in the Pensions Act 2014 to sixty-six by 2020 and sixty-seven by 2026–2028 (Gov.uk, 2014). The statutory retirement age, previously enforced by employers, has also been abolished completely through the Employment Equality (Repeal of Retirement Age Provisions) Regulations 2011 (No. 1069) as part of the UK government's Age Positive (DWP, 2012). At the time when much of the data used in this chapter was collected, approximately two-thirds of those aged fifty to sixty-four reported paid employment, while those working beyond pension age is increasing. Data from the UK Annual Population Survey reveals there were approximately 880,000 workers aged sixty-five or over in the United Kingdom in 2012, while these figures had increased to approximately 1.2 million in 2015 (NOMIS, 2013a, 2016). These policy measures have been taken in response to increasing life expectancy, and as a method of managing the cost of state pensions (Directgov, 2012). This has come further to the policy forefront following the publication of 'a new vision for older workers: retain, retrain, recruit' in 2015 (Altman, 2015).

A recent area of policy focus has been on employer-supported volunteering (ESV), which involves organizations providing their workers with support in the form of time-off for organized individual volunteering or through organizing group voluntary activities. While by no means a new method of promoting volunteering, ESV was highlighted in the UK Conservative Party manifesto in 2015 which outlined plans for three days per year to be allocated by employers for employees to engage in voluntary activity in large – those employing over 250 workers – private sector and public sector organizations (NCVO, 2016). These schemes have been shown to have positive effects in facilitating greater engagement in volunteering among employees (increasing their overall hours spent volunteering), and provide skill acquisition benefiting employees directly and employers through reductions in alternative training methods (Booth et al., 2009, 242–43). The outlined ESV policy, though, has yet to be more clearly defined or enacted in the United Kingdom.

6.3.2 Evidence from the British Social Attitudes Survey and English Community Life Survey

Patterns of engagement in volunteering from the 2012–2013 English Community Life Survey are summarized in table 6.2. The data shows that in the twelve months prior to survey approximately 70 percent of individuals engaged in some form of volunteering (formal or informal). Similar proportions were also reported in more recent data from both the 2013–2014 (69 percent) and 2014–2015 (74 percent) CLS (Cabinet Office, 2015, 6). With regard to frequency of engagement, approximately 44 percent of individuals reported formal volunteering at least once per month in 2012–2013, compared with 41 percent in 2010–2011,[5] with relatively consistent proportions among men and women. Women (39.2 percent), though, are more likely to engage in informal volunteering activity than men (32.5 percent). Formal volunteering is least prominent among those aged twenty-one to twenty-nine (only 20.9 percent report volunteering in the past month), those aged thirty to thirty-nine (28 percent), and the over seventies (28.8 percent). Younger individuals (sixteen to twenty) and those aged sixty to sixty-nine are particularly

Table 6.2 Engagement in Formal and Informal Volunteering

	Men	*Women*	*Overall*
Volunteered in past 12 months (%)	70.3	71.9	71.2
Volunteered in past month (%)	45.9***	51.5***	49.0
Formal volunteering			
Formal volunteering in past 12 months (%)	42.0***	45.4***	43.9
Formal volunteering in past month (%)	28.0*	30.0*	29.1
Formal volunteering hours (past 4 weeks) (mean)	9.0**	7.5**	8.2
Informal volunteering			
Informal volunteering in past 12 months (%)	60.8	62.0	61.5
Informal volunteering in past month (%)	32.5***	39.2***	36.2
Informal volunteering hours (past 4 weeks) (mean)	4.5***	6.0***	5.3
n	**3,076**	**3,839**	**6,915**

Note: Percentages are for those who report volunteering. χ^2 (for percentages engaging in volunteering) and ANOVA (for volunteering hours) significance levels between genders of 1 percent, 5 percent, and 10 percent are denoted by ***, **, and * respectively.
Source: Community Life Survey, 2012–2013.

engaged in volunteering, especially formal voluntary work (31.7 percent and 34.2 percent respectively), suggesting that these stages of the lifecourse may offer more opportunity for engagement in these acts, either alongside education/training (or as part of these activities) among the young, or following retirement (Van Willigen, 2000; Grimm et al., 2007).

Although fewer men report volunteering, those men who do volunteer appear more 'committed' to formal volunteering, evident in the hours reported volunteering (in past four weeks) in table 6.2. In contrast, women report greater hours of informal volunteering. Examination by age, summarized in figure 6.2, reveals that those aged thirty to thirty-nine, as well as reporting lower levels of participation in volunteering compared to most other age groups, report the lowest hours spent volunteering (in the past four weeks). The CLS usefully captures data on the reasons for volunteering, ending participation in volunteering, and barriers to volunteering, providing insight into the patterns observed, including the lesser time spent volunteering among the thirty to thirty-nine age group. The most common reasons reported for volunteering include: (1) I wanted to improve things/help (reported by 56.4 percent of respondents); (2) the cause was really important to me (38.5 percent); (3) it was connected with the needs of my family/friends (25.2 percent); (4) I felt there was a need in my community (25.9 percent); (5) I thought it would give me a chance to use my existing skills (25.3 percent); and (6) I had spare time to do it (33.9 percent). The reasons outlined are indicative of a number of intrinsic benefits arising from voluntary work. In contrast, extrinsic motivation is less evident, as the least common responses related to career development or gaining qualifications. The primary reason reported for ending participation in volunteering is a lack of time, in particular related to work

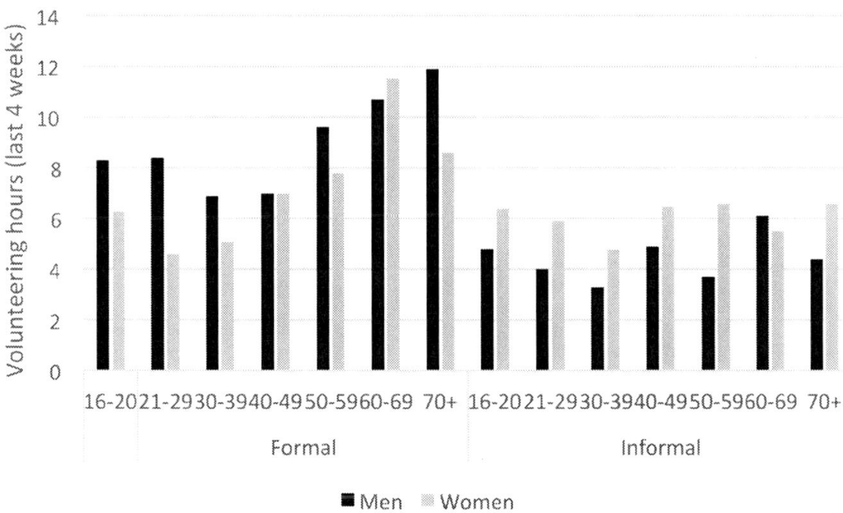

Figure 6.2. Volunteering Hours by Age (Bands).
***Source*: Community Life Survey, 2012–2013**

or home commitments (46.2 percent). Ill health and old age (17.4 percent), though, are also reported as reasons for ending engagement in volunteering.

Barriers to volunteering are summarized by age and gender in figure 6.3. The most common barrier to volunteering reported was 'I have work commitments', which was given more commonly among men (61.1 percent), although more than half of women (53.8 percent) also mentioned this as a barrier to volunteering. Significantly more women reported 'I have to look after children/the home' (37.6 percent compared to 25.3 percent among men) and 'I have to look after someone elderly or ill' (10.1 percent compared to 5.2 percent among men) as reasons for not volunteering. Meanwhile, more common among men was the response: 'I do other things with my spare time' (28.3 percent compared to 20.7 percent among women). As evident in figure 6.3, the combination of work commitments and looking after children/home creates particular barriers to volunteering among those aged thirty to thirty-nine and forty to forty-nine. These barriers significantly diminish among the over sixty-fives, although it should be noted that caring continues to impact the time-use of this age group through care provided for ill/elderly relatives and friends, and also time devoted to grandparenting, which is not collected in the CLS.

Data from the 2009 BSA survey does offer insight into patterns of grandparenting. It identifies that 64.5 percent of grandmothers provide care for their grandchildren, compared to 60.8 percent of grandfathers. The difference is driven by younger grandmothers, aged forty-five to fifty-four, who report a significantly greater propensity (78.9 percent) to provide childcare to grandchildren than their male counterparts (53.8 percent). Among older

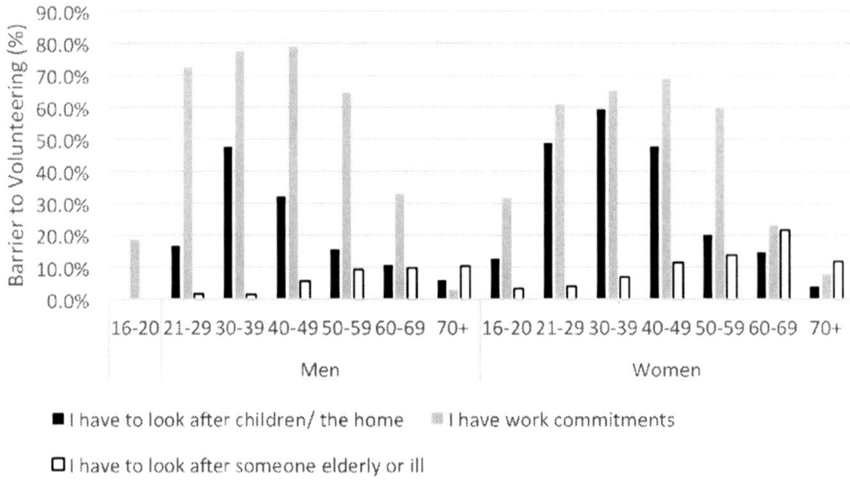

Figure 6.3. Barriers to Volunteering by Age (Bands).
***Source*: Community Life Survey, 2012–2013**

age groups the proportions providing care are comparable at approximately 75 percent. The BSA survey includes questions which focus on the number of hours of childcare given to grandchildren. Consistent with the findings of Carmichael et al. (2008, 26) with respect to informal carers in general, the data offers support to the notion that childcare among grandparents remains gendered: 19.6 percent of grandmothers report spending more than ten hours per week caring for their grandchildren, compared to 12.7 percent of grandfathers. Younger grandmothers, aged forty-five to fifty-four (34.2 percent), and grandmothers aged sixty to sixty-four (22.1 percent) are particularly likely to provide lengthier hours of childcare (over ten hours per week) for their grandchildren, but this is less common among grandfathers (7.8 percent). Approximately 47 percent of grandmothers providing care to grandchildren are retired. A further 22 percent are not in paid work accounting for many of the younger grandmothers, and offering some indication of the trade-off often present between paid work and unpaid care (Drinkwater, 2015). Among grandfathers similar proportions are retired (49 percent), but proportions not in paid work are notably lower (12 percent), while 38 percent report full-time employment (Wellard, 2011, 16). Extending the evidence from the BSA, it is also noteworthy that, in Understanding Society, approximately 43.1 percent of working age parents reported grandparents were a significant source of childcare during both school and holiday times in 2010–2011, offering some insight into the extended unpaid care networks associated with dependent children; an increase from 35 percent in 2009–2010 (Understanding Society, 2014, 41).

6.3.3 Evidence from the BHPS and Understanding Society: Panel Probit Analysis

A range of care activities within the household and for kin in other households are reported in the BHPS/US, including housework, unpaid (ill/elderly) care, childcare, and volunteering. Respondents are asked whether they engage in volunteering and about the frequency of these activities. Specifically respondents are asked, 'We are interested in the things people do in their leisure time, I'm going to read out a list of some leisure activities. Please look at the card and tell me how frequently you ... do unpaid voluntary work.'[6] The panel analysis considers this dependent variable against a number of focus variables. Separate models consider the relationship between key transitions throughout the lifecourse measured with reference to reported economic status (model 1) and engagement in volunteering and chronological age (model 2). The models also include measures relating to care, including hours spent providing ill/elderly care. The number of hours spent caring for dependent children is not collected in the BHPS/US. Instead the analysis considers responses to the question, 'Who is mainly responsible for looking after the child(ren)?' Measures of satisfaction with job, leisure, and life are included in the models, providing specific reflection on well-being.

The results of the panel probit models are summarized in table 6.3. The variables pertaining to economic status suggest that individuals are more likely to volunteer when in education, while retirement also appears a key trigger (model 1). Those reporting a long-term illness/disability that prevents them from engaging in paid work or being economically inactive are less likely to volunteer, perhaps indicative of these individuals more often acting as the recipients, rather than providers, of care. With respect to age (model 2) those aged twenty-one to twenty-nine are the only age category less likely to volunteer than those aged thirty to thirty-nine, although this finding is statistically insignificant among men. This evidences the other commitments present, specifically work and childcare which dominate the time-use of many individuals between the age of twenty-one and thirty-nine. With respect to childcare, the presence of young children aged zero to two and three to four among women (in model 1) significantly reduces frequency of volunteering. Older children, meanwhile, are positively related to frequency of volunteering, in some cases perhaps reflecting parents engaging in sports clubs or other volunteering activity related to their children (see Nichols and Shepherd, 2006). Provision of childcare by the respondent, or when shared with their partner, is positively associated with frequency of volunteering among women. Meanwhile, it is statistically insignificant among men. Only men reporting no children are likely to report greater frequency of volunteering, likely reflecting the greater engagement in volunteering among younger childless individuals and empty

Table 6.3 Ordered Probit Panel Models: Frequency of Volunteering (BHPS/US 1996–2010/2011)

	Ordered Probit Models: Frequency of Volunteering			
	Women		*Men*	
Variable	*Model 1*	*Model 2*	*Model 1*	*Model 2*
Economic status: reference is working				
Education	0.047**	–	0.100***	–
Retired	0.105***	–	0.129***	–
Illness/disability	–0.235***	–	–0.107**	–
Inactive	–0.109***	–	–0.122***	–
Age categories: reference is 30–39				
16–20	–	0.057*	–	0.169***
21–29	–	–0.154***	–	–0.038
40–49	–	0.153***	–	0.157***
50–59	–	0.247***	–	0.243***
60–69	–	0.381***	–	0.360***
70+	–	0.222***	–	0.276***
Working hours	–0.011***	–0.008***	–0.005***	–0.004***
Overtime	0.004*	0.004**	–0.003*	–0.002
Housework	0.003***	0.001*	0.006***	0.005***
Care (ill/elderly) hours: reference is zero				
1–4	0.000	0.000	–0.001	–0.001
5–9	0.007***	0.006**	0.010***	0.009***
10–19	0.060	0.051	0.092	0.089
20–34	0.009***	0.009***	–0.001	–0.001
35–49	–0.375***	–0.331***	–0.347***	–0.326***
50+	0.198***	0.176***	0.152***	0.141***
Annual income (£000s)	–0.002**	–0.004***	0.002***	0.001***
Highest level of education: reference is no qualifications				
Degree	0.825***	0.907***	0.731***	0.800***
A Level	0.530***	0.610***	0.513***	0.572***
GCSE	0.326***	0.382***	0.312***	0.362***
Marital status: reference is unmarried				
Married	0.106***	0.032**	0.190***	0.119***
Divorced	–0.006	–0.040**	–0.017	–0.045*
Widowed	–0.023	–0.000	–0.096***	–0.042
No. dependent children age 0–2	–0.246***	–0.183***	–0.122***	–0.085*
No. dependent children age 3–4	–0.096***	–0.041	–0.052	–0.018
No. dependent children age 5–11	0.064***	0.076***	0.082***	0.079***
No. dependent children age 12–15	0.014	0.014	0.066***	0.055***

	Ordered Probit Models: Frequency of Volunteering			
	Women		Men	
Variable	Model 1	Model 2	Model 1	Model 2
Who provides care in household? Reference is partner				
Respondent	0.256**	0.280***	–0.002	–0.008
Both	0.216*	0.217**	–0.000	–0.001
No child	0.315***	0.245**	0.140***	0.068***
Satisfaction variables				
Job	0.016**	0.013*	0.033***	0.030***
Life overall	0.027***	0.034***	0.027***	0.031***
Amount of leisure time	0.020***	0.014***	0.019***	0.017***
Model diagnostics				
Pseudo R-squared	0.030	0.033	0.029	0.032
LR statistic	2353.739	2611.460	1790.589	1936.965
Prob(LR statistic)	0.000	0.000	0.000	0.000
Log likelihood	–38119.510	–37673.780	–29853.410	–29515.280
Restr. log likelihood	–39296.380	–38979.510	–30748.710	–30483.760
Avg. log likelihood	–0.802	–0.799	–0.744	–0.743
No. observations	47,549	47,118	40,141	39,730

Notes: Significance levels of 1 percent, 5 percent, and 10 percent are denoted by ***, **, and * respectively. Missing values entered as zero (working hours, overtime) and mean (job satisfaction).
Source: British Household Panel Survey/Understanding Society, 1996–2010/2011.

nesters. Meanwhile, the provision of (ill/elderly) care has a nuanced relationship with volunteering. Provision of smaller amounts of care, in some cases (e.g., five to nine hours per week), is associated with greater volunteering activity. Meanwhile, women reporting provision of twenty to thirty-four hours of care per week are more likely to volunteer (this finding is not present among men). Both men and women reporting long caring hours (thirty-five to forty-nine hours per week) are less likely to volunteer, suggesting a possible trade-off is present between these activities with regard to time-use. However, those reporting the longest hours (fifty plus per week) of care provision are likely to volunteer more frequently. This latter group may reflect older individuals (aged sixty and over) who report both the greatest engagement in volunteering (especially formal) and the greatest hours of care on average, as they care for kin and non-kin who are ill and/or elderly.

The models indicate that working hours are negatively associated with frequency of volunteering. Extending this finding levels of overtime are also negative among men. Overall, these patterns are indicative of paid work acting as a barrier to volunteering, consistent with the CLS evidence. Interestingly, those reporting greater hours of housework are likely to volunteer more frequently. This may reflect the greater propensity to volunteer among individuals not engaged in paid work, including homemakers, and older adults including those who have retired who report some of the greatest time spent performing housework (see chapter 5). The tasks of social reproduction remain highly gendered, as discussed in chapter 5. It is important to note that a number of these activities are being performed by individuals for themselves and therefore do not represent care. However, the data suggests these activities are frequently performed on behalf of the household, including for children and other kin resident, and therefore some of this provisioning can be an expression of care for others. These activities, further, are often performed for non-residents including elderly relatives/friends, in particular grocery shopping and gardening. It is also important to note the marketization of certain activities captured within the caring sphere, including cleaning, DIY, and gardening.

Higher education levels are associated with a greater engagement in volunteering. Among men, higher annual income is also associated with greater levels of volunteering. These findings suggest that some men may volunteer as a way to give back to the community. In contrast, among women income is negatively associated with volunteering likely reflecting the greater engagement in volunteering among those limited in their labour market participation: those not engaged in paid work or working reduced hours. Meanwhile, married individuals are likely to volunteer more frequently compared to those who are unmarried, likely reflecting that those who are unmarried are, on average, younger. It is also noteworthy that widowers appear less likely to volunteer, while the models give some indication that divorced individuals may also be less likely to volunteer. With regard to the relationship between engagement in volunteering and subjective well-being, the models do provide some indication of the intrinsic benefits derived from volunteering. Satisfaction with job, amount of leisure and life are all positively associated with frequency of volunteering among both men and women. The finding pertaining to leisure may reflect the impact of transitions throughout the lifecourse, as volunteering often takes place when younger with fewer work and family responsibilities, and is triggered upon retirement when increased leisure time becomes available.

Overall, the models correspond with paid work acting as a barrier to volunteering, evident as those in education or retired are more frequently engaged in volunteering. This is also consistent with the negative association with working hours and overtime. Provision of both childcare and ill/elderly care, in some cases, also acts as a barrier to volunteering. Caring for young children, in particular, has a significant negative effect on frequency of volunteering. However, those providing the most care (ill/elderly) may actually volunteer more frequently as these individuals work shorter hours or do not (or may not be able to) engage in paid work. The findings also evidence an important relationship between volunteering and the lifecourse. Volunteering is more prominent early in life (while in education). The ability of individuals to volunteer is often significantly impacted by paid work, having children, and other commitments, especially during their twenties and thirties. Volunteering then increases upon retirement.[7] The evidence suggests some diversity, though, among individuals. Women with a lesser commitment to paid work may volunteer as well as providing care (both childcare and ill/elderly care), while other's time may be 'squeezed' at certain stages of the lifecourse, by caring for young children (peaking during their twenties and thirties) and grandparenting (evident in the data from BSA). Meanwhile, those who are working full-time may exhibit volunteering patterns which are more consistent with the overall pattern outlined above. This is also important, as the analysis suggests that volunteering is associated with well-being benefits, indicative of wider positive impacts (intrinsic benefits) from participation in these activities.

6.3.4 Qualitative Evidence from the Case Study

Extending the findings from the BSA, CLS, and the BHPS/US, evidence is drawn on the lived experience of volunteering of seven adults active in the case study community, in box 6.1, providing important temporal insights into the complex relationship between paid work, care, and volunteering. The empirical case study focuses on voluntary action in one community, referred to as Brightville. A case study approach was adopted to enhance understanding of the causal processes underlying the complex interactions between voluntary work, labour market participation, and other unpaid care within the family and community (Yin, 2008). Brightville developed in the nineteenth century, and had a diverse industrial base spanning coal mining and textiles. It coalesced with a nearby industrial town (Irontown), but to this day Brightville's residents retain a strong sense of a separate identity. Four case studies of volunteer organizations were conducted, where each organization was responsible for provision of social welfare services, employed paid workers, and used volunteers. All four, however, were engaged in welfare activities to support young families and older adults in the community. All employed paid workers and remain heavily reliant upon volunteers for service delivery. They were: a local community centre (Community Centre), a national government project (Government Project), a family support charity (Family Charity), and a community project (Community Project). All four attracted volunteers from within the boundaries of Brightville as well as from the neighbouring town.

In this chapter evidence is mainly, but not exclusively, drawn from the interviews with volunteers. The interviewees from these organizations were nineteen volunteers (fifteen women, four men) and eight paid workers (five women, three men). Five of the paid workers were also volunteers at the time of the interview, making a total of twenty-four volunteer interviewees (three paid workers interviewed were no longer volunteers but had originally come to the site in that role). The volunteers participated in management and trustee roles as well as delivering services to the public. Three-quarters of the interviewees were women. The interviews followed a 'life history' design adopted because of its capacity to capture the overlap between the individual and social and institutional structures (Dex, 1991; Musson, 1998). Interviews were recorded and transcribed in full and analysed by theme, paying careful attention to language used and emphasis given.

Selection of volunteers and former volunteers for interviews was guided by key informants (who were in some cases the gatekeepers who facilitated access). The sample comprised individuals with a range of characteristics (age, gender, employment status, volunteer role, caring responsibility, disability, and time commitment to volunteering). The length of volunteering experience varied from one who was just completing the training course, to others who had been volunteering for over a decade. Individuals' average weekly time commitment to volunteering ranged from two hours to around fifteen hours. Just seven of the nineteen volunteers were in waged work. Of the other twelve, only two expected to engage in the labour market in the future (one of whom was in training and the other receiving unemployment welfare payments). Others were retired (four), in receipt of incapacity benefit (three), one full-time carer for a severely disabled son, and two partnered mothers who expressed no interest in paid work. Pseudonyms are used to protect the identity of individuals, voluntary organizations, and the community.

Miranda and Sandra (box 6.1) highlight the trade-offs people make between paid work, care, and volunteering; and the gendered nature of the volunteering tasks they undertake when compared to Bernard, reinforcing the Understanding Society data. In all cases those volunteering are giving time, and part of themselves, by performing tasks for kin and non-kin, or using skills that others don't have, to help others. The potential benefits of volunteering for both service users and the volunteer are clear; Martin and Laura provide examples of both intrinsic and extrinsic reward being derived from volunteering, and for both of them volunteering is a substitute for paid work as both are beyond the labour market because of their disabilities. Grant similarly showed elements of both extrinsic (human capital) and intrinsic (well-being) motivations for volunteering. Meanwhile, Bernard and Miranda described specific intrinsic rewards from volunteering with satisfaction derived from the practical day-to-day activities. The importance of the household context for promoting volunteering is illustrated by the case of Bernard and Carol. Carol's volunteering propelled Bernard to also volunteer. Well-being and other benefits are, in addition, not restricted to only those volunteers as similar rewards were reported by other case study volunteers.

Box 6.1 Case Study Volunteers

Martin: Martin, in his twenties, lives in Brightville with his mother, and cannot take up paid work because of mental health problems. He values volunteering at the Community Project because it takes him out of the house. He has a history of voluntary work, helping elderly Brightville residents who are housebound, with whom he has great empathy, so every week he shops for them and helps them informally too. In addition to volunteering on a befriending project he also does occasional extra work for the Community Project, such as distributing leaflets. Through volunteering he has more self-esteem, and is now improving his basic literacy and numeracy skills. Martin commented, 'So I may be on Incapacity Benefit doing nothing and not working but I am doing things for the community and helping myself in the process.' Martin feels cared for and valued by the voluntary organization and its service users, and has gained self-esteem too.

Laura: Laura, in her late forties, said she was 'cut off' from paid work due to her disability (failing eyesight). She lives in Brightville with her husband and two sons. She stated, 'With me being classed as disabled, it gives me a bit of a boost to say that at least I can do something.' Volunteering represents a substantial time commitment for Laura. She spends four days per week undertaking formal voluntary work for three organizations (including the Community Project and Family Support Charity), and a more informal group, cooking on a budget, which helps families plan meals. Her weekday routine is structured around volunteering to a degree that is quite extreme and she says that sometimes her family takes second place to it. Laura reported personal rewards in terms of satisfaction in helping others, 'It gives me satisfaction to know that I've helped somebody or I've been able to take a bit of burden off their shoulders when I've gone to visit. It gives me … a bit of a boost to say that at least I can do something like that. I can't go out to get a job. But I can give myself back this way.'

Sandra: Sandra, in her early fifties, has three part-time cleaning jobs, and volunteers at a lunch club twice a week run by the Community Project, which involves preparing and serving meals, as well as providing social contact for elderly residents, some of whom receive few visitors, if any. Volunteering has been pivotal in her own growth in confidence: 'I was sort of "I hope they don't ask me questions" – you know? But now it doesn't bother me and I feel I can sit there and if we have any discussion I will say something. Whereas before I wouldn't say anything but now I'll say, "I've had this experience" and "I've done this."' But she *explained that her* daughter, her daughter's partner, and their baby were about to come to live with her because he had lost his job and they can no longer afford to be an independent household. Her daughter is looking for a job and expects Sandra to care for the baby while she is at work. 'If it comes to it I would have to do it [give up volunteering] to help my family but I don't want to.' Sandra's volunteer work may cease if the demands to care for her family increase.

Miranda: Miranda is a single mother in her fifties, who lives outside Brightville. She is the full-time carer of a disabled son. She is also a very committed volunteer to the Family Support Charity which supports distressed families in Brightville and beyond. She has been volunteering for them for over eleven years. This is the major external role she performs in the community. She reported supporting four families with young children and giving twelve to fifteen hours per week. She also undertakes informal volunteering, helping an elderly neighbour by cleaning, shopping (three times per week), and taking her on hospital visits. She identifies closely with 'her' families and is clearly proud of it. Evidencing the intrinsic benefits of her caring acts, her satisfaction is derived from the process of being able to help others with practical day-to-day activities. And when he is attending a day centre she spends much of her time volunteering with Bernard.

Grant: Grant, in his mid-fifties, lives with his second wife and two children. He reported having previously attempted to combine voluntary work and full-time employment. 'I did it for about a year. But then work, it was so demanding I used to [volunteer] on my two days off and I could not put in a 5 day week plus that. It sounds horrible but I couldn't'. He hoped that volunteering would enable him to become a social worker combined with feelings that he has something to offer families that need help, 'because I thought it could be a foot in the door for social work ... you are able to give something to those that maybe haven't got the support that I've got, or I've had'.

Bernard and Carol: Bernard and his wife Carol have lived for over forty years in Irontown, they are both in their sixties, and are comfortably off; Bernard was an accountant and Carol a full-time home maker. While Carole has been a volunteer for decades, Bernard is new to volunteering; he has 'followed' Carol into volunteering for a lunch club run by the Community Project when he semi-retired and began juggling voluntary work with working part-time (as an accountant). Since fully withdrawing from the labour market he has increased his voluntary commitments and now gives eight to ten hours a week to the lunch club, over three days. He now volunteers more than Carol does, but every Thursday Carol and Bernard volunteer together, 'we make a team', doing shopping for Brightville's housebound. The club is short of people with driving skills, and Bernard has taken on extra roles as he is a car owner; every Tuesday and Friday he helps at the Community Project's luncheon club for Brightville seniors. He transports two clients, who have difficulty walking to the luncheon club. He also takes meals out to three housebound residents. He feels that he is doing something useful helping three days a week. This commitment has provided a structure to his week replacing the structure paid work provided. Moreover he feels he is 'valued' both by the voluntary organization and the housebound of Brightville.

In summary, the evidence from the qualitative case study extends that presented in the previous section from the analysis of the BHPS/US panel data, and offers clear indication of the positive relationship between engaging in voluntary acts and well-being.

6.4 CHAPTER SUMMARY: WELL-BEING AND VOLUNTARY ACTS OF CARE

This chapter has contributed to our understanding of time spent performing acts of care and volunteering, using the conceptual lens of care to illuminate volunteering from a lifecourse perspective, including the role of 'transition' (education, paid work, retirement, childcare, eldercare).

A mixed method approach – using secondary data from three sources: British Social Attitudes, English Community Life Survey, and the combined panel of the British Household Panel Survey/Understanding Society, and qualitative data from an ESRC-funded case study conducted in a small former industrial town in the East Midlands region of the United Kingdom – has provided important evidence regarding patterns of care and volunteering, and the relationship between these activities and subjective well-being. The empirical analysis finds significant variations in engagement in volunteering, including differences in formal and informal volunteering, and the presence of trade-offs between paid work, care, and volunteering which are highly gendered. Volunteering is driven by the desire to help, socialize, and the needs of family or friends. Meanwhile, volunteering may provide benefits to subjective well-being: more frequent volunteering is positively associated with satisfaction with job, amount of leisure time, and life. The finding pertaining to leisure time, in particular, may reflect the relative stages of the lifecourse at which volunteering is more common, when adults are younger with fewer work and family responsibilities, and upon retirement where availability of leisure time is likely to increase significantly. Levels of engagement in volunteering appear closely linked to certain transitions of the lifecourse, including: (1) education, (2) paid work, (3) caring responsibilities associated with the presence of dependent children (both parenting and grandparenting) and ill/elderly relatives/friends, and (4) retirement. Paid work acts as a particular barrier, especially for men, while retirement acts as a specific trigger, especially for formal volunteering activity. Provision of childcare and looking after the home (especially when individuals are in their twenties and thirties), and caring for the ill/elderly (in older age) constrain women's ability to volunteer at certain stages in the lifecourse, evidencing the impact of the trade-offs present between time spent in these different activities. The evidence is also indicative of important overlap between informal care and more formal volunteering. Indeed, both the panel analysis and case study provide evidence of care driving voluntary work, including, for example, parents engaging in sports clubs their children attend, or an individual volunteering at a care centre attended by an ill/elderly relative or friend.

The findings presented are indicative of extrinsic rewards being derived from volunteering as evidenced in the case study and the CLS, however these rewards may not be particularly prevalent as the data from the CLS indicates. Perhaps more convincingly, the findings confirm the intrinsic rewards derived from volunteering: the panel analysis of the BHPS/US identified a statistically significant positive association between life (and specific domain) satisfaction and frequency of volunteering, while the case study suggests volunteering provides a range of well-being benefits, extending the findings of Meier and Stutzer (2008). The evidence suggests caring for others has an important health and well-being dimension for both the provider and those receiving care. These findings lend support to the notion that policy targeting increases in volunteering should recognize and nurture the intrinsic rewards of volunteering (Baines and Hardill, 2008).

There is likely to be increased need for volunteers to offer care because of the changing demographic profile in post-industrial economies, fragile economic environments, and fiscal constraints on welfare budgets. While not evidenced in this chapter, the impact of difficult labour market conditions (see chapter 4 for a fuller discussion), and recent and future changes to pensions and the welfare system in the United Kingdom, could have significant impacts on the ability of individuals currently exhibiting considerable engagement in volunteering to devote time to formal and informal care at certain stages in the lifecourse, for example, young and older adults, due to the growing financial pressures associated with paid work. Growth in employer-supported volunteering could offer a potential solution, but much remains unclear regarding the potential wider application of this form of voluntary activity. The concerns outlined are even more central given the findings presented which highlight the complex interplay between decisions to juggle care (in the home, other households, and volunteering) for kin and non-kin, paid work, and well-being benefits which can be derived by both the care provider/volunteer and the recipient of care.

NOTES

1. In this definition giving time to an employer through unpaid overtime would not be considered as voluntary activity.
2. Charities are governed in the United Kingdom by the Charities Act 2011 (which consolidated the Charities Act 1993 and other enactments which relate to charities), implemented in March 2012, which provides rules and regulations for the registration and operation of charities in England and Wales (Gov.uk, 2015).
3. Note that this list is not exhaustive. Other scholars identify other spatial scales, such as international care networks.
4. The English Community Life Survey was first commissioned in 2012–2013 (Cabinet Office, 2015).
5. It is noteworthy that some reductions in engagement in volunteering were recorded in 2009–2011 (Cabinet Office, 2015, 6), influenced by the 2007–2009 global economic crisis.

6. Possible responses to frequency of volunteering consist of the following options, 'never', 'once a year or less', 'several times a year', 'at least once a month' and 'at least once a week'.

7. Interestingly, considering the responses of retirees with respect to the perceived benefits of retirement, also collected in Understanding Society, it is evident that time for volunteering is not held as a central benefit, although 44.1 percent of women do consider it to be moderately or very important. Notably, among both men and women, time for family/friends is considered the most important benefit of retirement. This will include time used to care for friends/kin, including the provision of childcare by grandparents.

Chapter Seven

Where to Next? Travel-to-Work and Travel-for-Work

7.1 INTRODUCTION

Driven in part by technological change since the beginning of the Industrial Revolution, travel has developed to form an ever more important aspect of how we use our time. Travel is used to gain access to work, to conduct work, to participate in leisure pursuits, and fulfil household tasks, while travel itself can be engaged in as an activity. While acknowledging the wide range of ways in which we engage with travel, this chapter focuses on work-related mobility, specifically travel-to-work and travel-for-work, although some consideration is given to the blurring of certain activities, for example, combining the commute with the chauffeuring of children. The commute is necessary work-related time-use, acting as a bridge between home and work. The commute varies in distance and complexity throughout the lifecourse, including at certain stages the integration of household-focused activities such as the 'school run'. It is a 'fluid experience equally blended into home life and workplace and points in between' (Basmajian, 2010, 77). It is a product of past experience, present routines, and gender norms, and can be considered as both 'productive' and a 'waste of time' (76). Travel-for-work, in contrast, is work-related travel undertaken at the request of the employer in order to fulfil tasks of employment. It incorporates domestic and international business travel, teleworking, and working at multiple workplace locations. Among other things, it is used to meet with colleagues in other locations, work at customer sites, interact with clients and suppliers, undertake training, and attend and participate in conferences and exhibitions (Nicholas and McDowall, 2012, 336). It differs from the commute, and occupations that require lengthy assignments resulting in periods of absence and in some cases expatriation, as it can be irregular and therefore presents travellers and their households with specific challenges and benefits (Nicholas and McDowall, 2012, 350; Collings et al., 2011). It is not usually used to refer to short trips by employees, for example, meetings taking place within the same urban area (Jones, 2013, 63). Both travel-to-work and travel-for-work have important relationships with other elements of time-use, and impact on how we spend our time. This chapter considers the increasingly complex patterns of work-related travel present among many households, the impact of travel on time-use, and the relationship between these forms of travel and subjective well-being. The chapter extends work published in peer-reviewed journals including Wheatley (2013, 2014) and draws on findings from the Travel-for-Work Research Project (see chapter 1) and work published in Wheatley and Bickerton (2016b).

7.2 MOBILITY IN A CHANGING ECONOMIC ENVIRONMENT

Paid work has become increasingly mobile and unbounded as a product of internationalization, organizational trends including working in project teams, and inter-firm cooperation and knowledge sharing (Aguiléra, 2008). Indeed, paid work is 'leaking' out of organizations as information and communication technologies (ICTs) and mobile technologies enable employees to work on the move, in remote locations, during travel, on trains, in railway stations and airports, and at home (Felstead et al., 2005; Hislop and Axtell, 2009). This has resulted in the growth of 'instant offices' and airport hotels. Mobile workers use these locations when meeting with clients or colleagues from other workplace locations (Doyle and Nathan, 2001, 18). Workers are therefore able to travel, stay, and work in a single 'one stop shop'. Time once spent waiting may now, with the use of mobile technologies, be spent in work and/or leisure (Lloyd, 2003, 94). As recognized by Pooley et al. (2005, 2–3) human movements are increasingly complex, and cannot simply be divided into different categories. Instead concepts of mobility can be better understood as components of a 'mobility continuum' (see figure 7.1).

Mobility ranges from simple everyday movements, such as the commute, through longer distance (or time-distance) movements including travel-for-work, to migration and expatriation, and finally unbounded activities captured by the term 'virtual mobility'. The increasingly unbounded nature of paid work means that, for at least some workers, there has been a blurring of travel and home. Indeed, for many households work and travel have been transformed by new movements and mobilities (from Hardill, 2002):

- Commuting flows have become longer and more diffuse. Added complexity is present as commutes involve daily, weekly, and monthly movements, and may also be combined with other activities such as shopping and childcare.
- There has been a blurring of business travel with commuting, residential mobility, and migration. There is also a notable minority who use hotels/rented apartments for business assignments, sometimes provided by an employer.
- Worker mobility impacts on residential mobility with 'place' flexibility an increasing feature of life, especially among highly skilled households. This is illustrated by the notion of 'commuter' couples whose routines of work in some cases involve movements to be together at weekends. These complex routines challenge the idea of housing as a united space.

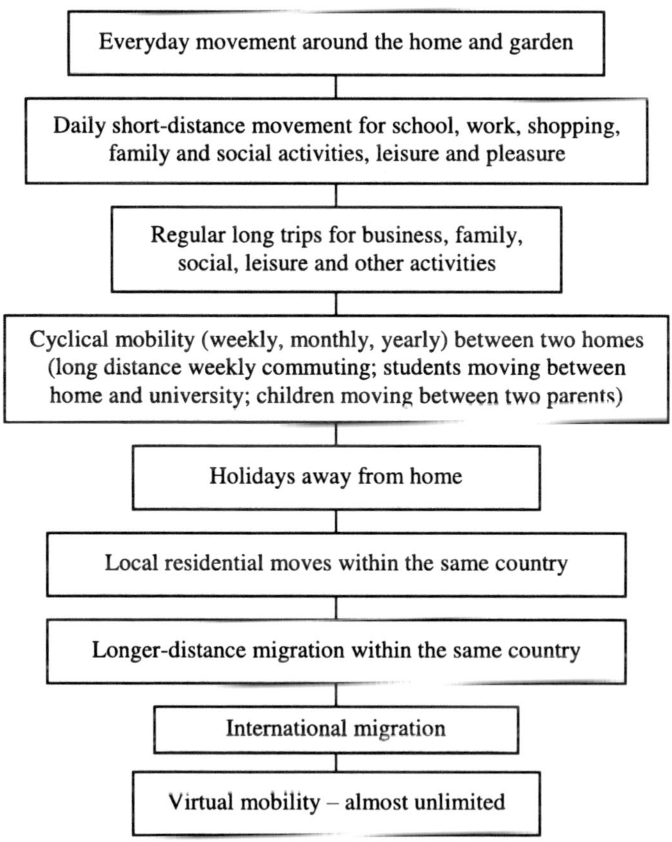

Figure 7.1. The Mobility Continuum. ***Source*****: Pooley et al. (2005, 3).**

Changes in mobility, aided by technological developments, have created a range of opportunities, including increasing the size of labour markets accessible to workers. Work is also increasingly unconstrained by place and space, through growth in mobile working, including teleworking. Teleworking, or telecommuting (a US equivalent), is commonly used to describe homeworking, but is broader in definition. It refers to distributed work: paid work outside of the normal place of work, at home, but also at client sites, on the move, and communicating using ICT (Pyöriä, 2003, 166; Bailey and Kurland, 2002). 'Teleworking' has been defined as a 'work arrangement in which employees perform their regular work at a site other than the ordinary workplace, supported by technological connections' (Fitzer, 1997, 65), and as 'remote work [that] involves the use of [ICT]' (Sullivan, 2003, 159). Informal telework has become more common and has created a blurring between work, travel, and leisure. However, although growth has been present, more formalized telework has remained a relatively marginal mode of work as a result of the lack of a contractual framework, and is currently common only among managerial and professional workers as these roles are subject to less control and supervision (Pyöriä, 2011, 2003; Hardill and Green, 2003). As well as creating opportunities, enhanced mobility creates additional challenges in the allocation of time at both the individual and household level. The patterns and impacts of work-related travel on the time-use of working households is, therefore, important to our understanding of how we use our time.

7.3 TRAVEL-TO-WORK

Commuting has considerable impacts on time allocation. The commute has increased in time-distance, initially as a result of the establishment and expansion of rail travel during the nineteenth century and subsequently driven by growth in the ownership of the car from the 1960s. These changes have enabled workers to travel further to work (Pooley et al., 2005, 114). Commutes, though, for the majority of workers remain in the form of frequent, often daily, journeys over relatively short distances (Green and Owen, 2006). Recent evidence confirms these commuting patterns. For example, the 2015 UK National Travel Survey recorded commutes averaging around thirty-one minutes per journey (ONS, 2016c). This is also consistent with the patterns evident from the BHPS/Understanding Society presented in chapter 4. In many post-industrial economies, including the United Kingdom and United States, the car remains the dominant mode of transport to work as it continues to be perceived as the most flexible and convenient way of travelling (Eriksson et al., 2013; Anable and Gatersleben, 2005). The choice of mode of transport is related to cost and availability. Individuals prefer individualized, independent travel, which provides personal space and security (Pooley et al., 2005).

However, international protocols have focused policy at central, regional, and local government levels toward reducing car use. In the United Kingdom, this was pushed to the policy forefront in the mid-2000s following the publication of the independent *Stern Review on the Economics of Climate Change* (H.M. Treasury, 2006), the *Eddington Transport Study* (DfT, 2006), and 'Towards a Sustainable Transport System' (DfT, 2007). A range of schemes specifically target reductions in car use (Pooley et al., 2005, 226–27), including the congestion charge in operation in London since 2003, and the Workplace Parking Levy implemented in Nottingham in 2012 (for details of the Workplace Parking Levy, see Nottingham City Council, 2016; Wheatley, 2012b). While many individuals may appreciate the benefits of reducing their car use – for example, the environmental and social benefits from reduced congestion – evidence suggests that many workers do not feel safe using public transport (e.g., waiting at bus stops), especially at night (Pooley et al., 2005, 140). Use of public transport is also hindered by the fact that it often requires multi-part journeys, for example, two bus journeys or a bus followed by a train. This may increase stress levels as workers face regular challenges in making connections due to, for example, unexpected delays (Eriksson et al., 2013). In a number of cases household responsibilities, including taking a child to school or day care or completing other errands, for example, shopping, also create a practical barrier to use of alternatives to the car (Pooley et al., 2005, 136; Wheatley, 2013, 2014). The continued dominance of the car as the preferred mode of transport used in travel-to-work, however, may have important implications with respect to both time-use and well-being.

The commute is also used for the completion of tasks for paid work. Travel time can be spent productively as 'activity time' to complete tasks, including informal teleworking such as contacting clients using mobile technologies. Past evidence from a study of twenty-six thousand rail passengers in the United Kingdom suggested that 13 percent of commuters work or study during most of their journey, and that nearly 30 percent undertake some form of work some of the time (Lyons et al., 2007). Many workers may view this time-use positively, as it enables work to be completed which may otherwise leak into, and therefore reduce, leisure time (Lyons and Urry, 2005). However, while used to work this time is not considered work-time by employers. While employers may not require workers to use this time productively, the blurring of this activity with paid work, it can be argued, essentially lengthens the working day.

Further complexity exists in the relationship between travel-to-work and residential location. Households may, for example, face challenges in combining two commutes (to different locations), often resulting in residential location close to transport hubs or nodes (Kloosterman and Musterd, 2001, 625). However, this may necessitate lengthier journeys. Long distance weekly commuting strategies may, alternatively, be adopted to avoid migration, although this may not deliver positive impacts for the individual and their household (Sandow and Westin, 2010; Sandow, 2014). Moreover, residential location may be driven, at least in part, by constraints due to the pressures of local housing markets which may render a lengthy commute a more practical and/or affordable option. Partners unable to find two jobs in a preferred location will often compromise with regard to their residential location. Where compromise is present, though, it is often greater on the part of women (Green, 2004, 636). Research from the Netherlands identified that in households where both partners engage in full-time work it is more likely both will exhibit comparable commuting patterns, potentially evident of more egalitarian attitudes towards task division between partners (de Meester and van Ham, 2009). However, dependent children continue to increase the likelihood of women moving to a part-time working arrangement, and performing a shorter commute. Women remain constrained in their working routines by the presence of children (Philp and Wheatley, 2011). Moreover, gender norms continue to limit women's spatial mobility, even among highly skilled individuals, resulting in both temporal and spatial constraint (see Wheatley, 2013).

7.3.1 Time-Use and the Commute

The cost of the commute has long been argued as rising dramatically with increases in both distance and time (Cameron and Muellbauer, 1998). This cost not only relates to the financial cost of travelling, for example, the cost of fuel or a rail ticket, but also the cost associated with other uses of time which are foregone. There is acknowledgement of the reluctance of many commuters to perform their travel routine (Kahneman et al., 2004; Wheatley, 2013). However, in many cases this travel is performed in order to maintain preferred standards of living which may not be possible if entering housing markets closer to their place of work. Drivers of this nature are especially common among those undertaking longer distance, and even weekly commutes (Sandow and Westin, 2010). Importantly many of the individuals involved in this movement of labour also must do so to gain access to labour market opportunities, especially those with highly specialized skills whose expertise may not be demanded in every location (Lindsay, 2003).

Mainstream analyses in economics including that of Becker (1976) focus on the cost of commuting, in relation to both time and monetary cost, which reduce the individual's level of income (see box 7.1). Other analyses,

Box 7.1 Mainstream Perspectives on the Commute

Becker's (1976) approach to the allocation of time, discussed in chapter 2, can also be applied to commuting behaviour. Becker uses the assumption that direct commuting costs, such as a train fare or purchasing petrol, vary positively, and indirect costs, such as space, vary negatively with distance commuted. The latter assumption is based on the premise that more outdoor space is available further away from the workplace, usually an urban area. Under these assumptions it is argued that if an individual experiences a rise in income this would increase the opportunity cost of commuting a given distance because the forgone value of the time involved would increase. The increase in commuting costs would discourage commuting. However, the increase in income may result in an increase in the demand for space, which would encourage more commuting. The outcome of an individual's choice over commuting and housing is, therefore, dependent on the relative strengths of the two conflicting forces.

Using a rational choice approach, Becker suggests that the distance commuted will only increase following an increase in income, if space has an income elasticity greater than unity. This is derived by looking at the effect of a change in full income on the time spent commuting, given by the equation (Becker, 1976, 106–8),

$$\frac{\delta t}{\delta S} = \frac{k(E_x - 1)}{p''x}$$

Time spent commuting is represented by t, S is full income, k is a constant, p'' is the cost per unit of space, and x is the quantity of space used. The cost per unit of space, p'', is assumed to be greater than 0, as space is considered desirable. Where E_x is the income elasticity of demand for space, an increase in income will increase the time spent commuting if, and only if, $E_x > 1$.

The result of Becker's analysis indicates that individuals consider outdoor space a 'luxury', and the demand for outdoor space rises with increases in income. If we assume the majority of workplaces are located in urban areas, then it follows that as income increases workers will locate further from their workplace in suburban and rural areas, but this will be achieved at the cost of lengthier commutes.

though, consider the commute in other contexts. For example, discussion of decision-making regarding the commute, and its impacts, is offered by Frey and Stutzer (2014) in relation to predictions and mispredictions of utility. It is argued that in the context of commuting, the individual may incorrectly predict levels of utility and disutility resulting in longer commutes than would be preferable, as individuals undervalue activities which provide a number of rewards to well-being, for example, leisure and family time. They identify a number of sources of this misprediction of utility: (1) adaptation is underestimated (mistakes in estimations of future utility); (2) distorted memory of past experiences; (3) rationalization of decisions (the individual feels a strong urge to justify their decisions); and (4) intuitive theories about the sources of future utility (individuals have diverse theories about what makes them happy). The outcome for many individuals is that they will undertake lengthy commutes which reduce time available for leisure and other activities that offer intrinsic reward (Frey and Stutzer, 2014, 946).

It has been suggested that there exists a limit to which individuals are willing to commute, defined as a 'commuting tolerance' (Clark et al., 2003; Johansson et al., 2003; Reitsma and Vergoossen, 1988; Lever, 1987). Originally identified by Getis (1969), a 'commuting tolerance' is a physical limit at which individuals become resistant to further increases in the time spent commuting. Commutes which exceed this limit would act as a significant source of stress (Reitsma and Vergoossen, 1988, 333) and dissatisfaction (Kahneman et al., 2004; Stutzer and Frey, 2008; Frey and Stutzer, 2014). Indeed, evidence has suggested that workers, in some cases, may switch between modes of transport to compensate for changes in commuting distance, for example, when they are subject to a change in workplace location or residence, in order to minimize increases in commute times (Vale, 2013, 39). Empirical observations suggest a 'tolerance zone' for the majority of individuals in the range of about thirty to forty-five minutes (Clark et al., 2003, 200). This effectively determines the size of the labour market area available to workers, although it should be noted that the 'commuting tolerance' will vary dependent on region of residence (and work), occupation, and a number of demographic factors (Clark et al., 2003; Lever, 1987, 264). Further evidence reported in Johansson et al. (2003), using data from Sweden, suggested that commuting tolerances are non-linear with time-distances. They are more sensitive for medium length commutes in comparison to very short or very long commutes. This indicates that individuals who perform medium length commutes have a lower commuting tolerance to changes in their commutes than those who experience commutes at either end of the time spectrum.

Figure 7.2 summarizes the relationship between willingness to commute and time travelled. The reluctance to change commuting patterns in the middle range (shown by the steeper gradient of the curve) may reflect the effects of different types of employment and/or the impact of gender norms. In the case of occupations, low paid or low skilled workers would be less willing to travel further as this would have a greater relative financial impact. This reluctance is also likely a product of these workers being relatively more able to find employment offering similar remuneration within the same locale. In the context of gender, women's household constraints may limit their movements. As a result they are more often restricted to local labour markets and employers (Hanson and Pratt, 1995, 13; Harris et al., 2007; Wheatley, 2013, 2014).

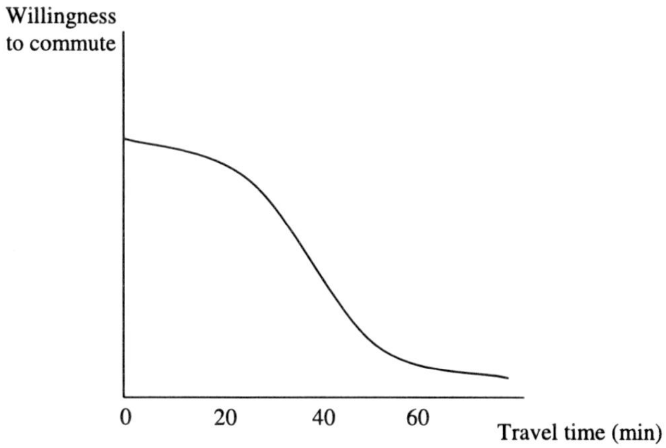

Figure 7.2. Willingness to Commute. ***Source*****: Adapted from Johansson et al. (2003).**

7.3.2 Gender and Travel-to-Work: The Spatial Entrapment Hypothesis

There has been significant debate regarding whether household responsibilities, including housework and care, impact travel-to-work among working women. While some a degree of equality is present in the economic lives of men and women (Lundberg and Pollak, 2007, 6–7) this may not have been realized with respect to the commute. For example, using data from Sweden (1978–2006) it has been shown that men continue to travel longer distances to work, and thus have access to wider labour markets than women (Frändberg and Vilhelmson, 2011). Evidence is indicative of many women remaining less mobile. Women unable to achieve the level of mobility required by employers may be perceived as being less committed to their organization (Sirianni and Negrey, 2000, 72). The presence of dependent children reduces work-time among women, but increases it among men, with potentially important career implications for working mothers (Jacobs and Gerson, 2001, 57). Research has conveyed some improvement in the gendered distribution of household labour (see Sullivan, 2010), including men performing a substantial proportion of the chauffeuring of children (Schwanen, 2007). However, many women continue to endure the 'double-shift' (Jones, 2003, 7). This constrains women's travel-to-work in respect to both time and distance (McDowell et al., 2005). Hjorthol and Vågane (2014) consider the case of men and women in Norway. They find that women are limited in regard to labour market opportunities as, on average, they do not travel as far as men (when considering comparable groups). Gender norms are also important in respect to access to a car for travel-to-work. Scheiner and Holz-Rau (2012, 258–59), for example, find that while patterns in car use among women are borne out of preference, these preferences are themselves a product of gender norms. In cases of one car households, women using a car will do so, often, as they are combining the commute with household activities.

Hanson and Pratt (1995, 10) described in their seminal US study of Worcester, Massachusetts, that many women remain highly dependent on local employment opportunities as a result of 'spatial entrapment'. Women typically travel short distances to work, as they attempt to manage paid employment alongside household labour, although it is acknowledged that their travel-to-work patterns are diverse (Hanson and Pratt, 1995, 155; Hjorthol and Vågane, 2014, 82; Frändberg and Vilhelmson, 2011). Women's spatial mobility is limited as their household responsibilities constrain travel-to-work. This is especially the case among women who are married and those with children (Hanson and Pratt, 1995, 99). Research is evident of women, in most cases, continuing to experience shorter commutes than men (Hjorthol and Vågane, 2014, 82) effectively limiting their access to labour markets (Frändberg and Vilhelmson, 2011). Limited spatial mobility may have severe career implications for some women, however, as employers demand high levels of flexibility and mobility from their workforce (Wheatley, 2012b). Evidence in the existing literature supports these assertions. For example, using empirical evidence from the United States, Carter and Butler (2008, 12–13) identify that dependent children are key drivers in variations in commutes between men and women. Even where children are not present, the household may still limit the mobility of women. Evidence from the United Kingdom identifies gender norms in the distribution of household tasks which reduce the available time for travel-to-work, effectively limiting the size of the labour market available to women. Moreover the household division of labour creates rigidity in time-use for women, for example, travel-to-work having to fit around the 'school run' (Dobbs, 2007, 95). Performing the school run and similar chauffeuring of children have been identified as some of the most temporally and spatially fixed activities (i.e., these activities take place at the same time and in the same location repeatedly) second only to sleep and personal care (Schwanen et al., 2008, 2119). Mixed methods research focusing on dual career households provides further reinforcement for the spatial entrapment thesis. Wheatley (2013) used UK evidence from the 2006 case study of Greater Nottingham (see chapter 1) and the 2006 Quarterly Labour Force Survey Household Data-Set. This research found evidence of spatial entrapment among career women, and identified school-age dependent children as representing a particular constraint, due to provision of care and performing the 'school run'. Household constraints, including the provision of care, result in reduced temporal and spatial flexibility among women, the latter potentially resulting in spatial entrapment (Wheatley, 2013).

7.3.3 Travel-to-Work and Subjective Well-Being

Travel can affect well-being in a range of ways. For example, access to transport and residential location, among other factors, influence the ability or potential of an individual to travel. Mode of transport, activities undertaken while travelling including mobile working, participation in work or leisure enabled by travel, and movements for leisure purposes where this activity acts as a source of utility, for example, recreational cycling all act as further influences on well-being (De Vos et al., 2013; Moktharian and Solomon, 2001). Travel-to-work is often perceived as generating dissatisfaction. Considered often as a 'waste of time' (Basmajian, 2010, 76), research has shown that the commute represents one of the least appreciated activities performed during the working day (Kahneman et al., 2004; Wheatley, 2013). Lengthier commutes reduce 'life' satisfaction, off-setting any benefits individuals receive from 'attractive' residential locations distant from their workplace (Stutzer and Frey, 2008; Frey and Stutzer, 2014, 953). Other research (see Ettema et al., 2012, 219–20), though, has identified that commutes may be viewed positively, although relative satisfaction is heavily associated with mode of transport, levels of stress, boredom and other negative feelings, and exogenous factors (e.g., road maintenance). Satisfaction may be particularly influenced by the extent to which the commute is perceived by the individual to be productive (Basmajian, 2010; Lyons and Urry, 2005), although conflicting evidence is found in this regard (see Ettema et al., 2012). Broader studies have, further, considered the impacts on well-being of transport disadvantage and social exclusion. Delbosc and Currie (2011, 560–61), for example, find that lack of access to transport and/or greater levels of social exclusion (including living in non-urban/rural areas) have detrimental impacts on well-being. Indeed, residential location has been found to affect well being through impacts on travel (De Vos et al., 2013). Returning to gender, Roberts et al. (2011, 1071) use data extracted from the BHPS to consider the psychological effects of commuting on men and women. They find that while commuting has an important detrimental effect on women, this finding is not present among men. It is posited that this is a result of women's greater household contribution, including childcare and housework. This is evident of the, at least perceived, constraining effect of these household activities spilling over into time spent travelling to work.

7.4 TRAVEL-FOR-WORK

A consequence of the changes in the nature of economic activity is an increase in travel-for-work including both domestic and international business travel (Beaverstock et al., 2009; Aguiléra, 2008). Organizations may include business travel within a broader 'travel plan', including promoting alternatives, for example, virtual meetings via Internet, video, or telephone (Cairns et al., 2010, 891; Gustafson, 2012a). Despite developments in ICTs, though, there remains demand from employers, driven in part by client need, for face-to-face contact in order to build personal relationships and create mutual trust (Aguiléra, 2008). Meanwhile, increases in worker mobility, specifically the increased incidence of travel-for-work, has itself been driven by technical developments including faster transportation networks which render frequent long distance (inter)national travel feasible (Bergström Casinowsky, 2013, 311). Travel-for-work now represents a significant activity undertaken as part of paid work. Evidence from the 2015 UK National Travel Survey identifies that business travel only accounts for approximately 3 percent of total journeys, however this represents 9 percent of total distance travelled and around 16 percent of long distance journeys undertaken (ONS, 2016c). Meanwhile, the 2015 International Passenger Survey revealed that 10.9 percent of journeys overseas by UK residents are for business, while 24.5 percent of inward travel to the United Kingdom is for business purposes (ONS, 2016d). Annual expenditure on business travel globally has been estimated at approximately USD 1.25 trillion in 2015. Meanwhile, UK spending on business travel remains second highest in Europe. In 2015 it was estimated at £30.8 billion (Global Business Travel Association, 2016). Travel-for-work requires both temporal and spatial availability, where availability in this context refers to the ability of a worker to be available in response to the demands, needs, or wishes of their employer (Bergman and Gustafson, 2008, 193–94). Travel-for-work is itself distinct from teleworking. Employees may telework during travel-for-work, but equally they may not depending on the nature of the travel, method, time of day, and preferences of the employer and employee.

Frequency is central to time spent travelling for work. It can be regular travel undertaken as part of a role requiring travel to be undertaken during the working day and/or work to be performed at multiple sites (and on the move). It also refers to less frequent domestic and international travel, often referred to as business travel, undertaken for a range of purposes outlined earlier in the chapter (Nicholas and McDowall, 2012, 336). A further distinction from the commute is present with respect to the extent of 'choice' associated with the action of performing travel-for-work. Travel-to-work is necessary work-related travel. Employees have a level of control over the time and distance they commute, subject to constraints associated with residential housing markets, local geography, and the commutes of others within their household (Green, 2004, 636). Meanwhile, with regard to travel-for-work individuals self-select their occupation incorporating into this decision whether travel may be required. In practice, however, labour market imperfections and the complexity of many occupations (including requirements for career development) result in employees working in roles that may not match their preferences, including those over travel-for-work. Indeed, some employers exert 'institutional pressure' on employees to be mobile (Lassen, 2009). Employees, in some cases, have reported a travel "threshold," reflecting the notion of a minimum amount of travel perceived at least by the employee as necessary to be successful, in particular through the generation and maintenance of professional networks (Storme et al., 2013, 16–17).

7.4.1 The Use of Time Spent Travelling for Work

Time spent travelling for work can be used productively, providing employees with time to work with a level of autonomy away from the office (Holley et al., 2008). Employees may derive positive experiences through using travel time as an opportunity for 'relaxation' and respite from their usual workplace and their family/home (Gustafson, 2012b, 210). Past research has shown that between 50 and 60 percent of employees use business travel time to work (Holley et al., 2008). However, the productive potential of travel is dependent upon a range of exogenous factors including the method of transport, time of day, and length of journey, as well as travellers' own preferences and choices regarding how they spend their time when travelling (Holley et al., 2008). Train (and similar) travel provides the greatest potential for productive 'working' travel time. It involves relatively less 'unusable' waiting time compared to air travel and requires lesser personal input, and is less stressful, than travel by car (Lyons et al., 2007; Gustafson, 2012b). The loss of useful time, though, resulting from time spent travelling intensifies both working time and family time (Gustafson, 2014, 73). Where frequent travel assignments are present a number of complications are reported including uncertainty over short-term work location (Bergman and Gustafson, 2008, 192). Alternatives to travel including the use of ICTs to hold virtual meetings may allow employees to avoid the need for frequent travel. However, evidence is conflicting. Several studies have found that the use of virtual meetings may actually create demands for travel as the availability of virtual methods of communication enhance opportunities to forge new relationships and extend networks (see, e.g., Lu and Peeta, 2009).

Some employees, however, actively choose not to use business travel time to work as they consider themselves to 'work a lot already' or may use this time only to think and plan work (Gustafson, 2012b, 210). One of the central concerns presented by travel-for-work is that there exists no clear divide between the 'work-time' owned by the employer, and 'leisure time' owned by the employee (Holley et al., 2008). Employers may require that employees use business travel time productively, although empirical evidence from a study of twelve organizations in Sweden reported in Gustafson (2012a, 214) suggests that most employers do not have expectations regarding employees completing work while travelling and allow travellers to choose how they use this time (see also Gustafson, 2014). Travel time is not considered as part of ordinary 'work-time'. Moreover, frequent travellers are often employed in managerial and professional occupations where remuneration is based on task completion and deliverables rather than hours worked (Gustafson, 2012b, 215). Defining 'work-time' when travelling for work is thus complex. Although expectations from employers may not be present, workloads may necessitate working on the move. Time 'lost' travelling is rarely compensated in regard to reductions in workload (Espino et al., 2002; Gustafson, 2006). Many employees use travel time to work, for example, checking emails, in order to avoid having to complete this work upon their return. Using case study evidence from three organizations in Sweden, Bergman and Gustafson (2008, 201) find that employees undertaking travel-for-work also report greater incidence of working over hours, and bringing work home. In some cases those travelling may thus complete work while travelling as this represents the only method of avoiding even more overtime and invasion of work into family and leisure time (Gustafson, 2014, 71). This raises the question of whether time off in lieu (TOIL) or similar is required for those undertaking frequent travel. Lengthy travel-for-work may require time off afterwards in order to allow for recuperation (Espino et al., 2002, 314). Some employers allow time off or working from home on an informal basis (Gustafson, 2012b). Employees, though, may seek to gain recognition of business travel time as 'work-time', but doing so could come at a significant cost. Employees would not wish for their employer to engage in consistent recording and monitoring of their work-time which could reduce autonomy and freedom in working routines. More stringent monitoring of the 'work-time' involved in travel-for-work could lead to closer monitoring of hours worked, for example, removing the ability to take occasional days/part days off without recording this in annual leave accounts.

7.4.2 Gender, the Household, and Travel-for-Work

Evidence suggests that while employees may make productive use of travel-for-work and even enjoy the time to complete work without the distractions present in the workplace, a primary focus of the majority of travellers is to minimize travel time and avoid overnight stays wherever possible. This is driven by family responsibilities, social obligations, and leisure preferences (Gustafson, 2012b, 216). Gender also plays a central role in determining both availability and preferences for travel-for-work. Using US data it has been shown that men display greater availability for, and frequency of, travel-for-work, and that married men in particular are likely to undertake frequent travel (Jeong et al., 2013, 148–49). A consistent pattern is present in the United Kingdom as the National Travel Survey shows men, in particular those aged between forty and fifty-nine years, are the most frequent business travellers (ONS, 2016c). In part as a result of family responsibilities, women who do undertake travel-for-work are more likely to avoid overnight stays, potentially resulting in lengthier journey times and distances (Bergström, 2006). Meanwhile, the presence of children has distinct effects for men and women. For men it may increase their willingness to travel as they take on the primary breadwinner role in the household. Women, in contrast, often become more closely tied to the home, reducing incidence of travel (Gustafson, 2006, 523).

Women may also be less likely to take on roles that require frequent travel, or be considered for them by employers, as a result of both their greater household contribution and the perceptions of employers regarding women's availability for travel-for-work (Gustafson, 2006). Recent research using data from the Swedish Labour Force Survey reported a greater likelihood of men undertaking travel-for-work, especially if it requires an overnight stay. Moreover, while men undertaking frequent travel-for-work reported lesser household contribution, for women frequent overnight stays do not result in a significant reduction in their household responsibilities. It has been suggested this may be the result of gender norms acting to maintain inequality in the household division of labour (Bergström Casinowsky, 2013, 318). The result is that business travel can create significant overwork among women, further evidencing the challenges of successfully combining work and home (Lewis and Humbert, 2010; MacDonald et al., 2005). The gender segregation evident in patterns of travel-for-work may act to limit the career progression of those less available for travel.

7.4.3 Travel-for-Work and Subjective Well-Being

Increasing temporal and spatial flexibility in paid work, including requirements to undertake work-related travel, presents a number of challenges for employees. They must be dynamic and able to manage moving between locations, on the move and at home (Halford, 2005). However, the unbounded nature of these forms of work-related activity can create difficulties for workers and their families (Tietze and Musson, 2010). While a range of research has considered the subjective well-being effects of travel-to-work (see, e.g., De Vos et al., 2013; Ettema et al., 2010, 2012; Roberts et al., 2011; Wheatley,

2014) there currently remain only few studies which focus on the subjective well-being effects of travel-for-work.

Travel-for-work can provide benefits to well-being associated with fulfilment and achievement at work (Gustafson, 2014, 70–71). Willingness and availability to travel may provide greater promotion prospects (Gustafson, 2006, 527; 2014, 74) through signalling organizational commitment (Gustafson, 2014, 73), enabling workers to access, maintain, and enhance knowledge networks (Lassen, 2009), and develop and enhance 'career' and/or 'mobility' capital (Dickmann and Doherty, 2008; Scott, 2006). Travellers gain access to, and experiences of, cultures and countries (Suutari and Taka, 2004), and practical and professional experience through meeting and working with individuals from other parts of their organization and other organizations (Gustafson, 2014, 74). Development of professional networks is one particular benefit associated with travel-for-work, although this requires a substantial and sustained time-input to achieve (Kirk, 2016, 690). International travel, in particular, may improve career prospects through skill acquisition and personal development (Bonache, 2005). Meanwhile, certain forms of business travel are associated with a heightened social status (Thurlow and Jaworski 2006), generating a more 'cosmopolitan' or 'jet-set' identity among travellers (Lassen, 2010). Benefits to career create a number of related benefits including greater income, which has been shown to be positively associated with both occurrence and frequency of travel-for-work including overnight stays (Bergström Casinowsky, 2013, 324; Jeong et al., 2013, 150; Gustafson, 2006, 522).

Travel-for-work can be stressful and may reflect increasing demands from employers for employees to be available for work (Bergman and Gustafson, 2008). Espino et al. (2002, 312), for example, reported that around three-quarters of a sample of World Banking Group employees reported high or very high stress levels associated with travel-for-work. Work-related stress can result from: (1) planning and preparation for travel; (2) practical problems during travel including delays; (3) cultural differences; (4) isolation; (5) health and safety (during travel and at the destination) including exhaustion from travelling and problems sleeping; (6) poor diet and difficulty exercising while away; and (7) accumulated work when returning from the period of travel (Ivancevich et al., 2003; Espino et al., 2002, 318). Business travel may increase difficulties surrounding schedule inflexibility reducing the ability of workers to manage competing role demands (Bonache, 2005). Travellers do, though, report developing 'travel competence' strategies in order to reduce stress when travelling. For example, when travelling by air individuals may take only hand luggage and carefully choose their airline (Gustafson, 2014, 70). Storme et al. (2013, 15), exploring the travel behaviours of academics using a mixed method approach, found that while approximately 30 percent of academics undertake little, and often relatively local, travel the majority of academics do travel regularly for work and are able to manage the demands for travel alongside their work and home obligations. Meanwhile, qualitative research focusing on the experiences of eight business travellers, reported in Nicholas and McDowall (2012, 350–51), identifies the role of negotiation and compromise between travellers and their partners, in particular in terms of the time spent with family when at home as a method of mediating work-family conflict arising from business travel.

Greater incidence of travel-for-work is associated with work-family conflict, negative spillover, and marital difficulties (Roehling and Bultman, 2002). Absences from home, especially if frequent, may result in stress and psychosocial problems in both travellers and their families (Black and Jamieson, 2007). Travel-for-work may be particularly stressful for those with children and for the children of employees undertaking travel-for-work (Espino et al., 2002, 316–18). Diamond et al. (2008) consider the psychological and physiological impacts among partners following a four- to seven-day separation due to work-related travel. They found significant impacts in relation to the quality of daily interactions, subjective stress, sleeping problems, and physical symptoms, especially for the travelling partner. Moreover, changes resulting from separation were more pronounced among those exhibiting higher levels of separation anxiety, suggesting that the relative impact of travel-for-work is likely to differ at the level of the individual. This is consistent with the findings reported by Gustafson (2014, 72) suggesting frequent travel can be associated with feelings of separation and loneliness. Impacts of travel-for-work also extend to relationships with friends and family not present within the home. Travellers with a family tend to prioritize their families when returning from business travel as leisure/family time is limited. Frequent travel-for-work constrains, in particular, the time available for social and leisure activities, especially in relation to 'collective activities', including social events or organized leisure activities with friends and relatives (73).

Reflecting on the specific impacts of working on the move, using a small-scale sample of teleworkers and non-teleworkers in the United States, Fonner and Roloff (2010, 353) found that high intensity teleworkers (individuals teleworking over 50 percent of the time) reported greater job satisfaction. They reported improved management of work-life boundaries, reduced stress, and reduced exposure to negative behaviours in the workplace including interruptions, distractions, and organizational politics. Meanwhile, Golden and Veiga (2005) suggest a curvilinear relationship is present with increased incidence of working on the move increasing satisfaction, but subject to diminishing returns. Challenges are faced by employees reporting working at multiple locations, particularly in respect to satisfaction with leisure time reflecting the potential double-edged sword of working flexibly (Wheatley, 2012a, 233).

The evidence is indicative of employees, in many cases, receiving a number of benefits from travel-for-work associated with enhancement of their careers, but that this use of time presents a number of challenges for both travellers and their households.

7.5 CASE STUDY EVIDENCE FROM THE UK MIDLANDS

The relationship between patterns of travel-to-work and travel-for-work and well-being has been explored in the psychology literature, but a lack of large-scale data containing information on both work-related travel and subjective well-being mean that this has not been fully explored in the economics and wider social science literature. For example, Kahneman et al. (2004) and Wheatley (2014) report on how the commute is one of the least appreciated activities undertaken during the working day, but this research does not report on travel-for-work. To address the gap in the existing literature a mixed methods research project (see Travel-for-Work Research Project in chapter 1) was undertaken in the Midlands region of the United Kingdom in 2015 (see box 7.2).

Box 7.2 Case Study: Travel-to-Work and Travel-for-Work Among Highly Skilled Workers in the United Kingdom (Craig Bickerton and Daniel Wheatley)

This case study reports findings from the Travel-for-Work Research Project, drawing on research published in Wheatley and Bickerton (2016b). Patterns of travel-to-work and travel-for-work have become increasingly complex over time, particularly for those employed in highly skilled managerial, professional, and associate professional occupations. These roles are subject to increasing amounts of travel as a result of globalization and the increasingly unbounded nature of work (Aguiléra, 2008; Felstead et al., 2005; Hislop and Axtell, 2009). In these circumstances there may be an expectation that employees make themselves available for this type of travel in order to be seen as candidates for career progression. The UK Midlands study comprised an online survey and detailed follow-up interviews with professional and managerial workers, that is, those most likely to be engaged in substantial amounts of travel-for-work as part of their job role. The survey received 141 complete responses and a 10 percent subsample of these were subject to a follow-up interview. The results from both the survey and follow-up interviews suggest that while there are some commonalities between the commute and travel-for-work there are a number of important differences that mean, overall, travel-for-work is viewed more positively than the commute.

Travel-to-work

Broadly consistent with patterns observed in the United Kingdom among highly skilled workers (see Wheatley, 2014), average home to work travel time among the

2015 survey of workers from the East Midlands was reported as 35.9 minutes (37.5 minutes, men; 33.4 minutes, women). The majority of respondents reported travelling to work by car (74.5 percent), while around 8 percent of respondents travelled by bus (7.8 percent) or train (8.5 percent), and the remainder walked or used a tram.

In general the commute is regarded as unproductive (especially for those who commute by car and are unable to work during this time), while it also lengthens the working day. It reduces the amount of time available for family and social activities and has a negative impact on health. Commuting is also generally performed as a solo activity, especially when travelling by car. Overall commuting is negatively correlated with subjective well-being, consistent with previous research (Basmajian, 2010; Kahneman et al., 2004; Wheatley, 2013). Participants in the research reported general dissatisfaction with the commute, including, for example:

> Whilst you try to make it productive you kind of feel it's dead time, it's neither at work, or with the family. [Interviewee 11]
>
> It does limit the leisure time or the willingness to pursue further leisure because you're tired … the real downside is your evenings are shorter and the opportunities to do things are restricted. [Interviewee 14]
>
> I think [because] my commute has an impact on my daughter as well, it can be a little bit more stressful. [Interviewee 12]

Where commutes are viewed more positively this was generally associated with alternative methods of transport which enabled productive use of travel time (train) and/or wider health and well-being benefits (walking, cycling):

> I haven't driven into work for months and I'm actually a great deal happier for it. That particularly is miserable, it's just endless congestion, endless dead time doing nothing productive you know, you're just there on your own in the car and it's horrible. [Interviewee 10]
>
> Walking and exercise makes me feel better and improves my productivity in work and mood and well-being at home. [Survey Respondent 97]

Travel-for-work

The most common forms of travel-for-work reported among the survey sample were '1 day (no overnight stay)' which was reported among 62.1 percent of respondents, followed by '2–3 days (requiring overnight stay)' reported by 23.4 percent of respondents. The bulk of respondents (77.4 percent) reported travelling locally, regionally, and nationally as part of their job. Meanwhile, a further 27 percent reported travelling internationally within the EU, and 18.5 percent internationally outside of the EU. The purpose of this work-related travel included: generating new business (reported by 46.8 percent of respondents), meeting with clients (56 percent), meeting with project teams (43.3 percent), visiting other sites within the organization (37.6 percent), training (47.5 percent), and attending conferences (58.2 percent).

Survey respondents and interviewees reported a number of negative impacts on their well-being associated with travel-for-work, including on their leisure time due to loss of time with family and friends, and to their health due to difficulty in eating in a healthy manner and exercising:

> If you're away it does limit your ability to get engaged in kind of gym work, jogging, playing football you know, any of the kind of health stuff that you could do if you lived round the corner from your work. [Interviewee 7]

While some of the disruption to family life and social activities also applies to travel-for-work, there are a number of benefits that offset these negative impacts. Travel-for-work allows for experience of new/different working cultures and environments (Suutari and Taka, 2004), and generates other positive career-related impacts through the development of professional networks and contacts (Gustafson, 2014, 74; Kirk, 2016, 690). Participants in the research reported:

> Travelling to different organizations and cultures, and meeting different people is stimulating and generates fresh thinking. This enhances career and overall happiness, at the expense of fatigue and absence from home. [Survey Respondent 4]
>
> Making the effort to travel is often noticed by my manager as putting in extra effort, especially as outside of normal hours, it is unpaid. [Survey Respondent 120]

Interviewees also conveyed the benefits of travelling with others over travel undertaken alone. Travelling for work with colleagues and/or peers in professional networks provides travellers with feelings of togetherness from socializing with others, as one interviewee commented:

> I think going with people you know, it's definitely more enjoyable because I think you can feel a bit more like you're with your friends. [Interviewee 5].

The benefits outlined above, along with the ability to plan travel and use travel time productively, account for the different perceptions of the commute and travel-for-work:

> Travel is essential to create business, and therefore, career opportunities. It also allows work to be undertaken without usual distractions. It takes me away from home too much, too often, but that comes with the job. [Survey Respondent 8]
>
> I don't mind travelling overseas because it feels like I am making a difference for my company, however the regular commute to the factory for meetings is tedious. [Survey Respondent 140]

Overall, the research evidences a number of important impacts of complex patterns of travel among highly skilled workers, including the differing perceptions of the commute and travel-for-work. The research also suggests areas for policy intervention: increasing the accessibility of public transport to ameliorate the effects of the commute and encouraging employers to recognize time-use associated with travel-for-work through, for example, more widespread use of time off in lieu (TOIL).

7.6 CHAPTER SUMMARY: COMPLEX PATTERNS OF TRAVEL AND SUBJECTIVE WELL-BEING

This chapter has explored the role of travel in impacting both patterns of time-use and reported well-being. The existing literature, and reflections from the case study of highly skilled workers reported in the Travel-for-Work Research Project, highlight the considerable but differential impact of both travel-to-work and travel-for-work with respect to how we spend our time. The commute generates widely negative impacts (Kahneman et al., 2004; Stutzer and Frey, 2008). Time spent commuting is not work-time: the nature of this form of travel, and its link to decisions over residential location, which influence the length of the commute and mode of transport used, provides a rationale for it not to be considered work-time. It is, though, time spent in necessary work-related activity. The commute essentially lengthens the working day. As a result it is widely considered as 'dead time' or a 'waste of time'. Negative impacts on well-being are particularly pronounced among those reporting lengthier commutes, as this reduces available leisure time, and time with family. Evidence in this regard points toward the presence of a commuting tolerance, that is, an amount of time up to which commuting is considered acceptable. Beyond this tolerance an individual would be unwilling to commute, although in practice a range of factors may result in individuals undertaking commutes which do not match their preferences and result in significant negative effects on well-being. Moreover, the most dominant mode of transport to work, the car, is associated with more negative impacts resulting from stress, inability to use travel time productively, and the potential for unplanned delays due to congestion. The lone nature of the commute also explains some of the negative perceptions of this activity as 'wasted time'. For some workers the commute also forms part of a complex multi-activity journey, especially working mothers who often combine the commute with childcare responsibilities including the school run. However, these demands, which continue to more often remain with women, can result in limited spatial mobility potentially affecting women's access to labour markets and restricting career opportunities (Wheatley, 2013), with potentially negative effects on well-being (Wheatley, 2014).

Travel-for-work, while sometimes undertaken outside of usual working hours, is often used productively. This productive use of this time does leave many workers feeling this time is not lost or wasted, consistent with the evidence in the case study. In addition, workers may receive a number of benefits associated with career development and wider exposure to other cultures and countries (Gustafson, 2014, 74; Kirk, 2016, 690; Suutari and Taka, 2004). The lesser frequency of travel-for-work among most workers renders its impact lesser in many cases, even where overnight stays are required. Where workers travel with colleagues, this can also mediate some of the negative impacts associated with travelling including feelings of isolation and loss of time for socializing. Travel-for-work, though, can result in intense schedules. Planning becomes increasingly important to offset the potential negative impacts including time available for family and leisure, and effects on physical and mental well-being including health and stress levels (Bergman and Gustafson, 2008; Gustafson, 2014). It is important that organizations acknowledge the impact of travel-for-work on workers. Organizations benefit from workers travelling as they generate new work, build and maintain relationships with clients, and enhance their knowledge and skills. Face-to-face contact remains preferred by many employers to achieve these outcomes. Alternatives, including use of ICTs, should though be considered where this is feasible as these can offer alternatives to travel in some cases which can be used to enhance inter- and intra-organization relationships.

Finally, in considering the differing well-being effects of travel-to-work and travel-for-work it is important to reflect on the findings which show that while travel-for-work offers some reciprocal benefits the commute is not seen as adding value. The commute is necessary work-related activity, time-use which is required to bridge home and work, but in the majority of cases it has no direct value adding function. The continued reliance on the car leaves the commute a widely negative experience. Improvements to alternative methods of transport, and greater use of flexible working arrangements which either render the commute unnecessary, for example, homeworking, or allow travel to be undertaken outside of peak journey times, offer routes to mediate the negative effects of the commute on well-being.

Chapter Eight

Leisure Time

The Pursuit of Happiness?

Craig Bickerton and Daniel Wheatley

8.1 INTRODUCTION

This chapter focuses on the relationship between time spent in different forms of leisure activity and subjective well-being. The economics literature on the relationship between work and well-being is now extensive but until recently economists have paid relatively little attention to how we use our leisure time. The relationship between leisure time and well-being is explored in this chapter with reference to existing literature and empirical data. In exploring this aspect of how we use our time, the chapter also contributes to our understanding of the 'leisure experience' derived from leisure activities, and offers insight into the 'cultural value' associated with activities including arts, heritage sites (e.g., museums, historical sites), and certain sports. Consideration of participation in both sport and culture is relevant as these activities have been shown to occupy the majority of the leisure time of individuals (Cabane et al., 2015; Cushman et al., 2005). Other uses of leisure time, including Internet use and time spent socializing with friends/family, are also considered in this chapter. The chapter, further, explores the relevance of frequency of engagement in leisure activities, and its relationship with subjective well-being, and whether a domain spillover is present between satisfaction with leisure and satisfaction with other aspects of life, including job satisfaction, and two measures of overall subjective well being, life satisfaction, and general happiness.

Although difficult to measure, assessing the value associated with time spent in leisure activities, including those outlined above, is central to our understanding of how we use, and derive enjoyment from, our time. As Throsby (2001, 33) argues, 'A view of economics which excludes the cultural dimension of the activities of individual economic agents and the institutions they inhabit is likely to be seriously deficient in explaining or understanding behaviour.' This chapter first provides a conceptual discussion of the leisure experience derived from time spent in leisure activities, drawing on the work of Ateca-Amestoy (2011; Ateca-Amestoy et al., 2008), and the cultural value associated with a range of leisure activities, drawing on the work of Throsby (2001, 2006). This is followed by an empirical exploration of the relationship between engagement in leisure activities and subjective well-being, using data extracted from Understanding Society which draws on work published in Wheatley and Bickerton (2016b).

8.2 THE LEISURE EXPERIENCE AND THE CULTURAL VALUE OF LEISURE ACTIVITIES

Leisure represents a complex human need, of variable definition, which is fulfilled through the consumption and production of leisure experiences (Ateca-Amestoy et al., 2008, 64). There exist four alternative definitions of leisure. The first defines 'leisure' in the context of 'leisure time', that is, time which is residual to time spent in work and/or is discretionary in nature in which there is freedom to choose how this time is used. The second definition is of leisure as an activity which takes place at a given time and location, where certain attributes of the activity define it as leisure. The third definition views leisure in the context of the experience of an individual, which is derived from a freely chosen activity. The fourth definition, sometimes referred to as 'leisure experience', integrates elements of all of the other three, where 'leisure is recognised as an action that takes place at a given time, is an activity that we can identify and, more importantly, brings pleasant experiences to the person involved in that action' (Ateca-Amestoy, 2011, 54–55). Within mainstream economics leisure is often referred to in the context of mainstream labour supply theory, that is, workers supply their labour in a trade-off between work (and income) and leisure. In this trade-off leisure is assumed as a source of utility (and work as a source of disutility), consistent with the first definition of leisure outlined above which focuses on leisure as time over which there is free choice. Under these assumptions greater hours of leisure are always preferable; this can be termed 'leisure-as-bliss' (Spencer, 2006). However, the marginal utility gained from leisure is heavily dependent on the nature of leisure time. Spare time for those on welfare payments, for example, is unlikely to be used in the same way as it would be by wealthier individuals. Meanwhile, unemployment is not the same as leisure time. As such unemployment cannot be classified as leisure (Spencer, 2006, 461–62). Leisure, therefore, is not simply free time, but is a product of personal perception of what is discretionary, enjoyable, pleasurable, and

Table 8.1 Characteristics of Cultural Value

Aesthetic	The aesthetic of the cultural work/asset, referring to the properties of beauty, harmony, and form
Authentic	The originality and integrity of a work/asset, which has an identifiable value in addition to the value derived from other cultural characteristics
Historical	Historical connections, including how it illuminates life at the time and in the present
Spiritual	The value of the work/asset in a religious context, by a faith, tribe, or other cultural grouping, or the spiritual value to all human beings
Social	Connecting to others, enabling us to understand society, and providing a sense of identity and place. In some cases value may be derived only when a work/asset is experienced as part of a group
Symbolic	Artworks and other cultural objects act as repositories and/or conveyors of meaning

Source: Adapted from Throsby (2001, 28–9).

satisfying (Kelly, 1982). Leisure experiences are both social and cultural in nature (Iwasaki, 2007, 257–58). Participation and engagement in cultural goods, including arts events, heritage sites, and certain sporting activities, form leisure experiences. Moreover, these activities are sources of both cultural and economic value. Cultural value in this context refers to certain activities and products associated with the 'intellectual, moral and artistic aspects of human life' (Throsby, 2001, 4; 2006). It is distinct from economic value. For example, Throsby (2001, 32) argues that some characteristics of cultural value are not measurable on a monetary scale as they do not generate any value for which there would be willingness to pay. Cultural value is generated through 'cultural characteristics' derived from a work, activity, or asset, as summarized in table 8.1.

Importantly, cultural value is derived from positive characteristics (Throsby, 2001, 27). Cultural goods including arts events, museums, historical sites, and certain sporting activities exhibit a number of these characteristics, but the cultural value associated with each remains difficult to measure. In addition, these goods have both use and non-use value. Users gain benefits through positive leisure experience. Meanwhile, as with other goods such as the environment, non-users derive utility from existence, option, and bequest values, that is, preservation of cultural/natural heritage. For example, individuals may derive utility from an area of parkland through knowing it exists, having the option to visit the amenity, and through preserving it for future generations (Ateca-Amestoy, 2011, 70). Evidence is indicative of positive leisure experience enhancing quality of life and subjective well-being (Ateca Amestoy et al., 2008; Iwasaki, 2007). Definitions and the relative outcomes enjoyed by those consuming leisure, though, differ between individuals, that is, one individual may enjoy participating in sport, while another attends a concert (Ateca-Amestoy, 2011, 54–57). Common to these definitions is the need for a time input to spend in leisure activities, but distinctions exist in other factors including the necessity of the presence of others and individual materialism which may influence both the way in which leisure is enjoyed and the value given to different experiences (57). Positive leisure experiences may, for example, be garnered from 'togetherness' involved in group or team activities (Hamermesh, 2002), which can be referred to in the context of 'enjoyable others' incorporating the social dimension of leisure including experiencing leisure with friends, family, and/or colleagues (Ateca-Amestoy, 2011, 56). 'Togetherness' may have particular relevance when considering engagement in certain arts events and various sports.

Two alternative theories have been advanced which attempt to offer an explanation of the relationship between leisure and subjective well-being, 'activity theory' and 'need theory'. Activity theory centres on the importance of frequency of participation, as well as engaging in more intimate activities, arguing that increases in both will increase subjective well-being. Need theory, in contrast, suggests that through satisfying our needs subjective well-being benefits are derived (Rodríguez et al., 2008). Some support has been found for both theories, for example, in Rodríguez et al. (2008), but equally some caution has been levelled in particular in respect to frequency of participation. While it has been identified that frequency is important in determining the satisfaction obtained from time spent in certain arts activities, for example, a more nuanced understanding is required: greater frequency does not always equate to greater satisfaction (Michalos and Kahlke, 2010, 2008; Michalos, 2005).

The public investment awarded to certain leisure activities, specifically arts, culture, and sport, may be evidence, in part, of the public good characteristics of arts, cultural, and sporting assets. For example, in the United Kingdom the Arts Council of England was allocated £1.04 billion of funding for arts and culture for the period 2012–2015 (Arts Council, 2013). Meanwhile, substantial investment in sport has been driven by agendas promoting a healthy, active lifestyle: £400 million of UK government funding was allocated for investment, through Sport England (2013), into national governing bodies (NGBs) of sports in England between 2013 and 2017. The extant literature is indicative, too, of the presence of cultural value arising from arts, culture, and sport. Marsh et al. (2010, 9–10) identify a range of external benefits at individual, community, and national levels. These include learning benefits generated through engagement in the arts, increased community cohesion, and potential health benefits, including, for example, application of the arts in the treatment of depression, and mental/physical benefits of sport and recreational fitness.

8.3 LEISURE TIME AND SUBJECTIVE WELL-BEING: CURRENT EVIDENCE

An area of research in the sub-discipline of cultural economics has begun to capture the potential relevance of leisure activities, including a range of arts, cultural, and sporting activities, to subjective well-being, although these findings are not without conflict and limitations. A survey of the cultural economics literature conducted by Blaug (2001) outlined the main areas of research activity developing in this sub-discipline, as summarized in table 8.2.

The benefits of leisure may be distinct to different groups of individuals, and those with differing household situations. For example, it has been argued that a 'hierarchy of needs' may be present between time used in leisure activities and household labour. Household labour has a significant impact in determining the maximum time available for leisure, evidencing the finite nature of non-work time. Specifically, 'leisure production requires the availability of discretionary time (i.e., time when individuals perceive themselves to be free of external demands and in control of their own situations) and not just of any residual, non-working time' (Ateca-Amestoy et al.,

Table 8.2 Research in Cultural Economics

Area of research	*Description*
Taste formation	How audiences for the arts tend to have higher levels in terms of income, age, occupation, and education
Demand and supply	Price and income elasticities of demand for theatre, dance, opera, and so on
Industrial organization	Pricing issues, especially where multiple objectives exist for organizations (e.g., museums) and the role of non-profit as a strategy
Art market	The nature of auctions for art, the rates of return of arts investments vs. financial investments, and the role of psychic income, that is, the non-monetary/non-material satisfaction associated with an occupation or economic activity
Economic history of the arts	Focusing on historical analysis of costs and prices, substitutes and complements and the finances of the arts
Artists labour markets	Applying human capital theory to the labour market for artists
Baumol's cost disease	Proposition that the failure to maintain technical progress in the arts with that of the economy as a whole, while wages rise everywhere (more or less) at the same rate, necessarily implies cost inflation in the arts
Public subsidies for the arts	The application of standard welfare approaches based on market failure/contingent valuation approaches, and research into the targeting of subsidies towards individuals or organizations

Source: Adapted from Blaug (2001).

2008, 77). In addition, it has been suggested that older people, in particular, may benefit from social interaction associated with certain leisure activities (Kemperman and Timmermans, 2008). Meanwhile, those in paid work may benefit from the ability to use leisure as a method of mediating work-related stress (Trenberth and Dewe, 2002).

Recent research has begun to capture the potential relevance of engagement in a range of leisure activities, including arts, cultural, and sporting activities. For example, Brajša-Žganec et al. (2011) consider time spent in a range of different leisure activities including playing sports, visiting the movies, attending concerts, watching TV, eating at restaurants, and attending church. Using sample survey data from Croatia, they found that cultural events significantly contribute to the explanation of subjective well-being among people aged between thirty and sixty years, as well as those aged over sixty years. More precisely, people who visit exhibitions, go to the theatre, read books, and attend concerts report higher levels of subjective well-being. These findings are consistent with those of Lloyd and Auld (2002) who reported a positive relationship between subjective well-being and engaging in social activities, including visiting and going out with friends. Robinson and Martin (2008), though, suggested in their research that happier people are those who are most active in the majority of social activities, bringing into question the causality in the relationships observed. Also relevant to the way we spend our leisure time is time spent using ICTs and watching television. Conflicting results are present with respect to Internet use. Some studies suggest negative impacts, for example, loneliness and social isolation (Putnam, 2000), while others suggests a number of benefits associated with increased social interaction (Amichai-Hamburge and Hayat, 2011, 587–88; Contarello and Sarrica, 2007, 1029), as outlined in chapter 1. Meanwhile, although watching television is one of the most frequently engaged in leisure activities (Brajša-Žganec et al., 2011, 88), it may generate few positive impacts (Knabe et al., 2010, 875; Frey and Benesch, 2008).

In the UK context, some tentative steps have also been taken to value these activities. Fujiwara (2013), for example, used data extracted from the UK Taking Part survey. This research, funded by the Arts Council of England, attempted to quantify the monetary value of the subjective well-being benefits of museum visits, participation in the arts, being an audience to the arts, and participation in sports. Using a CBA framework applying a non-standard willingness to pay valuation method, the findings estimated net well-being benefits of approximately £3,200, £1,500, £2,000, and £1,500 respectively per person per annum. While offering useful insight, the challenges associated with attempting monetary valuation of subjective well-being limits these findings. Work undertaken by the Scottish Executive in 2005 explored quality of life and well-being in the context of measuring the benefits of culture and sport, but concluded that evidence demonstrating a link between cultural participation and quality of life/subjective well-being is scarce (Galloway et al., 2006). The UK Department for Culture, Media and Sport (DCMS), in the context of understanding the value of time spent in culture and sport, published results based on analysis of the BHPS for the periods 1996–2000 and 2002–2007 (Marsh et al., 2010). Findings revealed that the positive effect of participation in cultural activities increases with the frequency of engagement. But, Marsh et al. also acknowledge the limited scope of their analysis due to the inclusion of only a narrow range of cultural activities in the BHPS. The DCMS research was extended in Marsh and Bertranou (2012) again using the BHPS. However, they suggest that the impact of engagement in culture may be overestimated in research and, further, that it is important to consider other factors including income. Other research, considering a range of measures of both overall and domain satisfaction (Michalos and Kahlke, 2010, 2008), found arts activities to have relatively little impact on overall life satisfaction. They qualify their findings, though, in that the size of these effects is 'relative' to other factors commonly found to have a large impact, for example, health and financial position, highlighting the relevance of their inclusion to analyses of subjective well-being.

8.3.1 Arts and Culture

A number of studies have presented results suggesting positive impacts from spending time in arts and culture. For example, recent research considering access to cultural activities (measured broadly in terms of number of times engaged per year) found cultural access to be second only to health status in factors affecting well-being (Grossi et al., 2012). Other recent research making use of momentary well-being measures reported on a number of activities that fall within the umbrella of arts and culture. Bryson and MacKerron (2013, 9), focusing on experiences of work, note that among thirty-nine types of activity, 'theatre, dance, concert' and 'exhibition, museum, library' are ranked second and third behind intimacy and love-making, among activities which increase happiness (relative to not doing these activities). As activities which exhibit cultural characteristics, visiting historical sites and museums may provide well-being benefits (Fujiwara, 2013). It has been suggested that overall engagement in the arts and culture is greater among women (DiMaggio, 2004), in part owing to different socialization between genders as well as differences driven by the occupations and industries in which men and women are employed (Christin, 2012). It has also been noted that those in higher socio-economic groups are more likely to visit museums and heritage sites (Marsh et al., 2010, 16). Lack of accessibility to some heritage sites may limit engagement, and therefore the potential well-being benefits, of certain groups less likely to have access to a car, for example, social housing tenants, older adults (19). Other research has identified positive associations between satisfaction levels and playing music, crafts, and purchasing works of art (Michalos, 2005; Creech et al., 2013). Meanwhile, in research focusing on direct professional engagement in the arts, Bille et al. (2013) explored job satisfaction among artists. Using European Value Survey data from 1999 and 2008 they found evidence of greater job satisfaction among artists, driven by the greater autonomy artists encounter within their occupation.

Wood and Smith (2004) explored live music performances at concerts, attempting to capture the well-being effects on performers (actively engaging) and audiences (passively engaging). They found well-being to be enhanced as musical performances are 'therapeutic in the broadest sense', providing immersion in the performance through the act of performing (for the performer) and emotional effects (for the audience). Other research is also indicative of the positive effects of playing instruments and listening to music. Creech et al. (2013) consider the impact of active music-making among the elderly, using case study evidence from the United Kingdom. They find positive effects on well-being from active music-making which provides a sense of purpose, autonomy, and social interaction, the latter finding consistent with Kemperman and Timmermans (2008). Meanwhile, Daykin et al. (2012) consider the impacts of music on young offenders through a systematic literature review. Positive associations are present within this literature, but results are not conclusive.

8.3.2 Sporting Activities

Sport and recreational exercise have also been identified as potentially important in improving health and subjective well-being (Taylor et al., 2015, 31; Wendel-Vos et al., 2004). A range of studies have shown sport and recreation generate both physical and mental benefits (see Taylor et al. (2015) for a full discussion). Individuals participating in these activities derive increased well-being from physical fitness (Kavetsos, 2011), and improved mental stimulation and satisfaction, in part associated with enhanced social networks (Gratton, 2004). Participation in sport has been shown to have positive effects in preventing and reducing work-related stress (Biddle and Asare, 2011). Downward and Rasciute (2011, 344), further, identify that happiness is enhanced by participation in sports. This is especially prominent among those engaging in sports that require social interaction (i.e., team sports), consistent with the benefits of 'togetherness' (Hamermesh, 2002). Bryson and MacKerron's (2013, 9) study, similarly, identified 'sports, running and exercise' as ranking highly (fourth) in their range of activities generating happiness. Kavetsos (2011) suggests that increased frequency of engagement in sports is associated with higher levels of happiness. It has, though, been suggested that childcare and housework may limit the participation in sports among women due to impacts on the availability of leisure time (Humphreys and Ruseski, 2006). Huang and Humphreys (2012) found close proximity to sports facilities to be a mediating factor in the impacts of participation in sports, suggesting access is important in generating positive effects. Meanwhile, Baker et al. (2005) found that being active is particularly beneficial for older adults. Hecht and Boies (2009, 421–22), further, examine non-work-to-work spillovers on well-being at work using a survey of Canadian university employees. They suggest positive effects associated with engagement in volunteering and that participating in sports, recreation, and fitness activities may generate positive spillover between domains thus increasing well-being at work, consistent with the findings of Trenberth and Dewe (2002).

The current evidence base pertaining to the relationship between cultural goods – including arts events, museums, historical sites, and certain sporting activities – and well-being is indicative of these activities generating positive leisure experiences, while a number of health and well-being benefits have been observed. However, the literature is often narrow in focus, considering only specific activities or groups of individuals. In contrast, this chapter reports empirical analysis on a wider range of arts, cultural, and sporting activities, in doing so extending the findings of the extant literature and increasing our understanding of how this aspect of how we use our time affects our well-being.

8.4 EMPIRICAL ANALYSIS: LEISURE ACTIVITIES AND SUBJECTIVE WELL-BEING

Empirical measurement of the impact of arts, cultural, and sporting activities is complex. It has been argued that economic impact studies only offer a partial measure of the value of engagement in, for example, arts activities as they cannot capture cultural value (Snowball, 2008, 39–42). Indeed, Throsby argues that a range of difficulties render willingness to pay measures inappropriate for measurement of cultural value: (1) individuals may not understand enough about the asset to provide an accurate assessment of willingness to pay; (2) some aspects of cultural value may not be able to be expressed adequately in reference to preferences; and (3) some characteristics are not measurable, and cannot be converted to, monetary scales (Throsby, 2001, 32). Throsby suggests five methods of investigation appropriate to the assessment of cultural value: (1) content analysis; (2) contextual analysis; (3) expert appraisal; (4) psychometric measurement; and (5) social survey methods

(29–30). Meanwhile, it has been asserted that the experience associated with engagement in leisure activities is most appropriately measured with reference to satisfaction levels as it allows the capture of a number of unobservable dimensions of leisure (Ateca-Amestoy, 2011, 53; Ateca-Amestoy et al., 2008). Leisure experience is derived from the meaning of the activity to the individual, not from the activity itself. Leisure, and the experience of it, is therefore distinct to the individual and satisfaction derived from a leisure experience may be an important determinant of individual happiness (Ateca-Amestoy et al., 2008, 65). Moreover, it has been argued that since leisure is a time-intensive activity, satisfaction with aspects of time-use is highly relevant in assessing relative outcomes (Ateca-Amestoy, 2011, 61). In this chapter the latter approach outlined by Throsby is applied, investigating time spent in arts, culture, and sport using social survey data extracted from wave 2 (2010–2011) of Understanding Society drawing on empirical results first presented in Wheatley and Bickerton (2016b). Wave 2 of the survey is used in this chapter as this was the only survey to include the module on uses of leisure time at the time the research was conducted. The data from Understanding Society, further, enables the analysis of domain satisfaction including aspects of time-use (e.g., leisure time) following Ateca-Amestoy et al. (2008; Ateca-Amestoy, 2011).

The measures of engagement with arts, cultural, and sporting activities are derived from questions of the variety, 'how often in the last 12 months have you been to events such as this?' with respondents given a list of possible activities which were grouped within Understanding Society. The arts, cultural, and sporting activities are grouped into five broad categories: (1) arts activities; (2) arts events; (3) museums, libraries, and archives; (4) historical sites; and (5) moderate and mild intensity sports. Engagement with arts activities comprises fourteen categories including dancing, singing, playing a musical instrument; arts events comprises a further fourteen categories including attending concerts, musicals/opera, cinema, reading for pleasure; visiting libraries, archives, museums comprise three categories in total; visiting historical sites includes seven categories; and engagement in moderate sport has twenty-three categories including football, basketball, tennis, and golf, while mild sport has nine categories including snooker, pool or billiards, bowling, yoga/pilates, and rambling/walking. A full description of the seventy activities included is provided in table 8.3. In addition, variables considering other leisure activities are included in the analysis, comprising a measure of the frequency of Internet use, and whether respondents have a drink/meal with friends or family at least once a month, providing some insight into the effects of time spent in these types of leisure activities (Brajša-Žganec et al., 2011; Lloyd and Auld, 2002; Amichai-Hamburge and Hayat, 2011, 587–88; Contarello and Sarrica, 2007, 1029; Putnam, 2000). However, measures of

Table 8.3 Categories of Arts, Cultural, and Sporting Activities

Arts Activities	**Arts Events**
Dance (including ballet)	Film at a cinema or other venue
Sang to an audience or rehearsed for a performance (not karaoke)	Exhibition or collection of art, photography, sculpture, or a craft exhibition
Played a musical instrument	Event which included video or electronic art
Wrote music	Event connected with books or writing
Rehearsed/performed in a play/drama, opera/operetta or musical theatre	Street arts or a public art display or installation
Taken part in a carnival/street arts event	Carnival or cultural specific festival
Learned or practiced circus skills	Circus (not animals)
Painting, drawing, printmaking, or sculpture	Play/drama, pantomime, or musical
Photography, film, or video making as an artistic activity	Opera/operetta
Used a computer to create original artworks or animation	Classical music performance
Textile crafts, wood crafts, or any other crafts such as embroidery, knitting	Rock, pop, or jazz performance
Read for pleasure (not newspapers, magazines, or comics)	Ballet
Wrote any stories, plays, or poetry	Contemporary dance
Been a member of a book club where people meet up to discuss and share books	African people's dance or South Asian and Chinese dance
Museum, Library, Archive	**Historical Sites**
Used a public library service	A city or town with historic character
Been to an archive centre or records office	A historic building open to the public (non-religious)
Visited a museum or gallery	A historic park or garden open to the public
	A place connected with industrial history
	A historic place of worship attended as a visitor (not to worship)
	A monument such as a castle, fort, or ruin
	A site of archaeological interest
	A site connected with sports heritage
Moderate Intensity Sports	**Mild Intensity Sports**
Health, fitness, gym, or conditioning activities	Snooker, pool, or billiards
Gymnastics	Darts
Swimming or diving	Ten-pin bowling
Cycling, bmx, or mountain biking (for sport or recreation)	Rambling, walking for pleasure or recreation
Football (including 5 or 6 a side)	Shooting
Rugby (union or league) or American football	Archery (if age <65)
Track and field athletics	Yoga or pilates (if age <65)

(continued)

Table 8.3 (continued)

Jogging, cross-country, and road running	Bowls (indoors or outdoors if age <65)
Hill trekking, backpacking, climbing, or mountaineering	Croquet (if age <65)
Golf (including pitch or putt)	
Boxing	
Martial arts	
Water sports, including yachting, dinghy sailing, canoeing, rowing, windsurfing	
Horse riding	
Basketball	
Netball	
Volleyball	
Cricket	
Hockey (exc ice, roller, or street)	
Baseball, softball, or rounders	
Racquet sports such as table tennis, tennis, badminton, or squash	
Ice-skating	
Skiing	
Motor sports	
Angling or fishing	
Archery (if age >64)	
Yoga or pilates (if age >64)	
Bowls (indoors or outdoors if age >64)	
Croquet (if age >64)	
Other sporting activity such as fencing, triathlon, lacrosse orienteering	

Source: Understanding Society (2012).

TV watching or listening to the radio, which have been shown to have relevance to subjective well-being (see, e.g., Frey and Benesch, 2008), were not included in the main (adult) questionnaire of wave 2 of Understanding Society and thus are absent in the analysis.

8.4.1 Evidence from Understanding Society

Understanding Society usefully collected data on the frequency of engagement in a wide range of different arts, cultural, and sporting activities in wave 2 of the survey. These are summarized in figures 8.1 and 8.2.[1] The data is evident of quite stark differences in engagement levels in different leisure activities.

For example, very few respondents report visiting archives (just 4.1 percent). In contrast, 70.5 percent of respondents report engaging in arts activities, and 67.9 percent in arts events. Within the patterns of engagement frequency also varies considerably. Frequency of engagement in arts events including attending concerts and the cinema, for example, is most common around three to four times per year. This is also the case for historical sites. Meanwhile, those engaging in arts activities, on average, do so with a higher frequency. This is likely to be driven by the nature of a number of these activities, including playing instruments and dancing, which form hobbies and often require lots of practice and a level of commitment in order to generate benefits in terms of positive leisure experiences. Engagement in sports follows a similar overall pattern whether mild or moderately intensive in nature: 58.8 percent of respondents report engaging in moderate sport and 55.4 percent engage in mild sport. Those engaging in more intensive sports do, though, report more frequent engagement. Around 31.5 percent of respondents report at least weekly engagement in moderate sports, compared with 21.1 percent in mild sports. Clearly there are a number of other ways people use their leisure time, including, for example, watching TV (Brajša-Žganec et al., 2011; Frey and Benesch, 2008), using the Internet and social media (Amichai-Hamburge and Hayat, 2011; Buglass et al., 2015; Contarello and Sarrica, 2007), and playing on games consoles. However, these are not directly captured by the Understanding Society survey as outlined in the previous section, although a measure of Internet use is included in the survey and in the analysis in this chapter. Internet use is most common among younger age groups as 74.4 percent of sixteen- to twenty-year-olds and 68.6 percent of those aged twenty-one to twenty-nine report using the Internet on a daily basis. In contrast only 21.3 percent of the over sixties report using the Internet on a daily basis, and 55.3 percent of those aged over sixty report no access or never using the Internet.

Both figures 8.1 and 8.2 also reveal important gendered patterns in participation in arts, culture, and sport. Figure 8.1 shows that relatively higher proportions of women spend time in arts and cultural activities, in particular in arts activities where 70 percent of women report at least monthly engagement compared with 56 percent of men. These findings are consistent with the assertion of higher engagement among women present in the existing literature (DiMaggio, 2004). It is worth noting, though, that the proportions visiting museums and historical sites, and the frequency of these visits, are consistent between genders. Past research has suggested that women may be more likely to engage in these 'highbrow cultural' activities (Christin, 2012), but this is not borne out in the data from Understanding Society. In contrast, participation in sport is more common among men, especially more frequent participation (one to three times per week; more than three times per week) in moderate sports, a finding likely reflecting the more limited time available

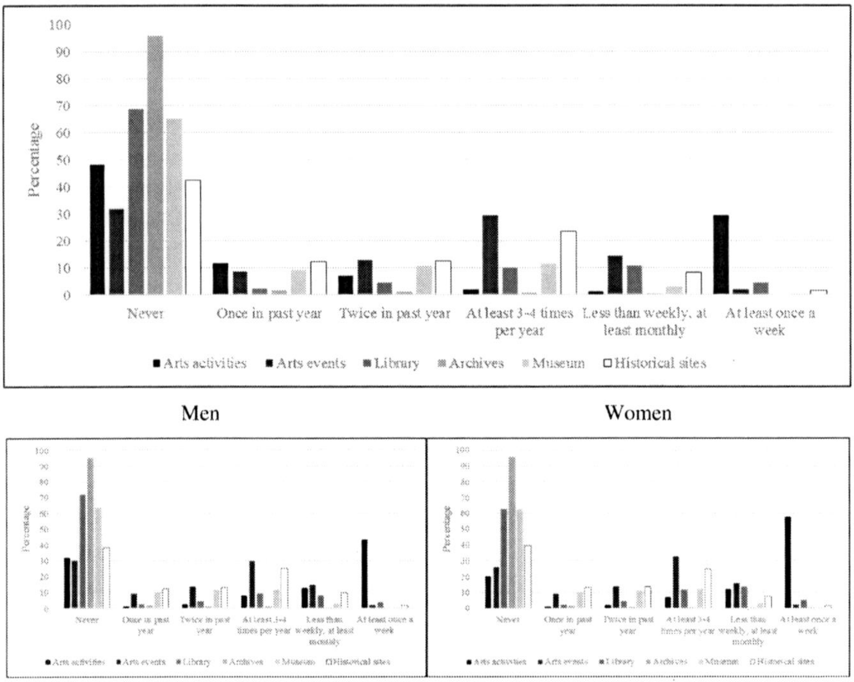

Figure 8.1. Frequency of Engagement in Arts and Cultural Activities.

to women to engage in sports resulting from their greater household contribution (Biddle and Asare, 2011).

With respect to the relationship between participation in leisure activities and well-being, figure 8.3 summarizes the mean reported satisfaction levels among those engaging in arts, cultural, and sporting activities, compared with those who do not. Consistent with, and extending, the findings present in the extant literature, the patterns evident in these charts suggest that participation and engagement in the range of activities captured in Understanding Society is associated with (statistically significant) higher levels of life satisfaction.[2] This finding is present among those reporting engagement in arts activities, visiting libraries, archives, museums and historical sites, and those participating in mild sports activities. This finding is not present, however, when considering engagement in arts events and moderate sports activities. Satisfaction with amount of leisure time, in contrast, is greater among those engaging in all of the activities considered, providing some initial evidence of the positive leisure experience associated with the whole range of these activities. Meanwhile, the impact of time spent in these activities on general happiness is similarly positive, with the exception of visiting archives.

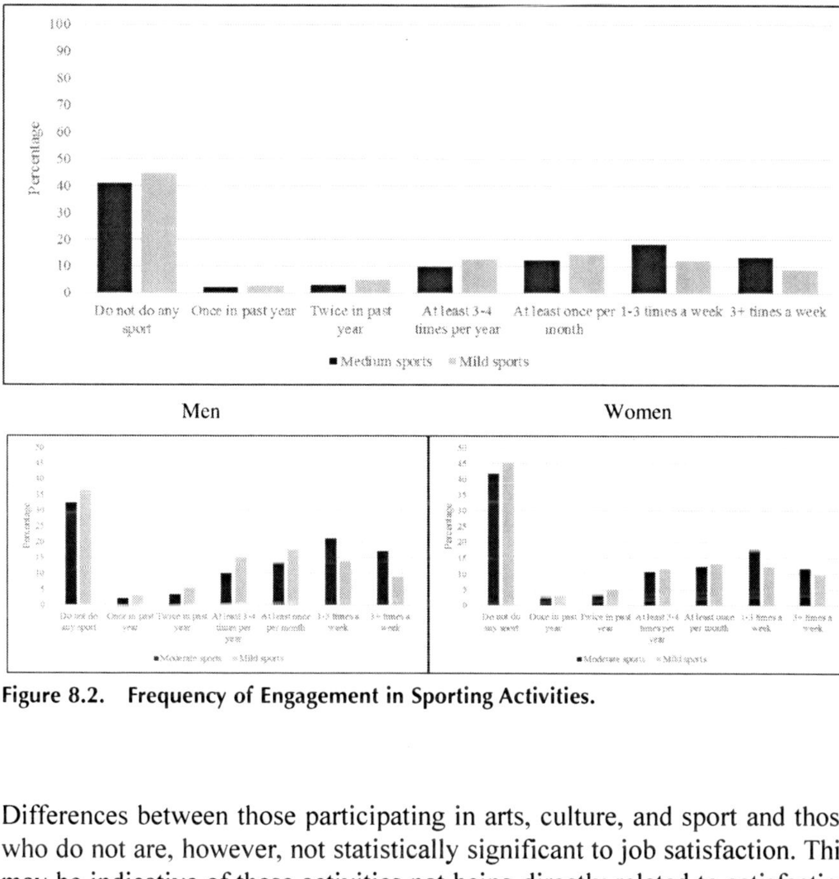

Figure 8.2. Frequency of Engagement in Sporting Activities.

Differences between those participating in arts, culture, and sport and those who do not are, however, not statistically significant to job satisfaction. This may be indicative of these activities not being directly related to satisfaction with work, that is, that positive spillover between domains is not experienced between work and leisure time. This finding provides evidence that is contra some of the findings reported by Hecht and Boies (2009) and Bryson and MacKerron (2013). The descriptive findings are indicative of a positive relationship between arts, cultural, and sporting activities and subjective well-being, but suggest this effect is not present in regards to job satisfaction.

8.4.2 Ordered Probit Regression Analysis

Extending the descriptive analysis, the results of the ordered probit models are summarized in table 8.4. The dependent variables considered are reported satisfaction with life, amount of leisure time, job, and a measure of general happiness, providing reflexive measures of well-being. The dependent variables are derived from responses to Likert scale questions, where 1 = completely unsatisfied, 4 = neither satisfied or unsatisfied, and 7 = completely

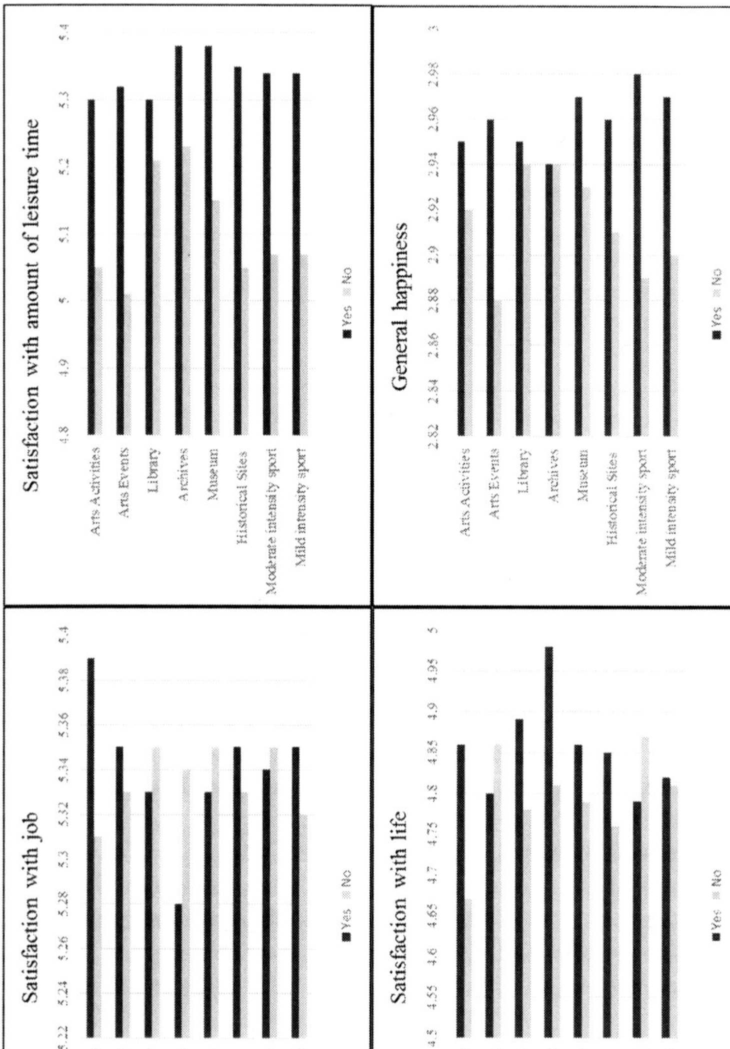

Figure 8.3. Engagement in Arts, Cultural, and Sporting Activities and Subjective Well-Being.

Table 8.4 Ordered Probit Models: Satisfaction and Engagement in Arts, Culture, and Sport

	Ordered Choice Probit Models			
	Satisfaction with Life	*Satisfaction with Amount of Leisure*	*Satisfaction with Job*	*General Happiness*
Age	−0.025***	−0.015***	−0.041***	−0.026***
Age²/100	0.029***	0.022***	0.055***	0.025***
Male	−0.055***	0.102***	−0.127***	0.054***
Long-term illness/disability	−0.373***	−0.221***	−0.150***	−0.321***
Highest educational qualifications: reference is no qualifications				
Degree or equivalent	0.044**	0.048**	0.035	0.029
A level	0.029	0.024	0.019	0.001
GCSE	0.025	0.020	0.039	0.007
Marital status: reference is single/never married or in civil partnership				
Married	0.190***	0.003	0.108***	0.042*
Separated/divorced	−0.071**	−0.098***	0.080**	−0.042
Widowed	−0.009	−0.013	0.211***	−0.052
Number of children in household aged 0–2	0.107***	−0.170***	0.024	0.081***
Number of children in household aged 3–4	−0.017	−0.169***	0.018	0.014
Number of children in household aged 5–11	−0.007	−0.116***	0.039***	−0.004
Number of children in household aged 12–15	−0.038**	−0.070***	0.040**	−0.041**
Government Office Region: reference is East Midlands				
North East	0.016	0.005	−0.075	−0.054
North West	−0.011	−0.036	−0.084**	−0.059
Yorkshire and the Humber	−0.034	0.000	−0.063	−0.100**
West Midlands	−0.054	−0.121***	−0.089**	−0.066
East of England	−0.025	−0.076**	−0.053	−0.096**
London	−0.153***	−0.152***	−0.085*	−0.067
South East	−0.042	−0.049	−0.059	−0.075**
South West	−0.014	0.022	−0.027	−0.089**
Wales	0.019	−0.026	0.040	−0.132***
Scotland	0.008	0.044	−0.011	−0.120***
Northern Ireland	−0.008	−0.013	−0.013	−0.109***
Current economic activity: reference is economically inactive (unemployed, illness/disability, family care)				
Working (employed, self-employed, family worker)	0.275***	−0.234***	—	0.304***
Education/training	0.535***	0.009	—	0.387***
Retired	0.507***	0.577***	—	0.297***
Annual labour income (£000s)	0.002***	−0.001	0.004***	−0.001

(continued)

Table 8.4 (continued)

	Ordered Choice Probit Models			
	Satisfaction with Life	*Satisfaction with Amount of Leisure*	*Satisfaction with Job*	*General Happiness*
Working hours	–0.002**	–0.012***	–0.004***	0.002**
Overtime hours	–0.005***	–0.015***	0.002	–0.004**
Arts, culture and sport variables				
Frequency of arts activities: reference is none				
At least once a week	0.060***	0.077***	0.027	0.001
Limited weekly, but at least monthly	0.020	0.024	0.018	0.000
At least 3/4 times per year	–0.018	–0.030	–0.070**	–0.025
Twice in past year	–0.010	–0.087*	–0.091	–0.060
Once in past year	0.048	–0.033	–0.053	0.038
Frequency of arts events: reference is none				
At least once a week	0.043	0.126**	0.094	0.112**
Limited weekly, but at least monthly	0.075***	0.090***	0.003	0.086***
At least 3/4 times per year	0.059***	0.077***	–0.012	0.021
Twice in past year	0.080***	0.052**	0.002	0.029
Once in past year	0.033	–0.001	0.007	0.003
Frequency of library: reference is none				
At least once a week	–0.050	0.046	0.025	0.038
Limited weekly, but at least monthly	–0.045**	–0.003	–0.018	0.015
At least 3/4 times per year	–0.041*	–0.025	–0.048*	–0.011
Twice in past year	–0.090***	–0.033	–0.043	–0.021
Once in past year	–0.043	–0.025	–0.101*	–0.074
Frequency of archives: reference is none				
At least once a week	–0.025	0.045	0.003	–0.058
Limited weekly, but at least monthly	–0.037	0.044	–0.009	–0.099
At least 3/4 times per year	0.004	–0.024	–0.099	–0.128
Twice in past year	–0.013	–0.074	–0.010	–0.121
Once in past year	0.008	0.007	–0.004	0.027
Frequency of museum: reference is none				
At least once a week	0.316***	0.073	–0.080	–0.009
Limited weekly, but at least monthly	0.080*	0.025	–0.040	0.027
At least 3/4 times per year	0.043*	0.049**	–0.047	0.059**
Twice in past year	0.017	–0.006	–0.036	–0.011
Once in past year	0.016	0.023	–0.039	–0.037
Frequency of historical sites: reference is none				
At least once a week	0.020	–0.041	0.046	0.084

(continued)

Table 8.4 (continued)

	Ordered Choice Probit Models			
	Satisfaction with Life	*Satisfaction with Amount of Leisure*	*Satisfaction with Job*	*General Happiness*
Limited weekly, but at least monthly	0.033	0.007	–0.002	0.036
At least 3/4 times per year	0.047**	0.002	–0.008	0.014
Twice in past year	0.065***	0.050**	0.005	0.083***
Once in past year	0.063***	0.013	0.009	0.042
Frequency of moderate intensity sports: reference is none				
3+ times per week	0.156***	0.269***	–0.003	0.095***
1–3 times per week	0.060***	0.113***	0.007	0.026
Limited weekly, but at least monthly	0.034	0.065***	0.028	0.018
At least 3/4 times per year	0.027	0.035	–0.005	0.004
Twice in past year	–0.017	0.066*	–0.084*	0.009
Once in past year	0.037	0.073	0.021	–0.003
Frequency of mild intensity sports: reference is none				
3+ times per week	0.157***	0.146***	0.054*	0.066**
1–3 times per week	0.131***	0.120***	0.045	0.029
Limited weekly, but at least monthly	0.056**	0.065***	0.020	0.033
At least 3/4 times per year	0.080***	0.048**	0.010	0.013
Twice in past year	0.003	0.034	0.027	–0.042
Once in past year	0.112***	0.010	0.126***	0.022
Other leisure activities Frequency of Internet use: reference is every day				
Several times a week	0.008	–0.016	–0.004	–0.004
Several times a month	0.033	–0.009	–0.043	0.010
Once a month	–0.018	–0.108**	–0.045	0.010
Less than once a month	0.009	–0.021	0.009	–0.043
Never/no access	0.092***	0.000	0.101***	0.062**
Drink/meal with family/ friends at least once a month	0.137***	0.103***	0.061***	0.076***
Model diagnostics				
–2 Log likelihood	73629.233	83194.232	47976.280	36229.716
Chi-square	2579.041	4096.841	487.577	1213.218
Sig.	0.000	0.000	0.000	0.000
Pseudo R-squares				
Cox and Snell	0.100	0.182	0.031	0.048
Nagelkerke	0.105	0.187	0.032	0.061
McFadden	0.034	0.056	0.010	0.032
No. observations	24,376	24,342	15,637	24,643

Notes: Significance levels of 1 percent, 5 percent, and 10 percent are denoted by ***, **, and * respectively. Missing values for income, working hours, and overtime entered as mean.
Sources: From Wheatley and Bickerton (2016b); Understanding Society, wave 2 (2010–2011).

satisfied. General happiness is reported on a 1–4 scale where 1 = much less than usual, 2 = less so than usual, 3 = about the same as usual, and 4 = more so than usual. The dependent variables are regressed against variables measuring engagement with arts, cultural, and sporting activities, and relevant control variables. The analysis provides a series of results consistent with those found in other research with regard to the relationship between a number of demographic and occupational factors. A non-linear relationship is present between satisfaction and age consistent with Blanchflower and Oswald (2008). Consistent with this finding, those with school-age dependent children (in particular children aged twelve to fifteen) also report lower life satisfaction and general happiness. As already noted in chapter 5, dependent children create additional time constraints which can negatively impact on both availability and use of leisure time (Garcia et al., 2007). Individuals who are married report higher levels of job and life satisfaction, and to a lesser extent general happiness. Interestingly, single/never married individuals are the least satisfied with their jobs, perhaps reflecting their career stage, given this group is on average younger, or potentially reflecting the less happy nature of those who remain unmarried as per the assertion of Stutzer and Frey (2006). Men report lower job and overall life satisfaction. This is again consistent with other research. Important gender divisions are also present in other measures of subjective well-being as women report lower satisfaction with the amount of leisure time, and general happiness, reflecting in the prior case their greater household contribution (see Garcia et al., 2007) which limits participation in certain leisure activities (Humphreys and Ruseski, 2006). The presence of a long-term illness/disability has a particularly strong negative association with satisfaction, consistent with the findings reported by Lucas (2007). Education provides less clear results, although those with degree or equivalent qualifications report greater life and leisure satisfaction. Regional variations reveal London as perhaps the most prominent outlier associated with lower life and leisure satisfaction, the latter likely driven by the relatively lengthier working hours and commutes experienced in this region of the United Kingdom (Harvie et al., 2009).

Elements of time-use follow similar patterns to those reported in chapter 4 and in the extant literature, including longer working hours and overtime creating dissatisfaction (see Philp and Wheatley, 2011). In addition, and consistent with the extant literature (Frey and Stutzer, 2002), economic activity variables suggest that those in work, education, or retirement are generally more satisfied than those unemployed or economically inactive. The magnitude of these effects is also particularly pronounced. One exception to this result is that leisure satisfaction is lower among those working than those unemployed. This is likely to reflect the negative impacts of paid work on the availability of leisure time, resulting from long hours, unpaid overtime, travel-to-work, and employer requirements for employees to be flexible and mobile (Wheatley, 2012b). It also suggests that individuals may consider leisure separately from other aspects of their lives, given they report satisfaction with life, job, and general happiness, but less so with leisure. This is further evidence that in some cases spillover between some subjective well-being domains may not be present.

Of primary interest to the analysis in this chapter are the variables which measure time spent in arts, culture, and sport. Engaging in arts activities is associated with greater satisfaction (although only statistically significant for life and amount of leisure). This finding is only present, though, when these activities are engaged with at least once per week, reflecting the importance of regular frequency for these non-passive activities. The majority of the activities comprising the arts activities category require active participation, for example, playing a musical instrument or acting in a play. Participating in these activities is likely to provide cumulative benefits in satisfaction through the act of performing, feelings of purpose, and social interaction (Wood and Smith, 2004; Creech et al., 2013). In contrast, more passive activities including attending arts events are more broadly associated with positive effects on satisfaction. A range of the arts activities, including singing and playing a musical instrument, and arts events, including attending concerts and musicals/opera, are music-centric. This finding is therefore consistent with, and extends, the extant research. This is evident in respect to life and leisure satisfaction, and to a lesser extent general happiness. Although the descriptive findings are indicative of greater life satisfaction among those visiting libraries and archives, this is not borne out in the regression analysis. The inclusion of controls actually suggests that these activities may be negatively associated with satisfaction, although statistically insignificant for archives. The exact drivers of this finding remain unclear, but could reflect some of those visiting libraries and archives being in lower socio-economic groups and thus other factors act as drivers of their relative satisfaction.

Museums and historical sites, which both exhibit a number of 'cultural characteristics', are associated with higher levels of satisfaction. A positive relationship with life satisfaction is present when museum visits are frequent, although high frequency isn't necessary in order for well-being benefits to be present as visiting museums at least three to four times per year is associated with greater life and leisure satisfaction and general happiness. Visiting historical sites less frequently (twice in the past year and once in past year, the latter for life satisfaction only) is also found to have a positive relationship with satisfaction. This finding could also be indicative of these types of heritage sites often being less frequently visited, in part as a result of the limited accessibility of some sites (Marsh et al., 2010, 19). Some of the strongest well-being effects are present with respect to participation in moderate and mild sport. Particularly positive leisure experiences appear to be generated from these types of activity, extending the extant literature (Downward and Rasciute, 2011; Bryson and MacKerron, 2013). In contrast to the other activities considered, participation in mild intensity sport does have a positive association with job satisfaction, consistent with Hecht and Boies (2009). This is likely to reflect involvement in recreational sporting activities organized within the workplace which generate positive impacts on well-being through improving social networks and generating feelings of 'togetherness' (Hamermesh, 2002; Downward and Rasciute, 2011). However, the analysis also suggests that the benefits of moderate non-passive sporting activities are only realized when engaged with regularly (more than three times per week, one to three times per week, and limited weekly, but at least once monthly).

Variables considering 'other' leisure activities, including the frequency of Internet use and whether respondents entertain family or friends for a drink/meal at least once a month, provide some interesting additional insight into aspects of subjective well-being. The presence of social networks, evident in the latter of the two measures, is associated with higher levels of well-being, especially life and leisure satisfaction, evident in the magnitude of the effects. This likely reflects the benefit of regular human interaction and corresponds with Headey (2008) who identifies family, friends, and community as being associated with greater satisfaction. With respect to Internet use significant associations are found between those who never use or have no access to the Internet and life and job satisfaction and general happiness. As the majority of those in this group are older individuals who are shown to report greater satisfaction (82.9 percent of the Understanding Society sample reporting never/no access are aged over fifty, with 43.8 percent aged seventy or over) this finding may be more a function of age than evidencing the specific effects of Internet use. The remaining associations for frequency of internet use are largely insignificant. The ordered probit models provide evidence in support of the suggested positive leisure experience generated from arts, culture, and sport. The exception to this, however, is job satisfaction, where few positive associations are found with the exception of mild intensity sport. It may be inferred from this that there may be limited or no spillover from the majority of these leisure activities into well-being at work. Mild sport, perhaps through strengthening social networks and 'togetherness' with colleagues, offers the exception. Remaining arts, cultural, and sporting activities may be considered 'peripheral' or 'separate' to job satisfaction, perhaps indicative of divisions in the way in which individuals consider work and leisure time.

8.5 CHAPTER SUMMARY: IS LEISURE THE SOURCE OF HAPPINESS?

According to mainstream approaches in economics, time spent engaged in leisure activities should, in principle, act as a significant source of utility. A number of factors can act to constrain the availability of leisure time and the way in which this time is spent, including spillover between other activities including work and household time into leisure time. To better understand the impact of different uses of leisure time, including time spent engaged in arts, cultural, and sporting activities, as well as Internet use and a measure of time spent with family/friends, this chapter has explored the relationship between how we use our leisure time and a number of measures of both domain and overall subjective well-being. The chapter has also contributed to our understanding of the leisure experience (Ateca-Amestoy, 2011) derived from participation and engagement in arts, cultural, and sporting activities, and the degree to which consumption of these activities generates a range of benefits, including to physical and mental well-being, potentially acting as a source of cultural value (Throsby, 2001, 2006). The evidence present in the existing literature has been extended through consideration of a broader range of activities drawing on the analysis of large-scale UK data from wave 2 (2010–2011) of Understanding Society reported in Wheatley and Bickerton (2016b).

Examining patterns of engagement reveals stark differences between activities which are frequent in their engagement, including arts events, arts activities, and moderate sports, and those that are infrequent including visiting libraries and archives. Analysis of the relationship between time spent in these activities and subjective well-being has generated a number of key findings. The analysis suggests that a positive leisure experience is derived from participation in arts, culture, and sport. The analysis identifies a positive relationship between satisfaction with life, amount of leisure time, and to a lesser extent general happiness, and those that attend arts events, visit historical sites and museums, and engage in moderate and mild sports. This corresponds with, and extends, previous research, and is indicative of the positive leisure experience derived from these activities. The presence of social networks is also found to have a positive relationship with the measures of subjective well-being considered, especially life and leisure satisfaction. Not all leisure pursuits appear to generate a positive leisure experience, however, as visiting libraries and archives is associated with lower satisfaction, although the exact drivers of this relationship remain unclear. Meanwhile, Internet use is found to be largely insignificant. Allied with the findings of research focusing on time spent watching television (Knabe et al., 2010, 875;

Frey and Benesch, 2008) this findings highlights that certain activities which account for a considerable amount of leisure time, may actually deliver few, if any, benefits to well-being.

The analysis also highlights the relevance of frequency of engagement in different leisure activities. Those participating in arts activities and sports on a regular basis report greater satisfaction. Indeed the characteristics of leisure activities, and frequency of engagement, are important in understanding the well-being benefits derived from them. This is also important given the gendered variations evident in engagement in the arts, which is more predominant among women, and sport which is more common among men. The results are indicative of non-passive activities which require greater personal effort, and/ or generate specific cumulative benefits, having positive well-being effects only when engaged with at least once per week. In contrast, less frequent engagement in more passive activities, including visiting historical sites, and to a lesser extent museums, generates benefits to well-being. Attendance of arts events is found to have a positive relationship irrespective of frequency, indicative of the general benefit of these leisure experiences. These findings do not contradict activity theory as such, but do suggest a more nuanced approach is needed when considering frequency of engagement in leisure activities (Michalos and Kahlke, 2010, 2008; Michalos, 2005).

The findings are indicative of activities which exhibit a number of 'cultural characteristics' as identified by Throsby (2001), including arts activities and events, visiting museums and historical sites, and certain sporting activities, delivering well-being benefits even when engaged with less frequently. These activities could, as such, act as a source of cultural value (Throsby, 2001, 27). It should be noted that, although generating well-being benefits including spillover to satisfaction with work, the cultural value of certain sports (and other activities) remains questionable due to their inherent characteristics. It is also not possible, given the limitations of the data presented, to measure the relative magnitude of the cultural value derived from the activities considered. Finally, the analysis suggests that with the exception of engagement in mild sport, spillover from leisure activities into job satisfaction is not present. The only exception to this is regular engagement in mild sports consistent with some of the findings presented by Hecht and Boies (2009) and Hamermesh (2002). While participation and engagement in arts, cultural, and sporting activities is found to have a positive relationship with life and leisure satisfaction and general happiness, this finding is not present in satisfaction with work. Adding to our understanding of the complex relationship between paid work and leisure, the negative relationship with leisure satisfaction found among workers compared with those unemployed may be indicative of the reduction in amount (and quality) of leisure time experienced by working individuals.

The causality present in the relationship between time spent in a number of leisure activities and subjective well-being does require further investigation. It is important that we obtain a greater understanding of whether engagement in leisure activities drives satisfaction, or whether lack of access, perhaps as a result of socio-economic factors, is manifest in lower satisfaction. This follows the assertion by Ateca-Amestoy (2011, 70) that access to cultural goods will increase quality of life as individuals have the option to use assets and also benefit from the 'symbolic' value of their existence. Nevertheless, the analysis presented contributes to our understanding of the relationship between a range of uses of leisure time and subjective well-being, evidencing the positive leisure experiences associated with a number of these activities.

NOTES

1. Frequency of engagement in sporting activities is asked using a different, seven-point, scale to arts and cultural activities, which are asked on a six-point scale.
2. Statistical significance in the patterns observed was confirmed using between groups ANOVA tests.

Chapter Nine

The Organization of Time and Subjective Well-Being

Key Findings and Implications for Public and Organizational Policy

9.1 INTRODUCTION

Time is spent in a range of activities which vary throughout the lifecourse of an individual. For the majority, the way time is spent follows a broadly consistent, ordered pattern. Individuals spend much of their formative lives in education and leisure, before transitioning into paid work. At certain stages of the lifecourse paid work is combined in some cases with childcare (and other caring acts), while breaks in paid work may be experienced for a range of reasons, for example, dependent children, ill health, unemployment, and so on. Finally, retirement brings with it increased leisure time, which offers greater opportunities to engage in activities such as voluntary work. This latter phase of the lifecourse is also associated with further demands to provide care and/or individuals becoming the recipients of care. While this broad pattern to time-use can be observed for many, as we have seen throughout this book, there are a number of important considerations which render our relationship with time complex, and gendered. How we use our time is a product not only of free choice, but reflects consideration for others and the presence of constraint, which have important consequences to our relative well-being. This book has combined exploration of existing literature with mixed method analysis of primary and secondary data drawn from a post-industrial society, the United Kingdom, providing insight into the relationships present between uses of time – including work, housework, care, volunteering, travel, and leisure – and subjective well-being. This final chapter draws together the key findings from each of the chapters of the book to consider, holistically, the relationship between how we use our time and our well-being. Specific consideration is also given within the chapter to both organizational and public policy implications arising from the analyses presented in the book, and some reflection is offered on the validity of subjective well-being measures in enhancing our understanding of well-being.

9.2 TIME WELL SPENT? KEY FINDINGS CONCERNING THE ORGANIZATION OF TIME

Throughout the book a range of forms of time-use have been explored with specific consideration given to the relationship between how we spend our time and our reported well-being. As outlined in chapter 1, the book is not exhaustive in its consideration of time. Detailed reflection has not, for example, been given to the impact of time spent sleeping, shown to have relevance to reported life satisfaction (Kahneman and Krueger, 2006). Meanwhile, certain forms of leisure time have not been considered in detail (e.g., television watching), although similarly these have been reflected upon, at least briefly, in both chapters 1 and 8. Initially centring on paid work, the exploration of time offered in the book has considered both the relationship between specific uses of time and well-being, and also the connections and spillovers present in the ways we use our time, generating a number of key findings.

9.2.1 Paid Work

Hours spent in paid work appear to have an inverse u-shaped relationship with subjective well-being (Meier and Stutzer, 2006). Both unemployment and underemployment (those expressing preferences for more hours of work) are associated with lower levels of well-being. This finding is relevant as growing flexibilization of the labour market has resulted in rising numbers of workers in the United Kingdom reporting working reduced hours due to a lack of full-time opportunities (ONS, 2015d). However, those subject to extensive hours of labour also report lower well-being, evidencing the complex relationship between work and how we use our time. Work, whether paid or unpaid, accounts for a considerable use of time, especially among those working full-time and in certain occupations. Evidence continues to show lengthy hours of work in the UK economy, especially in managerial and professional occupations (Ford and Collinson, 2011; Messenger, 2011; Philp and Wheatley, 2011). The presence of long hours is a concern as time spent working is forgone, that is, time spent in these activities cannot be spent undertaking other, potentially more pleasurable, acts. Long working hours, as a result, have particularly negative impacts on leisure satisfaction (Ateca-Amestoy et al., 2008; Van Praag and Ferrer-i-Carbonell, 2004), and may have wider negative impacts on satisfaction with job and life. However, as is clear from the findings in chapter 4, our understanding of paid work should not be oversimplified and it should not be considered solely as a source of disutility. Consistent with mainstream approaches in economics, the presence of work is important in providing necessary income to use in other areas of life. However, work itself can also act as a source of identity, fulfilment, and enjoyment, at least in some respects (Spencer, 2009), although this does depend to some degree on the relative 'fit' of a job with the preferences of a worker, that is, an individual undertaking a particular role due to a lack of alternative employment opportunities will likely report few, if any, positive effects on well-being. The intrinsic rewards that can be derived from work – including feelings of purpose and fulfilment, and providing a structure to time-use – often act as a driver for participation in voluntary work following an exit from paid employment, for example, due to retirement, or among those unable to engage in paid work, for example, as a result of a disability. While most individuals may outwardly show preferences for most other activities over work, a life without work is, for the majority, a highly undesirable outcome.

In addition to the extent of work, both the quality and intensity of work are also important to well-being. Intensive work routines may reduce job satisfaction, and create wider negative impacts as individuals may be too tired, for example, to engage in social activities. Evidence is reported in support of this assertion in both chapters 4 and 7, pertaining to patterns of travel-for-work in the latter case. The quality of work has implications for job satisfaction, but may also extend to other domains of well-being (Brown et al., 2012; Galletta et al., 2011; Gallie, 2007). Autonomy and control over aspects of paid work are significant, as higher degrees of autonomy offer greater scope to manage work, even intense work routines, around other aspects of life. Greater autonomy also allows individuals to tailor their working routines to their own preferences. In contrast, application of low discretion Taylorist work organization often demotivates employees, increasing shirking behaviours and reducing retention rates within organizations. Discretion over the timing, location, and way in which work is conducted is highly relevant to the relationship between paid work and well-being.

9.2.2 The Household Division of Labour and Flexibility in Work

While household models are increasingly divergent from the traditional male breadwinner, female homemaker model, the household division of labour remains central to understanding gendered patterns of time-use, and the implications these have for subjective well-being. Women continue to undertake the majority of housework in most households, accounting for up to two hours per day, and approximately double the time of men. Care, particularly for dependent children, also predominantly remains the domain of women, accounting for substantial demands on time (Garcia et al., 2007, 2011; Lundberg and Pollak, 2007, 6–7). Household constructs are increasingly varied, including one and a half worker, dual worker, and dual career households (Hardill and Wheatley, 2009; Hochschild and Machung, 1990; Lewis, 2001). However, even in the latter construct – which in principle should have no lead career present, and therefore no prioritization of one career over another – decisions over the household division of labour which impact upon paid work and careers, at least at certain stages during the lifecourse, are less than egalitarian (Hardill and Wheatley, 2009, 239; Wheatley and Wu, 2014).

The gendered household division of labour results in a considerable need for flexibility among many women, if they are to avoid labour market exit or at least the negative career implications often associated with short-term career gaps or reductions in participation in paid work (Atkinson and Hall, 2009, 663). Use of flexible working arrangements offer a range of potential benefits to well-being, for both men and women, through enabling better management of paid work alongside household responsibilities. However, those flexible working arrangements more often used by women, including reduced hours options, for example, part-time and job share, appear to have negative relationships with satisfaction with work and other aspects of life, reflecting less than ideal outcomes from the 'choice' to work flexibly (Fagan et al, 2012; Wheatley, 2016). Impacts are likely to remain highly gendered unless broader societal change is enacted to reduce the household burden many women continue to experience.

9.2.3 Care and Volunteering

Care and volunteering are activities which are closely tied, but are also distinct at least in certain respects, in their relationship with subjective well-being. Care takes many forms from childcare, to grandparenting, caring for ill/elderly kin and non-kin, and volunteering, although not all volunteering is associated with performing acts of care. Certain forms of care remain more commonly the responsibility of women, including childcare and grandparenting. As such time spent caring continues to reflect key disparities in the household division of labour (see chapters 5 and 6). Volunteering, meanwhile, is gendered but patterns of volunteering are perhaps more centrally influenced by the lifecourse than being a product of gender norms. The greater propensity to provide care among women can, though, limit the time available for volunteering. Patterns of volunteering vary considerably throughout the lifecourse (Neuberger, 2008), closely tied to periods of education, paid work (especially for men), caring responsibilities, and retirement which often acts as a trigger to volunteer. It also appears that in some cases undertaking unpaid caring acts for kin may limit engagement in volunteering, especially where paid work is also present creating particular demands on time-use. Individuals in their twenties and thirties are those most affected by dual responsibilities of paid work and care. A number of exceptions are found, though, including those who volunteer in organizations which are associated with their caring responsibilities, for example, parents volunteering at a sports club attended by their child(ren) (Nichols and Shepherd, 2006).

As a result of the differing drivers of informal care and volunteering, a contrasting relationship appears to be present between certain forms of care and subjective well-being. Where care is imposed on an individual, or it is perceived in this way, it is likely to act as a constraint to time-use, limiting labour market participation (Drinkwater, 2015), temporal and spatial mobility (Wheatley, 2013, 2014), time available for leisure activities (Wheatley and Wu, 2014), and opportunities to volunteer. Care, in some cases, is therefore associated with lower levels of well-being. Volunteering, meanwhile, by its nature is undertaken with a greater degree of choice (Zappala, 2000) at times in the lifecourse when more time is available to engage in this act, including following retirement. Findings suggest formal and informal volunteering offers both extrinsic rewards, for example, career/skill development, and intrinsic well-being benefits. In the latter case, evidence is indicative of a positive relationship between greater frequency of volunteering and life satisfaction. The qualitative evidence reported in chapter 6 supports and extends these findings, providing a number of examples of enjoyment and fulfilment being derived from these acts, including volunteering providing individuals with a role in the community (Grimm et al., 2007), and satisfaction being derived from helping others.

9.2.4 Travel

Human activity has become increasingly mobile in nature (Aguiléra, 2008; Felstead et al., 2005; Hislop and Axtell, 2009). Travel provides access to paid and unpaid work, including volunteering, and is used to conduct work, to access leisure activities, and fulfil household tasks, while travel itself can also be engaged in as a leisure activity. The ability to travel further afield and 'be more mobile' enabled by developments in technology, but also importantly by access to this technology, offers a range of benefits including the potential to engage with significantly larger labour market areas, enjoy more distant leisure activities, and choose residential locations which more closely match preferences. However, a number of constraints are present which limit the ability, at least of certain groups, to realize these benefits. Imperfections in labour and housing markets may render lengthier travel a necessity as individuals and households face challenges in gaining employment in a location close to their place of residence. These difficulties have led to a growth in commuter couples, and long distance commuting patterns (Hardill, 2002; Sandow and Westin, 2010; Sandow, 2014). Evidence suggests that the commute is a significant source of dissatisfaction. While most individuals have a commuting tolerance equivalent to around thirty to forty-five minutes per journey (Clark et al., 2003), lengthier commutes remain a feature for many workers, especially those whose work routines conform to the '9 to 5', resulting in peak-time travel on congested networks. The most common method of transport, the car, is also the source of the greatest dissatisfaction.

Limited mobility, in contrast, can also act as a significant source of dissatisfaction and may reflect socio-economic status or residential location which prohibits access to transport. Gender also has an important role. Women may be constrained in their labour market mobility, in regard to both regular travel-to-work (commuting) and travel-for-work, as a result of household responsibilities including caring for dependent children. Constraint of this nature, referred to as spatial entrapment, has important implications for time spent in work through limiting access to only local labour market areas, with potentially significant impacts on career development and the well-being derived from paid work (Hanson and Pratt, 1995; Wheatley, 2013, 2014). Moreover, the presence of substantive household responsibilities creates complex and highly demanding patterns of time-use as work, household, and travel time become blurred and time available for other activities including leisure is squeezed.

Travel-for-work, although often infrequent among workers, requires a substantial time input and has impacts on paid work, leisure, and family time, as well as broader well-being, including health (Bergman and Gustafson, 2008; Gustafson, 2014). It is associated with potentially important career benefits (Bonache, 2005; Gustafson, 2006, 2014; Lassen 2010; Thurlow and Jaworski 2006), and some of the negative impacts can be mediated by planning this travel and undertaking travel with others. Nevertheless travel-for-work can create work-family conflict through absence from home, reduced leisure time, and reduced quality of family/leisure time due to tiredness and other side effects. Travel also has other important impacts on leisure time, in particular, in influencing how we use our leisure time. For example, reduced access to transport as a result of socio-economic factors and/or geographical location has spillover effects into leisure time, as the ability to enjoy certain leisure experiences which are more distant, such as accessing historical sites, is restricted (Marsh et al., 2010).

9.2.5 Leisure

Leisure time has been considered in this book in regard to engagement in a wide range of arts, cultural, and sporting activities, as well as time spent using the Internet and socializing with family/friends. A range of leisure activities are found to have positive association with subjective well-being. Activities which involve more active participation, for example, playing an instrument, are found to have particularly positive relationships with well-being when undertaken frequently. Meanwhile, visiting museums and historical sites, and other more culturally focused activities, appear to return positive impacts when visited less frequently. Overall, leisure activities appear to be a significant source of satisfaction. In the case of certain activities including, for example, attending arts events, visiting historical sites or a museum, they may also act as a significant source of cultural value (Throsby, 2001, 2006; Wheatley and Bickerton, 2016a). Limited access in some cases may reduce the benefits felt from these activities, though, as outlined in the previous section.

Important in the context of connections between uses of time, leisure activities are not generally found to have direct relevance to satisfaction with work. Interestingly, more collaborative activities, including casual team sports, do appear to have a positive relationship with job satisfaction, perhaps associated with feelings of togetherness (Hamermesh, 2002). While the causality of this relationship could be questioned, that is, happier individuals may be more inclined to engage in these group activities, this finding nevertheless has relevance to organizations in evidencing the potential positive spillover into the workplace from providing employees with opportunities for social activities. It is also important to reflect on a number of leisure activities which account for substantial time-use, at least among certain groups, including television watching and time spent using the Internet, which have been shown to have potentially negative relationships with well-being (Frey and Benesch, 2008; Putnam, 2000), although evidence remains conflicting (Amichai-Hamburge and Hayat, 2011, 587–88; Contarello and Sarrica, 2007, 1029). The fact that these activities do not appear to provide well-being benefits is highly relevant given the increasing propensity for leisure time to be spent browsing the Internet including engaging with social media (Buglass et al., 2015).

9.2.6 Blurred Boundaries and Complex Interconnections in Time-Use

Although the way in which we use our time has been considered in a series of separate chapters in this book, it is important to reflect on the complex, and often blurred, connections present between different uses of time. The presence of spillover is responsible for a good degree of the complexity present in patterns of time-use. Researching time-use, in this regard, is challenging and imperfect, but nevertheless provides important insights into the way we spend our lives and how the organization of time affects our well-being.

Figure 9.1 summarizes the range of interactions between key elements of time-use considered in this book. It evidences the complex interplay and wide range of different activities that most individuals engage with on a regular basis. As already discussed paid work represents a substantial component of the time-use of many individuals, both on a short-term daily, weekly, or monthly basis, and also throughout the lifecourse. Aspects of paid work, in some cases, intersect with leisure activity. For example, an individual may spend some of their spare time undertaking research required in their job, common among academics, which may also act as a 'hobby' for the individual in their spare time. Moreover, the spillover between paid work and leisure time can extend into social activities as social networks are often closely tied to the workplace thus impacting the way in which time is spent outside of paid work. For many individuals, and particularly women, a substantial portion of time outside, or instead, of paid work is spent performing unpaid informal care (Garcia et al., 2011; Wheatley and Wu, 2014; Woolvin and Hardill, 2013). The provision of care, and more formal voluntary work, are similarly closely connected, although it should again be acknowledged that while volunteering can include voluntary acts of care, not all volunteering is associated with care. As evidenced in chapter 6 those undertaking acts of care for family or friends may extend this activity into more formal volunteering, for example, parents volunteering at a school or community centre their child attends, or an older adult providing support at a local day centre or luncheon club attended by an ill/elderly relative. Spillover is also present between volunteering and both paid work and leisure. For example, workplace groups or teams may participate in employee-supported volunteering (ESV) schemes (NCVO, 2016; Booth et al., 2009, 242–43), while households may participate in family volunteering.

Chapter 7 explored the impacts of time spent undertaking work-related travel, which extends the impact of paid work on time-use, as both commuting and travel-for-work are driven by the presence of paid work, and in the prior case the geographical separation usually present between workplace and home. The commute bridges home and work (Basmajian, 2010, 77), while it is also combined with household and caring acts, including the school run and shopping, creating further blurring and often representing a site of constraint and gender inequality (Wheatley, 2013, 2014). Travel-for-work is a requirement of the employer, but also facilitates the completion of work, generation of new work, generation/maintenance of networks, and skill development. It also highlights the continued need for face-to-face interaction as it remains favoured over alternatives including virtual meetings. Travel also spills over into leisure time, as it may be undertaken in order to access a leisure activity, while travel itself can act as a leisure activity, for example, enjoying a drive in the countryside (Moktharian and Solomon, 2001). Access to travel

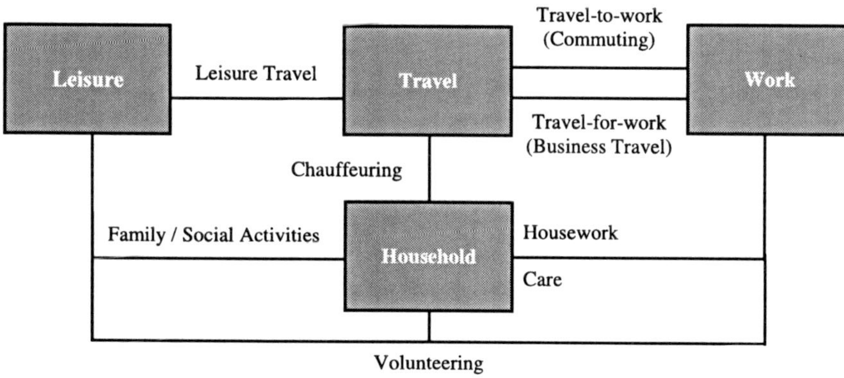

Figure 9.1. Interactions Between Work, Household, Travel and Leisure Time.

is, therefore, important to how we spend our leisure time, as reflected upon in chapter 8.

Blurred boundaries between forms of time-use have implications at individual, household, organizational, and societal level. They create challenges in designing policy both at (inter)national and workplace level, and also raise important questions regarding decision-making within households and at the level of the individual. It is also important to acknowledge that many forms of time-use can be marketized, and themselves represent paid work for those performing these acts, including, for example, household tasks such as cleaning, as discussed in chapter 5, as well as various caring and leisure activities. Substitution therefore occurs in some cases, as individuals/households exchange household labour for marketized labour; however this is only available to those that can afford to make such a substitution. At the same time many paid work activities can be performed voluntarily both formally and informally. Against a backdrop of recent public sector austerity measures taken in many post-industrial economies the role of voluntary work has become increasingly important. As noted earlier, how we quantify or define a use of time can, therefore, be argued as highly important to how it is perceived, and its relative impacts on well-being.

9.3 CHOICE, TOGETHERNESS, AND WELL-BEING

A number of important patterns and relationships have been identified between how we spend our time and subjective well-being. Certain underlying factors appear central to how different uses of time affect well being, though, including the level of choice involved in patterns of time-use observed and the role of personal relationships and social contact. Reflecting on patterns of time spent in paid work, household time including care, volunteering, travel, and leisure, the role of choice is undoubtedly a key factor in the relative well-being derived from an activity. Free-choice, subject to an opportunity cost arising from alternatives forgone, is a common assumption in mainstream models in economics. However, the evidence presented highlights that a range of constraints are faced by individuals at various stages in the lifecourse. The relative balance present between choice and constraint has important implications for well-being.

Reflecting on paid work, for example, greater levels of control and autonomy over paid work, and flexibility over both the arrangement of work-time and the location of paid work, provide well-being benefits reflected in reported job satisfaction and broader measures of happiness. Meanwhile, some workers may choose to 'volunteer' their time to their employer, working unpaid overtime, if they derive added value from this activity from feelings of fulfilment or improved career prospects, for example, in the case of travel-for-work. However, current evidence suggests that, on average, many workers continue to undertake patterns of paid employment which do not meet with their preferences. Hours remain long for some while others are underemployed, or unemployed, and unpaid overtime more often reflects a constraint and is thus strongly associated with negative well-being effects. Lack of choice regarding engagement in paid work, including reduced participation resulting from household and caring responsibilities, is also associated with negative impacts on well-being. Reflecting further on the household and care, the presence of constraint and inequality in household decision-making continues to burden women with a substantially greater household contribution. Women may therefore be limited in their access to paid work and its potential rewards, as already noted, while these patterns of time-use often create challenges in the organization of time which leave them experiencing significant work-life conflict, in particular during the middle part of their lives. Travel represents an interesting component of time-use with regard to choice. The commute, in principle, represents a choice as individuals determine where they live and work; however, this is subject to constraint and compromise related to household decision-making and imperfections in labour and housing markets. In practice, as a result, the commute is often undertaken under conditions of constraint. A degree of choice should similarly be present in travel-for-work, as individuals choose their occupation and when doing this should be aware of associated employer expectations surrounding travel. However, labour market imperfections result in compromise in the choice of occupation, and the presence of power among employers to exert pressure on workers to be flexible and mobile.

Both volunteering and time spent in leisure, generally, deliver benefits to well-being. Volunteering by its nature is undertaken by choice, although this may be influenced in some cases by social norms and the desire for extrinsic rewards. The evidence presented, extending existing literature, highlights a range of benefits to well-being for both the volunteer, and in cases of voluntary acts of care, the recipient. How we spend our leisure time similarly reflects a higher degree of choice, and is associated with a range of benefits to well-being, although how leisure time is spent is impacted by income, and in turn paid work, and associated access to certain leisure activities. Compromise may also be present as the preferences of others within the household, and in wider social networks, impact the use of leisure time. Leisure is also often the element of time-use which is squeezed when spillover is present from other activities, including paid work and care.

Personal relationships and contact with others also appear to be important determinants of the relative well-being effects of a range of uses of time. Spending time with family and friends is associated with a range of well-being benefits reported in existing literature and in the empirical analyses in this book. Meanwhile, the evidence presented has shown the relevance of togetherness to the experience of a range of activities. For example, participating in team sports with work colleagues has been found to have positive effects on job satisfaction. Meanwhile, undertaking travel-for-work with others can mediate some of the negative effects associated with this activity. There may also be opportunities to compound the well-being benefits associated with a number of activities through undertaking them with others. For example, engaging in group volunteering with family, friends, or colleagues (including ESV). In contrast, significant time spent in certain activities, even in leisure time, when a product of isolation and loneliness, for example, watching TV and using information and communication technologies (ICTs), can have negative effects on well-being. In the paid work sphere face-to-face contact continues to act as a primary driver for how time is spent. Despite the increasingly globalized nature of economic activity, the desire for face-to-face contact drives patterns of mobility, reflected in patterns of travel-for-work. It remains preferred over virtual alternatives offered by ICTs in order to build and maintain relationships and trust. Meanwhile, workers can benefit from extending professional networks facilitating career progression. In some cases a reliance on face-to-face interaction can limit opportunities for flexibility and could reflect a tendency for management to engage in excessive monitoring and supervision of workers. Balance is again essential in order to facilitate positive outcomes for both organizations and employees. Finally, it should also be noted that while these observations are consistent with the relationship between time-use and well-being for the majority, some individuals will derive well-being benefits in a contrasting manner, for example, enjoying time spent alone engaged in leisure activities or with animals e.g., walking a dog, or completing tasks alone for paid work.

9.4 IMPLICATIONS FOR ORGANIZATIONAL AND PUBLIC POLICY

9.4.1 Time-Use and Well-Being: Revisiting the UK Policy Context

Despite the United Kingdom's liberal stance on public policy intervention, especially concerning the labour market (Lewis and Campbell, 2008), a wide range of both public and organizational policy has both direct and indirect effects on time-use. Aggregated patterns show reductions in working hours in a historical context, evidencing the long-term effect of policy focused on work-time from the introduction of the Factory Acts in the nineteenth century to the more recent Working Time Regulations. However, there remains evidence of long hours (Ford and Collinson, 2011; Messenger, 2011; Philp and Wheatley, 2011), highlighting a continued need for policy focused on the extent of work-time. Indeed, while requirements for presence in the workplace may have reduced, this problem still persists. A growing concern, though, relates to presence of intensive labour extraction in many workplaces (Green, 2004; Kalleberg, 2012). It is increasingly the intensity of work, reflected in high workloads, tight deadlines, and deliverables, that raises perhaps greater concerns regarding worker well-being (Boxall and Macky, 2014; Grönlund, 2007; Kalleberg et al., 2009). Moreover, this is more problematic to effectively address through policy. It is challenging to consistently measure how hard an individual is working, and therefore, problematic to design and enact policy to address exploitation of workers in this regard. Measurement is particularly problematic in the service sector, which accounts for the greatest portion of employment in post-industrial societies.

Evidence in both the existing literature, and the analysis presented in chapter 5, identifies an increased awareness of the potential benefits of flexibility in paid work for both employee and employer (BIS, 2010; Glavin and Schieman, 2012; Jang et al., 2011; Woodland, 2003). Challenges are present, though, in current implementation as UK public policy through the Flexible Working Regulations remains subject to decision-making around 'business need'. Evidence reflects poor practice among some employers who have identified ways of using flexibility primarily as a method of reducing costs through a more flexible workforce, including use of zero hours contracts, agency, temporary and gig work (Fagan et al., 2012, 40; Friedman, 2014; Gregory and Milner, 2009, 123; Poelmans and Beham, 2008). Underemployment, as a result, is a growing feature of the UK labour market, which itself represents a significant public policy concern. Good practice does exist, and evidence supports the notion of win-win for both employee and employers when flexibility is used effectively, including the potential for employees to receive a number of well-being benefits, such as increased satisfaction with job and leisure time. Policy has been enacted, in particular in the past two decades, which has sought to provide greater opportunities to engage in paid work among those with significant caring responsibilities, including the Carers (Equal Opportunities) Act 2004, the Flexible Working Regulations which initially had a specific focus on providing flexibility in paid work for carers, and the recent Shared Parental Leave Regulations 2014. However, the evidence shows that care, including both childcare and ill/elderly care, often results in reduced participation in paid work, and can lead to labour market exit. This is particularly prevalent among women as they remain the primary caregivers in most households, reflecting important gender inequity in access to paid work throughout the lifecourse (Crosier and Warburton, 2001; Drinkwater, 2015, 281–84; Garcia et al., 2011; Hardill and Baines, 2011). Since the latter part of the twentieth century there have been concerted efforts to increase labour market participation among mothers – including single parents – as they are expected to either be in employment or looking for work, rather than relying on welfare (Lewis and Campbell, 2008, 5356). Public policy continues to struggle to enact effective change to address these issues, however, as many households remain less than egalitarian.

Both formal and informal volunteering have been considered in this book, with peaks of participation found present among young and older adults. Formal volunteering is often undertaken through an associated charity. Charities are governed in the United Kingdom by the Charities Act 2011, which provides rules and regulations for the registration and operation of Charities in England and Wales. For young people, the National Citizen Service, available to those aged sixteen to seventeen since 2011, offers a more formal extrinsic reward from engaging in formal voluntary activity. As well as extrinsic benefits, the evidence is indicative of significant intrinsic benefits (Meier and Stutzer, 2008), as the volunteer (and recipient) receive well-being benefits from voluntary acts. The findings pertaining to patterns of volunteering, and associated rewards, are also important as reductions in public sector provision and increased pressure for individuals to remain in the labour market, including into older age, are acting concurrently to increase demand, but potentially limit the supply of volunteers.

Government and international policy in recent decades has had a strong focus on reductions in car and air travel, as part of wider concerns relating to global warming (H.M. Treasury, 2006; DfT, 2006, 2007; Pooley et al., 2005, 226–27). However, these concerns have come to the policy forefront during a time when increasingly high levels of mobility are being witnessed as a result of globalization and other changes to the organization of paid work (Aguiléra, 2008; Felstead et al., 2005; Hislop and Axtell, 2009). With respect to the continued reliance on the car, from a practical perspective the key challenge remains around the ability of public transport to effectively support required levels of mobility. The evidence in this book, further, acknowledges a range of benefits and difficulties associated with highly mobile lifestyles (Gustafson, 2012a, 2014). Finally, while leisure time is less subject to direct policy intervention in comparison to other forms of time-use, it is affected indirectly by a range of policy as a result of leisure time being both directly and indirectly influenced by the way we spend the rest of our time. Reductions in public funding of the arts, as part of wider austerity measures, could result in reduced access to certain leisure amenities, including those that act as a source of cultural value, for example, museums and historical sites. Meanwhile, lengthy and/or intense work routines, for example, reduce leisure time and impact the way this time is used (Ateca-Amestoy et al., 2008; Van Praag and Ferrer-i-Carbonell, 2004; Wheatley et al., 2008). Meanwhile the provision of care can both limit leisure time with associated negative well-being effects (Garcia et al., 2007), and impact the ability to participate in paid work reducing income levels (Drinkwater, 2015) and therefore access to certain leisure activities. Policy pertaining to other elements of time-use is, therefore, highly significant to the relative amount and quality of leisure time.

9.4.2 Implications for Public Policy

The findings presented in this book have a number of important implications for public policy. The evidence, consistent with that in the existing literature, continues to show that long working hours have negative impacts on workers. Moreover, this type of extensive labour extraction may not actually benefit organizations, as some employers may believe, as overworked employees are less productive and less satisfied with, and committed to, their jobs. Continued regulation of work-time is, therefore, central in order to limit incidence of excessive work-time. Moreover, public policy must better acknowledge concerns surrounding unreported work-time. Employers, in some instances, require workers to work longer than contracted, or in cases of task-based salaried employment, which is not based on fixed hours, workers may be subject to high workloads which require both extensive and intensive work routines. To this extent, public policy also needs to be developed which adequately acknowledges the growing intensity of paid work.

With regard to other aspects of paid work and its relationship with the household, flexible working policy has been expanded on a number of occasions since its initial implementation in the United Kingdom in 2003 (Deakin and Morris, 2012, 750–52). Since 2014, all workers following twenty-six weeks of employment have the right to request a flexible working arrangement. Similarly efforts have been made to increase flexibility with respect to caring options for new parents through the recent Shared Parental Leave regulations, implemented in 2014. Evidence, though, continues to show that despite a series of expansions to the right to request a formal flexible working arrangement, allowance decisions made by employers remain centred on 'business need' (Poelmans and Beham, 2008; Wheatley 2012b). Meanwhile, organizations have also found an increasing number of ways to increase the flexibilization of their labour force, in some cases using flexible working primarily to their advantage (Gregory and Milner, 2009). The limitations of current policy results in the potential win-win of flexible working not being realized. Policy needs to be strengthened in order to address these issues, and ensure that benefits are received by both employers and employees. Societal change in the household division of labour, and expectations of men's and women's careers, is difficult to enact, although public policy has facilitated some positive change in recent decades. Challenges remain, though, with regard to the impact of the uneven household division of labour on women's careers. From a public policy perspective further consideration must be given to how women can be supported in their careers, and to ensure that career gaps or reductions in participation arising from household responsibilities, including care, do not continue to limit women's career progression.

The increasingly mobile nature of paid work also presents a number of public policy challenges. The commute is associated with widely negative effects on well-being, especially travel undertaken by car. Public transport offers a potential alternative, however the key challenge remains around the ability of public transport networks to effectively support required levels of mobility. Increased investment in these methods of transport is therefore required. The findings in this book pertaining to travel-for-work recommend some reduction in more distant (including international) travel where alternatives are feasible including, for example, use of virtual meetings. While the focus of these findings and recommendations has been on the well-being of workers, they also align with government and international protocols which have the environment and sustainability at their core.

The findings pertaining to volunteering lend support to the notion that policy targeting increases in volunteering should recognize and nurture its intrinsic rewards (Baines and Hardill, 2008). The National Citizen Service is an example of good practice, and evidence reflecting on voluntary acts of care in chapter 6 supports both the benefits for the individual in regard to skill development, but also the well-being rewards derived by both the volunteer and the recipients of care. However, while these positive impacts are evident, reductions in public spending is likely to put significant pressure on Voluntary and Community Sector Organizations (VCSOs) in the future. At the same time older adults, who currently show the greatest engagement in voluntary work, are under increased pressure to remain in paid work, which is likely to limit their ability to volunteer following changes to state pensions and removal of statutory retirement. Policy must, therefore, acknowledge the challenges faced by both VCSOs and volunteers if it is to nurture and increase engagement in these acts. As already noted, it is also important to acknowledge the positive well-being affects associated with engagement in arts, culture, and certain sports corresponding with wider calls for continued funding to support these activities. Although this evidence is not, alone, enough to suggest how and where government funding should be deployed. The findings also suggest that improving access to certain leisure amenities, including for the elderly, disabled, and unemployed/economically inactive, is essential so that the well-being benefits of engaging in a wide range of leisure activities, including those that act as sources of cultural value, can be realized by greater a share of society.

9.4.3 Implications for Organizations

At the organizational level the findings presented in this book offer a number of important implications, and suggestions for reflection on, and potential changes to, current practice. Extensive and intensive labour extraction can have potentially negative impacts on the well-being of employees. Ultimately tired, and in turn unhappy, workers are likely to be less productive, show lesser commitment to the organization, and potentially perform poorly including making errors within the workplace. Retention of workers is also likely to be adversely affected. It is therefore in the interest of employers to reflect on the well-being effects of their work environment, and consider alternative approaches where they are feasible in order to enhance productivity and improve retention of workers. Potential improvements could be made in a number of areas. For example, the evidence presented, extending that in the existing literature, suggests that autonomy and the quality of work are important to job satisfaction and broader well-being. Providing employees with a greater degree of control over certain aspects of their time spent in paid work creates a more positive working environment which facilitates high productivity levels among workers. In addition, offering greater flexibility in paid work is central if organizations are to benefit from greater well-being among employees. This is particularly important to those with caring responsibilities, in order to reduce incidence of reductions in participation in paid work, and even labour market exit, when caring becomes a necessity. Centrally, stigma must be removed from the 'choice' to work flexibly, and the quality of reduced hours options needs to be improved, as per previously reported findings (Fagan et al., 2012; Wheatley, 2016). Improving the accessibility of flexible working arrangements, and dissolving negative implications for those using these arrangements is central if the potential benefits of working flexibly are to be realized. Indeed, workers who are able to mould their working routines to their preferences and/or better manage non-work responsibilities are likely to be more productive, show greater commitment to the organization, and report greater satisfaction with their job. Given the range of potential benefits, it is increasingly difficult to rationalize employers limiting opportunities for flexibility and autonomy among employees, especially among highly skilled occupations. Short-run benefits through cost efficiency are unlikely to deliver longer-term benefits to the organization. The changes outlined do present certain challenges among smaller firms, though, and evidence suggests that this may continue to limit engagement among SMEs (Dex and Scheibl, 2001; Maxwell et al., 2007).

A range of benefits are associated with voluntary work, including to well-being. Employee-supported volunteering has the potential to generate extrinsic and intrinsic rewards among employees, and broader positive effects for organizations in enhancing corporate social responsibility. This could also reduce some of the pressure on VCSOs resulting from reductions in public sector provision of services. The findings are also indicative of the growing importance of both domestic and international mobility among workers. However, in the context of organizations it is important that the focus is on providing opportunities for, but not expectations of, travel and mobility. Face-to-face contact remains important to economic activity and career development is aided by travel, but extensive travel routines add to the growing intensity of paid work, and are associated with a number of negative impacts including to well-being. Employers should, therefore, consider use of alternatives to travel where feasible, for example, virtual meetings. Those less mobile, that is, women and those with significant household responsibilities, may otherwise be restricted in their career development in certain occupations/industries. Time-off-in-lieu (TOIL) is also an important tool in lessening the negative impacts of frequent travel. Currently it remains underutilized in many organizations, in part, as many employers prefer to award informal flexibility to travellers upon their return rather than using more formalized time rewards. However, informal reward suffers from certain limitations, as workers may not perceive the informal reward as reflecting adequate compensation for their efforts, and it can leave too much room for exploitation by the employer. Greater formality may, therefore, be more effective, although where high degrees of flexibility are already present this may not offer the same additional benefits. Finally, organizations may benefit from more formal organization of workplace social and sporting activities. Evidence supports the benefits of mild sporting activity, for example, to not only broader well-being but also job satisfaction, resulting from the development of social and professional networks which may have wider benefits to workers, and in turn organizations, through facilitating knowledge sharing and inter- and intra-organization communication. Wider use of ESV could also generate a number of these benefits, alongside the benefits noted earlier with regard to employees and the organization.

9.5 THE VALIDITY OF SUBJECTIVE WELL-BEING AS A MEASURE OF ECONOMIC WELL-BEING

This book has explored the relationship between patterns of time-use and empirical measures of self-assessed well-being, referred to as subjective well-being (Pavot and Diener, 2013, 134; Diener et al., 1999). A central question raised in regard to the findings presented in this book relates to the validity of these measures of well-being. Indeed, there are limitations to the use of self-reported well-being as opposed to revealed preference measures of satisfaction and happiness, although the latter measures are similarly subject to a number of important limitations as discussed in chapter 1 (see also Kahneman and Krueger, 2006). A central concern regarding the use of subjective well-being measures relates to causality in the relationships observed. As discussed in chapter 1, individuals may exhibit different happiness set-points at different times in the lifecourse. Relationships observed which identify positive association between variables and well-being measures could be argued as reflecting either that: (1) the impact of the variable in question is reflected in higher levels of well-being, or (2) those individuals reporting a higher level of well-being are more likely to show particular characteristics. For example, Stutzer and Frey (2006, 334–36) considered whether marriage increases happiness, or whether happier individuals are more likely to get married. Meanwhile, in research focused on time spent in social activities, Robinson and Martin (2008) found that happier people are those who are most engaged in the majority of social activities. Similarly, as discussed in chapter 8, the findings presented regarding engagement in certain leisure activities could be questioned as either evidence of these activities increasing satisfaction with leisure and life overall, or reflecting that those individuals who are happier as a result of other factors, for example, socio-economic status have greater access to certain leisure activities, although some of these factors were controlled for in the analysis.

It is also important to consider the range of other factors which must be effectively acknowledged in our interpretations of measures of self-reported well-being. Norms and expectations may influence relative satisfaction levels (Spencer, 2009, 130), while individuals may also 'adapt' to their environments and their preferences adjust over time (Schor, 1993, 129). Meanwhile, the presence of higher levels of subjective well-being can reflect both the presence of positive influence, but also an absence of negative influences (Pavot and Diener, 2013, 135). Finally, while some of the evidence presented in the book, in particular in chapters 7 and 8, conflicts with the notion that the closely related nature of subjective well-being measures necessarily results in changes in domain satisfaction influencing overall life satisfaction (Schimmack, 2008), it is nevertheless important to acknowledge that these measures are interconnected and changes to one measure can influence, or be reflected in changes to another.

Reflecting on the findings presented in this book, and supported by the findings of existing literature, the evidence suggests subjective well-being measures can be considered a suitable and valid way of researching well-being. Moreover, the findings also correspond with arguments for use of alternatives to GDP as a measure of economic well-being. Subjective well-being measures provide important insight and contribute to our understanding of the impacts of patterns of contemporary time-use. In addition use of mixed methods, as applied in this book, provide greater validity to findings through the ability to triangulate findings and, using qualitative approaches, gain greater insight into the reasons why individuals provide certain responses regarding their well-being. Combining methods in this way ensures that some of the limitations present in the use of subjective well-being measures, including causality in the relationships observed, are mediated and findings are both robust and offer important contributions to understanding.

9.6 LOOKING TO THE FUTURE

While the book has explored the relationship between a range of aspects of time-use and subjective well-being, it is by no means exhaustive. In addition, although the findings in this book offer a number of important contributions to our understanding, further research is required in order to provide a fuller understanding of the complex and often blurred boundaries which exist between the ways in which we use our time.

Work-time, which represents a substantial use of time for a significant proportion of individuals, is increasingly fragmented with evidence of more mobile and flexible working routines among employees (Wheatley, 2016). In some cases this reflects good practice and application of flexibility which can benefit both the employer and employee. However, a growing minority of the labour force are increasingly subject to highly flexibilized employment (Raess and Burgoon, 2015). Notwithstanding these changes work remains, for many, characterized by the '9 to 5'. Further research is needed to increase understanding of the impacts of the increasingly mobile and flexible nature of employment present in some occupations, but also to explore the quality of work and its impacts on well-being in organizations including those that continue to default to the work-time norms of the '9 to 5'. Consideration is needed of the effect of the overall quality of work, including the organization of work, arrangement of work-time, the nature of work tasks, workloads, requirements for mobility, the physical work environment, the presence or otherwise of social and professional networks, and other factors which may influence the quality of work. These insights are important in order to generate a more comprehensive understanding of paid work in contemporary post-industrial economies.

Mobility is increasingly relevant to understanding patterns of paid work, especially within highly skilled occupations. It is estimated that demand for travel including international air travel will increase in the next decade (Global Business Travel Association, 2016). However, further technological development, and changes in attitudes to none face-to-face contact, could reduce the need for such frequent travel among workers. This would also align with international protocols focused on the environment and sustainability. Further research is needed which explores the ways in which technology could be more effectively employed to create and maintain inter- and intra-organization relationships in order to facilitate these changes. Further changes in technology are also likely to continue to influence and change the way we work, and use our leisure time. For example, social media is leaking into how we work. Use of social media to publicize business and business activity, create and maintain networks, for example, LinkedIn, and for job seeking is becoming increasingly common. The relationship between this application of technology and the way paid work is conducted, and is experienced by workers, is of interest and requires investigation. With respect to leisure time evidence shows individuals are spending more time engaged in social media (Buglass et al., 2015) and using wireless technologies including smartphones. Research should consider the role of social media in acting as both a complement and substitute to other leisure activities, the intersection between work and leisure in this regard, and the impacts these patterns of time-use have on reported well-being. More detailed exploration of leisure time – using mixed methods to facilitate the capture of more detailed perspectives from those engaging in leisure activities, as well as those involved in the funding and management of these sectors – would extend the findings made in chapter 8 which draw only on secondary data derived from Understanding Society.

Social norms which influence the household division of labour, and continue to burden women with a greater household contribution, are likely to be slow to change based on evidence since the mid-twentieth century. Indeed, patterns of employment including proportions working reduced hours, and the gender pay gap, continue to evidence the impact of the uneven division of household labour. There appears to be no quick fix in this regard, but further research is required to explore the changing nature of household decision-making and improve our understanding of how workplace and public policy could be designed to facilitate positive change in existing gender norms. Research should also be conducted to explore the impacts of the recent expansion of the Flexible Working Regulations, and new regulations on Shared Parental Leave. Regardless of gender, individuals will become increasingly likely to remain in the labour market into older age as a result of changes to public policy and the welfare system. This is likely to have impacts in reducing the supply of volunteers, based on current patterns of volunteering which show retirement acting as a particular trigger, especially among men. If reductions in funding to care services continue, there will be increased demand for voluntary workers to provide some of these acts of care. Improving our understanding of the impacts of these changes on the recipients of care, the VCSOs organizing and providing these care services, and the volunteers providing care is, therefore, of considerable importance.

9.7 TIME AND SUBJECTIVE WELL-BEING IN SUMMARY

This book has contributed to our understanding of the relationship between how we use our time and subjective well-being. The findings provide important insight into how time is spent in contemporary post-industrial societies. Overall, the book has, though consideration of a range of uses of time – work-time, household time, care, volunteering, travel, and leisure – and the complex and blurred boundaries which exist between, presented an innovative exploration of well-being observed through the lens of time-use. It highlights that while the way time is spent follows a broadly consistent, ordered pattern throughout the lifecourse, our relationship with time is increasingly complex and remains highly gendered. The analyses reported in the book have generated a number of important findings, summarized earlier in the chapter. A key contribution has been in identifying the importance of both the degree of choice present in the way time is spent and personal relationships and social contact, to the impacts associated with the organization of time. There appear few uses of time which have a clear and consistent negative impact on well-being. Time used in an activity when reflecting choice appears more likely to generate improved well-being, while the presence of constraint has the opposite effect, or at least reduces the positive impacts received. Meanwhile, time spent engaged in activities with others, generating feelings of togetherness, offers a range of benefits to well-being. Whether time is well spent is a reflection, as much, of these factors as it is of the many complex and varied ways in which we organize our time.

Bibliography

Aguiléra, A. (2008). Business travel and mobile workers. *Transportation Research Part A*, 42(8), pp. 1109–16.

Alesina, A., Di Tella, R., MacCulloch, R. (2004). Inequality and happiness: Are Europeans and Americans different? *Journal of Public Economics*, 88, pp. 2009–42.

Altman, R. (2015). *A new vision for older workers: Retain, retrain, recruit* [online]. Available at: https://www.gov.uk/government/uploads/system/uploads/attachment_data/file/411420/a-new-vision-for-older-workers.pdf.

Amichai-Hamburge, Y., Hayat, Z. (2011). The impact of the Internet on the social lives of users: A representative sample from 13 countries. *Computers in Human Behavior*, 27(1), pp. 585–89.

Anable, J., Gatersleben, B. (2005). All work and no play? The role of instrumental and affective factors in work and leisure journeys by different travel modes. *Transportation Research Part A*, 39(2–3), pp. 163–81.

Anderson, D., Vinnicombe, S., Singh, V. (2010). Women partners leaving the firm: Choice, what choice? *Gender in Management: An International Journal*, 25(3), pp. 170–83.

Andrews, F. M., Withey, S. B. (1976). *Social indicators of well-being: Americans' perceptions of life quality*. New York: Plenum.

Angner, E. (2010). Subjective well-being. *The Journal of Socio-Economics*, 39(3), pp. 361–68.

Arenius P., Kovalainen, A. (2006). Similarities and differences across the factors associated with women's self-employment preference in the Nordic countries. *International Small Business Journal*, 24(31) pp. 31–59.

Arrowsmith, J. (2001). Government calls for better work-life balance [online]. *European Industrial Relations Observatory*. Available at: http://www.eurofound.europa.eu/eiro/2001/02/feature/uk0102115f.htm.

Arthur, M. (2008) Examining contemporary careers: A call for interdisciplinary inquiry. *Human Relations*, 61(2), pp. 163–86.

Arts Council of England (2013). Investment in arts and culture 2012–15 [online]. Available at: http://www.artscouncil.org.uk/funding/our-investment/investment-in-the-arts-2012-15/.

Ateca-Amestoy, V. (2011). Leisure and subjective well-being. In Cameron, S. (ed.), *Handbook on the Economics of Leisure.* Cheltenham: Edward Elgar Publishing, pp. 52–76.

Ateca-Amestoy, V., Serrano-del-Rosal, R., Vera-Toscano, E. (2008). The leisure experience. *Journal of Socio-Economics* 37(1), pp. 64–78.

Atherton, A., Faria, J., Wheatley, D., Wu, D., Wu, Z. (2016). Financial hardship and the decision to moonlight: Second job holding by the self-employed. *Industrial Relations Journal*, 47(3), pp. 279–99.

Atkinson, C., Hall, L. (2009). The role of gender in varying forms of flexible working. *Gender, Work and Organization*, 16(6), pp. 650–66.

Ayres, C. (1951). The co-ordinates of institutionalism. *American Economic Review*, 41, pp. 47–55.

Bailey, D., Kurland, N. (2002). A review of telework research: Findings, new directions, and lessons for the study of modern work. *Journal of Organizational Behavior*, 23(4), pp. 383–400.

Bain, P., Taylor, P. (2000). Entrapped by the "electronic panopticon"? Worker resistance in the call centre. *New Technology, Work and Employment*, 15(1), pp. 2–18.

Baines, S., Hardill, I. (2008). 'At least i can do something': The work of volunteering in a community beset by worklessness. *Social Policy and Society*, 7(3), pp. 307–17.

Baker, L. A., Cahalin, L. P., Gerst, K., Burr, J. A. (2005). Productive activities and subjective well-being among older adults: The influence of number of activities and time commitment. *Social Indicators Research*, 73, pp. 431–58.

Bank of England (2015). *Three Centuries of Macroeconomic Data* [online]. Available at: http://webarchive.nationalarchives.gov.uk/20160105160709/http://bankofengland.co.uk/research/Documents/onebank/threecenturies_v2.2.xlsx.

Bartling, B., Fehr, E., Schmidt, K. (2012). Screening, competition, and job design: Economic origins of good jobs. *The American Economic Review*, 102(2), pp. 834–64.

Baruch, Y. (2004). Transforming careers: From linear to multidirectional career paths – organizational and individual perspectives. *Career Development International*, 9(1), pp. 58–73.

Basmajian, C. (2010). "Turn on the radio, bust out a song": The experience of driving to work. *Transportation*, 37(1), pp. 59–84.

Bateson, M. (1990). *Composing a life.* New York: Grove Press.

Batt R. Valcour P. M. 2003 Human resources practices as predictors of work-family outcomes and employee turnover. *Industrial Relations*, 42(2), pp. 189–220.

Bazen, S., Thirlwall, T. (1989). *Deindustrialization.* Oxford: Heinemann Educational.

BBC (2013). Happiness index shows 'small improvement' in 2013, ONS says [online]. Available at: http://www.bbc.co.uk/news/uk-23501423.

Beaverstock, J., Derudder, B., Faulconbridge, J., Witlox, F. (2009). International business travel: Some explorations. Geografiska Annaler: Series B, *Human Geography*, 91(3), pp. 193–202.

Beck, U. (2000). *Brave new world of work*. Cambridge: Polity.

Becker, G. (1976). *The aconomic approach to human behaviour*. Chicago: The University of Chicago Press.

Becker, G. (1985). Human capital, effort and the sexual division of labor. *Journal of Labour Economics*, 3(1), pp. 33–58.

Bell, C. S. (1974) Economics, sex and gender. *Social Science Quarterly*, 55(3), pp. 615–31.

Bergman, A., Gustafson, P. (2008). Travel, availability and work-life balance. In Hislop, D. (ed.), *Mobility and technology in the workplace*. Routledge: Oxon, pp. 192–208.

Bergström, G. (2006). Ett arbetsliv i rörelse. Resandets positiva och negativa potential för arbetstillfredsställelsen bland resande säljare. *Arbetsmarknad & Arbetsliv*, 12(3), pp. 147–60.

Bergström Casinowsky, G. (2013). Working life on the move, domestic life at standstill? Work-related travel and responsibility for home and family. *Gender, Work and Organization*, 20(3), pp. 311–26.

Beyers, W. B. (2002). Services in the new economy: Elements of a research agenda. *Journal of Economic Geography*, 2(1), pp. 1–29.

Bianchi, S. M., Hotz, V. J., McGarry, K., Seltzer, J. A. (2008). Intergenerationalties: Theories, trends, and challenges. In Booth, A., Crouter, A., Bianchi, S., and Seltzer, J. (eds), *Intergenerational caregiving*. Washington, DC: Urban Institute, pp. 3–44.

Biddle, S., Asare, M. (2011). Physical activity and mental health in children and adolescent: A review of reviews. *British Journal of Sports Medicine*, 45(11), pp. 886–95.

Bielenski, H., Bosch, G., Wagner, A. (2002). *Working time preferences in sixteen European countries*. Luxembourg: Office for Official Publications of the European Communities.

Bienefeld, M. A. (1972). *Working hours in British industry*. London: Weidenfeld and Nicolson.

Bille, T., Fjaellegaard, C. B., Frey, B., Steiner, L. (2013). Happiness in the arts international evidence on artists' job satisfaction. *Economics Letters*, 121(1), pp. 15–18.

Black, I., Jamieson. S. (2007). Up, up and fading away: The work and family life of executive international travellers. *Policy and Practice in Health and Safety*, 5(2), pp. 63–78.

Blanchflower, D. G. (2000). Self-employment in OECD countries. *Labour Economics*, 7(5), pp. 471–505.

Blanchflower, D. G., Oswald, A. J. (2004). Money, sex and happiness: An empirical study. *The Scandinavian Journal of Economics*, 106(3), pp. 393–415.

Blanchflower, D. G., Oswald, A. J. (2008). Is well-being U-shaped over the life cycle? *Social Science & Medicine*, 66, pp. 1733–49.

Blaug, M. (2001). Where are we now on cultural economics? *Journal of Economic Surveys*, 15(2), pp. 123–43.

Böheim, R., Taylor, M. (2003). Option or obligation? The determinants of labour supply preferences in Britain. *The Manchester School*, March, 71(2), pp. 113–31.

Bonache, J. (2005). Job satisfaction among expatriates, repatriates and domestic employees. *Personnel Review*, 34(1), pp. 110–24.

Bonsang, E., Klein, T. J. (2012). Retirement and subjective well-being. *Journal of Economic Behavior & Organization*, 83(3), pp. 311–29.

Booth, J. E., Park, K. W., Glomb, T. M. (2009). Employer-supported volunteering benefits: Gift exchange among employers, employees, and volunteer organizations. *Human Resource Management*, 48(2), pp. 227–49.

Bosworth, D., Dawkins, P., Stromback, T. (1996). *The economics of the labour market*. Addison Wesley Longman Limited.

Boulin, J. (1993). The social organisation of time. *Futures*, 25(5), pp. 511–20.

Bowles, H., McGinn, K. (2008). Untapped potential in the study of negotiation and gender inequality in organizations. *Academy of Management Annals*, 2, pp. 99–132.

Boxall, P., Macky, K. 2014. High-involvement work processes, work intensification and employee well-being. *Work, Employment & Society* 28(6), pp. 963–84.

Brajša-Žganec, A., Merkaš, M., Šverko, I. (2011). Quality of life and leisure activities: How do leisure activities contribute to subjective well-being? *Social Indicators Research*, 102, pp. 81–91.

Brandth, B., Kvande, E. (2009). Norway: The making of the Father's Quota. In Kamerman, S., and Moss, P. (eds), *The politics of parental leave policies: Children, parenting, gender and the labour market*. Bristol: Policy Press, pp. 191–206.

Briscoe, J., Hall, D., Frautschy DeMuth, R. (2006). Protean and boundaryless careers: An empirical exploration. *Journal of Vocational Behavior*, 69, pp. 30–47.

British Household Panel Survey [computer file], ESRC Research Centre on Micro-social Change. Colchester: The Data Archive [distributor], (2010). Data files and associated documentation.

Broadbridge, A. (2008). Senior careers in retailing: An exploration of male and female executives' career facilitators and barriers. *Gender in Management*, 23(1), pp. 11–35.

Broadbridge, A., Hearn, J. (2008). Gender and management: New directions in research and continuing patterns in practice. *British Journal of Management*, 19(S1), pp. S38–S49.

Brown, A., Charlwood, A., Forde, C., Spencer, D. (2007). Job quality and the economics of New Labour: A critical appraisal using subjective survey data. *Cambridge Journal of Economics*, 31(6), pp. 941–71.

Brown, A., Charlwood, A., Spencer, D. (2012). Not all that it might seem: Why job satisfaction is worth studying despite it being a poor summary measure of job quality. *Work Employment & Society*, 26(6), pp. 1007–18.

Browning, M., Chiappori, P. A. (1998). Efficient intra-household allocations: A general characterization and empirical tests. *Econometrica*, 66(6), pp. 1241–78.

Bryman, A. (2012). *Social research methods* (4th ed.). Oxford: Oxford University Press.

Bryson, A., MacKerron, G. (2013). *Are you happy while you work?* CEP Discussion Paper No. 1187.

Buglass, S., Binder, J., Betts, J., Underwood, J. (2015). When 'friends' collide: Social heterogeneity and user vulnerability on social network sites. *Computers in Human Behaviour*, 54, pp. 62–72.

Bulger, C., Matthews, R., Hoffman, M. (2007) Work and personal life boundary management: Boundary strength, work/personal life balance, and the segmentation – integration continuum. *Journal of Occupational Health Psychology*, 12(4), pp. 365–75.

Burchell, B., Fagan, C. (2004). Gender and the intensification of work: Evidence from the European working conditions surveys. *Eastern Economic Journal*, 30(4), pp. 627–42.

Cabane, C., Hille, A., Lechner, M. (2015). *Mozart or Pele? The effects of teenagers' participation in music and sports*. SOEP Paper in Multidisciplinary Panel Data Research. Berlin: DIW Berlin.

Cabinet Office (2013), *Community Life Survey, 2012–2013* [computer file]. Colchester, Essex: UK Data Archive [distributor], October 2013. SN: 7405, http://dx.doi.org/10.5255/UKDA-SN-7405-1.

Cabinet Office (2013). *Community Life Survey, 2012–13 statistical summary* [online]. Available at: https://www.gov.uk/government/uploads/system/uploads/attachment_data/file/80777/Community-Life-Survey-Q2-2012-13-Statistical-summary.pdf.

Cabinet Office (2015). *Community Life Survey: 2014–2015 statistical bulletin* [online]. Available at: https://www.gov.uk/government/uploads/system/uploads/attachment_data/file/447010/Community_Life_Survey_2014-15_Bulletin.pdf.

Cabrera, E. (2007). Opting out and opting in: Understanding the complexities of women's career transitions. *Career Development International*, 12(3), pp. 218–37.

Cairns, S., Newson, C., Davies, A. (2010). Understanding successful workplace travel initiatives in the UK. *Transportation Research Part A*, 44(7), pp. 473–94.

Cameron, D. (2010). *Big society speech*, July 2010 [online]. Available at: http://www.number10.gov.uk/news/speeches-and-transcripts/2010/07/big-society-speech-53572.

Cameron, G., Muellbauer, J. (1998). Housing market and regional commuting and migration choices. *Scottish Journal of Political Economy*, 45(4), pp. 420–46.

Carers UK and the University of Leeds (2011). *Valuing carers 2011: Calculating the value of carers' support* [online]. CIRCLE, available at: http://circle.leeds.ac.uk/files/2012/08/110512-circle-carers-uk-valuing-carers.pdf.

Carmichael, F., Hulme, C., Sheppard, S., Connell, G. (2008). Work-life imbalance: Informal care and paid employment in the UK. *Feminist Economics*, 14(2), pp. 3–35.

Carnoy, M. (2000). *Sustaining the new economy*. USA: Russell Sage Foundation.

Carter, P., Butler, D. (2008). Women's work: The workplace and the spaces between. *The Industrial Geographer*, 5(2), pp. 3–18.

Castells, M. (2000). Materials for an explanatory theory of the network society. *British Journal of Sociology*, 51, pp. 5–22.

Castells, M., Aoyama, Y. (1994). Paths towards the Informational Society: Employment structure in G 7 countries 1920–90. *International Labor Review*, 133(1), pp. 5–33.

Cha, Y. (2010). Reinforcing separate spheres: The effect of spousal overwork on men's and women's employment in dual-earner households. *American Sociological Review*, 75(2), 303–9.

Chazan, D. (2016). *France reviews its 35-hour working week* [online]. Available at: http://www.telegraph.co.uk/news/worldnews/europe/france/12120927/France-reviews-its-35-hour-working-week.html.

Choi, S., Leiter, J., Tomaskovic-Devey, D. (2008). Contingent autonomy technology, bureaucracy, and relative power in the labor process. *Work and Occupations*, 35(4), pp. 422–55.

Christin, A. (2012). Gender and highbrow cultural participation in the United States. *Poetics*, 40(5), pp. 423–43.

CIPD (2012). *Unemployment drops to 2.51m, the lowest level for a year* [online]. Available at: http://www.cipd.co.uk/pm/peoplemanagement/b/weblog/archive/2012/11/14/unemployment-drops-to-2-51m-the-lowest-level-for-a-year-2012-11.aspx.

Clark, A., Oswald, A. (1994). Unhappiness and unemployment. *The Economic Journal*, 104(424), pp. 648–59.

Clark, A. E., Frijters, P., Shields, M. A. (2008). Relative income, happiness, and utility: An explanation for the Easterlin paradox and other puzzles. *Journal of Economic Literature*, 46(1), pp. 95–144.

Clark, S. C. (2000). Work/family border theory: A new theory of work/family balance. *Human Relations*, 53(6), pp. 747–70.

Clark, W., Huang, Y., Withers, S. (2003). Does commuting distance matter? Commuting tolerance and residential change. *Regional Science and Urban Economics*, 33(2), pp. 199–21.

Clarke, J. (2004). Dissolving the public realm? The logics and limits of neo-liberalism. *Journal of Social Policy*, 33(1), pp. 27–48.

Clary, E. G., Snyder, M. (1999). The motivations to volunteer: Theoretical and practical considerations. *Current Directions in Psychological Science*, 8(5), pp. 156–59.

Clutterbuck, D. (2003). *Managing work-life balance: A guide for HR in achieving organisational and individual change*. London: CIPD.

Cobb, J., Daly, H. (1989). *For the common good: Redirecting the economy toward community, the environment and a sustainable future*. Boston: Beacon Press.

Colander, D. (2000). The death of neoclassical economics. *Journal of the History of Economic Thought*, 22(2), pp. 127–43.

Collings, D., Doherty, N., Luethy, M., Osborn, D. (2011). Understanding and supporting the career implications of international assignments. *Journal of Vocational Behavior*, 78(3), pp. 361–71.

Comim, F. (2005). Capabilities and happiness: Potential synergies. *Review of Social Economy*, 63(2), pp. 161–76.

Commission of the European Communities (2005). Communication from the Commission to the Council on European Policies Concerning Youth. *Addressing the Concerns of Young People in Europe: Implementing the European Youth Pact and Promoting Active Citizens.* Brussels: Commission of the European Communities.

Commons, J. (1931). Institutional economics. *American Economic Review*, 21, pp. 648–57.

Connolly, S., Gregory, M. (2008) Moving down: Women's part-time work and occupational change in Britain 1991–2001. *Economic Journal*, 118(526), pp. F52–76.

Contarello, A., Sarrica, M. (2007). ICTs, social thinking and subjective well-being – the Internet and its representations in everyday life. *Computers in Human Behavior*, 23(2), pp. 1016—32.

Costa, G., Akerstedt, T., Nachreiner, F., Baltieri, F., Carvalhais, J., Folkard, S., Frings-Dresen, M., Gadbois, C., Gartner, J. (2003). As time goes by – flexible work hours, health and wellbeing. *Working Life Research in Europe Report*, 8, The National Institute for Working Life, Stockholm.

Costa, G., Sartori, S., Åkerstedt, T. (2006). Influence of flexibility and variability of working hours on health and well-being. *Chronobiology International*, 23(6), pp. 1125–37.

Coyle, D., Quah, D. (2002). *Getting the measure of the new economy*. iSociety at The Work Foundation.

Crafts, N. (1993). *Can de-industrialization seriously damage your wealth?* London: Institute of Economic Affairs.

Crafts, N. (1996). Deindustrialisation and economic growth. *The Economic Journal*, 106(434), pp. 172–83.

Creech, A., Hallam, S., Varvarigou, M., McQueen, H., Gaunt, H. (2013). Active music making: A route to enhanced subjective well-being among older people. *Perspectives in Public Health*, 133(1), pp. 36–43.

Cresswell, J. W. (2013). *Research design: Qualitative, quantitative, and mixed methods approaches* (4th ed.). London: Sage.

Cresswell, J. W., Plano Clark, V. (2011). *Designing and conducting mixed methods research* (2nd ed.). London: Sage.

Crompton, R., Harris, F. (1998). Explaining women's employment patterns: 'Orientations to work' revisited. *The British Journal of Sociology*, 49(1), pp. 118–36.

Crompton, R., Lewis, S., Lyonette, C. (2007). Continuities, change and transformations. In Cromption, R., Lewis, S., and Lyonette, C. (eds), *Women, men, work and family in Europe*. New York: Palgrave Macmillian.

Crompton, R., Lyonette, C. (2011). Women's career success and work-life adaptations in the accountancy and medical professions in Britain. *Gender, Work and Organization*, 18(2), pp. 231–54.

Crosier, T., Warburton, J. (2001). Are we too busy to volunteer? The relationship between time and volunteering using the 1997 ABS time use data. *Australian Journal of Social Issues*, 36(4), pp. 295–314.

Cushman, G., Veal, A., Zuzanek, J. (2005). *Free time and leisure participation: International perspectives*. Wallingford: CABI Publishing.

Daily, C., Trevis, C., Dalton, D. (2000). International experience in the executive suite: The path to prosperity? *Strategic Management Journal*, 21(4), pp. 515–23.

Daly, M. (2002). Care as a good for social policy. *Journal of Social Policy*, 31(2), pp. 251–70.

David, S., Boniwell, I., Ayers, A. C. (2013). *Oxford handbook of happiness*. Oxford: Oxford University Press.

Davis-Smith, J., Gay, P. (2005). *Active aging in active communities*. Bristol: The Policy Press.

Dawson, C., Henley, A. (2012). 'Push' versus 'pull' entrepreneurship: An ambiguous distinction? *International Journal of Entrepreneurial Behavior & Research*, 18(6), pp. 697–719.

Daykin, N., De Viggiana, N., Pilkington, P. Moriarty, Y. (2012). Music making for health, well-being and behaviour change in youth justice settings: A systematic review. *Health Promotion International*, 28(2), pp. 197–210.

De Meester, E., van Ham, M., (2009). Symmetry and asymmetry in working and commuting arrangements between partners in the Netherlands: Does the residential context matter? *Environment and Planning A*, 41(9), pp. 2181–200.

De Vos, J., Schwanen, T., Van Acker, V., Witlox, F. (2013). Travel and subjective well-being: A focus on findings, methods and future research needs. *Transport Reviews*, 33(4), 421–42.

Deakin, S., Morris, G. (2012). *Labour law* (6th ed.). Oxford: Hart.

Deaton A. (2008). Income, health, and well-being around the world: Evidence from the Gallup world poll. *Journal of Economic Perspectives*, 22(2), pp. 53–72.

Delbosc, A., Currie, G., (2011). Exploring the relative influences of transport disadvantage and social exclusion on well-being. *Transport Policy*, 18(4), pp. 555–62.

Della Giusta, M., Jewell, S., Kambhampati, U. (2011). Gender and life satisfaction in the UK. *Feminist Economics*, 17(3), pp. 1–34.

Delsen, L. (1998). When do men work part-time. In O'Reilly, J., and Fagan, C. (eds), *Part-time prospects: An international comparison of part-time work in Europe*. London: Routledge, pp. 57–76.

Den Dulk, L., de Ruijter, J. (2008). Managing work-life policies: Disruption versus dependency arguments. Explaining managerial attitudes towards employee utilization of work-life policies. *The International Journal of Human Resource Management*, 19(7), pp. 1222–36.

Department for Business, Innovation and Skills (BIS) (2010). *Flexible working and work-life balance* [online]. Available at: http://www.bis.gov.uk/.

Department for Business, Innovation and Skills (BIS) (2011a). *Flexible working and work-life balance* [online]. Available at: http://www.bis.gov.uk/.

Department for Business, Innovation and Skills (BIS) (2011b). *Working time regulations: Statutory instruments* [online]. Available at: http://www.bis.gov.uk/.

Department for Business, Innovation and Skills (BIS) (2014). *Zero hours employment contracts* [online]. Available at: https://www.gov.uk/government/consultations/zero-hours-employment-contracts.

Department for Transport (DfT) (2006). *Eddington transport study* [online]. Available at: http://www.dft.gov.uk/about/strategy/transportstrategy/eddingtonstudy.

Department for Transport (DfT) (2007). *Towards a sustainable transport system* [online]. Available at: http://www.dft.gov.uk/about/strategy/transportstrategy/pdf-sustaintranssystem.pdf.

Department for Work and Pensions (DWP) (2005). *Opportunity age – meeting the challenges of ageing in the 21st century*. Norwich: The Stationery Office.

Department for Work and Pensions (DWP) (2012). *Age positive: Managing without a fixed retirement age* [online]. Available at: http://www.dwp.gov.uk/policy/ageing-society/managing-without-fixed-retirement/.

Dex, S. (1991). *Life and work history analysis: Qualitative and quantitative development*. London: Routledge.

Dex, S., Scheibl, F. (2002). *SMEs and flexible working arrangements*. Bristol, UK: The Policy Press.

Di Tella, R., MacCulloch, R. (2006). Some uses of happiness data in economics. *Journal of Economic Perspectives*, 20(1), pp. 25–46.

Di Tella, R., MacCulloch, R., Oswald, A. (2003). The macroeconomics of happiness. *The Review of Economics and Statistics*, 85(4), pp. 809–27.

Diamond, L., Hicks, A., Otter-Henderson, K. (2008). Every time you go away: Changes in affect, behavior, and physiology associated with travel-related separations from romantic partners. *Journal of Personality and Social Psychology*, 95(2), pp. 385–403.

Dickmann, M., Doherty, N. (2008). Exploring the career capital impact of international assignments within distinct organisational contexts. *British Journal of Management*, 19(2), pp. 145–61.

Diener, E. (2009a). *Assessing well-being: The collected works of Ed Diener* (Social Indicators Research Series, Vol. 39). Amsterdam: The Netherlands: Springer.

Diener, E. (2009b). *Culture and well-being: The collected works of Ed Diener* (Social Indicators Research Series, Vol. 38). Amsterdam: The Netherlands: Springer.

Diener, E. (2009c). *The science of well-being: The collected works of Ed Diener* (Social Indicators Research Series, Vol. 37). Amsterdam: The Netherlands: Springer.

Diener, E. (2013). The remarkable changes in the science of subjective well-being. *Perspectives on Psychological Science*, 8(6), pp. 663–66.

Diener, E., Suh, E. M., Lucas, R. E., Smith, H. L. (1999). Subjective well-being: Three decades of progress. *Psychological Review*, 125, pp. 276–302.

Dikkers, J., van Engen, M., Vinkenburg, C. (2010). Flexible work: Ambitious parents' recipe for career success in the Netherlands. *Career Development International*, 15(6), 562–82.

DiMaggio, P. (2004). Gender, networks and cultural capitals. *Poetics*, 32(2), pp. 99–103.

Directgov (2012). *Changes to the planned increase in state pension age* [online]. Available at: www.direct.gov.uk.

Dobbs, L. (2007). Stuck in the slow lane: Reconceptualizing the links between gender, transport and employment. *Gender, Work & Organization*, 14(2), pp. 85–108.

Dolan, P., Peasgood, T., White, M. (2008). Do we really know what makes us happy? A review of the economic literature on the factors associated with subjective well-being. *Journal of Economic Psychology*, 29(1), pp. 94–122.

Dorn, D., Fischer, J. A., Kirchgassner, G., Sousa-Poza, A. (2007). Is it culture of democracy? The impact of democracy, and culture on happiness. *Social Indicators Research*, 82(3), pp. 505–26.

Downward, P., Mearman, A. (2007). Retroduction as mixed-methods triangulation in economic research: Reorienting economics into social science. *Cambridge Journal of Economics*, 31(1), pp. 77–99.

Downward, P., Rasciute, S. (2011). Does sport make you happy? An analysis of the well being derived from sports participation. *International Review of Applied Economics*, 25(3), pp. 331–48.

Doyle, J. (2000). *New community or new slavery: The emotional division of labour.* The Industrial Society. Loughton, Essex: CW Press.

Doyle, J., Nathan, M. (2001). *Wherever next: Work in a mobile world.* The Industrial Society. Loughton, Essex: CW Press.

Doyle, J., Reeves, R. (2001). *Time out: The case for time sovereignty.* The Industrial Society. Loughton, Essex: CW Press.

Drew, E. (1998). Changing family forms and the allocation of caring. In Drew, E., Emerek, R., and Mahon, E. (eds), *Women, work and the family in Europe*. London: Routledge, pp. 27–35.

Drinkwater, S. (2015). Informal caring and labour markets outcomes within England and Wales. *Regional Studies*, 49(2), pp. 273–86.

Dugger, W. (1979). Methodological differences between institutional and neoclassical economics. *Journal of Economic Issues*, 13(4), pp. 899–909.

Durand, M., Martin J., Saint-Martin, A. (2004). *The 35 hour week: Portrait of a French exception*. OECD Observer, 244, September.

Durbin, S., Tomlinson, J. (2010). Female part-time managers: Networks and career mobility. *Work, Employment & Society*, 24(4), pp. 621–40.

Dyck, I. (2005). Feminist geography, the 'everyday' and local–global relations: Hidden spaces of place-making. *The Canadian Geographer*, 49(3), pp. 233–43.

Easterlin, R. (1974). Does economic growth improve the human lot? Some empirical evidence. In David, P., and Reder, M. (eds), *Nations and households in economic growth*. New York: Academic Press, pp. 89–125.

Easterlin, R. A. (1995). Will raising the incomes of all increase the happiness of all? *Journal of Economic Behavior and Organization*, 27(1), pp. 35–47.

Easterlin, R. A. (2001). Income and happiness: Towards a unified theory. *The Economic Journal*, 111(473), pp. 465–84.

Eckersley, R. (2007). The politics of happiness. *Living Now*, 93, pp. 67.

Economic Intelligence Unit (EIU) (2012). *Women's economic opportunity index* [online]. Available at: www.eiu.com.

Ergeneli, A., Ilsev, A. (2010). Work–family conflict and job satisfaction relationship: The roles of gender and interpretive habits. *Gender, Work and Organization*, 17(6), pp. 679–95.

Eriksson, L., Friman, M., Gärling, T. (2013). Perceived attributes of bus and car mediating satisfaction with the work commute. *Transportation Research Part A: Policy and Practice*, 47(1), pp. 87–96.

Espino, C. M., Sundstrom, S. M., Frick, H. L., Jacobs, M., Peters, M. (2002). International business travel: Impact on families and travellers. *Occupational and Environmental Medicine*, 59, pp. 309–22.

Ettema, D., Friman, M., Gärling, T., Olsson, L. E., Fujii, S. (2012). How in-vehicle activities affect work commuters' satisfaction with public transport. *Journal of Transport Geography*, 24, pp. 215–22.

Ettema, D., Gärling, T., Olsson, L. E., Friman, M. (2010). Out-of-home activities, daily travel, and subjective well-being. *Transportation Research Part A*, 44, pp. 723–32.

European Commission (2003). *Adequate and sustainable pensions*. Luxembourg: Publications Office.

European Commission (2005). *Working time directive*. Available at: http://www.cec.org.uk/info/pubs/bbriefs/bb28.htm.

Eustace, E. (2012). Speaking allowed? Workplace regulation of regional dialect. *Work, Employment & Society*, 26(2), pp. 331–48.

Evans, S. (2011). *Is the German insult 'Raven mothers' holding back women at work?* [online]. British Broadcasting Corporation (BBC), March, Available at: http://www.bbc.co.uk/news/business-12703897.

Evetts, J. (2000). Analysing change in women's careers: Culture, structure and action dimensions. *Gender, Work and Organization*, 7(1), pp. 57–67.

Fagan, C., Burchell, B. (2002). *Gender, jobs and working conditions in the European Union* [online]. European Foundation for the Improvement of Living and Working conditions. Available at: http://www.eurofound.eu.int/publications/files/EF0249EN.pdf.

Fagan, C., Lyonette, C., Smith, M., Saldaña-Tejeda, A. (2012). *The influence of working time arrangements on work-life integration or 'balance': A review of the international evidence*. Conditions of Work and Employment No. 32: International Labour Organization.

Fagnani, J., Letablier, M. (2007). 'The French 35-hour working law and the work-life balance of parents: friend or foe?'. In Perrons, D., Fagan, C., McDowell, L., Ray, K., and Ward, K. (eds), *Gender divisions and working time in the new economy*. Cheltenham: Edward Elgar, pp. 79–90.

Faulkner, N. (1986). The women's studies movement: A decade inside the academy. *Frontiers: A Journal of Women Studies*, 8(3), pp. 55–61.

Felstead, A., Jewson, N., Walters S. (2005). *Changing places of work*, London: Palgrave.

Fenwick, T. (2006). Contradictions in portfolio careers: Work design and client relations. *Career Development International*, 11(1), pp. 65–79.

Ferber, M. A., Nelson, J. (2003). Beyond economic man: Ten years later. In Ferber, M. A., and Nelson, J. (eds), *Feminist economics today: Beyond economic man*. Chicago: University of Chicago Press, pp. 1–32.

Ferreira, S., Moro, M. (2010). On the use of subjective well-being data for environmental valuation. *Environmental Resource Economics*, 46(3), pp. 249–73.

Fielding, A. (1999). Why use arbitrary points scores? Ordered categories in models of educational progress. *Journal of the Royal Statistical Society: Series A (Statistics in Society)*, 162(3), pp. 303–28.

Figart, D. (2001). Wage-setting under Fordism: The rise of job evaluation and the ideology of equal pay. *Review of Political Economy*, 13(4), pp. 405–25.

Figart, D., Golden, L. (1998). The social economics of work time: Introduction. *Review of Social Economy*, Winter, 56(4), pp. 411–24.

Findlay, P., Findlay, J., Stewart, R. (2009). The consequences of caring: Skills, regulation and reward among early years workers. *Work, Employment and Society*, 23(3), pp. 422–41.

Fitzer, M. M. (1997). Managing from afar: Performance and rewards in a telecommuting environment. *Compensation and Benefits Review*, 29(1), pp. 65–73.

Flandez, R. (2009). Entrepreneurs take second jobs to stay afloat. *The Wall Street Journal*, 16 June.

Fleetwood, S. (2007). Why work-life balance now? *International Journal of Human Resource Management*, 18(3), pp. 387–400.

Folbre, N. (1991). The unproductive housewife: Her evolution in nineteenth-century economic thought. *Signs: Journal of Women in Culture and Society*, 16(3), pp. 463–84.

Folbre, N. (1994). *Who pays for the kids? Gender and the structures of constraint*. London: Routledge.

Folbre, N. (2001). *The invisible heart: Economics and family values*. New York: The New Press.

Folbre, N. (2012). Should women care less? Intrinsic motivation and gender inequality. *British Journal of Industrial Relations*, 50(4), pp. 597–619.

Fonner, K., Roloff, M. (2010). Why teleworkers are more satisfied with their jobs than are office-based workers: When less contact is beneficial. *Journal of Applied Communication Research*, 38(4), pp. 336–61.

Ford, J., Collinson, D. (2011). In search of the perfect manager? Work-life balance and managerial work. *Work, Employment & Society*, 25(2), pp. 257–73.

Foster, C., Whysall, P., Harris, L. (2007). Female career progression in retailing. *International Journal of Retail & Distribution Management*, 35(12), pp. 975–81.

Foster, R. (2013). *Household satellite accounts – valuing voluntary activity in the UK* [online]. Available at: http://www.ons.gov.uk/ons/dcp171766_345918.pdf.

Frändberg, L., Vilhelmson, B. (2011). More or less travel: Personal mobility trends in the Swedish population focusing gender and cohort. *Journal of Transport Geography*, 19(6), pp. 1235–44.

Fraser, J., Gold, M. (2001). 'Portfolio workers': Autonomy and control amongst freelance translators. *Work, Employment and Society*, 15(4), pp. 679–97.

Frey, B. (2008). *Happiness: A revolution in economics*. Cambridge: MIT Press.

Frey, B. S., Benesch, C. (2008). TV, time and happiness. *Homo Oeconomicus*, 25(3/4), pp. 413–24.

Frey, B. S., Stutzer, A. (2002a). *Happiness and economics*. Princeton: University Press.

Frey, B. S., Stutzer, A. (2002b). What can economists learn from happiness research? *Journal of Economic Literature*, 40(2), pp. 402–35.

Frey, B. S., Stutzer, A. (2014). Economic consequences of mispredicting utility. *Journal of Happiness Studies*, 15(4), pp. 937–56.

Friedman, G. (2014). Workers without employers: shadow corporations and the rise of the gig economy. *Review of Keynesian Economics,* 4(1), pp. 171–188.

Fujiwara, D. (2013). *Museums and happiness: The value of participating in museums and the arts* [online]. Museum of East Anglian Life, April. Available at: www.happymuseumproject.org.

Galinsky, E., Sakai, K., Wigton, T. (2011). Workplace flexibility: From research to action. *Work and Family*, 21(2), pp. 141–61.

Galletta, M., Portoghese, I., Battistelli, A. (2011). Intrinsic motivation, job autonomy and turnover intention in the italian healthcare: The mediating role of affective commitment. *Journal of Management Research*, 3(2), pp. 1–19.

Gallie, D. (2007). *Employment regimes and the quality of work*. Oxford: Oxford University Press.

Galloway S., Bell, D., Hamilton, C., Scullion, A. (2006). *Quality of life and wellbeing: Measuring the benefits of culture and sport: Literature review and thinkpiece*. Edinburgh: Scottish Executive Education Department.

Gambles, R., Lewis, S., Rapoport, R. (2006). *The myth of work-life balance: The challenge of our time for men, women and societies.* Hoboken, NJ: Wiley.

Garcia, I., Molina, H. A., Montuenga, V. (2011). Gender differences in childcare: Time allocation in five European countries. *Feminist Economics*, 17(1), pp. 119–50.

Garcia, I., Molina, A., Navarro, M. (2007). How satisfied are spouses with their leisure time? Evidence from Europe. *Journal of Family and Economic Issues*, 28, pp. 546–65.

Gardner, J., Oswald, A. J. (2006). Do divorcing couples become happier by breaking up? *Journal of the Royal Statistical Society: Series A*, 169(2), 319–36.

Gatenby, R. (2004). *Married only at the weekends? A study of the amount of time spent together by spouses*. London: Office for National Statistics (ONS).

Gershuny, J. (2011). *Time-use surveys and the measurement of national well-being*. Office of National Statistics.

Getis, A. (1969). Residential location and the journey from work. *Proceedings of the Association of American Geographers*, pp. 55–59.

Giele, J. Z., Elder, G. H. (1998). *Methods of life course research: Qualitative and quantitative approaches*. Thousand Oaks: Sage.

Glass, J. (2004). Blessing or curse: Work-family policies and mother's wage growth over time. *Work and Occupations*, 31(3), pp. 367–94.

Glavin, P., Schieman, S. (2012). Work–family role blurring and work–family conflict: The moderating influence of job resources and job demands. *Work and Occupations*, 39(1), pp. 71–98.

Global Business Travel Association (GBTA) (2016). *GBTA BTI™ outlook* [online]. Available at: http://www.gbta.org/europe/Pages/default.aspx.

Glucksmann, M. (1995). Why work? Gender and the total social organization of labour. *Gender, Work and Organization*, 2(2), pp. 63–75.

Golden, L. (2009). Flexible daily work schedules in U.S. jobs: Formal introductions needed? *Industrial Relations: A Journal of Economy and Society*, 48(1), pp. 27–54.

Golden, T. D., Veiga, J. F. (2005). The impact of extent of telecommuting on job satisfaction: Resolving inconsistent findings. *Journal of Management*, 31(2), pp. 301–18.

Goos, M., Manning, A. (2007). Lousy and lovely jobs: The rising polarization of work in Britain. *The Review of Economics and Statistics*, 89(1), pp. 118–33.

Gov.uk (2014). *Pensions Act 2014* [online]. Available at: https://www.gov.uk/government/collections/pensions-bill.

Gov.uk (2015). *Charities Act 2011* [online]. Available at: http://www.legislation.gov.uk/ukpga/2011/25.

Gov.uk (2016a). *National citizen service* [online]. Available at: http://www.ncsyes.co.uk/.

Gov.uk (2016b). *Shared parental leave* [online]. Available at: https://www.gov.uk/shared-parental-leave-and-pay-employer-guide/overview.

Graham, C., Chattopadhyay, S., Picon, M. (2010). Adapting to adversity: Happiness and the 2009 economic crisis in the United States. *Social Research*, 77(2), pp. 715–48.

Gratton, C. (2004). Sport, health and economic benefit. In Sport England, *Driving up participation. The challenge for sport*. London: Sport England.

Green, A. E., Berkeley, N. (2006). The West Midlands: The 'hinge' in the middle. In I. Hardill, I., Benneworth, P., Baker, M., and Budd, L. (eds), *The rise of the English regions?* London: Routledge, pp. 156–66.

Green, A. E., Owen, D. W. (2006). *The geography of poor skills and access to work*. York: Joseph Rowntree Foundation.

Green, F. (2001). It's been a hard days night: The concentration and intensification of work in late twentieth-century Britain. *British Journal of Industrial Relations*, 39(1), pp. 53–80.

Green, F. (2004). Work intensification, discretion, and the decline in well-being at work. *Eastern Economic Journal*, 30(4), pp. 615–25.

Green, F. (2006). *Demanding work. The paradox of job quality in the affluent society.* Princeton: Princeton University Press.

Greenfield, E. A., Marks, N. F. (2004). Formal volunteering as a protective factor for older adults' psychological well-being. *The Journals of Gerontology Series B: Psychological Sciences and Social Sciences*, 59(5), pp. S258–S264.

Greenhaus, J. H., Callanan, G., Godshalk, V. (2000). *Career management* (3rd ed.). Mason, OH: Thomson-South-Western.

Greenhaus, J. H., Ziegert, J. C., Allen, T. D. (2012). When family-supportive supervision matters: Relations between multiple sources of support and work–family balance. *Journal of Vocational Behavior*, 80(2), pp. 266–75.

Gregory, A., Milner, S. (2009). Trade unions and work-life balance: Changing times in France and the UK? *British Journal of Industrial Relations*, 47(1), pp. 122–46.

Gregory, M., Connolly, S. (2008). Feature: The price of reconciliation: Part-time work, families and women's satisfaction. *The Economic Journal*, 118(526), pp. F1–F7.

Gregson, N., Lowe, M. (1994). *Servicing the middle classes: Class, gender and waged domestic labour in contemporary Britain.* London: Routledge.

Grimm, R., Spring, K. Dietz, M (2007). *The health benefits of volunteering: A review of recent research.* Office of Research and Policy Development, Corporation for National and Community Service.

Grimshaw, D., Rubery, J. (2012). The end of the UK's liberal collectivist social model? The implications of the coalition government's policy during the austerity crisis. *Cambridge Journal of Economics*, 36(1), pp. 105–26.

Grönlund, A. (2007). More control, less conflict? Job demand-control, gender and work–family conflict. *Gender, Work and Organization*, 14(5), pp. 476–97.

Grossbard, S. (2010). Independent individual decision-makers in household models and the new home economics. *IZA Discussion Paper No. 5138.*

Grossi, E., Blessi, G., Sacco, P. L., Buscema, M. (2012). The interaction between culture, health and psychological well-being: Data mining from the Italian culture and well-being project. *Journal of Happiness Studies*, 13(1), pp. 129–48.

Guardian (2011). *Eurozone crisis: Cameron and Merkel agree framework for EU negotiations* [online], 20 November. Available at: http://www.guardian.co.uk/business/2011/nov/20/cameron-merkel-working-time-directive.

Guest, D. (2002). Perspectives on the study of work-life balance. *Social Science Information*, 41(2), pp. 255–79.

Gustafson, P. (2006). Work-related travel, gender and family obligations. *Work, Employment and Society*, 20(3), pp. 513–30.

Gustafson, P. (2012a). Managing business travel: Developments and dilemmas in corporate travel management. *Tourism Management*, 33(2), pp. 276–84.

Gustafson, P. (2012b). Travel time and working time: What business travellers do when they travel, and why. *Time & Society*, 21(2), pp. 203–22.

Gustafson, P. (2014). Business travel from the traveller's perspective: Stress, stimulation and normalization. *Mobilities*, 9(1), pp. 63–83.

Hakim, C. (2000). *Work-lifestyle choices in the 21st century: Preference theory*. New York: Oxford University Press.

Hakim, C. (2002). Lifestyle preferences as determinants of women's differentiated labor market careers. *Work and Occupations*, 29(4), pp. 428–59.

Hakim, C. (2004). *Key issues in women's work: Female diversity and the polarisation of women's employment*. London: GlassHouse Press.

Halford, S. (2005). Hybrid workspace: Re-spatialisations of work, organization and management. *New Technology, Work and Employment*, 20(1), pp. 19–33.

Hall, D. (2004). The protean career: A quarter-century journey. *Journal of Vocational Behavior*, 65, pp. 1–13.

Hall, L., Atkinson, C. (2006). Improving working lives: Flexible working and the role of employee control. *Employee Relations*, 28(4), pp. 374–86.

Haller, M., Hadler, M. (2006). How social relations and structures can produce happiness and unhappiness: An international comparative analysis. *Social Indicators Research*, 75, pp. 169–216.

Hamermesh, D. (2002). Timing, togetherness and time windfalls. *Journal of Population Economics*, 15(4), pp. 601–23.

Hammersley, M. (2008). Troubles with triangulation. In Bergman, M. (ed.), *Advances in mixed methods research*. London: Sage, pp. 22–36.

Hanson, S., Pratt, G. (1995). *Gender, work and space*. New York: Routledge.

Hardill, I. (2002). *Gender, migration and the dual career household*. International Studies of Women and Place series. London: Routledge.

Hardill I., Baines S. (2007). Volunteering for all? Explaining patterns of volunteering and identifying strategies to promote it. *Policy & Politics*, 35(3), pp. 395–412.

Hardill I., Baines S. (2011). *Enterprising care? Unpaid voluntary action in the 21st century*. Bristol: The Policy Press.

Hardill, I., Bentley, C., Cuthbert, M. (2006). The East Midlands: The missing middle? In I. Hardill, P. Benneworth, M. Baker, L. Budd, L.(eds), *The rise of the English regions?* London: Routledge, pp. 168–83.

Hardill, I., Graham, D., Kofman, E. (2001). *Human geography of the UK: An introduction*. Routledge: London.

Hardill, I., Green, A. (2003). Remote working: Altering the spatial contours of work and home in the new economy. *New Technology, Work and Employment*, 18(3), pp. 212–22.

Hardill, I., Monk, J. (2016). Lifecourse methods. In Douglas Richardson, D., Castree, N., Goodchild, M., Liu, W., Kobayashi, A., and Marston, M., *The Wiley-AAG International Encyclopedia of Geography*. Wiley-Blackwell and the Association of American Geographers

Hardill, I., Watson, R. (2004). Career priorities within dual career households: An analysis of the impact of child rearing upon gender participation rates and earnings. *Industrial Relations Journal*, 35(1), pp. 19–37.

Hardill, I., Wheatley, D. (2009). Dual-career couples, gender and migration. In Reuschke, D. (ed.), *Wohnen und Gender. Theoretische, politische, soziale und raumliche Aspekte*. Wiesbaden: VS Verlag für Sozialwissenschaften, pp. 239–59.

Harris, L., Foster, C., Whysall, P. (2007). Maximising women's potential in the UK's retail sector. *Employee Relations*, 29(5), pp. 492–505.

Harvie, D., Slater, G., Philp, B., Wheatley, D. (2009). Economic well-being and British regions: The problem with GDP per capita. *Review of Social Economy*, 67(4), pp. 483–505.

Hayden, A. (2006). France's 35-hour week: Attack on business? Win-win reform? Or betrayal of disadvantaged workers? *Politics and Society*, 34(4), pp. 503–42.

Headey, B. (2008). The set-point theory of well-being. Negative results and consequent revisions. *Social Indicators Research*, 86, pp. 389–403.

Hecht, T., Boies, K. (2009). Structure and correlates of spillover from nonwork to work: An examination of nonwork activities, well-being, and work outcomes. *Journal of Occupational Health Psychology*, 14(4), pp. 414–26.

Helliwell, J. (2003). How's life? Combining individual and national variables to explain subjective well-being. *Economic Modelling*, 20, pp. 331–60.

Helliwell, J., Layard, R., and Sachs, J. (eds) (2015). *World happiness report 2015* [online]. Available at: http://worldhappiness.report/wp-content/uploads/sites/2/2015/04/WHR15-Apr29-update.pdf.

Hewitt, P. (1993). *About time: The revolution in work and family life*. London: Rivers Oram Press.

Hicks, S., Tinkler, L., Allin, P. (2013). Measuring subjective well-being and its potential role in policy: Perspectives from the UK Office for National Statistics. *Social Indicators Research*, 114(1), pp. 73–86.

Himmelweit, S. (1995). The discovery of 'unpaid work': The social consequences of the expansion of work. *Feminist Economics*, 1(2), pp. 1–19.

Himmelweit, S., Sigala, M. (2002). The welfare implications of mother's decisions about work and childcare. *ESRC Future of Work Programme, Working Paper 20*.

Hislop, D., Axtell, C. (2009). To infinity and beyond? Workspace and the multi-location worker. *New Technology, Work and Employment*, 24(1), pp. 60–75.

Hjorthol, R., Vågane, L. (2014). Allocation of tasks, arrangement of working hours and commuting in different Norwegian households. *Journal of Transport Geography*, 35(1), pp. 75–83.

H.M. Treasury (2006). *Stern review on the economics of climate change* [online]. Available at: http://www.hm-treasury.gov.uk/independent_reviews/stern_review_economics_climate_change/stern_review_report.cfm.

Hobsbawm, E. (1968). *Labouring men*. London: Weidenfeld and Nicolson.

Hochschild, A. R. (2003). *The managed heart. Commercialization of human feeling*, Berkeley: University of California Press.

Hochschild, A. R., Machung, A. (1990). *The second shift, working parents and the revolution at home*. London: Piatkus.

Hodgson, G. (1988). *Economics and institutions*. Cambridge: Polity Press.

Hodgson, G. (1999). *Economics and utopia*. London: Routledge.

Hodson, R (2005). Gender differences in job satisfaction: Why aren't women more dissatisfied? *The Sociological Quarterly*, 30(3), pp. 385–99.

Hogarth, T., Hasluck, C., Pierre, G., Winterbotham, M., Vivian, D. (2001). *Work-life balance 2000: Results from the baseline study.* Department for Education and Employment Research Report Number 249. http://dera.ioe.ac.uk/4596/1/RR249.PDF.

Hogg, E. (2016). Constant, serial and trigger volunteers: Volunteering across the life-course and into older age. *Voluntary Sector Review*, 7(2), 169–90.

Holley, D., Jain, J., Lyons, G. (2008). Understanding business travel time and its place in the working day. *Time & Society*, 17(1), pp. 27–46.

Holman, D. (2013). Job types and job quality in Europe. *Human Relations*, 66(4), pp. 475–502.

Hoque, K., Kirkpatrick, I. (2003). Non-standard employment in the management and professional workforce: Training, consultation and gender implications. *Work, Employment and Society*, 17(4), pp. 667–89.

Houlihan, M. (2002). Tensions and variations in call centre management strategies. *Human Resource Management Journal*, 12(4), pp. 67–85.

Huang, H., Humphreys, B. R. (2012). Sports participation and happiness: Evidence from US microdata. *Journal of Economic Psychology*, 33(4), pp. 776–93.

Hughes, B., McKie, L., Hopkins, D., Watson, N. (2005). Love's labours lost? Feminism, the disabled people's movement and an ethic of care. *Sociology*, 39(2), pp. 259–75.

Humphrey, S. E., Nahrgang, J. D., Morgeson, F. P. (2007). Integrating motivational, social, and contextual work design features: A meta-analytic summary and theoretical extension of the work design literature. *Journal of Applied Psychology*, 92, pp. 1332–56.

Humphreys, B., Ruseski, J. (2006). *Economic determinants of participation in physical activity and sport*. International Association of Sports Economists Working Paper No. 0613.

Hundley, G. (2001). Why women earn less than men in self-employment. *Journal of Labour Research*, 22(4), pp. 817–29.

Hyman, J., Summers, J. (2004). Lacking balance? Work-life employment practices in the modern economy. *Personnel Review*, 33(4), pp. 418–29.

Hytti, U. (2010) Contextualizing entrepreneurship in the boundaryless career. *Gender in Management: An International Journal*, 25(1), pp. 64–81.

Ivancevich, J., Konpaske, R., DeFrank, R. (2003) Business travel stress: A model, propositions and managerial implications. *Work & Stress*, 17(2), pp. 138–57.

Iwasaki, Y. (2007). Leisure and quality of life in an international and multicultural context: What are major pathways linking leisure to quality of life? *Social Indicators Research*, 82(2), pp. 233–64.

Jacobs, J., Gerson, K. (2001). Overworked individuals or over-worked families? Explaining trends in work, leisure and family time. *Work and Occupations*, 28(1), pp. 40–63.

Jang, J. S., Park, R., Zippay, A. (2011). The interaction effects of scheduling control and work–life balance programs on job satisfaction and mental health. *International Journal of Social Welfare*, 20, pp. 135–43.

Jenkins, S., Delbridge, R., Roberts, A. (2010). Emotional management in a mass customised call centre: Examining skill and knowledgeability in interactive service work. *Work, Employment & Society*, 24(3), pp. 546–64.

Jeong, Y.-J., Zvonkovic, A., Sano, Y., Acock, A (2013). The occurrence and frequency of overnight job travel in the USA. *Work, Employment and Society*, 27(1), pp. 138–52.

Johansson, B., Klaesson, J., Olsson, M. (2003). Commuters' non-linear response to time distances. *Journal of Geographical Systems*, 5(3), pp. 315–30.

Jones, A. (2003). *About time for change*. London: The Work Foundation.

Jones, A. (2013). Conceptualising business mobilities: Towards an analytical framework. *Research in Transportation Business & Management*, 9, pp. 58–66.

Jorgensen, B., Jamieson, R., Martin, F. (2010). Income, sense of community and subjective well-being: Combining economic and psychological variables. *Journal of Economic Psychology*, 31(4), pp. 612–23.

José de Freitas Armstrong, N. (1999). Flexible work in the virtual workplace: Discourses and implications of teleworking. In Felstead, A., and Jewson, N. *Global Trends in Flexible Labour*. London: Macmillan Press, pp. 43–61.

Kahneman, D., Krueger, A. (2006). Developments in the measurement of subjective well-being. *Journal of Economic Perspectives*, 20(1), pp. 3–24.

Kahneman, D., Krueger, A. B., Schkade, D., Schwartz, N., Stone, A. (2004). Toward national well-being accounts. *The American Economic Review*, 94, pp. 429–34.

Kahneman, D., Krueger, A. B., Schkade, D., Schwarz, N., Stone, A. A. (2006). Would you be happier if you were richer? A focusing illusion. *Science*, 312 (5782), pp. 1908–10.

Kalleberg, A. L. (2012). Job quality and precarious work: Clarifications, controversies, and challenges. *Work and Occupations*, 39(4), pp. 427–48.

Kalleberg, A. L., Nesheim, T., Olsen, K. M. (2009). Is participation good or bad for workers? *Acta Sociologica* 52(2), pp. 99–116.

Kapp, K. W. (1968). In defence of institutional economics. *Swedish Journal of Economics*, 70, pp. 1–18.

Karasek, R. A., Theorell, T. (1990). *Healthy work: Stress, productivity, and the reconstruction of working life*. New York: Basic Books.

Kavetsos, G. (2011). Physical activity and subjective wellbeing: An empirical analysis. In Rodriguez, P., Kesenne, S., and Humphreys, B. R., *The economics of sport, health and happiness: The promotion of wellbeing through sporting activities*. Edward Elgar, pp. 213–22.

Kelliher, C., Anderson, D. (2008). For better or for worse? An analysis of how flexible working practices influence employees' perceptions of job quality. *The International Journal of Human Resource Management*, 19(3), pp. 419–31.

Kendall, J. (2010). *Volunteering in the noughties: What would Beveridge have thought?* Birmingham: Third Sector Research Centre.

Kelly, E. L., Moen, P., Tranby, E. (2011). Changing workplaces to reduce work-family conflict: Schedule control in a white-collar organization. *American Sociological Review*, 76(2), 265–90.

Kelly, G. M. (2000). Employment and concepts of work in the new global economy. *International Labour Review*, 139(1), pp. 5–32.

Kelly, J. R. (1982). *Leisure*. Englewood Cliffs, NJ: Prentice-Hall.

Kemperman, A., Timmermans, H. (2008). Influence of socio-demographic and residential environment on leisure activity participation. *Leisure Sciences*, 30, pp. 306–24.

Kesebir, P., Diener, E., (2008). In defense of happiness. In Bruni, L., Comim, F., and Pugno, M. (eds), *Capabilities and happiness*. Oxford: Oxford University Press, pp. 60–80.

Khattab, N., Fenton, S. (2009). What makes young adults happy? Employment and non-work as determinants of life satisfaction. *Sociology*, 43(1), pp. 11–26.

Kilpatrick, A., Lawson, T. (1980). On the nature of industrial decline in the UK. *Cambridge Journal of Economics*, 4, pp. 85–102.

Kim, J. E., Moen, P. (2001). Is retirement good or bad for subjective well-being? *Current Directions in Psychological Science*, 10(3), 83–6.

Kim, J. E., Moen, P. (2002). Retirement transitions, gender, and psychological well-being: A life-course, ecological model. *The Journals of Gerontology Series B: Psychological Sciences and Social Sciences*, 57(3), pp. P212–22.

Kirk, S. (2016). Career capital in global kaleidoscope careers: The role of HRM. *The International Journal of Human Resource Management*, 27(6), pp. 681–97.

Kitson, M., Wilkinson, F. (2007). The economics of new labour: policy and performance. *Cambridge Journal of Economics*, 31(6), 805–16.

Kjeldstad, R., Nymoen, E. (2012). Part-time work and gender: Worker versus job explanations. *International Labour Review*, 151(1–2), pp. 85–107.

Kloosterman, R. C., Musterd, S. (2001). The polycentric urban region: Towards a research agenda. *Urban Studies*, 38(4), pp. 623–33.

Knabe, A, Rätzel, S., Schöb, R., Weimann, J. (2010). Dissatisfied with life but having a good day: Time-use and well-being of the unemployed. *The Economic Journal*, 120, pp. 867–89.

Knoester, C., Eggebeen, D. (2006). The effects of the transition to parenthood and subsequent children on men's well-being and social participation. *Journal of Family Issues*, 27(11), pp. 1532–60.

Kodz, J., Kersley, B., Strebler, M. T., O'Regan, S. (1998). *Breaking the long hours culture.* London: Institute for Employment Studies.

Krueger, A., Mueller, A. (2012). Time use, emotional well-being, and unemployment: Evidence from longitudinal data. *The American Economic Review*, 102(3), pp. 594–99.

Kusku, F., Ozbilgin, M., Ozkale, L. (2007). Against the tide: Gendered prejudice and disadvantage in engineering. *Gender, Work and Organization*, 14(2), pp. 109–29.

Kyro, P. (2009). Gender lenses identify different waves and ways of understanding women entrepreneurship. *Journal of Enterprising Culture*, 17(4), pp. 393–418.

Laibman, D. (1992). *Value, technical change and crisis: Explorations in marxist economic theory*. New York: M.E. Sharpe.

LaJeunesse, R. (2009). *Work-time regulation as sustainable full employment strategy*. London: Routledge.

Lassen, C. (2009). Networking, knowledge organizations and aeromobility. Geografiska Annaler: Series B. *Human Geography*, 91(3), pp. 229–43.

Lassen, C. (2010). Individual rationalities of global business travel. In Beaverstock, J. V., Derudder, B., Faulconbridge, J., and Witlox, F. (eds), *International business travel in the global economy*. Farnham: Ashgate, pp. 177–94.

Lawson, T. (2003). *Reorienting economics*. London: Routledge.

Lawson, V. (2007). Geographies of care and responsibility. *Annals of the Association of American Geographers*, 97(1), pp. 1–11.

Leahy, M., Doughey, J. (2006). Women, work and preference formation: A critique of Catherine Hakim's preference theory. *Journal of Business Systems, Governance and Ethics*, 1(1), pp. 37–48.

Lee, S., McCann, D., Messenger, J. (2007). *Working time around the world: Trends in working hours, laws, and policies in a global comparative perspective*. Oxon, UK: Routledge.

Lee, Y. H., Lin, H. (2011). 'Gaming is my work': Identity work in internet-hobbyist game workers. *Work, Employment & Society*, 25(3), pp. 451–67.

Lever, W. (1987). New trends in the supply and demand patterns of labour in Western economies. In Fischer, M., and Nijkamp, P. (eds), *Regional Labour Markets*. New York: North-Holland, pp. 249–67.

Lewis, J. (2001). The decline of the male breadwinner model: The implications for work and care. *Social Politics*, 8(2), pp. 152–70.

Lewis, J. (2002). Gender and welfare state change. *European Societies*, 4(4), pp. 331–57.

Lewis, J., Campbell, M. (2008). What's in a name? 'Work and family' or 'work and life' balance policies in the UK since 1997 and the implications for the pursuit of gender equality. *Social Policy and Administration*, 42(5), pp. 524–41.

Lewis, J., Plomien, A. (2009). 'Flexicurity' as a policy strategy: The implications for gender equality. *Economy and Society*, 38(3), pp. 433–59.

Lewis, S., Humbert, L. (2010). Discourse or reality? Work life balance, flexible working policies and the gendered organization. *Equality, Diversity and Inclusion: An International Journal*, 29(3), pp. 239–54.

Li, Y., Ferraro, K. F. (2006). Volunteering in middle and later life: Is health a benefit, barrier or both? *Social Forces*, 85(1), pp. 497–519.

Liff, S., Ward K. (2001). Distorted views through the glass ceiling: The construction of women's understandings of promotion and senior management positions. *Gender, Work and Organization*, 8(1), pp. 19–36.

Lindsay, C. (2003). A century of labour market change. *Labour Market Trends*, March, pp. 133–44.

Lindsey, R., Metcalfe, E., Edwards, R. (2015). Time in mixed methods longitudinal research: Working across written narratives and large scale panel survey data to investigate attitudes to volunteering. In Worth, N., and Hardill, I. (eds), *Researching the lifecourse: Critical reflections from the social sciences*. Bristol, UK: Policy Press, pp. 43–61.

Lipietz, A. (1997). The post-Fordist world: Labor relations, international hierarchy and global ecology. *Review of International Political Economy*, 4(1), pp. 1–41.

Livingston, B. (2014). Bargaining behind the scenes: Spousal negotiation, labor, and work–family burnout. *Journal of Management*, 40(4), pp. 949–77.

Lloyd, J. (2003). Dwelltime: Airport technology, travel and consumption. *Space and Culture*, 6(2), pp. 93–109.

Lloyd, K., Auld, C. (2002). The role of leisure in determining quality of life: Issues of content and measurement. *Social Indicators Research*, 57, pp. 43–71.

Lowry, D., Moskos, M. (2008). Mobile phones, spillover and the 'work–life balance'. In Hislop, D. (ed.), *Mobility and technology in the workplace*. Oxford: Routledge, pp. 167–79.

Lu, J. L., Peeta, S. (2009). Analysis of the factors that influence the relationship between business air travel and videoconferencing. *Transportation Research Part A*, 43(8), pp. 709–21.

Lucas, R. (1987). *Models of business cycles*. Oxford: Basil Blackwell.

Lucas, R. (2007). Long-term disability is associated with lasting changes in subjective well-being: Evidence from two nationally representative longitudinal studies. *Journal of Personality and Social Psychology*, 92(4), pp. 717–30.

Lucas, R., Clark, A. E., Georgellis, Y., Diener, E. (2004). Unemployment alters the set point for life satisfaction. *Psychological Science*, 15(1), pp. 8–13.

Lundberg, S., Pollak, R. (2007). The American family and family economics. *Journal of Economic Perspectives*, 21(2), pp. 3–26.

Luttmer, E. (2005). Neighbors as negatives: Relative earnings and well-being. *The Quarterly Journal of Economics*, 20(3), pp. 963–1002.

Lyness, K., Gornick, J., Stone, P., Grotto, A. (2012). It's all about control: Worker control over schedule and hours in cross-national context. *American Sociological Review*, 20(10), pp. 1–27.

Lyon, D., Glucksmann, M. (2008). Comparative configuration of work across Europe. *Sociology*, 42(1), pp. 101–18.

Lyons, G., Jain, J., Holley, D. (2007). The use of travel time by rail passengers in Great Britain. *Transportation Research Part A: Policy and Practice*, 41(1), pp. 107–20.

Lyons, G., Urry, J. (2005). Travel time use in the information age. *Transportation Research Part A*, 39(2–3), pp. 257–76.

MacDonald, M., Phipps, S., Lethbridge, L. (2005). Taking its toll: The influence of paid and unpaid work on women's well-being. *Feminist Economics*, 11(1), pp. 63–94.

MacKerron, G. (2012). Happiness economics from 35,000 feet. *Journal of Economic Surveys*, 26(4), pp. 705–35.

Mainiero, L., Sullivan, S. (2005). Kaleidoscope careers: An alternate explanation for the 'opt-out' revolution. *Academy of Management Executive*, 19(1), pp. 106–23.

Mandel, H., Semyonov, M. (2005). Wage structures and gender gaps: Sources of earnings inequality in 20 countries. *American Sociological Review*, 70(6), pp. 949–67.

Marglin, S. (1974). What do bosses do? The origins and functions of hierarchy in capitalist production. *Review of Radical Political Economics*, 6(2), pp. 60–112.

Marsh, K., Bertranou, E. (2012). Can subjective well-being measures be used to value policy outcomes? The example of engagement in culture. *Cultural Trends*, 21(4), pp. 299–310.

Marsh, K., MacKay, S., Morton, D., Parry, W., Bertranou, E., Lewsie, J., Sarmah, R., Dolan, P. (2010). *CASE: Understanding the drivers, impact and value of engagement in culture and sport* [online]. Department for Culture, Media and Sport. Available at: https://www.gov.uk/government/uploads/system/uploads/attachment_data/file/71231/CASE-supersummaryFINAL-19-July2010.pdf.

Martin, M., Westerhof, G. (2003). Do you have to have them or should you believe you have them? Resources, their appraisal, and well-being in adulthood. *Journal of Adult Development*, 10, pp. 99–112.

Martin, R., Rowthorn, B. (eds) (1986). *The geography of de-industrialization*. London: Macmillan.

Marx, K. (1976). *Capital. Vol. 1*, trans. Ben Fowkes. London: Penguin.

Mason, C., Carter, S., Tagg, S. (2011). Invisible businesses: The characteristics of home-based businesses in the United Kingdom. *Regional Studies*, 45(5), pp. 625–39.

Massey, D. (1994). *Space, place and gender*. Cambridge: Polity Press.

Maxwell, G., Rankine, L., Bell, S. MacVicar, A. (2007). The incidence and impact of flexible working arrangements in smaller businesses. *Employee Relations*, 29(2), pp. 138–61.

McCarthy, A., Darcy, C., Grady, G. (2010). Work-life balance policy and practice: Understanding line manager attitudes and behaviors. *Human Resource Management Review*, 20(2), pp. 158–67.

McDonald, P., Bradley, L., Brown, K. (2009). Full-time is a given here': Part-time versus full-time job quality. *British Journal of Management*, 20(2), pp. 143–57.

McDowell, L. (2004). Work, workfare, work/life balance and an ethic of care. *Progress in Human Geography*, 28(2), pp. 145–63.

McDowell, L., Perrons, D., Fagan, C., Ray, K., Ward, K. (2005). The contradictions and intersections of class and gender in a global city: Placing working women's lives on the research agenda. *Environment & Planning A*, 37(3), pp. 441–61.

McDowell, L., Ward, K., Fagan, C., Perrons, D., Ray, K. (2006). Connecting time and space: The significance of transformations in women's work in the city. *International Journal of Urban and Regional Research*, 30(1), pp. 141–58.

McLaughlin, J. (2006). Conceptualising intensive caring activities: The changing lives of families with young disabled children [online]. *Sociological Research Online*, 11(1). Available at: http://www.socresonline.org.uk/11/1/mclaughlin.html.

McNamara, T., Pitt-Catsouphes, M., Brown, M., Matz-Costa, C. (2012). Access to and utilization of flexible work options. *Industrial Relations: A Journal of Economy and Society*, 51(4), pp. 936–65.

McQuaid, R., Greig, M., Adams, J. (2001). Unemployed job seeker attitudes towards potential travel-to-work times. *Growth and Change*, 32, pp. 355–68.

Meagher, G., Nelson, J. A. (2004). Survey article: Feminism in the dismal science. *Journal of Political Philosophy*, 12(1), pp. 102–26.

Meier, S., Stutzer, A. (2006). *Is volunteering rewarding in itself?* Center for Behavioral Economics and Decision-Making, Federal Reserve Bank of Boston.

Meier, S., Stutzer, A. (2008). Is volunteering rewarding in itself? *Economica*, 75(297), pp. 39–59.

Mentzakis, E., Moro, M. (2009). The poor, the rich and the happy: Exploring the link between income and subjective well-being. *The Journal of Socio-Economics*, 38(1), pp. 147–58.

Messenger, J. C. (2011). Working time trends and developments in Europe. *Cambridge Journal of Economics*, 35(2), pp. 295–316.

Michalos, A. (2005). Arts and the quality of life: An exploratory study. *Social Indicators Research*, 71, pp. 11–59.

Michalos, A., Kahlke, P. M. (2008). Impact of arts related activities on the perceived quality of life. *Social Indicators Research*, 89, 193–258.

Michalos, A., Kahlke, P. M. (2010). Arts and the Perceived Quality of Life in British Columbia. *Social Indicators Research*, 96, 1–39.

Mirowski, P. (1981). Is there a mathematical neoinstitutional economics? *Journal of Economic Issues*, 15(3), pp. 593–613.

Mitchell, W. C. (1925). Quantitative analysis in economics. *American Economic Review*, 15, pp. 1–12.

Moktharian, P., Salomon, I. (2001). How derived is the demand for travel? Some conceptual and measurement considerations. *Transportation Research Part A*, 35(8), pp. 695–719.

Morrison, A. (2006). A contextualization of entrepreneurship. *International Journal of Entrepreneurial Behaviour and Research*, 12(4), pp. 192–209.

Morrow-Howell, N., Hinterlong, J., Rozario, P., Tang, F. (2003). Effects of volunteering on the well-being of older adults. *Journal of Gerontology*, 58B(3), pp. S137–S145.

Musson, G. (1998). Life histories. In Symon, G., and Cassell, C. (eds), *Qualitative methods and analysis in organizational research.* London: SAGE, pp. 10–27.

National Centre for Social Research (2011). *British Social Attitudes Survey, 2009* [computer file]. Colchester, Essex: UK Data Archive [distributor], February 2011. SN:6695, http://dx.doi.org/10.5255/UKDA-SN-6695-1.

National Council for Voluntary Organisations (NCVO) (2016). *Employer-supported volunteering: What can research tell us about election 2015 policies?* [online]. Available at: http://blogs.ncvo.org.uk/2015/04/16/employer-supported-volunteering-what-can-research-tell-us-about-election-2015-policies/.

Nelson, J. A. (1995). Feminism and economics. *The Journal of Economic Perspectives*, 9(2), pp. 131–48.

Neuberger, J. (2008). *Report of the Commission on the Future of Volunteering and Manifesto for Change*. London: Volunteering England.

Nicholas, H., McDowall, A. (2012). When work keeps us apart: A thematic analysis of the experience of business travellers. *Community, Work and Family*, 15(3), pp. 335–55.

Nichols, G., Shepherd, M. (2006). Volunteering in sport: The use of ratio analysis to analyse volunteering and participation. *Managing Leisure*, 11(4), pp. 205–16.

Nolan, P., Slater, G. (2003). The labour market: History, structure and prospects. In *Industrial relations: Theory and practice* (2nd ed.). Oxford: Blackwell Publishers, pp. 58–80.

Nomaguchi, K., Milkie, M., Bianchi, S. (2005). Time strains and psychological well-being: Do dual-earner mothers and fathers differ? *Journal of Family Issues*, 26(6), pp. 756–92.

NOMIS (2013a). *Annual population survey: Economic activity and unemployment rates, October 2011–September 2012*. Office for National Statistics (ONS): Crown Copyright Reserved. Available at: http://www.nomisweb.co.uk.

NOMIS (2013b). *2011 Census of Population. DC3301EW – provision of unpaid care by general health by sex by age* [computer file]. Office for National Statistics: Crown Copyright Reserved. Available at: http://www.nomisweb.co.uk/census/2011/.

NOMIS (2014). *Mid-year population estimates, 2013* [online]. Office for National Statistics: Crown Copyright Reserved. Available at: https://www.nomisweb.co.uk/reports/lmp/gor/2092957698/report.aspx#tabrespop.

NOMIS (2015). *Annual population survey 2014: Employment by occupation and gender* [online]. Office for National Statistics: Crown Copyright Reserved. Available at: http://www.nomisweb.co.uk.

NOMIS (2016). *Annual population survey 2015: Economic activity and unemployment rates* [online]. Office for National Statistics: Crown Copyright Reserved. Available at: http://www.nomisweb.co.uk.

Nottingham City Council (2006). *Economy: Largest employers* [online]. Available at: http://www.nottinghamcity.gov.uk/index.aspx?articleid=7898#Largest%20Employers.

Nottingham City Council (2010). *Nottingham population estimates* [online]. Available at: http://www.nottinghamcity.gov.uk.

Nottingham City Council (2016). *Workplace parking levy* [online]. Available at: http://www.nottinghamcity.gov.uk/wpl.

Oakley, A. (1974). *The sociology of housework*. London: Martin Robertson.

OECD (2013). *Guidelines on measuring subjective well-being* [online]. Available at: http://www.oecd.org/statistics/Guidelines%20on%20Measuring%20Subjective%20Well-being.pdf.

Office for National Statistics (ONS) (2013a). *170 years of industrial change across England and Wales* [online]. Available at: http://www.ons.gov.uk/ons/rel/census/2011-census-analysis/170-years-of-industry/170-years-of-industrial-changeponent.html.

Office for National Statistics (ONS) (2013b). *Annual survey of hours and earnings, 2013 provisional results* [online]. Available at: http://www.ons.gov.uk/ons/dcp171778_335027.pdf.

Office for National Statistics (ONS) (2013c). *Women in the labour market* [online]. Available at: http://www.ons.gov.uk/ons/dcp171776_328352.pdf.

Office for National Statistics (ONS) (2014a). *Annual survey of hours and earnings, 2014 provisional results* [online]. Available at: http://www.ons.gov.uk/ons/dcp171778_385428.pdf.

Office for National Statistics (ONS) (2014b). *Self employed workers in the UK* [online]. Available at: http://www.ons.gov.uk/ons/dcp171776_374941.pdf.

Office for National Statistics (ONS) (2014c). *Measuring national well-being* [online]. Available at: http://www.ons.gov.uk/ons/guide-method/user-guidance/well-being/index.html.

Office for National Statistics (ONS) (2015a). *Annual survey of hours and earnings, 2015 provisional results* [online]. Available at: http://www.ons.gov.uk/ons/dcp171778_385428.pdf.

Office for National Statistics (ONS) (2015b). *Employee contracts that do not guarantee a minimum number of hours: 2015 update* [online]. Available at: http://www.ons.gov.uk/ons/dcp171776_415332.pdf.

Office for National Statistics (ONS) (2015d). *Time series: LFS: Part-time workers: % could not find full-time job: UK: All: SA* [online]. Available at: http://www.ons.gov.uk/employmentandlabourmarket/peopleinwork/employmentandemployeetypes/timeseries/ycda.

Office for National Statistics (ONS) (2015e). *UK labour market, June 2015* [online]. Available at: http://www.ons.gov.uk/employmentandlabourmarket/peopleinwork/employmentandemployeetypes/bulletins/uklabourmarket/2015-06-17.

Office for National Statistics (ONS) (2016a). Social survey division, Northern Ireland statistics and research agency. Central Survey Unit. *Quarterly Labour Force Survey, April–June 2015*. [data collection]. 3rd Ed. UK Data Service. SN: 7781, http://dx.doi.org/10.5255/UKDA-SN-7781-3.

Office for National Statistics (ONS) (2016b). *Time series: LFS: Usual hours of work: Self-employed: Over 45 hours*. [online]. Available at: https://www.ons.gov.uk/employmentandlabourmarket/peopleinwork/employmentandemployeetypes/timeseries/lzjm/lms.

Office for National Statistics (ONS) (2016c). *National travel survey, 2015* [online]. Available at: https://www.gov.uk/government/uploads/system/uploads/attachment_data/file/551437/national-travel-survey-2015.pdf.

Office for National Statistics (ONS) (2016d). *Travel trends, 2015* [online]. Available at: http://www.ons.gov.uk/peoplepopulationandcommunity/leisureandtourism/articles/traveltrends/2015.

Office for National Statistics (ONS) (2016e). *Annual survey of hours and earnings, 1997–2015: Secure Access*. [data collection]. 8th Ed. UK Data Service. SN: 6689, http://dx.doi.org/10.5255/UKDA-SN-6689-7.

Ogbonna, E., Harris, L. C. (2004). Work intensification and emotional labour among UK university lecturers: An exploratory study. *Organization Studies*, 25(7), pp. 1185–203.

Onyx, J., Leonard, R. (2000). Women, volunteering and social capital. In Warburton, J., and Oppenheimer, M. (eds), *Volunteers and Volunteering*. Annandale, NSW: Federation Press, pp. 113–24.

O'Reilly, J., Bothfeld, S. (2002). What happens after working part time? Integration, maintenance or exclusionary transitions in Britain and western Germany. *Cambridge Journal of Economics*, 26(4), pp. 409–39.

Oswald, A., Powdthavee, N. (2008). Does happiness adapt? A longitudinal study of disability with implications for economists and judges. *Journal of Public Economics*, 92, pp. 1061–77.

Padavic, I., Reskin, B. (2002). *Women and men at work* (2nd ed.). Thousand Oaks, CA: Pine Forge Press.

Pahl, R. mE. (1984). *Divisions of labour*. Oxford: Basil Blackwell.

Pascall, G. (2008). Gender and new labour: After the male breadwinner model? In Maltby, T., Kennett, P., and Rummery, K. (eds), *Social Policy Review 20*. Bristol: Policy Press, pp. 215–40.

Pavot, W., Diener, E. (2013). Happiness experienced: The science of subjective well-being. In David, S., Boniwell, I., and Conley Ayers, A. (eds), *The Oxford handbook of happiness*. Oxford: Oxford University Press, pp. 134–54.

Pawson, R., Tilley, N. (2006). *Realistic evaluation*. London: Sage.

Peel, S., Inkson, K. (2004). Contracting and careers: Choosing between self and organizational employment. *Career Development International*, 9(6), pp. 542–58.

Perrons, D. (2003). The new economy and the work-life balance: Conceptual explorations and a case study of new media. *Gender, Work and Organization*, 10(1), pp. 65–93.

Perrons, D. (2004). *Globalization and social change: People and places in a divided world*. London: Routledge.

Perrons, D., Fagan, C., McDowell, L, Ray, K., Ward, K. (2005). Work, life and time in the new economy. *Time and Society*, 14(1), pp. 51–64.

Perrons, D., Fagan, C., McDowell, L., Ray, K., Ward, K. (eds) (2006). *Gender divisions and working time in the new economy: Changing patterns of work, care and public policy in Europe and North America*. London: Edward Elgar.

Peterson, J., Lewis, M. (1999). *The Elgar companion to feminist economics*. Cheltenham: Edward Elgar.

Pfau-Effinger, B. (1998). Culture or structure as explanations for differences in part-time work in Germany, Finland and the Netherlands? In O'Reilly, J., and Fagan, C. (eds), *Part-time prospects: An international comparison of part-time work in Europe*. London: Routledge, pp. 177–98.

Philp, B. (2001). Marxism, neoclassical economics and the length of the working day. *Review of Political Economy*, 13(1), pp. 27–39.

Philp, B., Harvie, D., Slater, G. (2005). Preferences, power and the determination of working hours. *Journal of Economic Issues*, 39 (1), pp. 75–90.

Philp, B., Slater, G., Wheatley, D. (2015). New labour and work-time regulation: A quantitative analysis of capitalism in the UK, 1992–2009. *Cambridge Journal of Economics*, 39(3), pp. 711–32.

Philp, B., Wheatley, D. (2011). Time scarcity and the dual career household: Competing perspectives. *American Journal of Economics and Sociology*, 70(3), pp. 587–614.

Philp, B., Wheatley, D. (2013). European work time regulation and underemployment: A quantitative Marxist analysis. *Economic Issues*, 19(1), pp. 57–74.

Philpott, J. (2005). French lessons. *People Management*, October, 11(5).

Pichler, F. (2006). Subjective quality of life of young Europeans. Feeling happy but who knows why? *Social Indicators Research*, 75, pp. 419–44.

Plagnol, A. (2010). Subjective well-being over the life course: Conceptualizations and evaluations. *Social Research*, 77(2), pp. 749–68.

Poelmans, S., Beham, B. (2008). The moment of truth: Conceptualizing managerial work–life policy allowance decisions. *Journal of Occupational and Organizational Psychology*, 81(3), pp. 393–410.

Pooley, C. G., Turnbull, J., Adams, M. (2005). *A mobile century? Changes in everyday mobility in Britain in the twentieth century*. Hampshire: Ashgate Publishing.

Putnam, C. R. D. (2000). *Bowling alone: The collapse and revival of American community*. New York: Simon & Schuster.

Pyöriä, P. (2003). Knowledge work in distributed environments: Issues and illusions. *New Technology, Work and Employment*, 18(3), pp. 166–80.

Pyöriä, P. (2011). Managing telework: Risks, fears and rules. *Management Research Review*, 34(4), pp. 386–99.

Qari, S. (2014). Marriage, adaptation and happiness: Are there long-lasting gains to marriage? *Journal of Behavioral and Experimental Economics*, 50, pp. 29–39.

Quah, D. (2000). The weightless economy: In whose interest? *CEP's CentrePiece*, 5(1), pp. 28–30.

Quah, D. (2001). Technology dissemination and economic growth: Some lessons for the new economy [online]. Public Lecture, University of Hong Kong.

Raess, D., Burgoon, B. (2015). Flexible work and immigration in Europe. *British Journal of Industrial Relations*, 53(1), pp. 94–111.

Reid, D. (1996). Weddings, weekdays, work and leisure in urban England 1791–1911. *Past and Present*, 153, pp. 135–63.

Reitsma, R. F., Vergoossen, D. (1988). A causal typology of migration: The role of commuting. *Regional Studies*, 22(4), pp. 331–40.

Rifkin, J. (1995). *The end of work: The decline of the global labour force and the dawn of the post-market era*. New York: G. P. Putnams Sons.

Ritchie, J., Spencer, L. (eds) (2003). *Qualitative research practice*. London: Sage.

Roberts, J., Hodgson, R., Dolan, P. (2011). 'It's driving her mad': Gender differences in the effects of commuting on psychological health. *Journal of Health Economics*, 30(5), pp. 1064–76.

Robinson, J., Martin, S. (2008). What do happy people do? *Social Indicators Research*, 89, pp. 565–71.

Rochester, C., Ellis Paine, A., Howlett, S., Zimmeck, M. (2010). *Volunteering and society in the 21st century*. Basingstoke: Palgrave Macmillan.

Rodríguez, A., Látková, P., Sun, Y.-Y. (2008). The relationship between leisure and life satisfaction: Application of activity and need theory. *Social Indicators Research*, 86, pp. 163–75.

Roehling, P., Bultman, M. (2002). Does absence make the heart grow fonder? Work-related travel and marital satisfaction. *Sex Roles*, 46(9/10), pp. 279–93.

Rouwendal, J., Nijkamp, P. (2004). Living in two worlds: A review of home-to-work decisions. *Growth and Change*, 35(3), pp. 287–304.

Rueschemeyer, D. (2003). Can one or a few cases yield gains? In Mahoney, J., and Rueschemeyer, D. (eds), *Comparative historical analysis in the social sciences*. Cambridge: Cambridge University Press, pp. 305–36.

Rutherford, M. (2001). Institutional economics: Then and now. *Journal of Economic Perspectives*, 15(3), pp. 173–94.

Sallaz, J. (2002). The house rules: Autonomy and interests among service workers in the contemporary casino industry. *Work and Occupations*, 29(4), pp. 394–427.

Sampson, R. J., McAdam, D., MacIndoe, H., Weffer-Elizondo, S. (2005). Civil society reconsidered: The durable nature and community structure of collective civil action. *American Journal of Sociology*, 111, pp. 673–714.

Samuelson, P. A. (1948). Consumption theory in terms of revealed preferences. *Economica*, 15(60), pp. 243–53.

Sandow, E. (2014). Till work do us part: The social fallacy of long-distance commuting. *Urban Studies*, 51(3), pp. 526–43.

Sandow, E., Westin, K. (2010). The persevering commuter – duration of long-distance commuting. *Transportation Research Part A*, 44(6), pp. 433–45.

Sassoon, A. S. (1996). Complexity, contradictions, creativity: Transitions and the voluntary sector. *Soundings*, 4, pp. 183–94.

Schein, E. (1978). *Career dynamics: Matching individual and organizational needs*. London: Addison-Wesley.

Schein, E. (1996). Career anchors revisited: Implications for career development in the 21st century. *Academy of Management Executive*, 10(4), pp. 80–88.

Scheiner, J., Holz-Rau, C. (2012). Gendered travel mode choice: A focus on car deficient households. *Journal of Transport Geography*, 24, pp. 250–61.

Schimmack, U. (2008). The structure of subjective well-being. In Eid, M., and Larsen, R. J. (eds), *The science of subjective well-being*. New York: Guildford, pp. 97–123.

Schmid, G. (2010). Non-standard employment and labour force participation: A comparative view of the recent development in Europe. *IZA Discussion Paper No. 5087*.

Schoon, I., Hansson, L., Salmela-Aro, K. (2005). Combining work and family life: Life satisfaction among married and divorced men and women in Estonia, Finland and the UK. *European Psychologist*, 10, pp. 309–19.

Schor, J. (1993). *The overworked American: The unexpected decline of leisure*. New York: Basic Books.

Schwanen, T. (2007). Gender differences in chauffeuring children among dual-earner families. *The Professional Geographer*, 59(4), pp. 447–62.

Schwanen, T., Hardill, I., Lucas, S. (2012). Spatialities of ageing: The co-construction and co-evolution of old age and space. *Geoforum*, 43(6), pp. 1291–95.

Schwanen, T., Kwan, M. P., Ren, F., (2008). How fixed is fixed? Gendered rigidity of space–time constraints and geographies of everyday activities. *Geoforum*, 39(6), pp. 2109–21.

Scott, S. (2006). The social morphology of skilled migration: The case of the British middle class in Paris. *Journal of Ethnic and Migration Studies*, 32(7), pp. 1105–29.

Seiz, J. (1995). Bargaining models, feminism and institutionalism. *Journal of Economic Issues*, 29(2), pp. 609–18.

Sennett, R. (1998). *The corrosion of character*. New York: Norton.

Shields, M., Wheatley Price, S. (2005). Exploring the economic and social determinants of psychological wellbeing and perceived social support in England. *Journal of the Royal Statistical Society: Series A (Statistics in Society)*, 168(3), 513–37.

Shorthose, J. (2004). Like summer and good sex? The limitation of the work-life-balance campaign. *Capital & Class*, 82(1), pp. 1–9.

Singh, A. (1977). UK industry and the world economy: A case of de-industrialisation? *Cambridge Journal of Economics*, 1, pp. 113–36.

Singh, V., Vinnicombe, S. (2000). Gendered meanings of commitment from high technology engineering managers in the UK and Sweden. *Gender, Work and Organization*, 7(1), pp. 1–19.

Sirianni, C., Negrey, C. (2000). Working time as gendered time. *Feminist Economics*, 6(1), pp. 59–76.

Smith, A. (1981 [1776]). *An inquiry into the nature and the causes of the wealth of nations*. Liberty Fund: Indianapolis, Book I, Chapter 1–4.

Smith, C., Exton, C. (2013). *OECD guidelines for measuring subjective well-being* [online]. OECD Better Life Initiative. Available at: http://www.oecd.org/statistics/ Guidelines on Measuring Subjective Well-being.pdf.

Smith, P., Morton, G. (2006). Nine years of new labour: Neoliberalism and workers' rights. *British Journal of Industrial Relations*, 44(3), pp. 401–20.

Snowball, J. D. (2008). *Measuring the value of culture: Methods and examples in cultural economics*. Heidelberg: Springer.

Soobedar, Z. (2011). A semi-parametric analysis of the rising breadwinner role of women in the UK. *Review of the Economics of the Household*, 9(3), pp. 415–28.

Southerton, D. (2003). 'Squeezing time': Allocating practices, coordinating networks and scheduling society. *Time and Society*, 12(1), pp. 5–25.

Sparrowe, R. T., Liden, R. C., Wayne, S. J., Kraimer, M. L. (2001). Social networks and the performance of individuals and groups. *Academy of Management Journal*, 44(2), pp. 316–25.

Spencer, D. A. (2000). The demise of radical political economics? *Cambridge Journal of Economics*, 24, pp. 543–64.

Spencer, D. A. (2003). Love's labor's lost? The disutility of work and work avoidance in the economic analysis of labor supply. *Review of Social Economy*, 61(2), pp. 235–50.

Spencer, D. A. (2004a). Deconstructing the labour supply curve. *Metroeconomica*, 55(4), pp. 442–58.

Spencer, D. A. (2004b). From pain cost to opportunity cost: The eclipse of the quality of work as a factor in economic theory. *History of Political Economy*, 36(2), pp. 387–400.

Spencer, D. A. (2006). Work for all those who want it? Why the neoclassical labour supply curve is an inappropriate foundation for the theory of employment and unemployment. *Cambridge Journal of Economics*, 30, pp. 459–72.

Spencer, D. A. (2009). *The political economy of work*. London: Routledge.

Sport England (2013). *Sports we invest in* [online]. Available at: http://www.sportengland.org/funding/ngb_investment.aspx/.

Stanworth, C., Stanworth, J. (1995). The self-employed without employees – autonomous or atypical? *Industrial Relations Journal*, 26(3), pp. 221–29.

Steedman, I. (2001). *Consumption takes time: Implications for economic theory*. London: Routledge.

Stier, H., Yaish, M. (2014). Occupational segregation and gender inequality in job quality: A multi-level approach. *Work, Employment & Society*, 28(2), pp. 225–46.

Stiglitz, J., Sen, A., Fitoussi, J. P. (2009). Report by the Commission on the Measurement of Economic Performance and Social Progress [online]. Available at: http://www.stiglitz-sen-fitoussi.fr/documents/rapport_anglais.pdf.

Storme, T., Beaverstock, J., Derruder, B., Faulconbridge, J., Witlox, F. (2013). How to cope with mobility expectations in academia: Individual travel strategies of tenured academics at Ghent University, Flanders. *Research in Transportation Business & Management*, 9, pp. 12–20.

Sturges, J., Guest, D. (2004). Working to live or living to work? Work/life balance early in the career. *Human Resource Management Journal*, 14(4), pp. 5–13.

Stutzer, A. (2004). The role of income aspirations in individual happiness. *Journal of Economic Behaviour and Organisation*, 54(1), pp. 89–109.

Stutzer, A., Frey, B. S. (2006). Does marriage make people happy, or do happy people get married? *The Journal of Socio-Economics*, 35(2), pp. 326–47.

Stutzer, A., Frey, B. S. (2008). Stress that doesn't pay: The commuting paradox. *Scandinavian Journal of Economics*, 110(2), pp. 339–66.

Stutzer, A., Frey, B. S. (2010). Recent advances in the economics of individual subjective well-being. *Social Research*, 77(2), pp. 679–714.

Sullivan, C. (2003). What's in a name? Definitions and conceptualisations of teleworking and homeworking. *New Technology, Work and Employment*, 18(3), pp. 158–65.

Sullivan, C., Smithson, J. (2007) Perspectives of homeworkers and their partners on working flexibility and gender equity. *International Journal of Human Resource Management*, 18(3), pp. 448–61.

Sullivan, O. (1997). Time waits for no (wo)man: An investigation of the gendered experience of domestic time. *Sociology*, 31(2), pp. 221–39.

Sullivan, O. (2010). Changing differences by educational attainment in fathers' domestic labour and child care. *Sociology*, 44(4), pp. 716–33.

Sullivan, S., Forret, M., Carraher, S., Mainiero, L. (2009). Using the kaleidoscope career model to examine generational differences in work attitudes. *Career Development International*, 14(3), pp. 284–302.

Suutari, V., Taka, M. (2004). Career anchors of managers with global careers. *Journal of Management Development*, 23(9), pp. 833–47.

Taylor, F. (1967). *The principles of scientific management*. London: Norton.

Taylor, P., Davies, L., Wells, D., Gilbertson, J., Tayleur, W. (2015). *CASE: A review of the social impacts of culture and sport* [online]. Department for Culture, Media and Sport. Available at: https://www.gov.uk/government/uploads/system/uploads/attachment_data/file/416279/A_review_of_the_Social_Impacts_of_Culture_and_Sport.pdf.

Taylor, R. (2002). *Britain's world of work – myths and realities*. Swindon: Economic and Social Research Council (ESRC).

Taylor, R. (2004). Extending conceptual boundaries: Work, voluntary work and employment. *Work, Employment and Society*, 18(1), pp. 29–49.

Teasdale, N. (2013) Fragmented sisters? The implications of flexible working policies for professional women's workplace relationships. *Gender, Work and Organization*, 20(4), pp. 397–412.

Thompson, E. P. (1967). Time, work-discipline and industrial capitalism. *Past and Present*, 38(1), pp. 56–97.

Thoits, P. A., Hewitt, L. N. (2001). Volunteer work and well-being. *Journal of Health and Social Behavior*, 42(2), pp. 115–31.

Throsby, D. (2001). *Economics and culture*. Cambridge: Cambridge University Press.

Throsby, D. (2006). The value of cultural heritage: What can economics tell us? In Clark, K. (ed.), *Capturing the public value of heritage. The proceedings of the London Conference*. Available at: www.helm.org.uk/upload/pdf/Public-Value.pdf?1245528536.

Thurlow, C., Jaworski. A. (2006). The alchemy of the upwardly mobile: Symbolic capital and the stylization of elites in frequent-flyer programmes. *Discourse & Society*, 17(1), pp. 99–135.

Tietze, S., Musson, G. (2005). Recasting the home-work relationship: A case of mutual adjustment? *Organization Studies*, 26, pp. 1331–52.

Townsend, A. (1997). *Making a living in Europe*. London: Routledge.

Trade Union Congress (TUC) (2014). *Only one in every forty net jobs since the recession is for a full-time employee, says TUC* [online]. Available at: https://www.tuc.org.uk/economic-issues/labour-market-and-economic-reports/only-one-every-forty-net-jobs-recession-full-time.

Trenberth, L., Dewe, P. (2002). The importance of leisure as a means of coping with work related stress: An exploratory study. *Counselling Psychology Quarterly*, 15(1), pp. 59–72.

Tummers, M. P., Woittiez, I. (1991). A simultaneous wage and labor supply model with hours restrictions. *The Journal of Human Resources*, 26(3), pp. 393–423.

Understanding Society (2014). *Understanding Society Insights 2014* [online]. Available at: https://www.understandingsociety.ac.uk/d/140/Insights_-_2014.pdf?1414660258.

University of Essex. Institute for Social and Economic Research and NatCen Social Research, *Understanding Society: Waves 1-5, 2009–2014* [computer file]. 7th Edn. Colchester, Essex: UK Data Archive [distributor], November 2015. SN: 6614, http://dx.doi.org/10.5255/UKDA-SN-6614-7.

Vale, D. (2013). Does commuting time tolerance impede sustainable urban mobility? Analysing the impacts on commuting behaviour as a result of workplace relocation to a mixed-use centre in Lisbon. *Journal of Transport Geography*, 32, pp. 38–48.

van Hooff, J. (2011). Rationalising inequality: Heterosexual couples' explanations and justifications for the division of housework along traditionally gendered lines. *Journal of Gender Studies*, 20(1), pp. 19–30.

van Praag, B. M. S., Ferrer-i-Carbonell, A. (2004). *Happiness quantified. A satisfaction calculus approach*. Oxford: Oxford University Press.

van Praag, B. M. S., Frijters, P., Ferrer-i-Carbonell, A. (2003). The anatomy of subjective well-being. *Journal of Economic Behavior & Organization*, 51(1), pp. 29–49.

van Staveren, I. (2010). Post-Keynesianism meets feminist economics. *Cambridge Journal of Economics*, 34(6), pp. 1123–44.

Van Willigen, M. (2000). Differential benefits of volunteering across the life course. *The Journals of Gerontology Series B: Psychological Sciences and Social Sciences*, 55B(5), pp. S308–S318.

Veblen, T. (1899a). The preconceptions of economics science. *Quarterly Journal of Economics*, 13, pp. 121–52.

Veblen, T. (1899b). *The theory of the leisure class*. New York: Macmillan.

Veblen, T. (1909). The limitations of marginal utility. *The Journal of Political Economy*, 17(9), pp. 620–36.

Vermeulen, F. (2002). Collective household models: Principles and main results. *Journal of Economic Surveys*, 16, pp. 533–64.

Walby, S. (2002). Gender and the new economy: Regulation or deregulation? [online] ESRC seminar 'Work, life and time in the new economy', LSE, October. Available at: http://www.leeds.ac.uk/sociology/people/swdocs/.

Waring, M. (1988). *If women counted: A new feminist economics*. London: Macmillan.

Weale, M. (2016). What's in a Week's Work? [online]. Bank of England. Available at: http://www.bankofengland.co.uk/publications/Documents/speeches/2016/speech874.pdf.

Weber, M. (1976). *The Protestant ethic and the spirit of capitalism*. London: Allen and Unwin.

Weijers, D., Jarden, A. (2013). The science of happiness for policymakers: An overview. *Journal of Social Research & Policy*, 4(2), pp. 21–40.

Weiss, R., Kahn, R. (1960). Definitions of work and occupation. *Social Problems*, 8(2), pp. 142–51.

Wellard, S. (2011). *Doing it all? Grandparents, childcare and employment: An analysis of British Social Attitudes Survey Data from 1998 and 2009* [online]. Grandparents Plus. Available at: http://www.grandparentsplus.org.uk/wp-content/uploads/2011/03/Doing-it-all__Online.pdf.

Welsch, H. (2006). Environment and happiness: Valuation of air pollution using life satisfaction data. *Ecological Economics*, 58(4), pp. 801–13.

Wendel-Vos, G., Schuit, A, Tijhuis, M., Kromhout, D. (2004). Leisure time physical activity and health-related quality of life: Cross-sectional and longitudinal associations. *Quality of Life Research*, 13, 667–77.

WERS (2013). *The 2011 Workplace Employment Relations Study – information and advice* [online]. Available at: http://www.wers2011.info/.

Wheatley, D. (2012a). Good to be home? Time-use and satisfaction levels among home-based teleworkers. *New Technology, Work and Employment*, 27(3), pp. 224–41.

Wheatley, D. (2012b). Work-life balance, travel-to-work, and the dual career household. *Personnel Review*, 41(6), pp. 813–31.

Wheatley, D. (2013). Location, vocation, location? Spatial entrapment among women in dual career households. *Gender, Work and Organization*, 20(6), pp. 720–36.

Wheatley, D. (2014). Travel-to-work and subjective well-being: A study of UK dual career households. *Journal of Transport Geography*, 39, pp. 187–96.

Wheatley, D. (2016). Employee satisfaction and patterns in availability and use of flexible working arrangements. *Work, Employment and Society*, forthcoming. DOI: http://dx.doi.org/10.1177/0950017016631447.

Wheatley, D. (2017). Autonomy in paid work and employee subjective well-being. *Work and Occupations*, forthcoming.

Wheatley, D., Bickerton, C. (2016a). Subjective well-being and engagement in arts, culture and sport. *Journal of Cultural Economics*, forthcoming. DOI: http://dx.doi.org/10.1007/s10824-016-9270-0.

Wheatley, D., Bickerton, C. (2016b). Time-use and well-being impacts of travel-to-work and travel-for-work. *New Technology, Work and Employment*, 31(3), pp. 238–54.

Wheatley, D., Hardill, I., Green, A. (2008). Mobile work and challenges for public policy. In Hislop, D. (ed.), *Mobility and technology in the workplace*. Oxford: Routledge, pp. 227–39.

Wheatley, D., Hardill, I., Philp, B. (2011). 'Managing' reductions in working hours: A study of work time and leisure preferences in UK industry. *Review of Political Economy*, 23(3), pp. 409–20.

Wheatley, D., Wu, Z. (2014). Dual careers, time-use, and satisfaction levels: Evidence from the British Household Panel Survey. *Industrial Relations Journal*, 45(5), pp. 443–64.

White, B. (1995). The career development of successful women. *Women in Management Review*, 10(3), pp. 4–15.

White, M., Hill, S., McGovern, P., Mills, C., Smeaton, D. (2003). High performance management practices, working hours and work-life balance. *British Journal of Industrial Relations*, 41(2), pp. 175–95.

Wilensky, H. (1960). Work, careers and social integration. *International Social Science Journal*, 12, pp. 543–60.

Wight, V., Raley, S. (2009). When home becomes work: Work and family time among workers at home. *Social Indicators Research*, 93(1), pp. 197–202.

Williams, C. (2003). Developing community participation in deprived neighbourhoods: A critical evaluation of the third sector approach. *Space and Polity*, 7(1), pp. 65–73.

Williams, C. (2005). Harnessing the community sector. *Community, Work and Family*, 8, pp. 37–51.

Williams, C. (2011). Socio-spatial variations in community self-help: A total organisation of labour perspective. *Social Policy and Society*, 10(3), pp. 365–78.

Witte, E. (1954). Institutional economics as seen by an institutional economist. *Southern Economic Journal*, 21, pp. 131–40.

Wood, N., Smith, S. (2004). Instrumental routes to emotional geographies. *Social and Cultural Geography*, 5(4), pp. 534–48.

Woodland, S., Simmonds, N., Thornby, M., Fitzgerald, R., McGee, A. (2003). The second work-life balance study: Results from the employers' survey – main report. *Employment Relations Research Series, No. 22*, URN 03/1252, DTI, London.

Woolvin, M. (2011). Placing informal volunteering: Helping, deprivation and the lifecourse in Scotland. PhD thesis. Dundee: University of Dundee.

Woolvin, M., Hardill, I. (2013). Localism, voluntarism and devolution: Experiences, opportunities and challenges in a changing policy context. *Local Economy*, 28(3), pp. 273–88.

Worth, N., Hardill, I. (eds) (2015). *Researching the lifecourse: Critical reflections from the social sciences*. Bristol: Policy Press, pp. 1–22.

Yerkes, M. (2010). Diversity at work: The heterogeneity of women's employment patterns. *Gender, Work and Organization*, 17(6), pp. 696–720.

Yin, R. K. (2008). *Case study research: Design and methods* (4th ed.). Thousand Oaks, CA: Sage.

Young, M., Wilmott, P. (1957). *Family and kinship in East London*. London: Routledge & Kegan Paul.

Zappala, G. (2000). *How many people volunteer in Australia and why do they do it?* Camperdown: The Smith Family.

Zeytinoglu, I., Cooke, G., Mann, S. (2009). Flexibility: Whose choice is in anyway? *Industrial Relations*, 64(4), pp. 555–74.

Index

Age, 9, 16, 74, 85, 96, 105, 127–8, 134–40, 178, 185, 211
  Chronological age. *See* Lifecourse
Agency work. *See* Flexible labour
Annual Survey of Hours and Earnings. *See* Survey
Arts, 173, 175–80, 182–3, 185–6, 190, 193, 195–6
Austerity, 134, 207, 212
Autonomy. *See* Quality of work

Becker, Gary. *See* Mainstream economics
British Household Panel Survey. *See* Survey
British Social Attitudes Survey. *See* Survey
Bounded rationality, 7
Budget constraint. *See* Constraint
Business travel. *See* Travel-for-work

Capitalism, 4, 38, 44–5, 54, 66, 75–6
Car, 154–55, 160, 163, 169, 171–2, 180, 204, 211, 213
Cardinal. *See* Methods
Care
  Childcare, 4, 11, 37, 62, 70, 78, 84–8, 110–11, 138–9, 143–7, 161, 171, 181, 202–3, 211
  Grandparenting, 20, 24, 88, 103, 110, 125, 128, 130, 133–4, 137–8, 143, 147, 202
  for ill/elderly relative or friend, 70, 86, 92, 130, 134–7, 139, 141–3, 147, 202, 206, 211
  School-age children, 11, 112, 115–6, 161, 192
Career
  Anchor, 106
  Development, 80, 105–8, 134, 136, 163, 166, 170–1, 203–4, 206, 213, 215
  Kaleidoscope career, 106, 122
  Limitations, 76, 82, 98–9, 114, 160, 165, 203, 208, 213
  Protean career, 105–7
Carers (Equal Opportunities) Act 2004, 134, 211
Case study. *See* Methods
Causality, 3, 5, 14, 22, 38, 128, 143, 178, 197, 205, 216–7
Childcare. *See* Care
Choice, 3, 29, 42–50, 68, 79, 99, 102–7, 117, 132, 154–6, 162–3, 174, 199, 202–3, 207–9, 219
  Rational choice. *See* Mainstream economics
Coalition. *See* Government

Commitment, 49, 64, 70, 74–7, 79–80, 82, 105–8, 113, 121, 131–132, 137, 143–4, 146, 166, 185, 214–5
Community Life Survey. *See* Survey
Commute
Commuting tolerance, 158, 171, 204
and housing markets, 153, 156–7, 162, 203, 208
long distance commutes, 156, 162, 204
and mainstream economics, 156–9
School-run, 112, 115–16, 151, 155, 160–1, 171, 206
Spatial entrapment, 159–61, 204
Compressed hours. *See* Flexible working arrangements
Compromise, 17, 41, 49, 105–6, 131, 156, 167, 208–9
Concert, 16, 176, 178–80, 182–5, 193
Conservative. *See* Government
Constraint
Budget constraint, 3, 29, 31, 33–5, 44, 102
Resource constraint, 29, 37
and time-use, 3–4, 11, 25, 29–30, 34–42, 46, 48–9, 61, 71, 77, 88, 113, 156, 192, 199, 203, 208, 219
Corporate Social Responsibility, 215
Culture, 42–3, 51, 166, 179–93, 195, 214
Cultural activity, 179–80, 185–6
Cultural value, 173–6, 181, 195–6, 205, 212, 214
Long hours culture, 75–6, 107, 121–2
Workplace culture, 63–4, 170

Disability, 9–10, 68, 96, 130, 139, 144–5, 192, 201, 214
Discretion. *See* Quality of work
Divorced, 10–11, 142
Domain satisfaction. *See* Well-being
Domestic travel. *See* Travel-for-work
Dual career household. *See* Household models

Easterlin paradox. *See* Income
Economic crisis, 14, 66, 69, 77, 79, 83–5
Education, 8, 11–12, 62–3, 67, 69, 77, 88, 99, 104–5, 109, 115, 120, 128, 134, 139, 142, 147, 192, 202
Egalitarian. *See* Household models
Employer-supported volunteering. *See* Volunteering
Employment. *See* Paid work
Entrepreneur, 78, 123
Environment
Natural, 127, 155, 175, 213, 218
Work, 148, 170, 214, 217
Equal Pay Act, 62
Ethnicity, 8, 10, 61, 127
European Union, 2, 65–6, 74, 133–4, 169
European Working Time Directive, 65–66, 74
Opt-out, 65–7
Extensive labour extraction. *See* Quality of work
Extrinsic Reward. *See* Volunteering

Factory Act, 55, 71, 83, 210
Feminist economics, 3, 25, 30, 39–41, 46–50, 127–30
Finance, 12–13, 35, 47–8, 58, 60–1, 67–8, 70, 78–9, 110, 156–8, 177, 179
Financial pressure, 47, 65, 78, 101, 134, 148, 211, 213
Finland, 69–70
Flexible labour
Agency work, 85–6, 99, 210
Gig economy, 78, 84, 210
Insecure, 59, 80–1
Temporary work, 59, 77, 80, 84–5, 99
Zero hours contracts, 59, 85, 99, 114, 210
Flexible working arrangements
Compressed hours, 111–12, 115–19
Flexi-time, 111–12, 115–19, 121
Home-based teleworking, 111–12, 115–17, 122, 154, 172

Job share, 67, 111–12, 116–18, 202
Part-time work, 35, 40, 47, 59, 62–6, 70, 74, 78, 83–6, 88, 97–9, 103, 108–18, 145, 156, 202
Reduced hours, 35, 40, 55, 77, 83–5, 111–14, 119, 142, 200, 202, 214, 218
Term-time work, 111–12, 115–18
Flexible Working Regulations, 68–9, 71, 111, 123, 134, 210–11, 218
Flexibility, employer-oriented, 84–6, 89, 99, 114–15, 120–3, 160–3, 166, 193, 208, 210, 213–15
Flexi-time. *See* Flexible working arrangements,
Ford, Henry, 56, 71
France, 65, 67
Friend, 11, 15, 24, 48, 77, 86, 108, 110, 126, 129, 136–7, 145–7, 167, 170–6, 182, 194, 205
Full-time. *See* Working hours

Gender
Norms, 50, 65, 103, 116, 131, 151, 156, 158, 160, 165, 202
Pay gap, 19, 62, 101, 107, 218
Inequality, 4, 44–5, 49–51, 63, 105, 123, 131, 165, 206, 208
Germany, 69–70
Gig economy. *See* Flexible labour
Good job. *See* Quality of work
Government
Coalition, 65
Conservative, 57, 64, 135
New Labour, 62, 65, 67
Grandparenting. *See* Care
Gross Domestic Product. *See* Well-being

Habit. *See* Institutional economics
Hakim, Catherine. *See* Mainstream economics
Hakim's Preference Theory, 39–41
Happiness. *See* Well-being
Health, 2, 5, 6, 8–10, 12–13, 65–6, 76, 130–2, 134, 145, 148, 166, 169–70, 172, 176, 179–80, 199, 204
Historical site, 173, 175, 179, 181–3, 185–6, 193, 204–5, 212
Home-based teleworking. *See* Flexible working arrangements
Household division of labour, 3, 26, 46, 51, 56, 61, 63–4, 83, 97, 101, 103, 105–8, 122, 160, 165, 201–2, 213, 218
Household models
Dual career household, 22–3, 25, 63, 104–5, 109–10, 120, 160, 202
Egalitarian, 70, 102, 104–5, 122–3, 156, 202, 211
Male breadwinner, female homemaker, 48, 102–3, 165, 201
One and a half worker, 103, 202
Housework, 3, 15, 26, 39, 47, 64, 77, 84, 86–9, 92, 97, 102–5, 109–11, 122, 133, 139, 141–2, 161, 181, 199, 201–2
Horizontal segregation, 63, 69, 81–2, 107, 165
Human capital, 40, 131, 144, 177

Income, 2–3, 6, 8, 11–14, 29, 31–33, 36–7, 44, 57, 62–64, 67, 78–9, 96, 103, 107, 142, 157, 166, 171, 177, 201, 209, 212
Easterlin paradox, 8, 14
Income effect. *See* Labour supply theory
Indifference curve. *See* Labour supply theory
Inequality. *See* Gender
Information and Communication Technology (ICT), 8, 15, 53, 59–60, 63, 71, 76, 112, 121, 152, 154, 162–3, 172, 178, 209
Insecure. *See* Flexible labour
Institutional economics, 29–30, 38–9, 41–3, 45
Norms, 3, 8, 34, 42–5, 53–5, 71, 75, 81, 123, 216–17
Habit, 34, 42–3, 50

Intensive labour extraction. *See* Quality of work
International
 Policy, 211, 213, 218
 Travel. *See* Work-related travel
Internet, 15, 83, 162, 173, 182, 185, 194–5, 205
 Social media, 15, 185, 205, 218
Interview, semi-structured. *See* Methods
Intrinsic Reward. *See* Volunteering

Job quality. *See* Quality of work
Job satisfaction. *See* Well-being
Job share. *See* Flexible working arrangements

Kaleidoscope career. *See* Career

Labour Force Survey. *See* Survey
Labour market, 35, 40, 46–51, 59–79, 82–6, 99–107, 130–4, 143–6, 154–60, 177, 200–4, 210–11
Labour supply theory
 Assumptions of, 30–31
 Budget constraint. *See* Constraint
 Income effect, 32–3
 Indifference curve, 32–5, 43
 Limitations of, 33–4
 Substitution effect, 32
 and Utility, 29, 31–3
Leisure
 Leisure experience, 173–6, 181–2, 185–6, 194–7, 204
 Leisure time, 13, 15, 25, 31–33, 60, 67, 92, 117–9, 130, 139, 142, 147, 155, 164, 169–71, 173–97, 199, 204–12, 218, 978
 Satisfaction with amount of leisure. *See* Well-being
Liberal, 64–5, 67, 69, 101, 127, 210
Life satisfaction. *See* Well-being
Lifecourse
 and chronological age, 9, *127–8*, 134–40
 Older adult, 23, 128, 130, 132, 134, 142–3, 148, 180, 181, 206, 211, 213
 and research, 16–17, 126–8
 Transitions approach, 13, 16–17, 127–8, 133, 139, 142, 147–8
 Young, 68, 85, 99, 105, 109, 121, 128–30, 132–9, 142–5, 147–8, 180, 185, 192, 211
Long working hours. *See* Working hours
Loneliness. *See* Well-being

Mainstream economics
 Becker, Gary, 3, 29–30, 36–40, 47, 50–1, 102, 156–7
 Hakim, Catherine, 30, 39–41, 43, 50
 Labour supply theory. *See* Labour supply theory
 Rational choice, 3, 29, 31, 34, 39, 43–4, 47–51, 157
 Self-interest, 36, 39, 46, 48, 102, 129, 131
Male breadwinner, female homemaker. *See* Household models
Manager, 21–24, 38, 45, 49, 54, 56–61, 62–3, 74–7, 79, 81, 88–90, 92, 98, 104, 112–15, 120–23, 144, 154, 160, 168–70, 200, 218
Married, 10, 46–7, 49, 77, 96, 102, 142, 160, 165, 192, 216
Marx, Karl, 3, 30, 44–5, 75
Maternity leave, 62, 68–70
 See also Shared Parental Leave
Methods
 Cardinal, 6–7
 Case study, 17, 19, 21–6, 68, 119–22, 133, 143–8, 164, 168–71, 180
 Interview, semi-structured, 18, 20, 22–5, 120, 143–4, 168–70
 Mixed methods, 16–19, 22, 24, 125, 147, 160–1, 166, 168, 199, 217–18
 Ordinal, 6–7
 Primary data, 7, 21–5
 Quantitative, 16–19, 22–3, 43, 125, 133

Qualitative, 16–19, 22–4, 79, 105, 126, 133, 143, 146–7, 167, 203, 217
Regression, probit, 90, 92, 133, 187, 193
Secondary data, 16, 19–21, 25, 133, 147, 199, 218
Statistical significance, 10, 14, 17, 21, 46, 96, 114, 139, 148, 186–7, 193
Thematic coding method, 22, 25
Triangulation, 18, 25, 217
Momentary measure. *See* well-being
Museum, 173, 175, 177–9, 181–3, 185–7, 193, 196, 205, 212

New Labour. *See* Government
Norms. *See* Institutional economics
Norway, 69–70, 160

Occupation, 20, 23–4, 49, 57, 59, 61–3, 75–77, 79–83, 88–97, 104–7, 113–14, 151, 158, 163, 168, 177, 180, 190, 200, 208, 215, 217–18
Skilled, highly, 22–4, 49, 61, 63–4, 83, 89, 97, 104, 120–1, 153, 156, 168–71, 215, 218
Skilled, low, 55–6, 63–4, 114, 158
Older adult. *See* Lifecourse
Opt-out. *See* European Working Time Directive
Ordinal. *See* Methods
Organizations, 2, 22–4, 57, 75, 77, 106, 111, 113–14, 119–20, 122, 135, 152, 162–6, 170, 177, 201, 205, 209, 212–15
See also Voluntary and Community Sector Organizations (VCSOs)
Overtime, 3, 35, 67, 74–5, 83, 86, 88–9, 92, 97, 121, 141–2, 164, 192–3, 208

Qualitative. *See* Methods
Quality of work
Autonomy, 56, 74, 77–82, 90–3, 96–8, 115, 164, 180, 201, 214–15
Discretion, 34, 56, 75, 80–1, 90, 98, 201
Extensive labour extraction, 44, 71–2, 76, 92, 212
Good job, 45, 79–80
Intensive labour extraction, 55, 60, 67, 71–2, 74, 76–7, 78–9, 81–6, 90, 96–7, 121, 163, 167, 172, 201, 210–12, 214–15
Job quality, 79–82, 114
Training, 65, 70, 80, 132, 135–6, 151, 169
Quantitative. *See* Methods

Paid work
Employment, 13, 20–22, 35, 39–42, 47, 49, 55, 58–71, 73, 75–6, 78–80, 86, 97, 101–15, 128, 130, 134–5, 144, 151, 159–60, 201, 208–12, 217
Second job, 78–9, 85
Self-employment, 59, 73, 77–9, 83–4, 98, 107, 109
Part-time work. *See* Flexible working arrangements
Paternity leave, 68
See also Shared Parental Leave
Pensions Act, 134
Post-industrial society, 1, 16, 25, 65, 69, 71, 74, 81, 101, 104, 132, 148, 154, 199, 207, 210, 219
Definition of, 58–61
Preference Theory. *See* Hakim's Preference Theory
Presenteeism, 75, 121
Primary data. *See* Methods
Private sector, 22, 24, 65, 67, 96, 113–15, 117, 125, 135
Probit regression. *See* Regression
Professional, 23–4, 49, 59, 61–3, 74–81, 88–90, 92, 97, 104, 106, 112–15, 121, 154, 163–70, 180, 200, 210
Protean career. *See* Career
Public policy, 67, 133, 199, 210–14, 218–19

Public sector, 23, 69, 82, 84, 96, 114–16, 120, 134–5, 207, 211, 215

Radical economics, 3, 8, 25, 30, 40, 44–6, 50, 74–5
Rational choice. *See* Mainstream economics
Reduced hours. *See* Flexible working arrangements
Reflexive measure. *See* well-being
Regression. *See* Methods
Regulation, labour market
  See Carers (Equal Opportunities) Act 2004
  See Equal Pay Act
  See European Working Time Directive
  See Factory Acts
  See Flexible Working Regulations
  See Pensions Act
Relative (family member), 11, 40, 48–9, 86, 110, 137, 142, 147, 167, 206
Resource constraint. *See* Constraint
Retirement, 13, 24, 88, 109, 128, 130, 134, 136–9, 142–7, 192, 199, 201–3, 214, 219
Revealed preference. *See* Well-being

School-age children. *See* Care
School-run. *See* Commute
Second job. *See* Paid work
Secondary data. *See* Methods
Self-employment. *See* Paid work
Self-interest. *See* Mainstream economics
Shared Parental Leave, 69, 211–12, 219
Skilled, highly. *See* Occupations
Skilled, low. *See* Occupations
Sleep, 3, 33, 102, 110, 160, 166–7, 200
Spillover, 4, 89, 120, 167, 173, 181, 188, 193–6, 200, 204–6, 209
Sport
  Mild intensity sport, 182–6, 194–6, 215
  Moderate intensity sport, 182–6, 195
  Team sport, 176, 180, 205, 209
  and Togetherness. *See* Togetherness
Social media. *See* Internet
Socio-economic, 43, 179, 193, 197, 204, 216
Stated preference. *See* Well-being
Statistical significance. *See* Methods
Stress. *See* Well-being
Subjective well-being,
  Definition of, 4–5
  Factors affecting, 8–16
  Measurement of, 6–8
Substitution effect. *See* Labour supply theory
Surplus value, 44
Survey
  Annual Survey of Hours and Earnings, 19, 62–3
  British Household Panel Survey, 19–20, 34, 49, 74, 86–7, 108–110, 132–3, 161, 179
  British Social Attitudes Survey, 20, 132–3, 137–8, 143
  Community Life Survey, 20, 126, 132, 135–8
  Labour Force Survey, 19–20, 61, 74, 85–6, 160, 165
  Understanding Society, 2, 7, 20–1, 86–9, 92, 104, 109–11, 114–9, 134, 138, 139–43, 182–5, 189–94
  Workplace Employee Relations Survey, 21, 114
Sustainability, 213, 218
Sweden, 69–70, 101, 158–9, 164

Taylorist work organization, 56, 71, 76, 80–1, 86, 90, 201
  Taylor, Frederick, 55–6, 71
Technology, 1, 8, 15, 26, 42–3, 49, 53, 59–60, 76, 88–9, 121, 203, 218
Television, 15, 77, 178, 195, 200, 205
Temporary work. *See* Flexible labour
Term-time work. *See* Flexible working arrangements
Thematic coding method. *See* Methods

Togetherness, 170, 176, 180, 194, 205, 207–9, 219
Trade-off, 30, 32, 34–6, 76, 97, 108, 131, 176
Trade union, 55, 57, 65, 67, 85
Training. *See* Quality of work
Transitions approach. *See* Lifecourse
Travel-for-work
  Business travel, 1, 16, 151, 153, 162–70, 218
  Domestic travel, 151, 162, 215
  International travel, 1, 151, 162, 166, 169, 213, 215, 218
Triangulation. *See* Mixed methods
Trigger volunteer. *See* Volunteering
Trust, 129, 144, 162, 209

Uncertain, 78, 81, 134, 163
Underemployment, 67, 99, 200, 210
Understanding Society. *See* Survey
Unemployment, 12–14, 33, 67, 98, 133, 144, 174, 199–200
Unpaid work
  Care. *See* Care
  Housework. *See* Housework
  Unpaid overtime. *See* Overtime
  Voluntary work. *See* Volunteering
U-shape, 9, 12–14, 76, 200
Utility, 6, 29, 31–3, 35–9, 48, 102, 131, 157–8, 161, 174–5, 195, 201

Vertical segregation, 63, 69, 81–2, 107, 165
Voluntary and Community Sector (VCO), 120, 125, 127, 213
Voluntary and Community Sector Organizations (VCSOs), 125, 128–9, 143–4, 203, 213–5, 219
Volunteering
  Employer-supported volunteering, 135, 148, 206, 209, 215
  Extrinsic reward, 130–2, 134–5, 144, 147, 203, 209, 211, 215
  Intrinsic reward, 82, 130–2, 134, 136, 142–8, 158, 201, 203, 211, 213, 215
  Trade-off with care and paid work, 138, 141, 144, 147
  Trigger volunteer, 13, 128, 133, 139, 142, 147, 202, 219

Wage rate, 13–14, 31–33, 35
Walk, 146, 169, 182–3, 209
Welfare, 13–14, 23, 31–3, 41, 45, 62–7, 81, 101, 123–9, 133–4, 143, 148, 177, 211, 219
Well-being
  and GDP, 2, 6, 217
  Domain satisfaction, 4–5, 7, 9, 13, 25, 173, 179, 181–2, 187, 193, 201–2, 216
  Happiness, 2, 4–11, 13, 16, 25, 132, 170, 173, 179–82, 186–7, 192–3, 195–7, 208, 216
  Job satisfaction, 7, 76–7, 82–3, 96–8, 108, 113–14, 167, 173, 180, 187, 194, 196, 201, 205–9, 214–15
  Life satisfaction, 2, 5–7, 11–16, 25, 76, 92, 96–7, 119, 122, 131–2, 148, 161, 173, 179, 186, 192–3, 200, 203, 216
  Loneliness, 15, 167, 178, 209
  Momentary measure, 7, 179
  Reflexive measure, 7–8, 187
  Revealed preference, 4, 6–7, 27, 33–4, 216
  Satisfaction with amount of leisure, 5, 7, 76, 92, 98, 117–19, 142, 147, 187, 192–6, 200
  Stated preference, 4, 7, 27, 34
  Stress, 14–15, 49–50, 60, 67, 76–8, 80, 82, 108, 112, 122, 130, 155, 158, 161, 167–70, 178–80
  Subjective well-being. *See* Subjective Well-being
Working hours
  Full-time, 86, 107, 109, 115
  Long working hours, 15, 55, 64–6, 70–1, 74–8, 80, 86, 106, 121–2, 193, 200, 212

Work-life balance, 66–9, 77, 79, 107, 113–14, 121, 123
Workplace Employee Relations Survey. *See* Survey
Work-related travel
  Travel-for-work. *See* Travel-for-work
  Travel-to-work. *See* Commute
Young. *See* Lifecourse
Zero hours contracts. *See* Flexible labour

Lightning Source UK Ltd.
Milton Keynes UK
UKOW03n2241110417
298897UK00001B/13/P

9 781783 484256